The Dark Interval

Thinking Cinema

Series Editors

David Martin-Jones, University of Glasgow, UK
Sarah Cooper, King's College, University of London, UK

Volume 11

Titles in the Series:

Afterlives: Allegories of Film and Mortality in Early Weimar Germany by Steve Choe

Deleuze, Japanese Cinema, and the Atom Bomb by David Deamer

Ex-centric Cinema by Janet Harbord

The Body and the Screen by Kate Ince

The Grace of Destruction by Elena del Rio

Non-Cinema: Global Digital Filmmaking and the Multitude by William Brown

Sensuous Cinema: The Body in Contemporary Maghrebi Film by Kaya Davies Hayon

European Cinema and Continental Philosophy by Thomas Elsaesser

Limit Cinema: Transgression and the Nonhuman in Contemporary Global Film by Chelsea Birks

Fertile Visions: The Uterus as a Narrative Space in Cinema from the Americas by Anne Carruthers

The Dark Interval

Film Noir, Iconography, and Affect

Padraic Killeen

BLOOMSBURY ACADEMIC
NEW YORK · LONDON · OXFORD · NEW DELHI · SYDNEY

BLOOMSBURY ACADEMIC
Bloomsbury Publishing Inc
1385 Broadway, New York, NY 10018, USA
50 Bedford Square, London, WC1B 3DP, UK
29 Earlsfort Terrace, Dublin 2, Ireland

BLOOMSBURY, BLOOMSBURY ACADEMIC and the Diana logo are trademarks of
Bloomsbury Publishing Plc

First published in the United States of America 2022
Paperback edition published 2023

Copyright © Padraic Killeen, 2022

For legal purposes the Acknowledgements on p. viii constitute an
extension of this copyright page.

Cover design: Eleanor Rose
Cover image: Tony Leung in *2046* (2004), Dir. Wong Kar-Wia, Columbia
© AF archive / Alamy Stock Photo

All rights reserved. No part of this publication may be reproduced or transmitted in any form or by any means, electronic or mechanical, including photocopying, recording, or any information storage or retrieval system, without prior permission in writing from the publishers.

Bloomsbury Publishing Inc does not have any control over, or responsibility for, any third-party websites referred to or in this book. All internet addresses given in this book were correct at the time of going to press. The author and publisher regret any inconvenience caused if addresses have changed or sites have ceased to exist, but can accept no responsibility for any such changes.

Library of Congress Cataloging-in-Publication Data
Names: Killeen, Padraic, author.
Title: The dark interval : film noir, iconography, and affect / Padraic Killeen.
Description: New York : Bloomsbury Academic, 2022. |
Series: Thinking cinema ; volume 11 | Includes bibliographical references and index. |
Summary: "Invoking key concepts from the philosophical writings of Gilles Deleuze and Giorgio Agamben, The Dark Interval examines an iconography of radical passivity and temporal rupture that recurs in film noir, while examining the emergence of a specific cinematic figure - the 'intervallic' noir protagonist exposed to the redemptive force of his or her own passion"–Provided by publisher.
Identifiers: LCCN 2021056922 (print) | LCCN 2021056923 (ebook) |
ISBN 9781501349683 (hardback) | ISBN 9781501393037 (paperback) |
ISBN 9781501349690 (epub) | ISBN 9781501349706 (pdf) | ISBN 9781501349713
Subjects: LCSH: Film noir–History and criticism. | Motion pictures–Philosophy.
Classification: LCC PN1995.9.F54 K55 (print) | LCC PN1995.9.F54 (ebook) |
DDC 791.43/655–dc23/eng/20220126
LC record available at https://lccn.loc.gov/2021056922
LC ebook record available at https://lccn.loc.gov/2021056923

ISBN: HB: 978-1-5013-4968-3
PB: 978-1-5013-9303-7
ePDF: 978-1-5013-4970-6
eBook: 978-1-5013-4969-0

Series: Thinking Cinema

Typeset by Newgen KnowledgeWorks Pvt. Ltd., Chennai, India

To find out more about our authors and books visit www.bloomsbury.com
and sign up for our newsletters.

CONTENTS

List of Figures vi
Acknowledgements viii

Introduction 1

Prelude: The Interval as a Philosophical Concept 21

1. The 'Dark Interval' in Noir: From Iconography to Affect 31
2. The Passion of Ed Crane: Narrative Dissolution, Zero Affect and Beatitude in *The Man Who Wasn't There* 77
3. Vesperal Noir: Intervallic Suspension in *Cat People* 105
4. Saving Those Who Weep: The Interval of Affective Rupture in *Alphaville* 127
5. *2046*: Orphic Lingering in the Dark Interval (or, What 'Becomes' of Lemmy's Cigarettes) 149
6. Outside the Law: *The Long Goodbye*, Temporal Lapse and Force-of-~~Law~~ 179
7. Missing Persons and Deadbeats: 'Abiding' in the Dark Interval 205
8. Coda: Passion at the Impasse – Noir in Transit 233

Bibliography 247
Index 259

FIGURES

1. John Rosow (Michael Shannon) in *The Missing Person* 34
2. Philip Raven (Alan Ladd) in *This Gun for Hire* 34
3. Jef Costello (Alain Delon) in *Le Samouraï* 35
4. A contemplative Walter Neff (Fred MacMurray) in *Double Indemnity* 38
5. Uncle Charlie's ill-eased repose in *Shadow of a Doubt* 39
6. Young Charlie in a similar repose 40
7. Albrecht Dürer, *Melencolia I*, courtesy of The Metropolitan Museum of Art: www.metmuseum.org (Public Domain collections) 46
8. Rupture of the dark interval in *The Killers* 58
9. Fascination with the stars in *The Killers* 62
10. Fascination with the stars. *Close-Up* 63
11. Ed Crane in contemplation in *The Man Who Wasn't There* 86
12. Intersubjective space poised between light and dark in *The Man Who Wasn't There* 87
13. Attack on the space of reason and order in *Cat People* 112
14. Oliver uses an instrument of reason (a T-square) for protection. *Cat People* 112
15. The instrument of reason takes on religious qualities. *Cat People* 113
16. A return to reason and order in *Cat People* 113
17. Irena and Oliver in the dark interval. *Cat People* 115
18. As Lemmy and Natacha escape Alphaville, Natacha clings to the walls that house the supercomputer. *Alphaville* 153
19. In *2046*, the android wjw1967 (Faye Wong) grips the walls of the train corridor passionately, having been exposed to temporality and affect by her romantic encounter with a passenger 154
20. Interval of self-affection: Orphée sensually grips the mirror, gateway to 'the Zone', the underworld. *Orphée* 154
21. Natacha asleep on Lemmy's shoulder. *Alphaville* 170
22. Chow asleep on Bai Ling's shoulder. *2046* 171
23. Chow asleep on Su Li-Zhen's shoulder. *2046* 171

FIGURES

24	Chow alone, resting his head on the cab door. *2046* 172
25	Into the vortex. *2046* 172
26	Opening shot of Marlowe (Elliott Gould) in *The Long Goodbye* 187
27	Marlowe's strange exchange with a bandaged man, an impersonal figure of life. *The Long Goodbye* 195
28	Figuring the dark interval. *The Missing Person* 208
29	The child's replication of Hopper's painting *New York Movie* (1939) in *The Missing Person* 210
30	The detective's dream also replicates Hopper's painting. *The Missing Person* 210
31	Close of *The Missing Person*: the iconography of the dark interval 212
32	The Dude's channelling of the 'dark interval'. *The Big Lebowski* 219
33	The Dude a-slouches 221
34	… And a-slouches 222
35	… And still a-slouches 222
36	The Dude: 'the man for his time and place'. *The Big Lebowski* 225
37	Georg (Franz Rogowski) in one of many moments of suspension. *Transit* 238
38	Marie (Paula Beer) in a state of Hopperian lethargy and intermission. *Transit* 239

ACKNOWLEDGEMENTS

My thanks and gratitude to series editors David Martin-Jones and Sarah Cooper, who provided patient support and encouragement throughout the writing process, as did Katie Gallof, Erin Duffy, Stephanie Grace-Petinos and all at Bloomsbury. I would also like to acknowledge the contribution of the anonymous reviewers for Bloomsbury, who provided welcome encouragement and valuable advice at a very early juncture. This study would not have been possible without the contribution and support of many friends and colleagues in academia and beyond, in particular Ruth Barton, Julia Kilroy, Barry Monahan, Paula Quigley, Sean Ryder, Justin Tonra and Tony Tracy.

I owe the greatest debt to my wife Michelle and our two wonderful sons, Cathal and Kevin, who saturate every little interval of life with light and joy.

I dedicate this work to my parents, Margaret and Alfie.

Introduction

A passion for noir

If the history of film noir is in many respects the history of the struggle to define or categorize noir, I should confess at the outset that this book is not interested in rescuing any such definition. My study commences by making only this reasonably minor observation: *there is a passion for film noir*. Among filmgoers, and perhaps among cinephiles most of all, there remains an enduring passion for noir.

Nurtured in part by the eclectic manner in which noir aesthetics have continued to expand and mutate, noir has exerted a fascination on us for many decades now, eliciting passionate response from film viewers, cineastes and artists alike. The reason there is such a passion for noir is that noir itself – in all its many shapes and forms – is inextricably concerned with human beings caught up in states of passion. This is easy to recognize. Seduction. Corruption. Aggression. Submission. Degradation. Desolation. Bruised integrity. Bitter enmity. Obsession. Anguish. Regret. Fury. These are the high passions of film noir, and a book could be dedicated to each. This book seizes on a somewhat more elusive passion in noir, however – one that appears more muted perhaps, but which may in fact be noir's most profound expression of passion. It examines the seemingly paradoxical passion of *passivity* in film noir. And in doing so it places noir within certain currents of art history and philosophy that are similarly concerned with conceptions of the human arrested in strange states of passivity and halted temporality. This is certainly one area in which much remains to be said about noir. Stillness, arrest, passivity – these are underappreciated facets of film noir, both as an artistic form and as a philosophical discourse. Though it tends to escape attention, a passion for stillness, the passion *of* passivity, is one of noir's most alluring elements. Indeed, noir cinema has produced some of our culture's most riveting images of the human in strange intervals of stillness, detachment and suspended time.

In the book that follows, via attention to a number of iconographical gestures that recur across noir films of every era, I trace such depictions of passivity from within classics such as *This Gun for Hire* (Dir. Frank Tuttle, 1942), *The Killers* (Dir. Robert Siodmak, 1946) and *Cat People* (Dir. Jacques Tourneur, 1942), through early '*neo*-noir' films such as *Alphaville* (Dir. Jean-Luc Godard, 1965) and *The Long Goodbye* (Dir. Robert Altman, 1973), and on to modern noirs such as *The Man Who Wasn't There* (Dir. the Coen brothers, 2001), *2046* (Dir. Wong Kar-Wai, 2005) and *Transit* (Dir. Christian Petzold, 2018). In doing so, I develop a unique argument about the philosophical import of the depiction of states of passivity within noir and I extend the contexts for our further understanding of noir by teasing out its resonances with traditions in the visual arts. It is important to note that while retrieving the condition of passivity as a powerful and potentially redemptive passion that reverberates in noir, I do not suggest that such a concern with passivity – or with the philosophical qualities I associate with such passivity – is a feature of film noir in general. Rather it is something that distinguishes a certain quotient of noir films. As such, the book identifies and examines a certain tradition in noir, pursuing this disquisition via a number of themes that are at once artistic and philosophical in key: chiefly the related themes of iconography, temporality and affect. To draw this out, the book engages with a range of philosophers and thinkers across disciplines, invoking the works of Gilles Deleuze and Giorgio Agamben in particular.

Defining noir, or, the terminally indeterminable

In linguistics, the concept of 'semantic drift' is used to address the way in which the usage or meaning of a term has the capacity to mutate over time. As a result, any given term can accrue a meaning – or set of meanings – that is not entirely stable, but which can even appear multiple and contrary, precisely because of the knotted, schismatic legacy of the term's semantic development. All terms are necessarily open to semantic drift, and indeed any living language requires the possibilities of such drift for its survival. But certain terms – terms that exhibit exorbitant qualities of drift – are notable for the manner with which they seem to persist precisely *because* of the unstable meaning they generate and evoke. In modern English, few terms demonstrate this more entropic force of semantic drift quite like the term 'noir', which – in addition to being a term recruited into English from the French language – has become, in many respects, a cultural keyword, a sign, for a distinct indeterminacy at work in culture and communication itself.

Is it surprising, then, that the question 'What *is* noir?' should remain such a well-worn refrain?

Since the 1970s, this thorny query has been compounded by the manner in which the term has expanded promiscuously across an eclectic array of media and commodity forms, shaping everything from comic books and video games to perfumes and designer clothes. In this hazy way, as James Naremore has put it, noir has acquired the status of a 'worldwide mass memory'.[1] Needless to say, a philologist, art historian or film theorist may be able to trace a series of specific genealogies for each iteration of noir, and may – in doing so – broadly impart a functioning sense of what is connoted by the term in specific contexts. But the term itself – and the core concept it is presumed to describe – remains chimerical and elusive. In short, noir designates no straightforward object of inquiry. Noir, and – in particular – film noir, from which the term has acquired its mercurial cultural currency, is this strange concoction of associations, then: a term that drifts amorphously across diverse semantic registers, yet which nevertheless serves to address something significant in human experience, culture and aesthetics. My study in these pages is one that aims not to expel the indeterminacy that hovers around the enigmatic term 'noir' but rather to take such indeterminacy as my true object of inquiry. In particular, as a study primarily grounded in film iconography, I wish to attend to certain recurring images of the human figure caught in indeterminate, attenuated or 'in-between' states in film noir, and to examine the qualities of affect and temporality thereby invested in these images.

The French film critic Frank Nino is credited with coining the term 'film noir' in 1946, while discussing the emergence of what, for him, seemed a dark new range of American films fused with 'the dynamism of violent death'.[2] As Naremore has observed, however, the term's origin is a little more complex, and, in fact, French film critics had earlier applied the term 'film noir' to domestic crime melodramas such as *Pépé le Moko* (Dir. Julien Duvivier, 1936) and *Le jour se lève* (Dir. Marcel Carné, 1939).[3] Nevertheless, it was the same French writers who eventually came to identify the term more exclusively with American cinema, with Raymonde Borde and Etienne Chaumeton – in the first concerted study of noir – suggesting that films such as *The Maltese Falcon* (Dir. John Huston, 1941) and *This Gun for Hire* marked the occasion of noir's genesis.[4] In the decades that followed, the term gradually infiltrated film discourse in the Anglophone world, and in the 1970s and early 1980s it became the subject of frenetic scholarly research. Much of this early work on noir concerned itself with classification. There evolved three central approaches in this regard: the argument that film noir was a coherent genre;[5] the suggestion that it was not a genre but, instead, a distinct period or cycle of filmmaking (one obtaining during the years 1940–59);[6] and the idea that noir was, in fact, best understood as a visual style or sensibility.[7] In recent decades, however, this concern with classification has been overtaken by a more perplexing suggestion: the proposition that noir is, in fact, purely a phantom of film discourse and cinephilia.[8] For Stephen

Neale, noir is a chimera borne of cinema and its criticism, and doomed to 'incoherence'.[9] Thomas Elsaesser, meanwhile, declares something similar:

> [Noir's] most stable characteristic is its 'absent-centredness', its displacements, its over-determinedness, whose ghostly existence as too many discourses, instead of cancelling each other out, merely seems to amplify the term's resonance and suggestiveness.[10]

Without wishing to counter this suggestion that noir is, in some sense, fated to incoherence, I would suggest that part of the reason noir has been so 'over-determined' is that, very frequently, noir films – and noir images more generally – tend to relay conceptions of the human at its most indeterminate. Indeterminacy is itself a key thematic in noir. In this study I wish to embrace that condition of indeterminacy by approaching noir in terms of feeling and affect – qualities of experience that are seldom coherent but rather radial and dispersive. Indeed, the affective has always seemed the realm most appropriate to noir. Right from the outset, Borde and Chaumeton drew special attention to its 'oneiric, strange, erotic, ambivalent, and cruel' qualities.[11] In gauging noir in terms of affect, I also echo Henrik Gustafsson, who considers noir to be a peculiarly *affecting* category of cinematic experience and one, moreover, that frequently evinces a unique concern with the phenomenon of affect.[12] Gustafsson suggests that 'rather than defining what film noir is, establishing its centre and origin, it might be more helpful to ask what it does, how it engages and affects us'.[13] In pursuing such questions, his instincts chime well with the so-called 'affective turn' in cultural studies in recent decades. Affect theory makes central the human's embodied and sensorial experience, underlining the irreducible relational interactions of the human organism within its environment.[14] It exposes the human being's implication in a dynamic, intricate, emergent reality and in what the philosopher Gilles Deleuze might describe as the restless tumult of its own becoming. My interest throughout this study is in that tumult and in the curious passivity that one's inevitable and irrevocable exposure to it engenders in a certain kind of noir protagonist. In the chapters that follow I isolate a distinctive iconography of 'self-affective' passivity that recurs in classic noir and that has continued in noir of the modern era. Though it has often been too simply perceived as indicative of existential angst, sociocultural disenchantment or pathological detachment, this imagery of passivity, I suggest, might at times be better understood as demonstrative of a 'pure affectivity' – an affective attentiveness to one's own being and becoming: to one's own taking place. This would be a condition of 'radical passivity', as Thomas Carl Wall has defined it:

> Passivity in the radical sense, before it is simply opposed to activity, is passive with regard to *itself*, and thus it submits to itself as though it were an exterior power.[15]

Passivity, on these terms, is fundamentally an affective state. It is 'purely passionate', as Wall puts it.[16]

Here, then, contrary to orthodox understanding, passivity is deemed a passion. And it is a 'power'. Invoking an expression from the verse of the poet Rainer Maria Rilke, I term the noir protagonist's distinctive *exposure* and *attentiveness* to this passionate affective state as constituting a sustained experience of the 'dark interval'. The latter experience occurs when – in a condition of radical receptivity to the unfolding of one's own existence and to the potential inherent in that existence – one is suddenly *stilled*, becoming for a suspended moment merely 'the rest between two notes', as Rilke puts it.[17] In the grip of such a passionate passivity, the human quivers between the notes of the finite and the infinite, the temporal and the eternal, the possible and the impossible, the active and the inert, and ultimately intuits its 'self' as existing always and only as a body in a state of 'relation' – less as an identity and more as a process, one unfolding in a constant and complex relay across a field of potentials. As Brian Massumi would put it, the passionate awakening to 'intensity' that is experienced in this suspenseful interval alerts us to a resonant doubling of sensation that in fact ghosts alongside every moment of our lives. This sensation, a fizzling sense of the self-*as*-relation, lingers only on the edges of our perception. Following Spinoza, Massumi calls it affect.[18]

This dark interval, as it occurs in noir, is mirrored by a conception of an elusive 'interval' of exhilarating passivity that recurs in much contemporary philosophy – an interval of halted and charged duration that lays bare an enigmatic sense of potentiality. In the next chapter I will give a brief overview of this philosophical figure as it occurs in the work of Gilles Deleuze, Maurice Blanchot and a number of other thinkers. Throughout the book, in pursuing this trope of the dark interval in noir, I develop an implicit dialogue between Deleuze, Blanchot and a third philosopher, Giorgio Agamben. One of the key motifs in Agamben's work is that of a fundamental ontological 'suspension', a state of passive disruption or 'inoperativity' in which a mercurial sense of potentiality is glimpsed, arising when a human being becomes acutely sensitive to its own taking place. In Blanchot and Deleuze we find a concern with a similar experience of suspension – a suspension that, at rare moments, solicits an enigmatic experience of what Deleuze has termed 'beatitude'.

Potential and potentiality

This concept of 'beatitude' – which I will discuss in due course – is just one of many that Deleuze borrows from the work of the seventeenth-century philosopher Baruch Spinoza. Another of these important concepts is *potentia*, which for Spinoza indicates a power essential to the human being: its capacity *to be affected*. Within Spinoza's metaphysical model – where every 'mode' or element in existence is implicated in the existence of every other, each element being merely an expression of immanent, underlying forces and relations of which the universe consists – this capacity, the human body's *affectivity*, underwrites every aspect of human existence. As Elena del Río has put it, in a work that examines film performance in light of Deleuze/Spinoza's concepts, 'this capacity for existence expresses itself both in the body's *active power* to affect, and in its *passive power* to be affected by, other bodies. Affects are thus the *powers of the body*.'[19]

As del Río observes, for Deleuze/Spinoza this quality of *potentia*, the fundamentally 'open' condition of affective possibility that informs the human's existence, is not reducible to – and, indeed, is very frequently in conflict with – another more restrictive form of power (*potestas*) that also serves to condition existence. The latter form of power, *potestas*, might best be understood as producing a more rigid and deterministic regime of possibility, one that is delimited and codified by the dominant ideological social structures that emerge in any given period, and in accordance with the specific discourses and orders of representation that have secured the stability of such social structures. (Of course, as Mark Bould has persuasively demonstrated, a dominant concern in film noir centres on the experience of human subjects whose possibilities are routinely enclosed by a social field of complex determinants.)[20]

In del Río's work on film, she examines the ways in which certain qualities of cinematic performance, primarily arising from gesture, can be understood to express and disclose the human's more radical and liberating affective potential as *potentia*: the capacity to be affected. In my study, the term 'potential' is similarly intended to evoke Deleuze/Spinoza's concept of *potentia* as a form of affective possibility that is proper to the human and irreducible – not to mention resistant – to more constrictive and hegemonic manifestations of power. Significantly, where many thinkers of affective potential, including del Río, are drawn primarily to examples of the human's *active* powers of affection, in my disquisition on film noir I am primarily examining the more *passive* power of *being affected*, specifically with the intent of highlighting the fact that this passive power – as Wall's notion of 'radical passivity' suggests – involves (somewhat enigmatically) an even more undistilled sense of power and potential still: a disclosure of potential in its most raw and rarefied state. It is a passivity, then, that is radically *receptive*. Far from denoting a condition of impotence, we might even regard this state as equivalent to the Nietzschean 'will to power'. This is how Deleuze, too, has understood the somewhat counterintuitive passivity inherent in the Nietzschean concept:

> For Nietzsche, the capacity for being affected is not necessarily a passivity but an affectivity, a sensibility, a sensation ... a *feeling of power* ... This

is why Nietzsche always says that the will to power is 'the primitive affective form' from which all other feelings derive. Or better still: 'The will to power is not a being, not a becoming, but a *pathos*. Pathos is the most elementary fact from which a being arises'.[21]

I examine the significance of this pathos – this elementary and mercurial capacity to be affected – specifically in relation to a subtle but distinct iconography of passivity, stillness and quietude that recurs across noir films of every era.

Before moving on, it may prove useful here to observe the resonances between Deleuze/Spinoza's concept of 'potential' and Giorgio Agamben's concept of 'potentiality'. As Leland De La Durantaye has observed, 'potentiality' is the dominant leitmotif in Agamben's thought. And yet, as De La Durantaye also quite rightly notes, identifying the centrality of this idea 'is a far cry from understanding it'.[22] While it is a difficult and slippery concept, potentiality in Agamben's work tends to involve an impassioned intuition of one's own possibility – one that enthrals the human being during an experience of profound self-affection. This passion can be understood as, in effect, what the human itself *is*. That is to say, in such moments – those 'dark intervals' during which the human glimpses or intuits this very passion that both informs and encapsulates it – the human can be regarded as nothing other than 'a pure passion affecting itself'.[23] What is disclosed to us in such an experience of 'pure passion' is the potential that our passion shelters. Potential here is not simply possibility but something in excess of possibility. As we have observed, possibility – in the quotidian sense of the term – always describes a field of potential events and actions circumscribed by the dominant ideologies, discourses and paradigms of the day. But potentiality itself exceeds such circumstance. For example, it discloses possibilities that draw not solely from the 'actual' but which may instead reverberate across the more irreducible register of the 'virtual'. Moreover, as Agamben points out repeatedly in his many works, 'potentiality' is in every instance twinned with its own 'impotentiality'.[24] The latter category would account for all those potentials – disclosed to the human being in its thoughts, its sensations, its feelings, its understanding – that do not *pass over* into actuality as 'acts' but which, nevertheless, remain invested with the same 'pure potential' as those that do. (This notion is resonant with Agamben's understanding of the influence of 'non-lived experience' elsewhere in his work.)[25] At an anecdotal level, we might think of the way a person can nurse fantasies or regrets founded on moments where a certain action was not taken – all the 'what-might-have-beens' that accumulate in a life. (This is a common experience in classic noir, of course, very much to the fore in Fritz Lang films such as *The Woman in the Window* (1944) and *Scarlet Street* (1945).) Such potentials may not have been *realized*, but they remain a significant force or power in a person's life. Thus, insomuch as impotentiality accounts for all potentials – those that pass into actuality and those that do not – this impotentiality has a kind of primacy even beyond potentiality. It is the font of potential itself, we might say. And, insomuch as the human is one who can – in this manner – plumb the depths of its own impotentiality, then what truly distinguishes the human from other beings is the ability to *suspend* the terms of what is possible for it. In other words, the human is marked by its facility to conceive both of its being as it is and of its being *other* than it is, just as it is no less marked by what Friedrich Nietzsche would call its 'untimely' inclination to lapse out of historicist conceptions of chronological time and to experience genuine happiness instead only as a forgetting of time and history.[26] This *impotentiality* is an ontological feature of human experience that has far-reaching consequences, not the least of which are ethical. The key point is that, on these terms, our capacity for action is first and foremost an incapacity. Again, we might call it a 'radical passivity', as Wall has gleaned it, or even a 'powerlessness', in the contexts in which both Maurice Blanchot and Gilles Deleuze use this term. This power founded in a strange 'incapacity' or 'powerlessness' – this 'pure passion' – arises from our irreducible exposure to affect: from our unavowable, involuntary capacity to be affected. Significantly, as we shall see, this latter notion of an intractable yet strangely redemptive powerlessness is one that Deleuze insists has come to haunt the protagonist of much modern cinema. As I argue, it can be understood, in particular, to haunt a certain vein of noir protagonist, who – in a perverse but also strangely exalted condition of passivity – seems to relent to or lapse into a radical state: that of 'a pure passion affecting itself'.

The 'lapse' of the dark interval

One way to think of the experience of the interval in film noir is indeed as a 'lapse', with all the rich connotations that this word carries. In fact, if there is an overriding narrative phenomenon that could be located in every film noir, I would suggest it is the phenomenon of *lapse*. The protagonists of noir are people who lapse into crime, collapse into love, fall from grace, lose their way, lose their minds. The focus of my study here is on another kind of lapse, however. It is often configured as a temporal lapse, a lapse into a time that seems *outside* of time. It is also configured as an ontological lapse – a lapse into a zone of indistinction, between familiar registers (man/animal, living/dead), where the very concept of 'the human' itself comes into question. Importantly, such a lapse should not be understood as irreducibly pessimistic or simply melancholic. In the Oxford English Dictionary, we can retrieve a sense of the verb 'lapse' that would mean something else entirely: 'To glide, to pass with an effortless motion.'[27] In noir, the shuddering lapse of the dark interval may consume and destroy protagonists, but there are a great many, too, who learn to glide, who adjust to the perpetual scintillations of their own *elapsing*.

Sometimes this lapse is staged as an enigmatic and ecstatic 'moment': an interval, in which the protagonist encounters something – a thought, a sensation, a force – which he or she (though it is usually a 'he') cannot apprehend. Thereafter, the protagonist is marked as *intervallic*, in the terms that I will develop throughout this study. We should note here a strong resonance with the force of the 'time-image' as Gilles Deleuze has defined it in his influential taxonomy of cinema. In essence, Deleuze argues that in the post-war period, the classical cinema (which he terms the 'regime of the movement-image'), marked by its consistent spatiotemporal relations and stable narrative logic, was both complemented and challenged by the emergence of a more disruptive regime, that of the 'time-image'. The latter regime – which Deleuze associates very closely with cinema's rendering of the body's affective states, and, in particular, the body's 'tirednesses and waitings' – gives access to a 'direct image' of time.[28]

Significantly, the transition between the regime of the movement-image and that of the time-image occurs precisely as a result of a change in the status and the functioning of a formal condition of cinematic editing that Deleuze terms 'the interval'. In classical narrative cinema, such an interval is invariably constituted by a shot (or series of shots) which serves to facilitate the smooth and coherent connection between a character's perception and their affective response to it. (In broad terms, the interval stitches together a sense of there being a 'natural' transition between actions and reactions, causes and effects.) For this reason, the interval is very often constituted by an 'affection-image', frequently a close-up of the human face, which – as Deleuze puts it – 'occupies' the interval 'without filling it up'.[29] Deleuze argues that within the regime of 'the movement-image', the more radical transitional force of possibility resident in the interval is generally subdued or unexplored; instead, the interval is turned towards providing and preserving a sense of temporal coherence and a stable sensorimotor logic at the heart of the film's narrative world. With the advent of the regime of the 'time-image', however, the interval no longer provides any such certainty. In this more radical interval, connections between action and reaction, perception and response, no longer follow predictable trajectories and rational conventions of montage, but are disrupted and disturbed, as the immense potential resident in the interval suddenly flares up. Into this space – the space of the now somewhat dysfunctional interval – there rushes sensations and affects (forces of potential) that are dynamic and dispersive, both for the characters on-screen and for the film's viewers.

Of course, such qualities are the hallmarks of the modernist cinema that rose to the fore in Europe and elsewhere during the 1950s and 1960s, and, indeed, Deleuze traces the emergence of 'time-images' to the films of the Italian neorealist movement that blossomed at the end of the Second World War.[30]

Yet, as Elena del Río has observed, one can make a compelling argument that the time-image also has its origins in film noir.[31] And, indeed, we should be very sensitive, I argue, to the very evocative resonances between the archetypal noir antihero and that figure that Deleuze has called 'the seer'.[32] The seer, for Deleuze, is a cinematic protagonist who – having been made bereft of agency by the dissociative force of the time-image – nevertheless survives this condition by becoming a consummate *surveyor* of time. The exemplary figure in this regard may well be Sandro (Gabriele Ferzetti) in *L'Avventura* (Dir. Michelangelo Antonioni, 1960), but we can trace this figure's lineage back to *intervallic* noir protagonists such as the disarmingly passive protagonist, Ole Andersson (Burt Lancaster) in *The Killers* (Dir. Robert Siodmak, 1946). There is a distinctly ecstatic but also markedly elegiac quality to the seer's experience. Sensitive to the processual force of time-as-becoming and to the intensive canter and recoil of one's own duration, this surveyor of time becomes the channel of untimely temporal affects unmoored from narratives of human provenance, progress and destiny.

Notably, in noir we do not always witness the rupture of the interval, the force or convulsion of the lapse, but are introduced instead to protagonists that are already *intervallic*. Such protagonists are relayed through a distinctive iconography, which I delineate in the first chapter. Recurrently, this iconography alights on images of self-affection, withdrawal and passivity. But this passivity – often rendered through a slowness, a restraint and a dense, affective embodiment in the actors' performances – is deceptive. Very often, despite their stillness, and despite the melancholy that shimmers around them like an aura, these passive figures – these intervallic noir icons – are vibrant with an acute sense of life. The dark interval exposes this vitality that underwrites life: it discloses to the noir protagonist the intensive quality of his or her 'being-as-such', whereby he or she grasps a sense of their being neither an 'agent' nor a 'subject' but something more mercurial: a 'singularity', a singular *expression* of life, immersed always in the tumult and transition of an impersonal becoming. The predicament for these characters is whether they can appropriate the singular potential or indeterminate conflux of potentials that inform their life – 'a life', as Deleuze might call it. *How does one appropriate the 'passion' that one is?* This tasking question is one uniquely attuned to the wavelength of noir.

Ultimately, what the intervallic noir protagonist is often imbued with, as a result of this task, is a somewhat elegiac modality: a poignant, yet not necessarily pessimistic, adjustment to one's own becoming that is more akin to a 'manner' than an identity. Inevitably, this is a disposition that can be melancholic, but also a disposition that may be hopeful and charged with potentiality. Such a disposition might be regarded as investing the noir protagonist with a wonderful quality of 'poise'. The latter term denotes an elegance and grace in one's bearing, as well as an ability to inhabit a state of physical suspension: to negotiate and deliver the appropriate gesture at a moment loaded with suspense. Significantly, both poise and composure are terms that hail etymologically from the Old French term for weight (*peser*). This points, too, to the significance of embodiment – the 'weightedness' of the noir body – in noir performance. Composure is not strictly an internal property of the mind, an interior calmness; it is as much a property of the body: an ability to compose one's body within one's environment, or to make it appear composed. Indeed, in Spinoza's philosophy, all anybody can and does do (as a body, as a 'mode' of being) is enter into intensive relations with other beings, producing transient 'compositions' which – even in their drift towards decomposition and recomposition – serve to mark and alter each being involved in the encounter. Moreover, acceptance of this principle, as Deleuze understood it, involves an ethics that is also an aesthetics: the requirement to artfully pursue and arrange 'good encounters' and to experiment with potential relations.[33] Indeed, it is in such compositional potential – 'a social field defined … by the lines of flight running through it' – that Deleuze and Félix Guattari locate a sociopolitical and communal solidarity available to humans, and available to them precisely as desiring bodies capable of countering oppressive or disciplinary assemblages with fresh alliances and bold strategies of composition.[34] Amidst the flux of composition and decomposition, and in the forging of a disposition to one's environment that is always at the same time a stoic alliance with the forces of difference and indeterminacy, we can glimpse the intervallic qualities of composure and lapse that respond so dexterously to the shifting terrain of human experience. In film noir, encounters are seldom simply 'good', of course. But a certain variety of noir protagonist – often an ascetic yet profoundly emotional figure – nevertheless seems acutely sensitive to these values.

Noir: Classic and modern

While the dark interval – both as a narrative phenomenon and as a distinct iconography – is very visible in the films of the 'classic' era of noir, I argue that it has become a more complex and more self-conscious trope since the advent of the 'modern noir' in the late 1960s. Before fleshing out this point, let me make a short digression to reflect upon the distinction between 'classic' and 'modern' noir.

In my view, the long-standing division between classic film noir and some newer variety of noir, '*neo*-noir', has become unsustainable. If *neo*-noir is perceived as gathering momentum early in the 1970s in the shape of films such as *Chinatown* (Dir. Roman Polanski, 1973), *The Long Goodbye* (Dir. Robert Altman, 1973) and *The Conversation* (Dir. Francis Ford Coppola, 1974), that means that *neo*-noir has been around for fifty years, at least twice as long as the so-called 'classic' cycle of noir. However, if noir is to be understood in terms of the affective scope of its iconography rather than in historicist terms that are purely – and too reductively – chronological, then film noir might be considered to exist fluidly from the late 1930s through to today. By now, the term has come to function in a way similar to a term such as 'baroque': it can be understood to refer to a period *and* to the style or mood that this particular period bequeathed to future generations as its aesthetic legacy.

Notwithstanding the necessity to move beyond the creaky distinction between noir and *neo*-noir, I believe that *Point Blank* (Dir. John Boorman, 1967) does provide a useful marker for distinguishing a decisive transition that takes place in noir in the years after the 'classic' cycle ran its course. *Point Blank*, as Andrew Spicer has observed, finds noir becoming radically more self-conscious.[35] I would suggest that it is specifically self-conscious in its exposition of an iconography (and the tropes and themes associated with it) that always resided, if often only incipiently, in films of the classic era: the iconography of the dark interval, the moment of profound self-affection. As its title suggests, *Point Blank* makes the dark interval central. It takes it as its subject. By the film's end the entire duration of the narrative, which extends over many days, will recoil upon itself, revealed as a single moment. Allied to this, the most provocative aspect of Boorman's film is that it constitutes a narrative that effaces itself, a narrative that ultimately stages its own disappearance. By way of a ruse, the film appears to chart the determined revenge of a heist-man (Lee Marvin) who – having been shot and left for dead by his accomplices – manages to make his way from the abandoned island penitentiary of Alcatraz to the city of Los Angeles, whereupon he delivers vengeance. All is not quite as it seems, however. The film's formal play – disjunctive POV, abstract scenography, strange visual and narrative repetitions – emphasizes a dreamlike, looping quality to Walker's progress. Eventually, we understand that his revenge narrative is but the fantasy of a fatally wounded man in the final moment of his life. What is vital to acknowledge about *Point Blank*, however, is that its devastation of the site of narrative is more than a gratifying narrative pleasure. The narrative of *Point Blank* vacates itself in such a manner that what it exposes – however tenuously, however spectrally – is the trace of a potentiality that underwrites narrative itself and, more fundamentally, underwrites human experience of every order. It reveals that Walker's life has, in a very specific sense, as much potential in the interval of his final moment as it does in any prior moment of his life.[36] Potential is virtual as well as actual. This is *how* the film brings into view something that has always been ineluctably at the very core of noir – the 'blank point', the dark interval of a strange intuition of potential – and how it explicitly makes this trope the philosophical centre of the film.

In the wake of Boorman's film and its attention to a blank point – which is to say, its attention to the 'dark interval' – the modern era of noir has been marked by a remarkable formal concern with precisely this interval, this blank point or existential caesura. Many of the most well-regarded 'noirs' of recent decades are notable for staging their own effacement just as *Point Blank* does, their narratives evaporating indeterminately into a 'zero point' of narration at their conclusion. Prominent examples would include *Romeo's Bleeding* (Dir. Peter Medak, 1993), *The Usual Suspects* (Dir. Bryan Singer, 1995), *Lost Highway* (Dir. David Lynch, 1997), *Memento* (Dir. Christopher Nolan, 2000), *Mulholland Drive* (Dir. David Lynch, 2001), *The Man Who Wasn't There* (Dir. Joel Coen, 2001), *Shutter Island* (Dir. Martin Scorsese, 2010), *Inception* (Dir. Christopher Nolan, 2010), *Nocturnal Animals* (Dir. Tom Ford, 2016), *You Were Never Really Here* (Dir. Lynne Ramsay, 2017), *Destroyer* (Dir. Karyn Kusama, 2018) and *Transit* (Dir. Christian Petzold, 2018). An important point to grasp about modern noir films, however, is that even when they do not dissolve before us at the close in this way, their narratives tend to deal thematically with the significance of this dark interval, this conceptual 'vanishing point'. Very often, at the level of iconography, they appear fixated upon the *intervallic* passivity and detachment of their protagonists. Indeed, these qualities inform many of the films deemed to constitute the first wave of '*neo*-noir', among them *The Long Goodbye, Chinatown, The Conversation, Night Moves* (Dir. Arthur Penn, 1975), *The Passenger* (Dir. Michelangelo Antonioni, 1975) and *The American Friend* (Dir. Wim Wenders, 1977), albeit in ways quite discrete to each film. And these attributes continue to mark many contemporary noirs.

It is on these terms, then, that a distinction between 'classic' and 'modern' noir is evoked in my study. Ironically, one could argue that the great majority of contemporary noir films are, in fact, not modern at all, but instead quite continuous with a somewhat 'generic' understanding of noir as a cinema marked visually by high contrast lighting or dynamic use of colour, a cinema concerned thematically with crime, psychology and sexuality, and a cinema marked narratively by intrigue, deception and dramatic reversals. This is, indeed, the popular understanding of what film noir 'means' and it is therefore no surprise that in the critical reception of contemporary noir 'movies' we find that the descriptive term 'film noir', or often simply 'noir', has increasingly reasserted itself, usurping the term '*neo*-noir' that was such a mainstay of film criticism throughout the 1980s and 1990s. However, even while the historical distinctions between film noir and *neo*-noir may gradually fall into disuse, perhaps a more valid distinction can be retained in the term 'modern noir' as I employ it.

Žižek's hard kernel

Notably, the significance of a 'blank' or 'void' condition in noir has been observed before by Slavoj Žižek. Indeed, some of the finest insights into film noir have been delivered by Žižek, and the Lacanian/Kantian analysis of noir that he produces in a celebrated essay anticipates, to some extent, elements of my own analysis here. In '"The Thing That Thinks": The Kantian Background of the Noir Subject', Žižek examines the way in which the protagonists of modern noirs such as *Blade Runner* (Dir. Ridley Scott, 1982) and *Angel Heart* (Dir. Alan Parker, 1987) find themselves bound to an 'irreducible gap',[37] ejected from the conventional ideological narrative of the social order (the Lacanian 'Symbolic' realm), and left instead to grapple with the 'Cartesian-Kantian problematic of the subject qua pure, substanceless "I think"'.[38] The noir protagonist thus becomes an expression of the 'cogito', *pure thought* at its most paranoiac; 'nothing but a gaze paradoxically entitled to observe the world in which I do not exist', as Žižek puts it.[39] In contrast to the vein of 'classical logic-and-deduction detective fiction', where the detective remains integrated within the symbolic order, Žižek says,

> The noir narrative reduces the hero to a passive observer transfixed by the succession of fantasy scenes, to a gaze powerlessly gaping at them: even when the hero seems 'active', one cannot avoid the impression that he simultaneously occupies the position of a disengaged observer, witnessing with incredulity the strange, almost submarine, succession of events in which he remains trapped.[40]

This passivity is an articulation of the Freudian 'drive', as opposed to 'desire', says Žižek. Unlike 'desire', 'drive is not "progressive" but rather "regressive", bound to circulate endlessly around some fixed point of attraction, immobilised by its power of fascination'.[41]

This conception of the noir hero – particularly the male hero – as a figure governed by a regressive passivity, a passivity wrought of an arresting, debilitating drive, is one that has been observed elsewhere, of course. Janey Place, for instance, notes the 'general passivity and impotence which characterises the film noir male',[42] while Elizabeth Cowie and Frank Krutnik have each pointed to this hero's tendency towards 'masochism'.[43] While there is no question that passivity in noir – particularly as it pertains to the male protagonist – is often couched in an apparent masochism or fatalism,[44] not all passivity in noir is simply a situational symptom of trauma or loss or a sign of existential capitulation. On the register of affect or *pathos*, passivity can mark a more affirmative openness to potential and power, as Spinoza and Nietzsche would have it. (This is the lens through which I approach a certain iconography of noir passivity in Chapter 1.) What is interesting, furthermore, if we return to Žižek, is his assignment of this decidedly debilitating passivity of the 'drive' to the noir hero, in the wake of their approaching the impossible limit experience, the 'hard kernel' of the Lacanian 'Real'.[45] Yet, by contrast, in his analysis, elsewhere, of *Stromboli* (Dir. Roberto Rossellini, 1950), Žižek argues that when Karin (Ingrid Bergman) approaches a similar limit, her own submission to 'symbolic suicide' is a paradigmatic 'act' of freedom.[46] The 'act', says Žižek, invoking the Hegelian trope of 'abstract negativity', occurs in 'the moment when the subject who is its bearer *suspends* the network of symbolic fictions which serve as a support to his daily life and confronts again the radical negativity upon which they are founded'.[47] It is the moment itself – the moment of 'tarrying with the negative', as Žižek puts it – which makes Karin's suspension an *act*. Afterwards, she, too, by Žižek's logic, will face a return to desire (the Symbolic) or a collapse into the destructive stalling of the drives (dysfunction in the Real), but during the interval of suspension in which the act of freedom is *borne* out, what emerges for Karin is 'supreme bliss'. This is the bliss that surges to the fore '*as soon as we renounce all symbolic ties ... The act in the Lacanian sense is nothing but this withdrawal of the fact that we have nothing to lose in a loss*'.[48] I do not see why we could not argue that such an experience of liberation – the realization that there is 'nothing to lose in a loss', rather than merely a masochistic repetition of loss – is also available to those passive noir icons who so often find themselves similarly suspended in a moment that exceeds the symbolic reach of the signifier, those moments of self-affection that I term the 'dark interval'. Indeed, many noir protagonists appear idiosyncratically invested with a unique quality to *persist* in this state of 'suspension', and so to inhabit an amorphous condition of 'freedom', as Žižek might have it. In my study I develop implicitly a conception of such 'freedom' – howsoever spectral or transient – through reflection on the Spinozist experience of 'beatitude' that both Deleuze and Agamben have invoked in their work.[49] Freedom on these terms would be reconceived as an attentiveness to the force of potentiality and the capacities of one's own passion. While I do not further invoke Žižek's stimulating analysis in 'The Thing That Thinks', the reader is invited to bear in mind both the resonances and the points of disagreement outlined above.

Suspension in the interval

In the chapters that follow, I pursue a range of examples of the 'potentiality' that is opened up to noir protagonists who – undergoing a suspension in the 'dark interval' – are confronted with the radical passivity and passionate becoming that subtends their sense of 'self' and indeed their very concept of existence. I begin in Chapter 1 by identifying an iconography of the interval as it emerges in classic noir, before then relating it to an older iconography of the *intervallic*: the imagery of melancholy and *acedia* that recurs in Medieval and Renaissance art. I proceed from there to examine passivity in the classic noir protagonist, closing with an analysis of the opening shot of *The Killers* (Dir. Robert Siodmak, 1944) in which I argue that its noir antihero (Burt Lancaster) experiences a quasi-redemptive beatitude at the point of death.

In each of the subsequent chapters I reflect upon specific iterations of the dark interval. In Chapter 2 I examine how the protagonist of the Coen brothers' *The Man Who Wasn't There* – the profoundly passive Ed Crane (Billy Bob Thornton) – finds himself exposed to the dark interval, an exposure that gradually renders his narrative identity increasingly obsolete, the more he defers to his 'passion'. (A concern with the collapse of narrative identity has been integral to noir since the classic era.[50]) Drawing comparisons between the Coens' film and Carl Theodor Dreyer's *The Passion of Joan of Arc* (1928), I draw heavily upon Deleuze's arsenal of film concepts.

In Chapter 3 I return to older noir terrain to examine noir-horror hybrid *Cat People* (Dir. Jacques Tourneur, 1942) together with Giorgio Agamben's reflections on the Rilkean concept of 'the Open'. The latter – for Rilke – constitutes a prelapsarian affective space of immediate plenitude, one from which the human has become divorced. *Cat People*'s chief concern, I suggest, is with the evocation of this problematic space and with the exposure of the uncertain ontological interval that both conjoins and separates man and animal, that caesura by which the category of 'the human' itself is assured and yet forever left in question. As such, the film stages a tragic representation of the human's alienation from its more fundamental implication in circuits of affect and becoming. Yet I also observe how, within the film, the condition of lassitude and the work of art are presented as a potentially redemptive means of resolving this pivotal breach.

Chapters 4 and 5 are conceived as counterparts whereby I bring *Alphaville* (Dir. Jean-Luc Godard, 1965) and *2046* (Dir. Wong Kar-Wai, 2004) into a dialogue that examines the role of the 'affective interval' in noir. Each film invokes noir in very specific ways – essentially as a myth of the 'dark interval'. In Godard's film the interval is a source of salvation, exposing the human to its affective potential and its powers of change and transformation. In *2046*, by contrast, the interval is somewhat more melancholy. It reveals the capacity for the human to find itself arrested *in* the interval, consumed by the experience of its own taking place, savouring the powers inherent in repetition and drift, while succumbing to the recursive temporality that the interval involves. The noir protagonists of *2046* tend to 'bide time' in a manner that halts and ritualizes the force of change itself, auto-affectively repeating their experiences of the intervallic, rather than daring to 'advance to live' (the mantra of Godard's romantic couple).

In Chapter 6, I investigate another inflection of the dark interval in noir: this time as a lapse in the socio-juridical order. In particular, I explore how this lapse is represented via metaphors of time and temporality, beginning with examples from classic noir (*The Big Clock* (Dir. John Farrow, 1948), *The Stranger* (Dir. Orson Welles, 1946) and *The Unknown Man* (Dir. Richard Thorpe, 1951)) before moving to the modern noir *The Long Goodbye* (Dir. Robert Altman, 1973). In doing so, I meditate upon yet another inflection of the interval: the anarchic potentiality resident in the interval of 'pure violence', as Walter Benjamin and Agamben understand it. In Chapter 7, I reflect on the 'ends' of noir as they emerge in *The Missing Person* (Dir. Noah Buschel, 2010) and *The Big Lebowski* (Dir. the Coen brothers, 1998) respectively. Each film offers very resonant and yet very divergent visions of community in a modern era that, as Agamben has described it, is characterized by a post-historical or 'messianic time' of arrest, suspension and inoperativity. Finally, in the closing 'coda' of the book I point to the ways in which Christian Petzold's *Transit* (2018) brings together many of the themes pursued throughout my study and does so specifically via an engagement with the noir iconography of the dark interval.

I should observe that while I tend to treat classic noir and modern noir interchangeably throughout, it is evident within my analysis that – as I suggested in relation to *Point Blank* – I believe the modern noir engages more self-consciously with the trope of the 'dark interval'. I should also like to point out that I am not arguing that the iconography and associated affective qualities of the dark interval are necessarily central to every film noir or that this concept should overbearingly influence our understanding of noir *in general*. I believe it is present in a certain strain or quotient of noir only, and even in films that may at times appear only partially indebted to noir, as is the case with *2046*. Given the expansiveness of the way in which the term 'noir' is applied, however, I believe it is important to examine the phenomenon at its peripheries as well as at its centre. This book wilfully digs around the edges of noir.

Finally, I would like to draw attention to the grander approach informing this study. While I argue for the significance of this figure of the 'dark interval' in noir, the respective chapters are each conceived as 'meditations', or riffs, on a specific inflection of the dark interval and the potentiality it exposes. It is hoped that they interlink well and that together they constitute a lyrical engagement with what remains, stubbornly, one of film history's most enigmatic objects of inquiry.

Notes

1. James Naremore, *More Than Night: Film Noir in Its Contexts* (London: University of California Press, 1998), 39.
2. Quoted in Raymonde Borde and Etienne Chaumeton, *A Panorama of American Film Noir*, trans. Paul Hammond (San Francisco, CA: City Lights Books, 2002), 5.
3. Naremore, *More Than Night*, 15–16.
4. Borde and Chaumeton, *A Panorama of American Film Noir*, 29.
5. See Foster Hirsch, *The Dark Side of the Screen: Film Noir* (New York: De Capo Press, 1981), and James Damico, 'Film Noir: A Modest Proposal', *Film Reader*, no. 3 (1978), 48–57.

6 On noir as 'a specific period of film history', see Paul Schrader, 'Notes on Film Noir', *Film Comment*, 8.1 (1972), reprinted in *Film Noir Reader*, ed. Alain Silver and James Ursini (New York: Limelight, 1996), 53–63.
7 Schrader also argues that visual style and mood were the twin hallmarks of noir. This suggestion resonates with the earlier view of Raymond Durgnat, who argued that noir required classification 'by motif and tone'. See Raymond Durgnat, 'Paint It Black: The Family Tree of the Film Noir', *Cinema*, 6.7 (1970), reprinted in *Film Noir Reader*, 38.
8 Marc Vernet, 'Film Noir on the Edge of Doom', in *Shades of Noir*, ed. Joan Copjec (London: Verso, 1993), 26.
9 Stephen Neale, *Genre and Hollywood* (London: Routledge, 2000), 153.
10 Thomas Elsaesser, *Weimar Cinema and After: Germany's Historical Imaginary* (London: Routledge, 2000), 423.
11 Borde and Chaumeton, *A Panorama of American Film Noir*, 2.
12 Henrik Gustafsson, 'A Wet Emptiness: The Phenomenology of Film Noir', in *A Companion to Film Noir*, ed. Andrew Spicer and Helen Hanson (Oxford: Wiley Blackwell, 2013), 50–66.
13 Ibid., 52.
14 A good overview is provided in *The Affect Theory Reader*, ed. Melissa Gregg and Gregory J. Seigworth (Durham, NC: Duke University Press, 2010). An early and influential work on affect is Brian Massumi's *Parables for the Virtual: Movement, Affect, Sensation* (Durham, NC: Duke University Press, 2002).
15 Thomas Carl Wall, *Radical Passivity: Levinas, Blanchot and Agamben* (Albany: State University of New York, 1999), 1.
16 Ibid.
17 Rainer Maria Rilke, 'My Life Is Not This Steeply Sloping Hour', trans. Robert Bly, *Selected Poems of Rainer Maria Rilke* (New York: Harper and Row, 1981), 30–1.
18 Massumi, *Parables for the Virtual*, 32.
19 Elena del Río, *Deleuze and the Cinemas of Performance: Powers of Affection* (Edinburgh: Edinburgh University Press, 2008), 8.
20 Mark Bould, *Film Noir: From Berlin to Sin City* (New York: Columbia University Press, 2005).
21 Gilles Deleuze, *Nietzsche and Philosophy*, trans. Hugh Tomlinson (London: Athlone Press, 1983), 77.
22 Leland De La Durantaye, *Giorgio Agamben: A Critical Introduction* (Stanford, CA: Stanford University Press, 2009), 5.
23 Giorgio Agamben, 'Eternal Return and the Paradox of Passion', *Stanford Italian Review*, 6.1–2 (1986), 17.
24 Agamben, *Potentialities: Collected Essays in Philosophy*, trans. Daniel Heller-Roazen (Stanford, CA: Stanford University Press, 1999), 181–4.

25 Agamben, *The Signature of All Things: On Method*, trans. Luca D'Isanto with Kevin Attell (New York: Zone Books, 2009), 101.
26 Friedrich Nietzsche, *Untimely Meditations*, trans. R. J. Hollingdale, ed. Daniel Breazeale (Cambridge: Cambridge University Press, 1997), 62.
27 "lapse, v." *OED Online*. Oxford University Press. Web. 21 November 2014.
28 Deleuze, *Cinema II: The Time-Image*, trans. Hugh Tomlinson and Robert Galeta (London: Athlone Press, 2000), xi–xii.
29 Deleuze, *Cinema I: The Movement-Image*, trans. Hugh Tomlinson and Barbara Habberjam (London: Athlone Press, 1986), 65.
30 David Martin-Jones has noted the unintended consequence of Eurocentrism inherent in Deleuze's location of the origins of the time-image in the ruins of post-war Europe. See *Deleuze and World Cinemas* (London: Continuum, 2011), 10–19.
31 Elena del Río, 'Feminine Energies, or the Outside of Noir', in *Deleuze and Film*, ed. David Martin-Jones and William Brown (Edinburgh: Edinburgh University Press, 2012), 155–72.
32 Deleuze, *Cinema II*, 123.
33 Deleuze, *Spinoza: Practical Philosophy*, trans. Robert Hurley (San Francisco, CA: City Lights Books, 1988), 119.
34 Gilles Deleuze and Félix Guattari, *A Thousand Plateaus: Capitalism and Schizophrenia*, trans. Brian Massumi (Minneapolis: University of Minnesota Press, 1987), 90.
35 Andrew Spicer, *Historical Dictionary of Film Noir* (Lanham MD: Scarecrow Press, 2010), xlv–xlvi.
36 This is why Jack Shadoian is mistaken when he says that Walker, in death, 'imagines a potency that was never his in life'. In fact, he discovers the potentiality that underwrites – and has always underwritten – his being and becoming. See Jack Shadoian, *Dreams and Dead Ends: The American Gangster Film* (Oxford: Oxford University Press, 2003), 255–6.
37 Žižek, 'The Thing That Thinks', in *Shades of Noir*, 212.
38 Ibid., 202.
39 Ibid., 222.
40 Ibid., 223.
41 Ibid., 222.
42 Janey Place, 'Women in Film Noir', in *Women in Film Noir*, ed. E. Ann Kaplan (London: BFI, 1998), 63.
43 See Elizabeth Cowie, 'Film Noir and Women', in *Shades of Noir*, 125; Frank Krutnik, *In a Lonely Street, Film Noir, Genre, Masculinity* (London: Routledge, 2006), 102.
44 Robert B. Pippin, *Fatalism in American Film Noir: Some Cinematic Philosophy* (Charlottesville: University of Virginia Press, 2012).
45 Žižek, 'The Thing That Thinks', 107.

46 Slavoj Žižek, *Enjoy Your Symptom! Jacques Lacan in Hollywood and Out* (London: Routledge, 2001), 42–3.
47 Ibid., 53.
48 Ibid., 43.
49 Žižek himself has referred to 'beatitude' on occasion, although his use of it seems somewhat inconsistent – perhaps due to the prominence of the motif of *jouissance* (bliss) in Lacanian thought. In 'The Thing That Thinks', the subject's return to the Symbolic is described as occurring through the detour of 'fairy beatitude', that is to say fantasy. (See 'The Thing That Thinks', 217.) Elsewhere, in *Tarrying with the Negative*, Žižek explicitly critiques the strain of 'Spinozist beatitude' he sees at work in Deleuze, whereby, as Žižek summarizes it, the 'subject' gives way to an impersonal register of affect. Ultimately, Žižek seems to suggest here that Deleuzian beatitude itself constitutes an implicit and impotent allegiance with the 'Symbolic', a powerless capitulation to the order of representation. See Žižek, *Tarrying with the Negative* (Durham, NC: Duke University Press, 1993), 216–19. Žižek's reflections on 'beatitude' become far more unstable when we consider that, in describing the 'supreme bliss' experienced in an 'act' of subjective destitution, in his treatment of *Stromboli*, Žižek seems much closer to Deleuze than he would perhaps wish to admit. One thinks of Deleuze's reference to Rossellini's 'lonely woman' characters in *Cinema II* who become seers, conduits for the time-image. See Deleuze, *Cinema II*, 2.
50 Žižek, 'The Thing That Thinks', 2.

Prelude: The Interval as a Philosophical Concept

In what follows I provide a brief survey of 'the interval' as a nuanced philosophical concept that has quietly gathered force in continental thought since the middle of the last century. Despite its recurrence, however, it is important to state that the figure of 'the interval' is *not* a unifying principle that carries the same meaning for every philosopher who employs it. Conceptions of it vary considerably. At the same time, the resonances between certain articulations of the concept are also striking. Arguably, the most influential proponent of the interval is Maurice Blanchot. The latter employs the term in a variety of contexts, such that the Blanchotian interval may be understood to allude to categories of the ontological,[1] the aesthetic,[2] or the ethical,[3] depending on the discussion in which it emerges. In every case, what the interval discloses for Blanchot is an arrest or rupture in human experience: a hiatus or gap that has its origins in the divisions wrought in the human by speech and temporality. What makes itself *immediate* in the interval is a fragile, attenuated sense of presence or of becoming, impossible to grasp in itself but to which one may submit in fascination.

A similar conception of 'the interval' – one related both to the technics of cinema and to temporal experience in its most rarefied state – also heavily informs the philosophy of Gilles Deleuze and his poetics of film. Deleuze's interest in 'the cinematic interval' in *The Movement Image* is mirrored in his philosophy by a core concern with the chimerical experience of a 'meanwhile', a 'dead time', that is a kind of passenger in our everyday temporal experience. But this passenger is also, crucially, the time of 'the event'. In *What Is Philosophy?* Deleuze and Félix Guattari describe this strange temporality that seems to persist *outside* of time itself:

The meanwhile is not part of the eternal, but neither is it part of time – it belongs to becoming. The meanwhile, the event, is always a dead time; it is there where nothing takes place, an infinite awaiting that is already infinitely past, awaiting and reserve. This dead time does not come after what happens; it coexists with the instant or time of the accident, but as the immensity of the empty time in which we see it as still to come and as having already happened, in the strange indifference of an intellectual intuition.[4]

The terminology of Deleuze and Guattari here – for example, 'an infinite awaiting' – cannot but evoke the earlier work of Blanchot. It is vital to grasp that the 'waiting' here is not a literal one but rather denotes an experience in which we become suddenly attentive to this time in which *something is happening*. We become attentive, in other words, to the very interval of time's taking place, attentive to a 'dead time' that underscores our experience of progression itself as past, present, and future, and in which, by a strange alchemy that collapses temporal orders, 'the present' can be intuited to coexist with itself as both 'past' and 'yet to come'.[5] (As I will outline in the next chapter, this intuition has its correlate in Henri Bergson's concept of 'paramnesia' as Deleuze employs it in his *Cinema* books.)[6]

One of the cognates for this mercurial interval, of course, is certainly 'the moment', which, as Peter Poellner rightly points out, 'occupies a position of elevated significance' within the discourse of modernism.[7] I would suggest that the late modernist writer Italo Calvino's short story 't zero' grapples uniquely with the force of such a moment, this intervallic dead time. Indeed, the story can be used here to shed some light on this enigmatic concept. Calvino's opening line – 'I have the impression this isn't the first time I've found myself in this situation'[8] – summarizes very succinctly the quality of this experience of the interval. It cannot be reduced merely to the commonplace phenomenon of déjà vu. Rather it is an irruption of what we might call 'the occasion' of presence or consciousness itself and a sudden realization that this occasion is one that necessarily *recurs*.

The situation in Calvino's tale is that of an archer who, in a privileged epiphanic moment, becomes radically aware of precisely this: his 'situation'. The entire text describes a moment that in cinematic language might be described as a 'freeze-frame'. Calvino's tribal archer calls the moment 't_0', so as to distinguish it from the subsequent moments in a series that would proceed from that moment (i.e. t_1, t_2, t_3, etc.). The archer describes the details he is aware of in this moment. His arm holds a bow. Before him, at about a third of its trajectory, is an arrow, and a little farther away still, there is a lion in the midst of leaping, its jaws agape. The archer is aware that many countless *possible outcomes* attend upon this moment. 'I am therefore in one of those situations of uncertainty and expectation where one really doesn't know what to think. And the thought that immediately occurs to me is this: it doesn't seem the first time to me.'⁹ This *is* the first time the archer has experienced this particular instant and yet in it he senses something familiar – something that has already taken place or, as Blanchot would put it, something that has *always already* taken place. Every instant is a repetition of the same transitory, *transitional* instant *between* instants and of the potential ever inherent in all such unheralded passages. In Blanchot's terms, something happens to Calvino's archer here, but it is something 'that he can only recapture by relinquishing [his] power to say "I". And what happens has always already happened.'¹⁰ What has erupted for this archer, we might say, is at once a heightened sense of presence and at the same time a sense of the very tenuousness of this presence, of its fragility: its enigmatic sense of having passed already and yet being infinitely to come. The present is fragile because beneath our conceptions of time as series – past, future, present – there is another time: a non-time, a dead time, a meanwhile which resists the human conception of linear chronology and which shadows it. This is the 'other' time which the archer suddenly intuits and, as I shall suggest in the next chapter, it is the same 'time zero' (t_0) that is disclosed to a certain strain of noir protagonist, a protagonist who is thereafter aligned with their exposure to this time, this time of 'the interval'. It renders them *intervallic*. What erupts before thought in such a moment is a glimpse of the illusory quality of the present itself, its tenuousness as a category of time and space. And yet everything in human consciousness and understanding is predicated on this sense of presence. Indeed, it is the very site and occasion of *predication*.¹¹ Jacques Derrida uses the figure of the intervallic to address precisely this functional yet decidedly phantasmatic presence.

> An interval must separate the present from what it is not in order for the present to be itself, but this interval that constitutes it as present must, by the same token, divide the present in and of itself, thereby also dividing, along with the present, everything that is thought on the basis of the present, that is, in our metaphysical language, every being, and singularly substance or the subject.¹²

In the wake of this initial division, this division that divides 'every being', including ourselves, Derrida says, there remains yet a trace – or traces – of its taking place, and trace(s) of what its taking place has eclipsed. Derrida has created numerous ciphers and neologisms to address this trace, among them *différance*, 'the parergon'¹³ and 'hauntology'.¹⁴ In Calvino's story, the archer, too, tries to find a vocabulary for his sudden stumbling on to this trace of the interval. The sensation is one of 'a slight doubling of images', he says.¹⁵ He feels that he, the lion and the arrow have crossed upon some kind of spatiotemporal 'void'.¹⁶ Yet for him the moment is by no means a supernatural one, even though it has triggered these peculiar feelings. Instead what this accented, *accentuated* moment reveals is merely the enigma of time itself:

> The accent remains, as of a cadence I seem to feel beating on the instant I am living through. I still wouldn't like what I have said to make this moment seem endowed with a special temporal consistency in the series of moments that precede it and follow it: from the point of view of time it is actually a moment that lasts as long as the others, indifferent to its content, suspended in its course between past and future; what it seems to me I've discovered is only its punctual recurrence in a series that is repeated, identical to itself every time.[17]

This experience of a 'slight doubling' and of a cadence *felt* 'beating on the instant' is consistent with Massumi's characterization of affect as we have already noted it. We should note, too, that in the passage above Calvino also clearly invokes the Nietzschean thesis of eternal recurrence. Deleuze – like Pierre Klossowski – was instrumental in recalibrating Nietzsche's original doctrine of the eternal return so that what *eternal return* signifies is not the rather suspect mechanistic notion that in infinite cyclical time each and every instant in the universe is fated to be repeated eternally but rather a more quotidian and yet more subtle thesis still: eternal return describes that moment in which human presence – or, as Deleuze would prefer, 'becoming' – becomes alert to its own unfolding in time: alert to the difficulty of its own positing and to its immersion in the teeming, differential potential of material existence. This moment is one of *return* because this moment, whenever it occurs, is always the same shuddering exposure to the tumult of becoming, even though, at the very same time, what it discloses is an essential difference: the difference inherent in every return, whereby the one who experiences it is no longer the same 'one'. (Indeed, one is no longer 'one' at all.) For Deleuze, it is a moment that demands affirmation. Nietzsche, too, saw in this moment – this moment which carries the 'greatest weight' – a fundamental affirmative power and joy.[18] Disregarding the cosmological interpretation of Nietzsche's model, Deleuze, among many others (e.g. Klossowski, Agamben), regards eternal recurrence – this 'thought of thoughts' – as a doctrine of a unique and affirmative attunement to the present moment (when 'presence' is understood not as static or stable but as merely the transitory and tenuous vehicle of becoming and of potential).

Returning to Calvino's story, the archer contemplates the fantastic possibility of remaining in t_0 – time zero. Rather than proceeding in a temporal series, he wishes instead to inhabit the infinite expanse of this suspended moment. And so he describes the myriad details – seen and unseen – of his emergent environment; from zebras to militias, underground seeds to exploding supernovae. Enclosing himself in this moment he also realizes he no longer needs a subjective position, since he no longer needs to worry about what will happen to his 'self' at future moments. He thereby stumbles upon a certain freedom, one steeped in an impersonal, nigh on pantheistic splendour. 'There's no use in my assuming the subjective point of view that has guided me so far, now I can identify myself with myself as well as with the lion or with the grain of sand or the cost-of-living index or with the enemy or with the enemy's enemy.'[19] What the archer experiences here is consistent with that elevated stage of knowledge that Spinoza defines as viewing the world *sub specie aeternitatis* – that is, from the standpoint of eternity. In his *Ethics*, Spinoza outlines three different forms of knowledge that a human may acquire. The first form is comprised of 'inadequate ideas', whereby we observe the affective relations and compositions that underlie our existence as mere representations. The second form, whereby one experiences 'adequate ideas', is acquired when we progress to shared insights borne of intelligence (what Spinoza calls 'common notions'). Through adequate ideas we come to understand our implication in this intensive circuit of affects that act upon us constantly in our bodily relations. And this understanding can prompt us to behave in ways that enhance our power to act and to assume control over our passions, maximizing affects that are joyful and our capacity for active affections. Yet a third kind of knowledge may emerge, however, when – via our abilities to hone adequate ideas and to deliver our bodily existence to a condition of active affection – we may come to see our lives *sub specie aeternitatis*, viewing our existence as if from the vantage point of God: as merely an idea, an impersonal field of relations and intensities, implicated and resonating across a plane of forces. Whenever our understanding reaches – however intermittently – a knowledge of our existence *sub specie aeternitatis*, it involves a radically dispossessing experience that Spinoza terms 'beatitude'. Such an experience of beatitude is invariably short-lived and we remain at the mercy of the affective relations in which we are entangled.[20] Nevertheless, the experience carries a transformative charge, allowing us to arrest the purely representational notions of selfhood that tend to govern our lives and to recognize our impersonal enmeshment in a greater field of intensities and becomings.

Having stumbled upon such beatitude, Calvino's archer, then, can be forgiven for wishing to remain in 'time zero', in the vein of a neutral, impersonal observer. However, he swiftly realizes that in order to do so he would first have to move to yet a further division in time, another interval from which to survey this same *time zero*. Obviously, this exposes as delusory the fancy that one can enclose oneself within a moment, and it scuppers, too, any attempt at persisting in a condition of pure objectivity or impersonal neutrality. The archer thus – with knowing irony – resolves: 'I must adopt some kind of subjective viewpoint so I might as well keep my own ... [T]o stay still in time I must move with time, to become objective I must remain subjective.'[21] In the end, the archer realizes that, because of the paradoxical necessity of retaining subjectivity in order to experience the objective, he is thereby inevitably exposed to a progressive linear time also and to preserving some notion of the self.

If the interval discloses an experience of beatitude and potentiality to us, then, the best one can do is attempt to retain the insight it discloses, by embracing the principles of profound relationality and transformation it reveals: in short, by embracing the principle of becoming. It is noteworthy that, in visualizing such a disruptive intuition of an all-encompassing and impersonal becoming, and endorsing, too, the importance of embracing it, Deleuze and Guattari employ an image extremely similar to that of Calvino's thought-experiment, while also invoking Spinoza's third form of knowledge. To experience becoming on these terms is to 'be present at the dawn of the world', they say.

> To reduce oneself to an abstract line, a trait, in order to find one's zone of indiscernibility with other traits, and in this way enter the haecceity and impersonality of the creator. One is then like grass: one has made the world, everybody/everything, into a becoming ... one has suppressed in oneself everything that prevents us from slipping between things and growing in the midst of things. One has combined 'everything' *(le 'tout')*: the indefinite article, the infinitive-becoming, and the proper name to which one is reduced.[22]

This is an experience of becoming that is radically dispossessive – a *becoming-indeterminate* or *becoming-imperceptible*. It is to 'slip' between things, or to 'lapse' between things, as I might put it. To become zero.

In such a becoming, then, Calvino's archer is fated to spill ever forward into other moments, while retaining the force of time zero and its irruption. The relevance of this to my study of film noir is that for many of noir's protagonists – and it is particularly true in a certain strain of modern noir – a desire not unlike that of the archer's, that is, the desire 'to stay still in time', and yet do so while *moving with time*, is frequently manifest. In many respects my meditation on film noir is an attempt to use noir iconography to further theorize the significance of this chimerical time zero or 'zero point' – the 'dark interval', as I term it. Such an opening may grant access to the Spinozist dimensions of a view *sub specie aeternitatis*, but it might also be regarded as escorting us to a different if not unrelated space. This would be Blanchot's no less enigmatic space of 'the Outside', a conceptual topos that, for Blanchot, mirrors the space of death. Fundamentally, this outside constitutes 'the space of literature', which is to say, *l'espace* (the gap) in which the creative act takes *its* place. (Indeed, it is to the compulsive intuition of this conceptual space that, at its core, the creative act responds.) For Blanchot, literature – no less than painting or cinema – addresses this strange space, and channels it: by occupying it, mimicking it and, in the end, by effacing it and thus effacing itself. The latter is significant because – as

I noted earlier – one of the 'legacy narratives' of classic noir is the modern noir which draws back on itself to a zero point, an interval where all becomes uncertain and evaporates before us.[23]

Within the noir narratives that I examine there is, too, a preponderant concern with a time that has become 'intervallic' and with characters that dwell and linger in such a time, often to their cost. The Swede in *The Killers* is such a one and it is true that in the classic noir this submission to an intervallic time is primarily melancholic or elegiac. Nevertheless, it contains the germ of a related experience – that of beatitude – an intuition of potentiality as resident in the very thrum of the dark interval itself. Beatitude is not a concept one finds associated with the so-called 'gritty' and pessimistic world of noir, of course, yet it is an experience of enlightenment, I argue, that has come increasingly to the fore as a key thematic in contemporary noir. We can say that noir beatitude – if it occurs at all – is found in the tension between a Spinozist accession to an experience *sub specie aeternitatis* and the more earthy dimensions of Blanchot's trespassing onto a *thought outside of thought*. Jean-Luc Nancy has noted the resonances between these two movements (the Spinozist and the Blanchotian interval, we might say), observing that Blanchot retains Spinoza's desire for a conception of reality as pure immanence and becoming but modifies it such that 'passion would be more on the side of pleasure [*jouissance*] and death than joy and life'.[24] Noir's intervallic antiheroes, alert to potentiality, may veer towards the Blanchotian expenditure of passion in the face of finitude, but both dispositions are available, and certainly a perversely joyful stoicism is also a means of discharging passion in noir.

If this section has identified some of the philosophical resonances and concatenations of the term 'interval' as I use it in this study, I should note that – in theorizing this quality of the 'intervallic' in noir, principally by paying particular attention to a certain tradition in noir iconography – I will also be engaging with the art theory of Aby Warburg and, in particular, his idea of the 'pathos formula'. This concept, too, is one that fundamentally centres on an experience of a charged interval of duration, as we will observe during the course of the next chapter.

Notes

1 Blanchot, *The Infinite Conversation*, trans. Susan Hanson (Minneapolis: University of Minnesota Press, 1993), 25–32.
2 Blanchot, *The Space of Literature*, trans. Ann Smock (Lincoln: University of Nebraska, 1989), 251–76.
3 Blanchot, *Friendship*, trans. Elizabeth Rottenberg (Stanford, CA: Stanford University Press, 1997), 289–92.

4 Gilles Deleuze and Félix Guattari, *What Is Philosophy?*, trans. Hugh Tomlinson and Graham Burchell (New York: Columbia University Press, 1994), 158.
5 Deleuze, *Nietzsche and Philosophy*, 48.
6 Deleuze, *Cinema II*, 79.
7 Peter Poellner, 'Existential Moments', in *The Moment: Time and Rupture in Modern Thought*, ed. Heidrun Freise (Liverpool: Liverpool University Press, 2001), 53.
8 Italo Calvino, 't zero', in *t zero*, trans. William Weaver (New York: Harcourt, Brace and World, 1969), 95.
9 Ibid., 96.
10 Blanchot, *The Infinite Conversation*, 384–5.
11 By which I mean to suggest that it is upon this site of our presumed 'presence' that the original potentiality of the verb ('to be', 'to do') and the verbal ('to speak', 'to commune') flares up and continues to find affirmation, producing the basis of conscious agency.
12 Jacques Derrida, *Margins of Philosophy*, trans. Alan Bass (Chicago: University of Chicago Press, 1982), 13. In this guise, the interval is merely a cognate for Derrida's master trope, *différance*. This figure of infinite deferral is founded on the interval – the space *between* – which is as much a typographical as a spatial or temporal gap. See *Margins of Philosophy*, 1–28. The resonances between Derrida and Blanchot are particularly strong here on the notion of the interval as an originary division. See Blanchot, *The Infinite Conversation*, xiv–xv.
13 See Jacques Derrida, 'The Parergon', trans. Craig Owens, *October 9* (1979), 3–41.
14 Derrida's concept of 'hauntology' is developed in *Spectres of Marx: The State of the Debt, the Work of Mourning and the New International*, trans. Peggy Kamuf (New York: Routledge, 1994).
15 Calvino, 't zero', 97.
16 Ibid., 98.
17 Ibid., 99.
18 Friedrich Nietzsche, *The Gay Science*, trans. W. Kaufmann (New York: Vintage Books, 1974), 273–4.
19 Calvino, 't zero', 108.
20 For an excellent overview of Spinoza's forms of knowledge and an overview of Deleuze's engagement with Spinoza more generally, see Stephen Zepke, *Art as Abstract Machine: Ontology and Aesthetics in Deleuze and Guattari* (London: Routledge, 2005), 41–76.
21 Calvino, 't zero', 109.
22 Deleuze and Guattari, *A Thousand Plateaus*, 280.
23 Indeed, no cinema plays with the paradoxes of time quite as electrically as noir. Noir is fundamentally a cinema centred on temporal experience. And,

in this, it exemplifies the tensions that Mary Ann Doane argues came to characterize the classical cinema: the desire to represent a frozen condition of presence, instantaneity and the contingent on the one hand, while, on the other, attempting to systematize the shock qualities of the contingent itself. See Mary Ann Doane, *The Emergence of Cinematic Time: Modernity, Contingency, the* Archive (Cambridge, MA: Harvard University Press, 2002), 206–33.

24 Jean-Luc Nancy, *The Disavowed Community*, trans. Philip Armstrong (New York: Fordham University Press, 2016), 101–2.

1

The 'Dark Interval' in Noir: From Iconography to Affect

Iconography and iconology

During the early twentieth century, in the wake of work by art historians Aby Warburg, Erwin Panofsky and others, iconography evolved as a methodology for the analysis of painting and the visual arts.[1] It has since become ingrained in the wider discourses of semiology, media studies and cultural studies. It should be noted that what we now commonly regard as analysis of an image's iconography might be more accurately called iconology, at least were we to adhere to the distinction originally made by Warburg and still frequently employed by art theorists.[2] Warburg regarded iconography as pertaining to the observation of icons – pictorial gestures and emblems – that are to be found in images, and iconology as pertaining to the study of what those gestures and emblems signify in particular contexts, whether socio-historical, philosophical, anthropological or otherwise. However, as has become a familiar practice, particularly in film studies, I use the term 'iconography' in a manner that fuses both categories, iconography and iconology. That is to say, I treat the term 'iconography' as by itself referring both to the recognition of the visual elements to be found within a film *and* to the analysis of the economy of meaning that these elements produce and participate in. Ultimately, it should suffice to say that, in tracing and interrogating a specific iconography that recurs morphologically in film noir of every era, I am also performing a critical aesthetic and philosophical examination of that iconography – one that at times may be deemed properly *iconological* in practice, even if I refrain from using the term. The terms were used interchangeably for centuries, and as Matthew Rampley has observed, even iconology's most renowned advocate, Panofsky, 'frequently elide[d]' the difference between the two categories.[3] Moreover, as Whitney Davis has noted, iconography – as an inquiry into 'the transhistorical and transcultural transmission of pictorial motifs' – is an essential element of iconology (the interpretation of motifs raised to the power of symbols), but iconology itself is not essential to iconographical observation.[4]

Warburg's interest in iconography was primarily focused on exploring the persistence of certain motifs and formulas across historical periods via a principle of 'after-life' or 'survival' (*Nachleben*), as Warburg termed it. Fundamentally, his work was motivated by a concern with 'how and why symbolic images of great pathos persist in Western cultural memory', as Christopher D. Johnson puts it.[5] Yet Warburg's project was not merely committed to documenting intertextual relations. For Warburg, the unique potency of the surviving image resides specifically in its temporal-aesthetic capacity to capture and discharge expressive impressions of feeling and lived experience, functioning as a kind of time capsule that channels both pathos and temporality itself. A 'survival' of certain motifs, we might say, uniquely imbues an image with a distinctive pulse of duration. This afterlife of the image is what interested Warburg in iconography. As Georges Didi-Huberman notes, whereas Panofsky 'sought to understand only the "meaning" of images, ... Warburg also sought to understand their "life", that impersonal "force" or "power" ... that he occasionally speaks of but regularly declines to define'.[6]

In film studies, iconographical analysis became a prominent methodology from the 1960s onwards, chiefly through the efforts of a series of scholars, among them Lawrence Alloway, Ed Buscombe and Colin McArthur.[7] This was iconography in the tradition of Panofsky rather than Warburg, and each invoked iconography primarily with the intent of developing genre as a discursive category of film analysis. I would stress here that my engagement with iconography is *not* an attempt to locate a visual register that would offer a basis for locating a genre called film noir. Rather, I am attending to a specific set of films that – in their critical reception – have been identified as 'noir' and, within these films, I examine certain visual motifs that they share, tropes related to the theme of 'the dark interval', as I perceive it. In fact, despite the great range of analysis of film noir in recent decades, there remains outstanding a demand for a more radical investigation of the nuanced iconographic elements that carry a specific force in noir. Needless to say, Janey Place and Lowell Peterson's influential 1974 essay 'Some Visual Motifs of Film Noir' certainly remains a hugely important dissection of the noir visual aesthetic.[8] Yet because it is focused on how technical issues such as lighting and framing in classic noir came to establish an expressionist mood and *milieu* in the films in question, it has led inadvertently to a too totalizing perspective on noir visual codes, with expressionism judged always to be the final word on the matter. However, as Patrick Keating's interrogation of assumptions about noir and low-key lighting has demonstrated, noir visual aesthetics remains open to further inquiry.[9]

In this chapter I will engage with a specific visual that recurs in noir – that of the arrested figure, caught in melancholy repose or in a state of rapt fascination. As a visual motif, it connotes a mysterious and pressing sense of quietude and temporal rupture unique to a certain strain of film noir. As the chapter progresses, I will argue that such imagery is indicative of an iconography of the 'dark interval' that recurs in noir. The stilled human figures I examine can be understood to connote lassitude, listlessness and melancholy, no doubt, but also a profound passivity that perhaps harbours a strange redemptive quality.

Shadows of doubt – The figure of *acedic* arrest in noir

Some years ago, Marc Vernet conducted an absorbing study of 'quietude' in the opening sequences of classic film noirs.[10] Admittedly, his premise (that the openings of noir films are inordinately marked by 'signs of tranquillity') is forced to elide the openings of countless noirs that would trouble such a thesis, and his hope to detect a kind of Proppian structural logic at work in noir narrative also seems quite misplaced. Nevertheless, his central impulse remains insightful: images of quietude – and, moreover, passivity and stillness – *do* seem to occupy a privileged position in film noir. In the following section, I draw attention to one very specific visual inflection of this quietude in noir: the image, repeated morphologically throughout numerous noir films, of a human figure lying in bed in a condition of pronounced stillness or inertia.

Let me begin by drawing attention to a single visual tableau that is shared by three noir films which, between them, span a period of almost seventy years. These texts range from the classic cycle of noir in the form of *This Gun for Hire* (Dir. Frank Tuttle, 1942) to the more modern in *Le Samouraï* (Dir. Jean-Pierre Melville, 1967), to the still more contemporary in *The Missing Person* (Dir. Noah Buschel, 2009). Each film commences with a stylized shot of its central male protagonist lying inert on a bed in a dingy lodging. In each case the protagonist seems perversely habituated to that inertia (Figures 1–3).

Indeed, detective John Rosow's opening line in *The Missing Person*, delivered in the weary voice-over of noir convention, goes, 'I could have lied there forever' (Figure 1).

This sentiment seems to capture the mood of profound repose and withdrawal in each of these three shots, as well as the manner in which such repose appears to baulk at the demands of a linear and progressive temporality. This is underlined by the placement of the alarm clock on the dresser in the scene from *This Gun for Hire* (Figure 2).

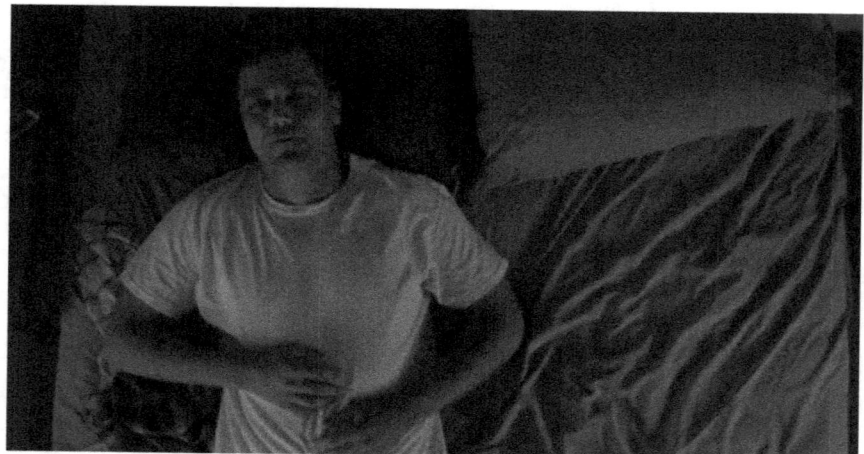

FIGURE 1 *John Rosow (Michael Shannon) in* The Missing Person.

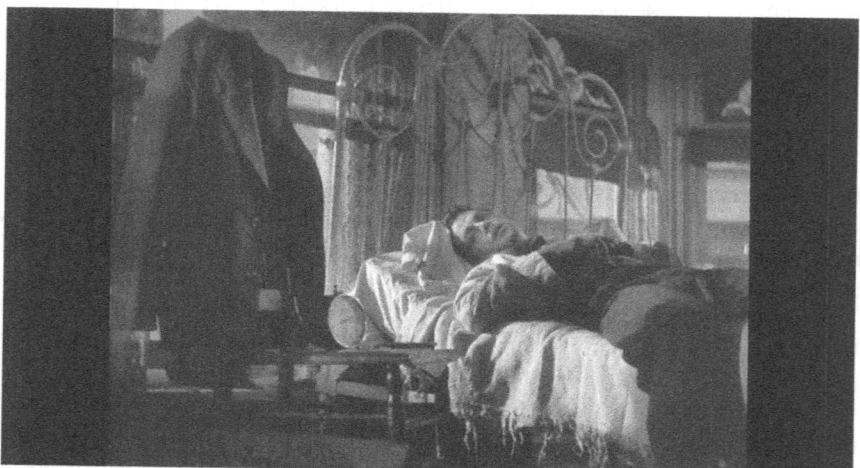

FIGURE 2 *Philip Raven (Alan Ladd) in* This Gun for Hire.

The clock is at odds with Alan Ladd's condition of wearied and disturbed withdrawal, and its alarm call is indeed his summons to a grim appointment. The scene carries a sly surrealist energy, too: the result of unorthodox framing and the prominence of a large jacket in the foreground, the latter dominating the space and floating in the air like one of René Magritte's empty suits. Ladd's character, Raven, is a strange, eerie hitman, at once volatile and sedate. In their seminal study of noir, Raymonde Borde and Etienne Chaumeton were enormously impressed with this sequence.

FIGURE 3 *Jef Costello (Alain Delon) in* Le Samouraï.

We will not easily forget the opening sequence of the film: in a seedy, barely furnished attic Philip Raven has just got up. He checks his gun one last time and gives a bit of milk to his cat. Before going off to do his killing, he icily entrusts the creature to the cleaning woman. As soon as his back is turned, she wreaks her revenge by driving the animal away. He returns, however, and catches her at it. Without a word, he slaps her twice, sending her sobbing at his feet. He pours more milk for the kitten, strokes it for a moment, and again leaves.[11]

Certainly, the sequence was not forgotten. The charm that Borde and Chaumeton find in the play of signifiers – that is, the juxtaposition of violence (the gun, the slap) with tenderness (the cat, the milk) – has been a recurrent character trait, the very shtick of the 'angelic killer', in hitman narratives ever since.[12] Yet a further element still that has endured from the scene is the initial fleeting image of Ladd's supreme detachment and inertia. This image, and the iconographic force it carries, appears to have become something of an incidental visual template for noir, repeated in a number of films throughout the classic cycle and into the modern era.

Famously, Melville's *Le Samouraï* was directly inspired by *This Gun for Hire*, and the French director opens his film in a similar manner to its model, while accentuating the detachment of the lone figure in the isolation of a personal cell that carries an almost monastic force. Here, in the long shot that opens the film, a total disregard for chronological time is emphasized (Figure 3).

And where Ladd's listless repose was only captured fleetingly in *This Gun for Hire*, Melville intensifies the supreme inertia of his own protagonist

(Alain Delon) via the provocatively lengthy duration of the take. Never altering elements within the initial composition, the director lets the single shot run for almost three minutes. The mise-en-scène is both drab and ascetically spare. We see a large bed, a wardrobe, a dressing table, an armchair and at the centre of the frame, between two large windows, a birdcage in which a bird's silhouette can be discerned. The colour design is one of muted blues. Light in the frame is muted, too. There are very few highlights in the shot other than a sensuous cloud of white light ghosting in from the two large windows. The effect is to make the physical presence of Alain Delon's character – who lies stretched out on the bed – almost imperceptible. Indeed, it is only his repeated exhalation of cigarette smoke that draws any attention to him at all.[13] There is an evocative affective blankness, then, to the whole composition, a quality of indetermination that is emboldened by the whooshing sound of the cars that pass on the streets below the apartment windows, the audio of which is stylized so as to resemble the sound of waves crashing gently upon a shore. The only thing breaking this undulating rhythm of the passing cars is the cheeping of the bird in the cage. The cheeping is analogous to the cigarette smoke that rises habitually from Delon's face, the only evidence of the latter being a living, breathing being. Melville offers us at once, then, an image of a spatiotemporal locus of ineffable blankness and, in the bird's unobtrusive cheeps and Delon's unobtrusive smoking, something (a life) that is attempting to adjust itself to this blankness, to 'blend in', to become indiscernible.

This blending in (and perhaps also its impossibility) is, in fact, key to each of these three scenes and their mobilization of the same iconographic gesture. It is my suggestion that the depiction of inertia in these sequences is indicative of a distinctive iconography in noir – one that stresses the noir protagonist's susceptibility to the experience of self-affection: a mercurial, profoundly somatic sense of awareness which, among other things, serves to sever the character from the impulses and contingencies of social and personal narrative. While the image certainly asserts a distinctive melancholy, the experience it depicts is not, for all that, without a potential for joy and for a particular expression of agency.

In any event, the tableau of the figure lying in bed is an iconographic gesture that is noteworthy for opening noir films of every era. Even when such tableaux are not the opening image in a film, it is often the case that the first scene in which the protagonist is introduced will find them in just such a repose. (It is, almost always, a 'him'.) Further examples would include the opening shot of boxer Charley Davis (John Garfield) in *Body and Soul* (Dir. Robert Rossen, 1947), the introductory shot of Robert Ryan's own beleaguered boxer in *The Set-Up* (Dir. Robert Wise, 1949), Bernardo Bertolucci's first shot of Marcello (Jean-Louis Trintignant) in the noir-accented *Il Conformista* (1971), our introduction to Philip Marlowe (Elliott Gould) in *The Long Goodbye* (Dir. Robert Altman, 1973) and our introduction to Guy Pearce's amnesiac detective in *Memento* (Dir. Christopher Nolan, 2000).[14] A variation on this opening – featuring a close-up of Joaquin Phoenix's troubled antihero gasping for breath, in an act of self-inflicted masochistic suspension – can be found, too, in *You Were Never Really Here* (Dir. Lynne Ramsay, 2017). Female protagonists, too, can be found in a condition of jaded repose during a film's opening sequence, as is the case – very markedly – in Jane Campion's *In the Cut* (2003), where Meg Ryan's submerged, almost somnambulant college professor lays in bed, stalled in a hypnopompic trance-state that establishes the delirious tonal qualities that will govern the film thereafter. In *Femme Fatale* (2002), meanwhile, the meta-noir impulses of Brian De Palma's film commence with his wry mobilizing of this iconography, the opening scene finding complex heroine Laure (Rebecca Romijn) lying in a hotel bed naked, idly drawing on a cigarette, while captivated by a sequence from *Double Indemnity* on the television.

It's worth noting that, like any iconographic element used in narrative cinema, the significance of this visual motif can often only be gleaned in the context of the wider elements of the diegesis in which it participates. Thus, not every use of this iconography can be said to invite the same meaning. While repeating the gesture, a film may mobilize it to suggest something quite different to a prior articulation. Certainly, the three tableaux I initially highlighted share the iconography in a manner that seems to italicize themes of disaffection, retreat, disengagement, detachment and so on, and this is borne out in each of these films as a whole, even if – in the cases of *Le Samouraï* and *The Missing Person* – these qualities are complemented by a sense of blissful inertia. By contrast, if we take the example of *Body and Soul*, we can note that Robert Rossen's film employs a different inflection of this iconography. *Body and Soul* opens with a shot of an empty outdoor boxing ring. A punching bag fixed in the centre of the ring sways with the breeze. The camera pans slowly through the low-lit yard to the veranda where behind the glass windows of a sunroom the film's protagonist, Charley (Garfield), lies stretched out asleep on a lounger. The film cuts to his face, which – in addition to bearing the scars of his many boxing fights – is visibly fraught with distress. He is in the midst of a nightmare. We hardly linger on the image long at all, however, before, his distress having been established, the man awakes, screaming the name 'Ben'.[15]

We can quickly establish here a number of differences between this particular image of the 'bed-bound' protagonist and the three images we first observed. The chief difference is that, while the three men in Figures 1–3 are awake, Garfield's boxer is asleep when we initially view him. Another difference is that, from the off, Charley's distressed repose is indicative of an as-yet unknown psychological predicament. While the figures in the other three films are not exactly models of contentment, there is nothing in the depiction of their lassitude that suggests a predicament and there is only a little that portends to character psychology. By contrast, Davis's mid-nightmare distress and his uttering of the name 'Ben' immediately ground us in a character psychology of torment, fear and guilt, and in a narrative intrigue (Who is Ben? What has happened to him? And how is Garfield's guilt-ridden figure involved?).

We might say that time in the image in Body and Soul is inscribed as urgent and motivated, pulsating with narrative questions from the start, while in the three films we originally identified the image of the bed-bound figure is one in which time is left 'open', enigmatic. They seem almost to speak to an evacuation of time and space. And it is this element that I wish to focus on as we proceed.

Notably, this particular iconographic tableau is but one visual in an iconography of arrest and lassitude distinctive to noir that stresses a strange, heightened, sometimes enrapt passivity. For instance, it is a counterpart to the image of the fascinated figure – his or her face stricken dramatically by wonder, awe or terror – which similarly recurs in noir, and which we will also examine later in this chapter in relation to Siodmak's *The Killers*. It is also a counterpart to the conventional image of a protagonist lost in thought, a cigarette held in hand or clasped at the lips, his or her torso framed against a window or shaded backdrop (Figure 4).

Of course, it is very often the fate of this latter visual to be accented, narratively, as a gesture of intense contemplation or of temptation, and thus to produce an index of subjectivity, one grounded in character psychology. But the gesture itself – once disentangled from narrative and functioning as an independent noir 'visual' – has increasingly evolved to become an icon

FIGURE 4 *A contemplative Walter Neff (Fred MacMurray) in* Double Indemnity.

less of psychological contemplation and more of self-affective absorption, as it is in the lyrical noirs of Wong Kar-Wai, for instance. A related noir visual is that of a lone figure seated at a bar or in a café, frequently clasping a cup of coffee, while caught in a strange state of detachment; this is an image that is also notable for marking the opening of many noir films, from *Detour* to Christian Petzold's *Transit* (2018).

For the moment, our concern remains with the figure laying in strange sensual inertia. Though it's a complex example, the weight and significance of this iconographic image is made explicit in Hitchcock's proto-noir, *Shadow of a Doubt* (1943). Just as in the opening shots of *This Gun for Hire*, *Le Samouraï* and *The Missing Person*, the opening sequence of *Shadow of a Doubt*, too, introduces us to that film's protagonist, Uncle Charlie (Joseph Cotten), as he lies stretched out on a bed in a boarding house (Figure 5).

Unlike the three virtually motionless, erotically passive figures examined previously, Charlie's twitchy fidgeting with a cigar during the shot suggests that he is somewhat more ill at ease. This unease is instructive. For one thing, it graphically underlines a psychological frustration at work in Charlie's inertia, whereas, in the three images identified earlier, the inertia seems steeped in a more impassive affective register. (Admittedly, we can trace a distinct distress in Alan Ladd's Raven also.) Charlie's fidgeting – his unease – is furtherly instructive because the key narrative issue that emerges in *Shadow of a Doubt* resides in the possibility that this man's niece, also called Charlie (Teresa Wright), may lapse into the same maudlin world view that afflicts him. It is this world view which – we are later invited to assume – has directly led to Uncle Charlie becoming a pathological serial

FIGURE 5 *Uncle Charlie's ill-eased repose in* Shadow of a Doubt.

FIGURE 6 *Young Charlie in a similar repose.*

killer. This is made clear in the graphical resonances that Hitchcock deftly draws between Uncle Charlie's repose here and, just a few shots later, the repose of the film's heroine, the young, intelligent woman who holds her exotic uncle in such high regard. When we first encounter the latter, she too lays supine on her bed (Figure 6).

The shot is carefully framed so that it pointedly mirrors the perspective of the earlier one. In fact, Robin Wood has identified the care with which the sophisticated rhythm of the film's editing stresses a resonance between the two shots.[16] Indeed, in addition to the parallels wrought by iconography and editing, the two characters appear to be almost telepathically linked, as is suggested in a later sequence where Young Charlie receives a telegram from her uncle at precisely the moment she is about to telegram him. That they are affectively attuned to one another, meanwhile, is evident in the exchange of a melody ('The Merry Widow Waltz') that is unconsciously transferred between them shortly after Uncle Charlie's return to his home town of Santa Rosa. Over the years a host of critical material has gathered upon this motif of the doubling of the Charlies in *Shadow of a Doubt*.[17] For our present purposes, the key thing to recognize is that the paralleling device commences with the visual rhyming of these two shots at the outset of the film: shots that depict the two characters' confinement to bed – this staple, if elusive, image in noir. If we return to the tableau of Figure 6, we see that, like her uncle, this young girl lying in her bed is also in a ruminative state. Her opening dialogue dramatically underlines this agitation. During an exchange with her father, Young Charlie bemoans the drudgery of her family life and her small-town existence in Santa Rosa. She resents the all-consuming *ennui* that this has forced upon her. Responding to her father's conciliatory remark that things aren't all that bad, and that at least the family is doing well in financial terms, she scowls, 'Money. How can you talk about money when I'm talking about souls? We eat and sleep and that's about all. We don't even have any real conversations. Just talk.'[18]

Though we do not realize it at this point, Charlie's lamentations are an indication of her being exposed to a malaise that, if not addressed, may perhaps evolve into the virulent misanthropic malice of her uncle. Additionally, we will come to understand that Uncle Charlie's malice, too, has emerged from a similar disenchantment with the world and that, as a result, the film therefore affords some moderate sympathy towards him. Instructively, in the two images above we note that Uncle Charlie's arms are 'closed' across his chest, as if he were already a corpse, while Young Charlie's are 'open'. The gestures attest to variations in possibility. It is too late for Uncle Charlie to be saved, we might gather, but not too late for his niece.

Ultimately, by the narrative's end, Young Charlie will have been 'saved'. Indeed, as Wood notes, the narrative as a whole 'attempts to impose itself and render things "safe"'.[19] This salvation is complex, however, and by the finale Uncle Charlie will have irreversibly prised open his niece's eyes to the inherent darkness that lurks beneath the façade of polite society. In their very influential analysis of the film, Claude Chabrol and Eric Rohmer argue that an overriding motif in Hitchcock's work – a 'Catholic' element they term 'the transference of guilt' – is at work, too, upon Charlie in *Shadow of a Doubt*, whereby she is laid open to 'the discovery of the innate defect of the universe'.[20] Importantly, Hitchcock's film doesn't attempt to expel this defect. It candidly acknowledges it. Thus, while the narrative may conjure a rather gruesome end for Uncle Charlie, the film at no point offers a straightforward condemnation of his 'deviant' criminal psychology. Rather, what Hitchcock provides is a nuanced and provocative meditation on the question of existential doubt itself: of doubt in other people, of doubt in the function of the assorted cultural practices that unite a 'family', a 'community', a 'nation' and so on. Significantly, as the film's iconography indicates, doubt here is an affective quality as much as it is a psychological one. The film suggests a terror resident in such doubt: that is, the possibility that one might succumb to its phantasmatic 'shadow' and in the process become a shadow oneself. This is precisely what has happened to Uncle Charlie. He is perhaps the darkest variation on Hitchcock's 'man who knows too much'. Significantly, he even specifically warns his curious niece of the dangers of knowing 'too much', a warning that finds resonance with a similar censure by Joe, the paternal head of the Newton household, to his younger daughter Ann. Early in the film Joe casts suspicion on Ann's practice of reading books, telling her that 'you'll ruin your eyes'. Later in the film, Uncle Charlie, who we learn was in his own youth an avid reader, also, will reveal his own pathological 'vision' of the world: 'Do you know that the world is a foul sty? Do you know if you ripped the fronts off houses you'd find swine? The world is a hell.'

The motif of 'doubt' involved here, I would insist, should not simply be relegated to the doubt of existentialist thought, that is, a crisis in meaning to which one either succumbs or which one totemically overcomes via an assertion of agency, an assertion of one's freedom.[21] Certainly, at the film's end, such an existential 'way out' is perhaps the cure – the only cure – that Young Charlie can turn to for her exposure to doubt. Hitchcock's ambivalent ending seems at once a validation of this move (the retention of belief in the world, albeit on new terms) and a querying of it. Yet the fact is that Uncle Charlie – somewhat like the figures in melancholy repose that we looked at earlier – is undergoing another kind of doubt also. It is a still more radical condition, I suggest, and, as we will see, the scenes of recumbent lassitude allude to it. This doubt coincides with and discloses a more incipient experience – that of self-affection: the acute experience of one's own passivity which Giorgio Agamben has characterized as the state of 'shame'. For Agamben, such an experience of shame is 'the hidden structure of all subjectivity' and consists in the very recognition of one's being 'consigned to something which cannot be assumed ... an extreme and irreducible presence of the "I" to itself'.[22] It is fundamentally an affective experience, rather than an intellectual or psychological one. (Notably, when aligned with other motifs that emerge in Agamben's thought, this shame might even be regarded as an experience that contains the germ of a more hopeful scenario, a more consoling fate.)

In *The Coming Community* Agamben discusses another experience, that of 'erotic anamnesis', in a manner that seems resonant, too, with his concept of shame:

> The movement Plato describes as erotic anamnesis is the movement that transports the object not toward another thing or another place, but toward its own taking-place.[23]

It is certainly possible to consider the passive figures in the images identified above as undergoing just such an experience of 'erotic anamnesis', an affective experience whereby one is halted by the phenomenon of one's own 'taking-place'. Of course, the irruption of this experience – whether one calls it shame, doubt, self-affection or erotic anamnesis – is usually treated as an unambiguously negative one in noirs of the classic era. Hitchcock's film itself preserves only moderate ambivalence about it, and in the narratives of most classic noirs doubt is something to be swiftly countered or eliminated. In many contemporary noirs, however, I would suggest that this experience – principally that of self-affection – has become a much more ambivalent element. It now even frequently provides the thematic focus of a film's narrative, where once it had been merely a thematic subcurrent. As Gilles Deleuze might put it, the cinematic regime of modern noir is no longer that of the rational 'movement-image', seeking to sow the solace of subjectivity in the fertile ground of 'action' and 'reaction' and a vision of the world as 'whole', but rather that of the dispersive 'time-image', which fillets human subjectivity, conferring the status of subjectivity solely on time itself, exposing the human to a thought that is at once both cataclysmic and strangely redemptive.

Acedia and noir

The shadow of doubt, this overwhelming experience of self-affection, is equivalent to the debilitating phantasm – 'the noonday demon' – that was said to fascinate and terrorize medieval monks who fell prey to *acedia*. The latter is a condition of sloth and profound sorrow upon which Agamben reflects at length in one of his earliest works, *Stanzas*.[24] During the medieval period, *acedia* (sloth) was considered one of the great evils facing the Christian devout, a sinful condition that manifested itself in the radical boredom, disaffection, passivity or melancholy of the sufferer. This malady is reclaimed by Agamben, however, as a trope that – though certainly melancholic – may help to recalibrate our understanding of human experience and to resituate human agency in the wake of the manifold 'crises of meaning' that underlie contemporary Western anxieties. I would like to argue that, via the recurrent inscription of visual motifs such as the one we have examined above, we might consider film noir to have fostered its own distinctive iconography for this condition of *acedia*. Moreover, the noir iconography of *acedia* is one that is visually continuous with classical renderings of this peculiar condition. In both medieval and Renaissance art the depiction of *acedia* often overlapped with depictions of melancholia and the saturnine, as Panofsky, Raymond Klibansky and Fritz Saxl observe in their momentous study, *Saturn and Melancholy*.[25] One of the key artworks in this tradition is Giulio Campagnola's early-sixteenth-century engraving, *Saturn*, in which the Roman god – traditionally associated with agriculture, rebirth, astrology and melancholy – lays idle in a pastoral setting, his gaze fixed listlessly on a point outside the frame, his head supported by his hand, the latter a well-worn gesture of melancholy since antiquity.[26]

The state of affective stillness evoked in Campagnola's image is quite conversant with the images of arrested repose and enigmatic detachment that we earlier identified in a number of noir films. We might therefore regard the latter as 'surviving images', as Warburg and Didi-Huberman employ this term. Of course, to point out that the iconography of noir participates in a long-standing tradition of visual representations of melancholy may not seem an especially novel or fruitful observation. Nevertheless, it is an important one, I insist, as it opens up the possibility to investigate noir through the lens of '*acedic* arrest', an investigation that proves illuminating, particularly in relation to modern noir and many of the themes that a certain strain of modern noir pursues.

Notably, as Agamben observes, a key dimension of *acedia* is the strange, disruptive and halted temporality that it heralds. The latter resonates with a pronounced tension in noir between a conventional temporality located in a linear chronology and a more elusive temporality which would rupture it, resisting history, bucking any fluid temporal progression into the future and emphasizing a reckless or unreckonable present. In her influential essay on the 'chronotope' of noir, Vivian Sobchack has, in an analogous way, described this other temporality that tends to derail the protagonists of noir, bound as they are so often to transient spaces ('bars, diners, and seedy hotels') conducive to an affectively charged temporal disposition that Sobchack calls 'lounge time'.[27]

Of course, it should be noted that the narrative of *Shadow of a Doubt* explicitly presents us with the possibility that it is not a spiritual malaise such as *acedia*, but rather a physical injury, that might account for Uncle Charlie's psychosis. During the film we learn that he suffered a bicycle accident in his childhood, one that left him with a fractured skull. Yet, as his sister Emmy suggests, his subsequent problems stemmed not from any impairment this injury left him with but rather from his period of forced repose while he recuperated:

> He was laid up so long. And then, when he was getting well, there was no holding him. And it was just as though all the rest he had was too much for him, and he had to get into mischief to blow off steam.

Here it is Uncle Charlie's very lying down for so long that is rendered suspect – the experience that laid him open to the shock of doubt in the first place. We cannot fail to observe once more the parallels with our introduction to Young Charlie. When Joe asks his younger daughter, Ann, where Charlie is, the youngster replies, 'She's in her room – thinking.' When Joe then locates Charlie in her bed, she immediately underlines that this indeed has been her activity and that it's brought her to a morose pass: 'I've just been thinking for hours and I've come to the conclusion I give up. I simply give up.'[28]

Indeed, lying too long in bed, or simply sleeping in late, is frequently connoted as a 'taboo' activity – or *inactivity* – in film noir. The narratives of both *Nora Prentiss* (Dir. Vincent Sherman, 1947) and *Pitfall* (Dir. André De Toth, 1948) – two hard-boiled melodramas about adultery and domestic collapse – open with scenes in which a middle-class family man is late coming down to breakfast, testing the patience of his wife who calls him from the domestic space of the kitchen/dining room. Delayed by the stirring of spring outside his bedroom window, the doomed protagonist of *Nora Prentiss*, Dr Richard Talbot (Kent Smith), is aligned with sensitivity, feeling and romance, in short, with an affective register that rejects the impingement of 'clock-time' and the oppressive values of a modernity in which clock-time had established itself both as a form of currency and as a technocratic determinant.[29] Elsewhere, as if to demonstrate graphically the dangers that idling in one's bedroom embodies, many noir films also depict the criminal set as being marked by a perverse bedroom languor. In his analysis of *The Big Heat* (Dir. Fritz Lang, 1953), Colin McArthur notes how the film mobilizes just this strategy in relation to its introductory shot of vicious mob boss Mike Lagana (Alexander Scourby) in his elegant bedroom. According to McArthur, this 'tradition of representing crime bosses as languidly luxurious' is one that originated with the classic gangster movies of the 1930s and 1940s.[30] It is not just the gangsters, however. An air of exorbitant inertia also suffuses the countless images of female protagonists in sensual repose in classic noir, particularly those of the femme fatale. Fritz Lang's *Scarlet Street* (1945) underlines this quality when the film's scheming villain (Dan Duryea) chides Joan Bennett's languorous femme fatale: 'Can't you get those lazy legs off that couch?' Indeed, the character will eventually meet her grisly end while lazing in bed. (In general, this framing of vamp protagonists in noir is consistent with an older visual arts tradition of depicting the charged eroticism of the feminine as obtaining precisely in the languid female body, perhaps best exemplified in the works of Gustav Moreau.)

In both cases – that of the gangster and the femme fatale – these images of sensual repose are generally inflected to suggest venality and unchecked libido. Invariably, such scenes also include visual elements that mark the subject's concerns as being materialistic or unambiguously sexual. These images are thus presented as continuous with the broader narrative impulses of the film, speaking to a given character's drive towards power or to their absorption in a deviant desire. As such, they prop up a narrative logic founded on coherent temporal progression and an investment in sharply determined identities and subjectivities. The images of *acedic* arrest that I attend to, however, speak to something rather different. They demonstrate a secession of identity and agency – or, at any rate, a secession of the identity and agency of a 'narrative' subject. These are images in which narrative and time itself seem in crisis. In the case of the gangster and the sultry femme fatale, it is power and sexuality that is deviant, but in the images of *acedia* in noir it is temporality itself that has deviated. Time falls. It lapses. It becomes 'out of joint'.

Such a deviant temporality of pronounced arrest and suspension can be found in perhaps the most famous historical artwork to engage with the theme of *acedia*: Albrecht Dürer's 1514 engraving *Melencolia I*, in which a downcast angel sits in profound stillness, her head resting on her hand as in Campagnola's painting of Saturn. Scattered on the floor beside her are a

FIGURE 7 Albrecht Dürer, Melencolia I, *courtesy of The Metropolitan Museum of Art: www.metmuseum.org (Public Domain collections).*

host of scientific instruments, the latter discarded as if insufficient to the task of gauging the intensity of feeling she endures (Figure 7).

Agamben notes in this latter picture 'an atemporal dimension, as though something, interrupting the continuum of history, had frozen the surrounding reality in a kind of messianic arrest'.[31] This latter concept of 'messianic arrest' is a central cog in Agamben's thought. His meditations on such arrest are a response to the oppressive discursive regimes that Agamben believes situate the beleaguered 'subject' of modernity, regimes that are, in effect, actually constitutive of subjectivity itself. Via the motif of 'messianic arrest' and a number of related concepts, Agamben is intent on thinking an alternative to such subjectivity, one that delves into what might be regarded as a category of 'the posthuman', though Agamben himself would perhaps not use this term. This strain in Agamben's thought, and its post-historical overtones, will be returned to in greater detail in a later chapter. In the meantime, and specifically in relation to the temporal anomalies induced by *acedia*, we should consider Agamben's enumeration of the many traits that medieval theologians once attributed to this condition. Two that are of inevitable interest to a study of noir are:

> ... *desperatio*, the dark and presumptuous certainty of being already condemned beforehand and the complacent sinking into one's own destruction ... [and] ... *torpor*, the obtuse and somnolent stupor that paralyses any gesture that might heal us.[32]

The latter traits, of course, are characteristics that so frequently mark the melancholy noir protagonist. Indeed, Agamben insists that the state of *acedia* is one that finds resonances with the alienated condition of man in modernity, and he relates it to Martin Heidegger's influential analysis of the existential condition of the human being (Dasein) when fallen into the everydayness of the 'they-self'.[33] (The parallels and interchanges between film noir and existentialist thought are by now well-established, of course.)

Yet, while *acedia* is a condition fundamentally oriented upon negativity and alienation, Agamben notes in it nevertheless 'a fundamental ambiguity', whereby that which marks the *acidiosus* (the slothful one) is a desperate awareness of the unobtainability of its object (God's grace) but not for all that a total retreat from its pursuit. Instead, and somewhat paradoxically, because 'its desire remains fixed in that which has rendered itself inaccessible, *acedia* is not only a flight from, but also a flight toward, which communicates with its object in the form of negation and lack'.[34] As a result, as Agamben explains, even in the medieval period *acedia* was recognized by the church fathers as hosting within itself the possibility of salvation:

> Next to *tristitia mortifera* (deadly sorrow) ... the fathers placed a *tristitia salutifera* (saving sorrow) ... that was the operator of salvation and the 'golden goad of the soul', and, as such, 'it should be counted not a vice but a virtue'.[35]

This potential virtue, this 'saving sorrow', is very pertinent to a certain strain of noir, I would suggest, one that has become more self-conscious in the modern era.

For Agamben, the 'saving sorrow' of *acedia* (or melancholia, with which it increasingly fuses in the Renaissance period) resides precisely in its qualities for temporal arrest and, concomitant with that, its capacity to open up a space for the unreal. In this regard, it may be useful here to note that Dürer's engraving of the angel of melancholy inspired quite distinct interpretations between Warburg and Panofsky. As Margaret Iversen and Stephen Melville point out, where Warburg discovered in it 'the representation of a struggle between reason and demonic forces that managed to compress their energies in a state of "robust composure"', Panofsky viewed the image as imparting the sense of a being fraught with despair due to the melancholic's 'consciousness of a sphere beyond their reach'.[36] In his own meditation on Dürer's masterpiece, Agamben diverts from both, and very much departs from Panofsky's conception of an idealist 'beyond' that torments the melancholic. Instead, Agamben suggests, in an excavation of the symbols at play in the image, *Melencolia I* reveals to us a phantasmatic space that is prised apart by melancholy, creativity and the play of language, and which obtains in an indeterminate third register between the objective and the subjective.

Throughout his work in *Stanzas*, Agamben pursues this notion of the space of the unreal – a 'placeless place' – through examination of a range of areas, from the medical doctrine of the four humours to the practice of the Italian 'Stilnovist' poets, and he observes the overlooked relations between melancholia, romance and eroticism, and the profound contemplation of self-affection. This 'intermediate epiphanic space', located between our self-affection and our mercurial relations to the objective world, becomes ultimately the space of human art and culture itself.[37] It constitutes an indeterminate zone of experience, one that Agamben traces from medieval thinking through to the important concepts of transitional phenomena and 'potential space' in the work of D. W. Winnicott. As in the stanzas of the Stilnovist poets, such a space of self-affection, fundamentally a space of transition, discloses a sense of potentiality itself. The formal principle of the 'stanza' thus becomes a metaphor for a conception of the human in a most amorphous and intervallic state.

In what way can melancholy open or initiate this space? Invoking Freud's influential examination of melancholy, Agamben points out its continuity, too, with theological conceptions of *acedia* in the medieval period. Melancholy, according to Freud, arises when a lost object is not successfully mourned but instead is uncannily internalized by the mourner, the object taking on a phantasmatic power thereafter. As Agamben points out, however, *acedia* is still more complex. The melancholy of *acedia* is a mourning for an object that was never possessed in the first place, that was never obtainable and therefore never capable of being lost. This leads, says Agamben, to the creation of an unprecedented space for the 'unreal'.

> Covering its object with the funereal trappings of mourning, melancholy confers upon it the phantasmagorical reality of what is lost; but insofar as such mourning is for an unobtainable object the strategy of melancholy opens a space for the existence of the unreal and marks out a scene in which the ego may enter into relation with it and attempt an appropriation such as no other possession could rival and no loss possibly threaten.[38]

This phantasmatic rendering of the unreal is a common feature of film noir and one of the ways in which noir, horror and Gothic elements frequently coalesce in the classic cycle. Often it is rendered metonymically as a specific phantasmatic presence. For instance, the phantasm is very vividly represented in Hitchcock's *Shadow of a Doubt* in the form of Dimitri Tiomkin's subversive treatment of 'The Merry Widow Waltz' (Franz Lehar), which flares up at moments of tension in the film. In the film's occasional glimpses of imagery from *within* Uncle Charlie's mind, the melody is accompanied by a surreal vision of couples waltzing. Uncle Charlie's peculiar vision is a phantasm of a time long past, a time of purported innocence, which is made clear in his gift to Emma upon his arrival in Santa Rosa: an old photograph of their parents from 1888. As Young Charlie admires it, her uncle tells her: 'Everyone was sweet and pretty then, Charlie. The whole world. A wonderful world. Not like the world today. Not like the world now.' Of course, despite his romantic appreciation of it, this is a historical period that preceded Uncle Charlie's birth. And yet he seems to recall it and to be haunted by it. This image, then, with its acoustic fellow traveller 'The Merry Widow Waltz', is the phantasm that Charlie's *acedia* has bestowed upon him. And, as we observed earlier, Young Charlie will come suddenly to be imbued with it, too. During the dinner scene the melody of 'The Merry Widow Waltz' suddenly streams its way into her own thoughts ('I can't get that tune out of my head') and her ensuing desire for its expulsion mirrors the narrative's own impetus to eliminate Uncle Charlie.[39]

The condition of *acedia*, then, is productive of such phantasms. That the phantasm is here articulated as an inescapable melody is symptomatic, too, of noir. As I have pointed out in a previous study, the motif of the 'haunting melody' is one that recurs in noir films of every era.[40] In the case of *Shadow of a Doubt*, Uncle Charlie's trafficking with this phantom melody breeds a pathological hatred in him and the trope – as it relates to the figure of the *acedic* noir protagonist – is thereby debilitating and quite negatively charged. Yet, as we will see in the next chapter, in *The Man Who Wasn't There*, the Coen brothers employ the same convention very pointedly, and very poignantly, to summon a strange sense of solace for that film's protagonist. In the latter film, Beethoven's 'Pathétique Sonata' becomes both the quasi-redemptive expression of the protagonist's hypersensitive affective life and a kind of counterpoint to the film's ostensible narrative and, indeed, a counterpoint to the preponderance of 'narrative' categories that are referenced within the film. It becomes within the film an evocation of the *placeless place* of self-affection, the dark interval.

Before we get to *The Man Who Wasn't There*, however, we will continue with our excavation of an iconography of the 'dark interval' in noir, moving to yet another of its articulations – the gazing figure – and the strange brand of affective experience that this iconographic trope evokes.

Zero affect: A 'pathos formula' for noir

What does the image of *acedic* arrest in noir convey? Depictions of *acedia* in visual art – whether ingrained in the artworks of the Renaissance or in noir iconography – might be considered to constitute an enigmatic example of what Warburg termed 'pathos formulae' (*pathosformeln*). The latter can be understood as 'emotive formulas' that persist as intertextual fragments of cultural memory, while in effect constituting visual strategies for the depiction of certain affective states or experiences. The formulas that primarily interested Warburg resided in physical gestures from artworks in classical antiquity that had been revived in the Renaissance period. These formulas are not simply depictions of human gesture, it should be noted. They also include inanimate elements in a visual composition that are nevertheless latent with pathos. Warburg's most famous example of the latter relates to Botticelli's *Birth of Venus*, wherein the human figure's intensive emotional state is projected or 'displaced' on to windswept clothing and hair, Warburg tracing the debt of these visual elements to more ancient works.[41]

There is a distinct quality of affective relation in pathos formulae, then. As such, while the influence of Ernst Gombrich's interpretations of Warburg's project has been criticized by Didi-Huberman, Gombrich's insistence that the *pathosformeln* centre on a pathetic relation between the human figure and its surrounding environment nevertheless remains valuable; it underlines the centrality of *relation* itself as a fundamental principle of affect and affective experience.[42] As both Didi-Huberman and Agamben are at pains to stress, however, the *pathosformel* is not simply a technique for conveying emotional tonalities. As Didi-Huberman puts it, the *pathosformel* is the very 'incarnation' of Warburg's concept of 'survival' (*Nachleben*).[43] In other words, it is through these emotive formulas that the lived intensities of earlier ages are passed on as disruptive 'untimely' phantoms to later epochs. Similarly, Agamben notes that the *pathosformel* 'designates an indissoluble intertwining of an emotional charge and an iconographic formula in which it is impossible to distinguish between form and content.'[44] *Pathosformeln*, on these terms, are anything but mere artistic acts of mimesis or transmissions of cultural memory, then, but rather visual compositions heaving with a *living* stamp of temporality and affect.

Notably, Warburg conceived of his famous *Mnemosyne Atlas* – wherein he gathered together images from different periods, grouping them in accordance with the 'emotive formulas' they solicited – as functioning via an 'iconology of the interval'. This enigmatic phrase has often been understood to denote the interval as the blank space between the images that we find on each plate in Warburg's catalogue, functioning as a sort of historical spacing that facilitates a sense of context. However, in an intriguing interpretation, Didi-Huberman argues that the interval, as Warburg intends it, is not simply a blank space between the images in Warburg's atlas but is in fact a feature of potentially every image within it, insomuch as any image can be said to function as an imprint of an interval of time. On these terms, the interval resides in the charge of feeling and of temporality channelled in every surviving image. But it does so only because such images – as intervals – disclose the force of the interval itself and its recurrence as constituting the very 'material of time'. Moreover, in doing so, these images demonstrate the way in which the interval operates contrapuntally against chronological organizations of time.[45] Didi-Huberman's insights here are very much consistent with our examination of the interval as a philosophical figure in the previous chapter: The image-*as*-interval is equivalent to the Nietzschean moment of eternal return; it discloses the 'meanwhile', the time of 'the event' that – as Deleuze and Félix Guattari suggest – underscores temporal experience itself while challenging our linear conceptions of time.

At any rate, we can say that Warburg's pathos formulae are enigmatically ingrained with temporality and affect. And, more to the point, they transmit the force and intensity of an intervallic experience. It should be noted that the examples of *pathosformeln* foregrounded by Warburg pertained to figures in movement, and very often in agonistic or ecstatic states. What was revolutionary about the Renaissance for Warburg was precisely the way its artists aspired to capture human movements in the still form of painting. Nevertheless, Warburg also understood the pathos formulae to involve passive states and gestures.[46] Moreover, if we employ the pathos formula in a study of film, we should be attentive to the fact that Warburg had developed his concept in large part as a means of examining the enigmatic psychic qualities of movement when configured in still images; in cinema, however, we are already dealing with moving images. As such, we might regard images of stillness and passivity in cinema to reverse the logics in play here. In cinema, stilled photograms or slowed motions and gestures can discharge a peculiarly visceral affective quality of suspension precisely because they arrest the image in motion. Indeed, a number of theorists, among them Laura Mulvey and Raymond Bellour, have claimed just this: that cinema frequently unlocks a mercurial affective force when the movement of the film is 'delayed' (Mulvey) or 'interrupted' (Bellour), either by technical means on the part of the viewer or when qualities of stillness are courted within the film's own design. Agamben, too, observes a similar phenomenon at work in the distinctive video works of Bill Viola wherein human figures are captured in a strange condition between movement and stillness, producing images that are 'charged' or 'tremoring' with time.[47]

In addition to this, we might also note that – while less demonstrative – gestures and visual articulations of passivity (or indeed 'impassivity', as it so often is construed in noir) can be regarded as an affective or 'pathetic' response to a sudden and overwhelming sense of the human's affective exposure to its environment and to its own ontological and temporal condition. Such passivity might be understood, for instance, as an overwhelming alertness to the inscrutable, indifferent *thereness* of objective reality – that which Maurice Blanchot calls 'the inertia of being'.[48] This is a pathos formula that we often encounter in the copious representations of human inertia, lassitude, withdrawal and various affective states of torpor, disaffection and detachment in noir. Such representations are most obviously associated with the weirdly enervated male protagonist, but, as already noted, they are perceptible, too, in the exotic languidness of the femme fatale and in the strange sensuality – whether sedate or exorbitant – which marks the villainous in noir. (As Johnson observes, Warburg was always interested in the 'syncretic' dimensions of a pathos formula, its ability to survive and recur morphologically in new variations, thereby eliciting 'multiple, competing meanings'.)[49]

Just as affectlessness, as Kant knew,[50] is not the absence of affect but a more mercurial, 'sublime' manifestation of it still, so too intense experiences of pathos do not actually require any emphatic physical demonstration but may well occur with a minimal degree of expression where pathos is perhaps even at its most incipient and insistent. Blanchot gives a good indication of this more deceptive aspect of pathos – deceptive because it appears subdued – when he reflects on the 'time without event, without project, without possibility' that is experienced during states of suffering:

> This experience has a pathetic appearance, but on condition that one also give the word pathos its non-pathetic sense. It is a question not of that paroxysmic state where the self cries out and is torn apart, but rather of a suffering that is almost indifferent, not suffered, but neutral (a phantom of suffering) insofar as the one who is exposed to it, precisely through this suffering, is deprived of the 'I' that would make him suffer it.[51]

Blanchot's conception of pathos here is of a neutral and indifferent state that, nevertheless, seems imbued with what we might call a quality of immense 'passion'. Such a seemingly paradoxical conception is supported, however, by Erich Auerbach's reflections upon the semantic associations between *pathos* and *passio* in antiquity. In stark contrast to the connotations of dynamic or obsessive energy it has acquired, the original meaning of 'passion', as Auerbach points out, was – like 'pathos' – bound up in a sense of passive suffering.[52]

The pathos formula that a certain strand of noir – noir of the dark interval – frequently evinces, then, I suggest, is one that centres on the human figure removed to a state of strangely indifferent suffering, a deceptively *passionate passivity* that deprives one of an 'I', bleaching subjectivity and erecting in its place an enigmatically neutered, automatist or autonomic state. Such passivity perhaps discloses, too, an attitude of essential neutrality towards objective 'reality', a fundamental detachment that is often accented in myriad ways in noir texts. It manifests itself, for instance, in the profound resignation of the jaded noir hero, who ruefully accepts the meaninglessness of life and does his best to persist nevertheless in a finite, fallen world via a measure of self-containment. Robert Altman's deconstruction of the most exemplary of noir detectives – Philip Marlowe – in *The Long Goodbye* is a ferocious reckoning with just this kind of figure. At yet another extreme, this passivity manifests itself in the Zen-like disposition of certain noir protagonists, the most hyperbolic of which may well be the mysterious figure of Gorodish in *Diva* (Dir. Jean-Jacques Beineix, 1981). Gorodish (Richard Bohringer) is a captivating blend of Zen master and *deus ex machina* who abides on the fringes of the film's narrative. His strange quasi-divinity appears actually to stem solely from his immersion in the specific iconography of the noir hero, one pronounced aspect of which is an ascetic detachment from everyday social reality.[53]

In any event, howsoever it manifests itself, a predominant pathos formula within noir – rendered through a specific iconography of *acedic* arrest – is one whereby the figure depicted enters upon, accedes to, attains, or strives to attain, a strange state of self-affection, one that I will term 'zero affect'. *'Zero affect', I contend, is a unique pathos formula that finds idiosyncratic expression in film noir.*

It is crucial that in teasing out this pathos formula we do not misunderstand this 'zero affect' as denoting a lack of affect or indeed any spurious 'waning of affect'.[54] Rather, it is a radical attunement to affect – an exposure and an openness to affect and to one's own affectivity – that occurs in this state. Zero affect would communicate the experience of self-affection, the human's dramatic intuition of its own relational implication in a greater field of affective intensities, at its most arresting. This arrest, however, need not simply denote the momentary or the momentous. To the contrary, such arrest perhaps might even be sustained indefinitely as a mode of existence, a 'way of being', such that one might inhabit, or seek to inhabit, this condition. If, as Gregory J. Seigworth and Melissa Gregg have suggested, affect by definition 'arises in the midst of in-between-ness: in the capacities to act and be acted upon', then zero affect – as a visual formula – would relay a fascination with the sensation of this *in-between-ness*, a passion for the 'dark intervals' that underwrite the conditions of our own affective recurrence in time.[55] One manner in which this zero affect is articulated in noir is through images of figures in arrested, listless or detached repose, as in those images we have just looked at. But it is also demonstrated in a related iconography, the image of the gazing figure, peering with a strange, neutered awe at an object of fascination. We will shortly examine the most iconic example of this image in noir – that of the Swede's gaze into death in *The Killers*. Before then, we will take a useful detour and consider the paintings of Edward Hopper and how they, too, treat images of strange, sensuous inertia and the fascinated gaze.

Excursion into 'Hopper-noir'

It is by now a critical commonplace to identify Hopper's work as deeply conversant with many of the aesthetic tendencies that noir also invokes. Slavoj Žižek, for instance, insists that Hopper should be 'included among the noir auteurs'.[56] This does not overstate the case. As Nicholas Christopher has noted, director Abraham Polonsky escorted his cinematographer on *Force of Evil* (1948), George Barnes, to a Hopper exhibition, precisely to develop the look of the film.[57] Indeed, the critical commentaries surrounding Hopper and noir have become so implicated in one another that *The Missing Person* (Dir. Noah Buschel, 2009) pointedly conflates both its noir conventions and Hopper's imagery in a manner that makes the one absolutely equivalent with the other. (*The Missing Person* is examined in a later chapter.)

Significantly, a characteristic motif in Hopper's work is that of a human figure in mundane yet deeply involved repose. Often the figure is seated. Frequently the figure's face seems diverted – transfixed even – by something outside the purview of the painting's spectator. In works such as *Evening Wind* (1921) it is, as Ivo Kranzfelder describes it, 'an outside space purposelessly left undefined'.[58] Very often, the space alluded to is situated on the other side of a window.[59] This gaze through a window into an undefined exterior in Hopper has particularly strong resonances with many works in German Romanticism, where contemplation of an indiscernible outside – as, for instance, in *Woman at a Window* (1822) by Caspar David Friedrich – discloses the advent of thought into a transcendental realm. It carries overtones with the more contemporaneous work of the Surrealists, too, who – as Martin Jay notes – were fixated on the idea of the window as 'a transitional or liminal plane'.[60] In any event, Hopper's window motif is at least as old as Vittore Carpaccio's 1502 painting *Saint Augustine in His Study*, in which the venerable saint is depicted breaking off from his intellectual labour to gaze out his window, having suddenly intuited the passing and beatification of his friend, St Jerome.

In Carpaccio's painting, this gaze into an undefined space discloses an interruption of the transcendental. In his own images, however, Hopper mutes the lurch towards the transcendental, at least in the most conventional sense of the term as a move towards, or intuition of, a space 'beyond' the material world. Rather, Hopper's conception of the 'transcendental' is more akin to the 'transcendental materialism' that Gilles Deleuze asserts in a number of his philosophical works, including those with Félix Guattari: a transcendence that is, at its core, only a registration of one's irrevocable implication in an immanent and indeterminate realm of forces and affects. A fundamental element of Deleuze's thought is this positing of a 'transcendental field' within human cognition, which he defines as 'a pure stream of a-subjective consciousness, a pre-reflexive impersonal consciousness, a qualitative duration of consciousness without a self'.[61] It is a figural conception of transcendence that Deleuze explicitly borrows from Jean-Paul Sartre, while altering its import. Similarly resisting the classical sense of transcendence as a surpassing of material reality, Hopper's painting nevertheless retains a profound sense of the ineffable. Hence, in Hopper's works, the transfixed human figure is frequently bound by the magnetism of thought itself (as is the male figure in *Excursion into Philosophy* (1959) or the female figure in *Automat* (1927)).

A good example of the latter – of the absorptive shock of thought – is *New York Movie* (1939), the painting which informs the plot and the distinctive meta-noir elements of *The Missing Person*. Here an usherette in a cinema is engaged enigmatically with her own thoughts, oblivious to the screen at which the film's audience stares. As is evident in the painting, the enigmatic pathos formula that one finds in Hopper's imagery is quite resonant with that of the noir iconography I examined earlier. And, just as in those noir staples, Hopper's images are also continuous with medieval and Renaissance images of *acedia* and the saturnine, as the usherette's holding her face with one hand in *New York Movie* rather pointedly indicates. Among other things, what Hopper's paintings bring out in these older iterations of the pathos formula are strange qualities of suspended or automatist states of distraction and withdrawal that work against the grain of commodified practices of attention and activity in modernity.

Notably, Kranzfelder engages Warburg's concept of the *pathosformel* to account for the inscription of the ineffable in the billowing curtains in *Evening Wind*. The suggested movement of the curtains helps to convey the affective intensity fizzing within the stillness of a human figure gazing – distractedly, and yet also attentively – into a mesmerizing 'outside'. No thinker other than Blanchot has made a more daring attempt to approach the 'gaze' into this enigmatic 'outside'. His philosophical corpus features a huge battery of terms – 'the Outside', 'the other night', 'the space of literature', 'the il y a', 'the incessant', 'the impossible', 'the disaster' and, above all, 'the interval' – which struggle to denote this 'outside' even while respecting the radical dislocation of the experience it embodies.[62] Blanchot's terms are very much equivalent to Edward Hopper's repeated employment of the pathos formula of the gazing figure, I would suggest. We can look upon a Hopper painting and observe the gestural response that this passionate relation to 'the outside' triggers in the human figure. It is one of a paradoxical stillness and passivity: one hovering between neutered indifference and strange attention. Late in his career, in a 1963 painting in which a lone woman in an otherwise empty cinema sits staring vacantly at a presumably blank screen, Hopper finally gives this passivity a name: *Intermission*.

In the face of Hopper's intermission, or Blanchot's 'interval', in the face of the inscrutable impassivity of time and being itself, the human can only withstand by becoming, in turn, similarly impassive, even if such impassivity masks an experience of tremulous passion and may perhaps only ever be sustained for a short period. This, then, is the affective experience communicated through imagery of 'zero affect'. At the heart of noir, I argue, we so often encounter figures who – voluntarily or involuntarily – become alert to this passivity and often come to abide, or attempt to abide, in it. It is a state of pronounced suspension, of radical waiting, a lapse into the dark interval.

This notion of 'abiding' in the interval is itself a suggestive underlying theme of the Coen brothers' highly self-aware engagements with noir in both *The Big Lebowski* and *The Man Who Wasn't There*. Certainly, the noir iconography of the 'dark interval' is one that the Coen brothers very graphically invoke in the latter film. Indeed, Billy Bob Thornton's performance of the radically passive Ed Crane is a hyperbolic rendering of the languid corporeality that so many male leads of the classic noir cycle made their trademark. Geoffrey O'Brien drolly captures one paradigm of the latter perfectly when he pays tribute to the 'irredeemable materiality' of Dana Andrews, star of *Laura* (Dir. Otto Preminger, 1944) and many other noirs. Andrews, he says, demonstrates on-screen little other than his own body, 'this body that must carry the weight of Dana Andrews through the world, and his coat and hat too, and the extra pack of cigarettes for later'.[63] This accent here on automatism and on the tolls of embodiment is very telling, its principal purpose being to stress how affect, much more than psychology, governs noir agency, however frayed the latter tends to be. The laconic physical acting styles of Robert Mitchum, Lancaster and Andrews – so emblematic of noir – could be regarded as exemplary of what Richard Maltby describes as 'autonomous performance', a mode of screen performance that aligns itself with spectacle and display, and thus inherently centres on the body. Maltby distinguishes the latter from 'integrated' performance, a mode that is more deeply invested in serving character and narrative.[64] Maltby's concept is useful not just because it helps to situate a noir performance style of accentuated lassitude and inertia but because it also evokes a sense of the body's affective 'autonomy' in the face of narrative itself.[65] Indeed, in a study of cinematic performance that draws inspiration from Deleuze, Elena del Río identifies performance as not simply autonomous but as a site where an 'expression-event' of affective intensity takes place, one that remains entirely 'unassimilable' to language.⁶⁶ Despite an apparent paradox when it comes to the fatigued, affectless performance of the noir protagonist, there is no reason not to read such intense inertia and passivity as itself constituting a site of affective intensity. One thinks for instance of an observation made by W. J. T. Mitchell, offered in the context of the imposingly aloof human figures in many of Anthony Gormley's famous 'corpographs': 'The eloquence and the power of the figure seems ... inversely proportional to its dramatic or gestural insistence. It is as if the more passive, noncommittal, and self-absorbed the figure, the more "dominion" it exerts over the space around it.'⁶⁷

In any event, as a result of iconography and performance, one of the specific visual legacies of noir is the protagonist whose physical presence is visually underlined as imbued with a distinctive weariness. Even when the protagonist is elsewhere in the narrative a livewire, charged with a dynamic athletic vitality that enables him to act faster than his rival, his default disposition is one of a phlegmatic, jaded waiting. Mitchum's character, Jeff Bailey, in *Out of the Past* (Dir. Jacques Tourneur, 1947), is perhaps the finest example of this paradoxical fusion of action and inertia.⁶⁸ Indeed, if one subscribes to Deleuze's thesis that in the post-war period, the classical cinema of consistent spatial relations and stable narrative logic was complimented and challenged by a new regime, that of the time-image which gives access to a 'direct image' of time, a 'little time in the pure state', then this jadedness of the human body in film noir is one site within cinema where the time-image can be seen already to assert itself. Commenting on the protagonists of Michelangelo Antonioni's films, Deleuze notes that in the regime of the time-image,

> Even the body is no longer what moves; subject of movement or the instrument of action, it becomes rather the developer [*révélateur*] of time, it shows time through its tirednesses and waitings.⁶⁹

We could, very readily, apply Deleuze's comments here to the laconic, densely freighted physical performances of noir protagonists such as Andrews and Mitchum. The wearied protagonists of noir are similarly laid open to a radical conception of time, and we should note here that there are suggestive correspondences between Deleuze's rooting of the time-image in the fatigue of the body and Vivian Sobchack's phenomenological conception of noir temporality ('lounge time') as it occurs in places of transition and waiting.⁷⁰

The 'dark interval' in *The Killers*

The noir protagonist is usually considered to be caught up in 'webs' of intersubjective intrigue, but actually, at a far more incipient level still, the noir protagonist is always suffused in a more expansive and amorphous affective register. At privileged moments in noir narratives a protagonist might suddenly catch a glimpse of this suffusion – a glimpse of 'the outside' that triggers an experience of the 'dark interval'. The most paradigmatic example of this 'privileged moment' in noir is that of Burt Lancaster's gaze into his own death in *The Killers*. Significantly, this privileged moment is – once again – staged in *The Killers* via that familiar noir tableau of the figure lying in bed in a strange passivity. Indeed, the scene constitutes perhaps the most iconic example of this iconography, noir's most quintessential demonstration of this tableau. The passivity of 'the Swede' (Burt Lancaster) as he lies in bed awaiting his executioners is utterly mesmerizing.[71] Aware of the imminent threat to his life, the Swede doesn't attempt to escape his motel room. Instead, having heard the two assassins approach the door, he lifts himself up on his bed (in a manner vaguely reminiscent of the female figure in Hopper's *Evening Wind*), leans forward and peers into the unknown (Figure 8).

The suspensive dynamic of his relation to this 'unknown' is given figural representation in the form of the closed bedroom door he stares at intently, and in the thin gleam of light that ghosts through it. The film then cross-cuts between shots of the Swede's stare and POV shots of this door before the latter opens, bringing with it intense light and then – the more prosaic reality – the two hit-men who immediately unleash a hail of gunfire. It is not this murder, however, but the image of the transfixed and passive Lancaster that becomes the central impetus of the film. It raises an enigma that motivates the film's subsequent flashback narrative. How are we – via our surrogate, investigator Reardon (Edmond O'Brien) – to account for the Swede's mesmerizing passivity in the face of certain death? What has the

FIGURE 8 *Rupture of the dark interval in* The Killers.

Swede seen? And yet the image, too, while motivating the narrative, also comes to haunt and undermine the film's hermeneutic impulse. The stubborn inscrutability of the Swede's gaze into oblivion subverts the various flashback accounts and perceptions of numerous characters who knew him – accounts and perceptions that would try to explain and circumscribe the singularity of his existence.

But what does the Swede see? His enigmatic passivity is emboldened by the fact that we know he has chosen not to escape. Yet it would be a mistake, for all that, to perceive this passivity as straightforward fatalism, as Michael Walker does when he declares: 'We are now at the heart of the noir world, where a man so lacks the will to live that he just waits for the end.'[72] It would be a mistake because it is not so much death that the Swede fatalistically 'embraces' as much as it is its captivating and irreducible otherness to which he submits. He does so, as Oliver Harris has rightly noted, *not* in a state of dejected resignation but in an enraptured state of fascination,[73] which Foster Hirsch has elsewhere recognized as a strange kind of 'exaltation'.[74]

For Harris, the Swede's gazing stillness is emblematic of this trope of 'fascination' in noir, a trope which he says 'has been at once massively overexposed and almost completely overlooked'.[75] Moreover, the image of the noir protagonist rapt in fascination becomes itself a 'fascinating image' for the viewer. Significantly, for Harris, who invokes the philosophy of Blanchot throughout, this fascinated gaze takes place in what Blanchot calls 'time's absence'.[76] Here, then, once again, we find the critical observation that, whether it is inscribed at the level of narrative or at the level of iconography, or both, in noir there is something that disrupts or subverts narrative, ruptures linear conceptions of time and marks the emergence of an atemporal or extra-temporal quality. A further example of such a tendency can be identified in *Double Indemnity* (Dir. Billy Wilder, 1944), where – in a typically self-reflexive moment – Wilder cuts the sound of the protagonist's footsteps from the soundtrack to indicate the character's anxiety following the murder he has just committed. In voice-over, the guilty man (Fred MacMurray) describes the strange experience:

> Nothing had slipped, nothing had been overlooked, there was nothing to give us away. And yet, Keyes, as I was walking down the street to the drug store, suddenly it came over me that everything would go wrong. It sounds crazy, Keyes, but it's true, so help me: I couldn't hear my own footsteps. It was the walk of a dead man.

At the level of the narrative, the scene is clearly geared towards underlining the protagonist's sense of transgression, guilt and impending downfall. At an extra-diegetic level, however, the scene calls attention to 'the moment' itself – that is, to the moment of time's own occurring – and to a phantasmatic quality resident in this moment and, by extension, in every moment. In his second book on cinema, Deleuze employs Henri Bergson's concept of 'paramnesia' to describe how the human is always aware of the present moment at two levels: both as the present-that-passes (*the actual*) and, residually, as the past-that-it-already-is (*the virtual*):

> The past does not follow the present that it is no longer, it coexists with the present it was. The present is the actual image, and its contemporaneous past is the virtual image, the image in a mirror. According to Bergson, 'paramnesia' (the illusion of déjà vu or already having been there) simply makes this obvious point perceptible: there is a recollection of the present, contemporaneous with the present itself, as closely coupled as a role to an actor. 'Our actual existence, then, whilst it is unrolled in time, duplicates itself along with a virtual existence, a mirror-image. Every moment of our life presents the two aspects, it is actual and virtual, perception on the one side and recollection on the other … Whoever becomes conscious of the continual duplicating of his present into perception and recollection … will compare himself to an actor playing his part automatically, listening to himself and beholding himself playing'.[77]

For Deleuze, this spectral, autonomic facility of *paramnesia* reveals to us the degree to which a dim awareness (or recollection) of the most passive, unheralded, insignificant moments of our everyday lived experience – our suffusion in the diaphanous flows of becoming – ghosts us constantly, serving as an affective 'virtual' register quite in contrast to the conventional 'narrativized' accounts of 'actuality' with which we mediate our existence. Such a hazy awareness of the spectral quality of the present moment is in fact characteristic of classic noir, but it is seldom as self-consciously articulated as it is here in *Double Indemnity*. Instead, it is usually relayed with more subtlety, as it is in the Swede's death-scene in *The Killers*. By contrast, in modern noir, we find a proliferation of scenes that very explicitly evince a profound concern with this spectral extra-temporal experience – the 'dark interval' – so often rendered as a moment of ecstatic self-affection.[78] To cite just two prominent examples, it is just such a moment, a weirdly banal yet epiphanic moment, that essentially kick-starts the narrative in meta-noir *The Man Who Wasn't There*. In the scene in question, the protagonist, barber Ed Crane, is suddenly overcome by *paramnesia* while cutting a customer's hair. It is the first in a series of such moments in the film – moments that are freighted with a sense of extra-temporal shock. Another example, more pointed still, of a modern noir that foregrounds its concern with this spectral moment is *The Aura* (Dir. Fabián Bielinsky, 2005). The film's disconcerting hero, Esteban Espinosa (Ricardo Darín), is an epileptic taxidermist who gets involved in a high-stakes heist. His epileptic attacks, we learn, are preceded by a strange moment of sensuous plenitude and calm, as he explains to his potential love interest, Diana (Dolores Fonzi):

Esteban: A few seconds before it happens I know I'm going to have an attack. There's a moment ... A shift. The doctors call it an aura. Things suddenly change. It's as if ... as if everything stopped and a door opened in your head, letting things in ...
Diana: What things?
Esteban: Sounds ... Music ... Voices ... Images ... Smells ... The smell of school, of kitchen, of family ... It tells me the fit is coming and there's nothing you can do ... to stop it ... nothing. It's horrible ... And it's perfect ... because during those few seconds, you're free ... There's no choice, there's no alternative, nothing for you to decide. Everything tightens up, gets narrower ... And you surrender yourself.

Here again we have the familiar reference to time's cessation and it is far from accidental. *The Aura*, heavily stylized as a film noir, is conversant with a significant strain of modern noir that concerns itself centrally with the enigmatic, spectral and quasi-illusory status of time, and which lays particular emphasis on the idea of a moment of strange and acute presence, at once ablaze with plenitude and yet phantasmatic and unreal.[79] Esteban's 'aura' also self-consciously refers to another quality that has always been implicit in such images of arrest in noir – a strange, 'horrible', 'perfect' experience of freedom to which one can only 'surrender'.

While bearing in mind this trope of freedom, it's worth drawing attention to the similarities between Esteban's description of the epileptic's experience of aura and the strange passivity of the Swede during this cardinal scene in *The Killers*. For Harris, the short sequence in which the Swede – in a condition of 'extraordinary immobility' – sits up on his bed and stares into the impossibility of his death is:

> cinema's most intense visualization of Blanchot's gaze of interminable fascination, 'a dead gaze, a gaze become the ghost of an eternal vision', that belongs to the man who 'enters the nocturnal realm of fascination wherein he dies in a passion bereft of will'.[80]

Significantly, the Swede's enigmatic drift into an autonomic gaze or reverie occurs not just once in the film but recurs throughout. Harris is attentive to one other of these moments. It is the more obvious one: the famous siren scene in which the Swede encounters the film's femme fatale, Kitty Collins (Ava Gardner), for the first time and is transfixed. However, the film also contains yet another scene that centres on the Swede's transfixed gaze. And, in fact, it is far more suggestive than the scene with Kitty, as it replicates

FIGURE 9 *Fascination with the stars in* The Killers.

almost entirely the composition of the film's key scene – that of the Swede staring into the certainty (and yet the seemingly eternal deferral) of his own death.[81] It can be found almost exactly halfway into the film's *Citizen Kane*-esque flashback through the Swede's 'life story'. In the scene, the Swede sits up attentively on his bunk in prison and gazes at the night outside through the bars of his cell. The compositional symmetry with the Swede's deathbed scene must surely have been intended by director Siodmak,[82] as Lancaster's posture is virtually a mirror image of his posture in the earlier scene (Figure 9).

Moreover, as his cellmate Charleston (Vince Barnett) regales him with tales of star-systems, the Swede gazes out on to the night sky with precisely the same opaque absorption that he looks upon Kitty the first time he sees her – that same fascinated glaze with which he will eventually stare into the certainty of his own death (Figure 10).

Most striking perhaps is the shadows of the prison bars that fall across the figure of the Swede. His gaze here is a prohibited one. In Blanchot's terms, the Swede's gaze in the enigmatic sequence at the beginning of the film marks an exchange with 'the incessant' or 'the interminable'.[83] Both are terms that I would suggest we might roughly equate with the experience of *paramnesia*. In *paramnesia* is glimpsed something of that quasi-transcendence I discussed earlier. It is a chink in experience whereby the personal gives way to the impersonal – an opening on to Deleuze's 'transcendental field': 'a pure stream of a-subjective consciousness, a pre-reflexive impersonal consciousness, a qualitative duration of consciousness without a self'.[84] Of course, it carries distinct echoes, too, of Spinoza's third kind of knowledge: the view *sub specie aeternitatis*.

FIGURE 10 *Fascination with the stars*. Close-Up.

In *The Killers* Siodmak very deliberately lingers on images of the Swede's transfixed gaze three times in the film, emphasizing the 'transcendental' qualities of his experience of fascination. When the three images of the Swede in a state of fascination are overlaid – that is, the Swede's first glimpse of Kitty (*eros*), his prison-bed gaze into the cosmos (*infinity*) and his eternal stare into the onset of death (*finitude*) – one realizes that this conceptual triptych testifies precisely to the extra-temporal quality of fascination itself. Lancaster is photographed in resonant tableaux each time he is exposed to it in the narrative, the graphic repetitions at once stressing both the momentousness and the (eternal) recurrence of this experience. Moreover, Lancaster's physical action in each of these three scenes is precisely the same – a craning of the neck, a leaning forward to see something. It carries obvious echoes with the pathos formulae of passive, sensuous absorption that we have observed in Hopper's paintings and – while it carries a somewhat more active affective quality – it is also continuous with the images of *acedic* detachment that we earlier addressed in *This Gun for Hire*, *Le Samouraï* and *The Missing Person*. All of these images in noir articulate the irruption of the 'dark interval': that strange extra-temporal moment during which a figure – in the grip of self-affection – is captivated by a sudden alertness to their suffusion in the impersonal, indecipherable and indeterminate folds of an affective order that threatens the narrative coherence of social and psychological identities. In *The Time-Image*, Deleuze explicitly broaches this encounter as a brush with a 'thought from outside', the 'unthought within thought'.[85] The latter is a motif he borrows from Blanchot, and if we want to understand the experience of the 'dark interval' in noir, then

Blanchot's concept of 'the Outside' – already astutely associated with noir by Harris – may help us.

The Outside, for Blanchot, is a radical immanent darkness lying exterior to every discourse. It is impenetrable. Its contours cannot be marked. One approaches it analogically or asymptotically. (Importantly, the act of writing, or what Blanchot calls 'the space of literature', mirrors and echoes this Outside.) Nevertheless, it is an outside that bleeds into the interiority of human experience. Emmanuel Levinas parses it well in his essay on Blanchot:

> It is what appears – but in a singular fashion – when all the real has been denied: realisation of that unreality. Its way of being, its nature, consists in being present without being given, in not delivering itself up to the powers, ... in being the domain of the impossible, on which power can get no purchase, in being a perpetual dismissal of the one who discloses it. Hence, for one who gazes upon the impossible, an essential solitude, incommensurable with the feeling of isolation and abandonment – haughty or desperate – in the world.[86]

Noir iconography is rife with this gazing upon the impossible, this peering into an inapprehensible Outside during the 'dark interval'. In *The Killers* the Swede's absorbed, compulsive gaze in the face of death constitutes an enigmatic interval that absorbs us, also, as viewers. Certainly, the scene is replete with much drama, a drama that is only accentuated by Siodmak's use of parallel editing during the scene. And it triggers the film's seductive investigative narrative. But it is the 'affective' charge of Lancaster's repose, the 'pathos formula' at work in it, that more firmly grips us. Three times in the film the Swede glimpses the outside, and – needless to say – these recurrent glimpses are the real 'killers' that do for him. Meanwhile, the film's viewer in turn is waylaid, if only temporarily, by the fascination that this very image of fascination engenders. As Lesley Stern has observed, the cinema viewer is always implicated in such 'a circuit of affects'.[87] It is a phenomenon of affective contagion, not unlike Carl Plantinga's thesis of how affective mimicry operates upon the viewer during 'the scene of empathy'.[88] Yet on this occasion it is not one that performs a function of absorbing us into the film's narrative reality. What the viewer is struck by is the unruly nature of fascination itself. Fascination – contrary to its conventional understanding – is never a fascination with one thing. It never unifies. It disperses among a play of forces. Its objective quarry, if it deceivingly appears to be unitary, is only ever isolated by virtue of its constituting a sudden discharge of forces in an unreckonable flux. Ultimately, *fascination takes no object other than the interval of its own fascination*. When it flares up, it does so in moments such as that one the Swede endures in *The Killers*. It is a fascination that neither is directed upon an object, nor is it simply self-directed. Rather it marks a self-affective secession to the sensation – the force, the passion – of affective encounters that do not *belong* to a person but which instead mark an impersonal becoming upon a plane of immanence.

Noir beatitude

The noir protagonist who encounters this rupture of fascination – especially the fascination of death – can undergo it only via a profound and detached passivity, akin to what Thomas Carl Wall describes as 'radical passivity'.[89] (Of course, in the finish, nobody can withstand fascination, which is – by way of a terse truism – the underlying 'lesson' of almost every film noir.)

How might one describe such 'radical' passivity?

In Blanchot's 'The Instant of My Death', a short essay that – in his typically lyrical yet precise prose – deals with an experience of Blanchot's own during the Second World War, the writer describes the strange 'sovereign elation' involved in such passivity.[90] Having been placed before a firing squad of enemy soldiers, a young Frenchman (in reality, Blanchot himself) experiences

> a feeling of extraordinary lightness, a sort of beatitude (nothing happy, however) – sovereign elation? The encounter of death with death? … He was perhaps suddenly invincible. Dead – immortal. Perhaps ecstasy. Rather the feeling of compassion for suffering humanity, the happiness of not being immortal or eternal. Henceforth, he was bound to death by a surreptitious friendship.[91]

Though Harris doesn't mention 'The Instant of My Death' in his essay on *The Killers*, the narrative circumstances are remarkably similar to those in that pivotal scene where the Swede peers expectantly into his own death. Indeed, in his detailed analysis of Blanchot's story, Jacques Derrida even describes the scene in cinematic terms that call to mind the Swede's own encounter with death:

> Death has already taken place, however unexperienced its experience may remain in the absolute acceleration of a time infinitely contracted into the point of an instant. The screenplay is so clear.[92]

However, even as Blanchot's autobiographical protagonist awaits certain death in a condition of strange rapture, a sudden eruption of combat in the vicinity intervenes, and the execution does not take place. Yet, despite this unexpected reprieve, Blanchot confesses that the recollection of that curious 'light' feeling remained profoundly with him for the rest of his life, changing 'what there remained for him of existence. As if the death outside of him could only henceforth collide with the death in him.'[93] Beatitude is the term that Blanchot gives to this 'light' feeling. And 'beatitude' is perhaps ultimately a term that describes the affective quality that we find, too, in the Swede's gazing visage in *The Killers*. Significantly, as we noted in the last chapter, beatitude is also a term that punctuates (or perhaps even *punctures*) the work of Gilles Deleuze in a small but telling number of places, stemming from the influence of Spinoza upon his work. It is of key importance in his final publication, the short essay 'Immanence: A Life ...'. As I noted earlier, in this essay Deleuze strives to assert a functional concept of the transcendental, yet one that would not imply the transcendent as involving any supranatural, non-material 'beyond'. Instead, he argues that it is possible to posit a 'transcendental field' that 'doesn't refer to an object or belong to a subject'. Such a field would appear 'as a pure stream of a-subjective consciousness, a pre-reflexive impersonal consciousness without a self'.[94] And, for Deleuze, a critical concept already exists for such a 'transcendental field'. The concept is 'immanence', but an immanence that Deleuze is careful to strip of any theological or metaphysical baggage:

> Immanence is not related to Some Thing as a unity superior to all things or to a Subject as an act that brings about a synthesis of things: it is only when immanence is no longer immanence to anything other than itself that we can speak of a plane of immanence ... the plane of immanence [cannot] be defined by a subject or an object that is able to contain it.[95]

'Pure immanence', he goes on to say, is 'a life'. As a paradigmatic example of precisely what this means, he cites the case of Riderhood in Charles Dickens's *Our Mutual Friend*. The latter is a rogue despised by his fellows but when his life is suddenly endangered, 'everybody bustles about to save him, to the point where, in his deepest coma, this wicked man himself senses something soft and sweet penetrating him'. Once he returns to health, however, 'his saviours turn colder, and he becomes once again mean and crude'.[96]

> Between his life and his death, there is a moment that is only that of a life playing with death. The life of the individual gives way to an impersonal and yet singular life that releases a pure event freed from the accidents of internal and external life, that is, from the subjectivity and objectivity of what happens: a 'Homo Tantum' with whom everyone empathises and who attains a sort of beatitude. It is a haecceity no longer of individuation but of singularisation: a life of pure immanence, neutral, beyond good and evil, for it was only the subject that incarnated it in the midst of things that made it good or bad. The life of such individuality fades away in favour of the singular life immanent to a man who no longer has a name, though he can be mistaken for no other. A singular essence, a life.[97]

It is this impersonal *life-as-singularity* – this more neutral expression of *a life* that in its very neutrality boasts 'a sort of beatitude' – that we catch sight of in the Swede's own gaze. Moreover, it is precisely such an experience of the singular that the Swede himself is repeatedly laid open to during his excursions into fascination. As such, it may serve as a succinct description of precisely what is at stake in the noir protagonist's exposure to the 'dark interval'. Yet it is important to note, too, that Deleuze insists that such a moment of an alertness to beatitude – a moment when a singularity within the plane of immanence becomes immanent to itself – should not be restricted only to those moments when life touches death. 'A life is everywhere', he says. It is present 'in all the moments that a given living subject goes through and that are measured by given lived objects: an immanent life carrying with it the events or singularities that are merely actualised in subjects and objects'.[98]

I will develop this concept of 'beatitude' in the following chapter in my analysis of *The Man Who Wasn't There* and I will chart its recurrence in noir – particularly modern noir – as my study progresses. Before that, I would like to point out an earlier occasion in Deleuze's work when he turns, in passing, to this notion of beatitude.[99] In the chapter 'Repetition for Itself' in *Difference and Repetition*, Deleuze outlines a central philosophical tenet of the book: the concept that in the human it is the 'passive synthesis' of myriad elemental, pre-individual, impersonal and non-reflexive 'contractions' that ultimately provides the bedrock for consciousness and what we come to know as 'the self'. These latter qualities (consciousness and subjectivity) are virtually epiphenomenal, borne upon the back of these multiple contractions (essentially, habits) that occur on the plane of immanence at both an organic and non-organic level. According to Deleuze, passive synthesis constitutes for the human 'our habit of living, our expectation that "it" will continue'.[100] The human in this view is pre-governed by what Deleuze calls 'larval selves', the vast multiplicity of minute, impersonal and passive contractions that constitute who each of us is long before the human categories of reflection, psychology and communication enter into it.

> Underneath the self which acts are little selves which contemplate and which render possible both the action and the active subject. We speak of our 'self' only in virtue of these thousands of little witnesses which contemplate within us: it is always a third party who says 'me'.[101]

The upshot, as Branka Arsić has put it, is that

> Our laughter is never the outcome of our decision to laugh; but what is more important, we can feel that we are crying only if we are already crying: laughter is laughing, crying is crying, little smiles are smiling. That

is what we are: a bunch of laughter, tears, smiles or anger. A bundle of contractions. A constituent passivity.[102]

According to Deleuze, there is a distinctive pleasure taken in these countless repetitive and habitual contractions. It is the pleasure of 'contemplation'. Contemplation here is not the contemplation of a psychological subject who directs thought upon a specific object. Contemplation is more akin to an impersonal register that acknowledges the supremacy of these essentially imperceptible contractions, and it can trigger a strange pleasure. 'There is a beatitude associated with passive synthesis,' says Deleuze, 'and we are all Narcissus in virtue of the pleasure (auto-satisfaction) we experience in contemplating, even though we contemplate things quite apart from ourselves.'[103]

This is the beatitude that is staged in the images we have looked at in this chapter – images of the human figure in a state of passive or autonomic transfixion, absorbed by something: an outside which could not be more intimate, an outside that is not representable within the frame. It is not the beatitude of a contemplative subject but rather the beatitude wrought incipiently by the contemplation(s) of multiple larval selves, caught up in a complex affective relay. It is a picture of immanence that has become immanent to itself. This is the image of beatitude par excellence. And it is, moreover, a pathos formula, in Warburg's terms: the pathos formula that I have termed 'zero affect'. The latter – which would account not simply for certain iconographies of noir but perhaps also older images of *acedia* – captures and relays the 'affectivity' of the human being in that moment where it has become suddenly and dramatically attuned to itself, attuned to its implication in a greater passional network, and gripped both by an unsettling doubt and perhaps also by the force of potential resident in the experience. It is an 'affectivity' that may uncover melancholy, then, but also joy, and perhaps also a prospect for a revised conception of agency.

In relation to noir, Deleuze's notion of the pre-individuated human – that singularity comprised of countless 'contemplative souls' or 'larval selves' – becomes particularly interesting when it is invoked in conjunction with his very influential studies on cinema. In Deleuze's film theory, the circulations of affect are of key significance, and the influential cinematic element he calls 'the interval' is vital to understanding how affect operates. Following Deleuze, Blanchot and Agamben, in the subsequent chapters I will suggest that at a cinematic level it is the affective interval, the 'dark interval', which in noir produces the categories of both self-affection (*acedia*) and a potential beatitude ('the saving sorrow') that is disclosed within it. I will begin to do so in the next chapter, an analysis of *The Man Who Wasn't There*. The film reveals how self-affection, and the sense of 'potentiality' that it discloses, is frequently diminished, and always at risk of being diminished, by narrative acts that underwrite and prop up our conceptions of human subjectivity.

Notes

1. See Erwin Panofsky, 'Iconography and Iconology: An Introduction to the Study of Renaissance Art', in *Meaning in the Visual Arts* (London: Penguin, 1993), 51–81.
2. Iconology remains a mainstay in the work of many influential theorists, most notably W. J. T. Mitchell. See Mitchell's *Iconology: Image, Text, Ideology* (Chicago: University of Chicago Press, 1987).
3. See Matthew Rampley, 'Iconology of the Interval: Aby Warburg's Legacy', *Word & Image: A Journal of Verbal/Visual Enquiry*, 17.4 (2001), 303–4.
4. Whitney Davis, *A General Theory of Visual Culture* (Princeton, NJ: Princeton University Press, 2011), 204.
5. Christopher D. Johnson, *Memory, Metaphor, and Aby Warburg's Atlas of Images* (Ithaca, NY: Cornell University Press, 2012), ix.
6. Georges Didi-Huberman, *The Surviving Image: Phantoms of Time and Time of Phantoms – Aby Warburg's History of Art*, trans. Harvey L. Mendelsohn (University Park: Pennsylvania State University Press, 2017), 59.
7. Lawrence Alloway, 'Iconography and the Movies', *Movie*, no. 7 (1963), 4–6; Edward Buscombe, 'The Idea of Genre in the American Cinema', *Screen*, 11.2 (1970), 33–45; Colin McArthur, 'Iconography', in *Underworld USA* (London: Secker and Warburg/BFI, 1972), 23–33.
8. Janey Place and Lowell Peterson, 'Some Visual Motifs in Film Noir', in *Film Noir Reader*, ed. Alain Silver and James Ursini (New York: Limelight, 1996), 65–76.
9. Patrick Keating, 'Out of the Shadows: Noir Lighting and Hollywood Cinematography', in *A Companion to Film Noir*, 267–83.
10. Marc Vernet, 'The Filmic Transaction: On the Openings of Film Noirs', trans. David Rodowick, *The Velvet Light Trap*, 20 (1983), 2–9.
11. Borde and Chaumeton, *A Panorama of American Film Noir*, 37–8.
12. Andrew Spicer, 'The Angel of Death: Targeting the Hitman', in *Crime Cultures: Figuring Criminality in Fiction and Film*, ed. Bran Nicol, Patricia Pulman and Eugene McNulty (London: Continuum, 2010), 155–74.
13. In fact, first-time viewers of the film often do not notice him initially. See Ginette Vincendeau, *Jean-Pierre Melville: 'An American in Paris'* (London: BFI, 2003), 180.
14. In the case of *Memento* the scene with Lenny (Guy Pearce) on the bed is actually the second sequence in the film. It's important to note, however, that the film unfolds along two discreet and interweaving narrative timelines. Lenny's appearance on the bed is the first scene in the second timeline, then, which we might call 'the voice-over timeline'. It is the thread, rendered in black and white, that produces the film's narrative and which specifically serves to root the film in a noir idiom.

15 By coincidence or by design, Garfield's final film, another noir, *He Ran All the Way* (Dir. John Berry, 1951), opens with a shot that is virtually a quote of the opening shot in *Body and Soul*: a panning shot tracks to Garfield's protagonist, Nick Robey, who mutters portentously in his sleep, tossing and turning uneasily in his bed, evidently caught in a bad dream.

16 Robin Wood, 'Ideology, Genre, Auteur', in *Film Genre Reader III*, ed. Keith Barry Grant (Austin: University of Texas, 2003), 69.

17 Francois Truffaut was one of the first to call detailed attention to the 'doubledness' of the two Charlies. See Claude Chabrol and Eric Rohmer, *Hitchcock: The First Forty-four Films*, trans. Stanley Hochman (New York: Ungar, 1979), 72.

18 Significantly, her decrying of material wealth has been pre-emptively mirrored in the glimpse of the banknotes on Uncle Charlie's bedside table in the prior shot. Uncle Charlie's demeanour makes him appear contemptuous of this money. Some of it has even fallen to the floor. Its iconographic significance clearly resides in the fact that his gaze is averted from it.

19 Wood, 'Ideology, Genre, Auteur', 69.

20 Chabrol and Rohmer, *Hitchcock*, 74.

21 On the significance of 'existential choice' in relation to the articulation of 'freedom' in noir, see Robert Porfirio, 'No Way Out: Existential Motifs in the Film Noir', in *Film Noir Reader*, 87.

22 Giorgio Agamben, *Remnants of Auschwitz: The Witness and the Archive*, trans. Daniel Heller-Roazen (New York: Zone, 1999), 105–6.

23 Giorgio Agamben, *The Coming Community*, trans. Michael Hardt (Minnesota: University of Minnesota, 1993), 2.

24 Giorgio Agamben, *Stanzas: Word and Phantasm in Western Culture*, trans. Ronald L. Martinez (Minneapolis: University of Minnesota, 1993), 3–28.

25 Raymond Klibansky, Erwin Panofsky and Fritz Saxl, *Saturn and Melancholy: Studies in the History of Natural Philosophy, Religion, and Art* (Nendeln/Lichtenstein: Kraus, 1979), 247–50.

26 See ibid., 286–8; and Agamben, *Stanzas*, 7.

27 Vivian Sobchack, 'Lounge Time: Postwar Crises and the Chronotype of Film Noir', in *Refiguring American Film Genres*, ed. Nick Browne (Berkeley: University of California, 1988), 129–67. Sobchack's observation that noir's temporality – 'lounge time' – emerges in a period when 'the "security state" becomes a generally accepted way of life' (166) also resonates very sharply with my analysis of *The Long Goodbye*.

28 Charlie's line here is quoted virtually verbatim by Philippe Noiret's enigmatic and profoundly listless police officer in Bertrand Tavernier's knowing modern noir, *Coup de torchon* (1982).

29 As Mary Ann Doane has observed, the relationship between the rationalization of time in modernity and cinema as a technics is a complex one, with classical cinema to some degree complicit in establishing such a rationalized temporality. See Doane, *The Emergence of Cinematic Time*, 4–7.

30 Colin McArthur, *The Big Heat* (London: BFI, 1992), 51.
31 Giorgio Agamben, *The Man without Content*, trans. Georgia Albert (Stanford, CA: Stanford University Press, 1999), 109–10.
32 Agamben, *Stanzas*, 4–5.
33 Agamben, *Stanzas*, 5. See also Martin Heidegger, *Being and Time*, trans. John Macquarrie and Edward Robinson (Blackwell, 1962), 210–19.
34 This is perhaps what distinguishes Agamben's concept of *acedia* from Walter Benjamin's implicit critique of *acedia* in his essay, 'Theses on the Concept of History'. In the latter, Benjamin refers to *acedia* as a kind of overwhelming resignation – what happens when one 'despairs of grasping and holding the genuine historical image as it flares up briefly'. See 'Theses on the Concept of History', in *Illuminations*, trans. Harry Zohn, ed. Hannah Arendt (New York: Schocken, 2007), 256. This 'genuine historical image', as Benjamin esoterically defines it, is something which 'arrests' thought, producing a 'shock' within which nestles a revolutionary potential (256–62). In *Stanzas*, Agamben preserves the power of such an arrest within his own more detailed and better delineated concept of *acedia*.
35 Agamben, *Stanzas*, 7.
36 Margaret Iversen and Stephen Melville, *Writing Art History: Disciplinary Departures* (Chicago: University of Chicago Press, 2001), 48–50.
37 Ibid., 25.
38 Ibid., 20.
39 For an excellent analysis of the use of 'The Merry Widow's Waltz' in *Shadow of a Doubt*, see Richard R. Ness, 'A Lotta Night Music: The Sound of Film Noir', *Cinema Journal*, 47.2 (2008), 52–73.
40 Diverse expressions of this motif can be found in noir, including in films such as *Nocturne* (Dir. Edwin L. Marin, 1945), *Detour* (Dir. Edgar G. Ulmer, 1945), *Black Angel* (Dir. Roy William Neill, 1946), *The Locket* (Dir. John Brahm 1946), *The Long Goodbye* (Dir. Robert Altman, 1973) and *Angel Heart* (Dir. Alan Parker, 1987). See my video essay, 'Suffering in Rhythm: The "Haunting Melody" in Film Noir', *[in]Transition: Journal of Videographic Film and Moving Image Studies*, 5.2 (2018).
41 See Aby Warburg, *The Renewal of Pagan Antiquity: Contributions to the Cultural History of the European Renaissance*, ed. Kurt W. Foster; trans. David Britt (Los Angeles: Getty Research Institute for the History of Art and the Humanities, 1999), 89–156.
42 See Ernst Hans Gombrich, *Aby Warburg: An Intellectual Biography* (Oxford: Phaidon Press, 1970), 71.
43 Didi-Huberman, *The Surviving Image*, 123.
44 Agamben, *Potentialities*, 90.
45 Didi-Huberman, *The Surviving Image*, 325–35.
46 Warburg: 'The legacy of antiquity offers the artist, through the medium of historical recollection, experiences of a passionate, active or passive

orientation towards the world, which are just as essential a part of the modern social psyche as childhood recollections are to the life of the adult.' Quoted in Rampley, 'Iconology of the Interval', 322. Consider also Warburg's admiration for the subtle intensity aglow in Botticelli's 'tranquil moods'. See Warburg, *The Renewal of Pagan Antiquity*, 143. Or his observations on the 'enfolding' stillness and 'atmospheric harmony' captured in Pierre Puvis de Chavannes's mural *The Pastoral Life of Saint Geneviève* (1877), the latter coalescing to impart a 'feeling of rapt adoration'. Warburg, *The Renewal of Pagan Antiquity*, 713.

47 See Laura Mulvey, *Death 24 X A Second: Stillness and the Moving Image* (London: Reaktion Books, 2005) and Raymond Bellour, *Between-the-Images* (Zurich: JPR Ringier, 2011). Agamben, 'Nymphs', in *Releasing the Image: From Literature to New Media*, ed. Jacques Khalip and Robert Mitchell (Stanford: Stanford University Press, 2011), 61.

48 Blanchot, *The Space of Literature*, 110. Eleanor Kaufman has examined the significance of this inertia to Blanchot, drawing the contrast between the image of fundamental ontological passivity in his work and that of a more active becoming in Deleuze's writing. See Kaufman, 'Midnight, or the Inertia of Being', *Parallax*, 12.2 (2006), 98–111.

49 See Johnson, *Memory, Metaphor, and Aby Warburg's Atlas of Images*, 104.

50 In the *Critique of Judgment*, Kant remarks that 'the absence of emotion … when found in a mood that adheres emphatically to its principles, cannot only be sublime but most admirably so'. The translation is Paul de Man's, quoted in Rei Terada, *Feeling in Theory: Emotion after the 'Death of the Subject'* (Cambridge, MA: Harvard University Press, 2001), 83.

51 Blanchot, *The Infinite Conversation*, 44–5.

52 Erich Auerbach, '*Passio* as Passion', in *Time, History, and Literature: Selected Essays of Erich Auerbach*, ed. James I. Porter, trans. Jane O. Newman (Princeton, NJ: Princeton University Press, 2014), 166.

53 The character was identified as a 'deus ex machina' by Pauline Kael. See Pauline Kael, *Diva* Review, *The New Yorker*, 19 April 1982.

54 A 'waning of affect' is, famously, one of the characteristics Frederic Jameson observes as central to the processes of postmodernism. Fredric Jameson, *Postmodernism, or, the Cultural Logic of Late Capitalism* (Durham, NC: Duke University Press, 1991), 37.

55 Seigworth and Gregg, 'An Inventory of Shimmers', in *The Affect Theory Reader*, ed. Gregg and Seigworth (Durham, NC: Duke University Press, 2010), 1.

56 Žižek, *Enjoy Your Symptom!*, 152.

57 Nicholas Christopher, *Somewhere in the Night: Film Noir and the American City* (New York: Simon & Schuster, 1997), 15.

58 Ivo Kranzfelder, *Edward Hopper, 1882–1967: Vision of Reality* (New York: Taschen, 1998), 42.

59 Indeed, Žižek has noted how Hopper's most profound connection to noir involves his inscription of a frame within his paintings, and his particular 'obsession with the motif of the window qua boundary and link between the interior and the exterior'. See *Enjoy Your Symptom!*, 154.

60 Martin Jay, *Downcast Eyes: The Denigration of Vision in Twentieth-Century French Thought* (Berkeley: University of California Press, 1993), 245.

61 Gilles Deleuze, 'Immanence: A Life', in *Pure Immanence: Essays on Life*, intro. John Rajchman, trans. Anne Boyman (New York: Zone, 2001), 25.

62 See Blanchot, *The Space of Literature*, *The Infinite Conversation*, and *The Writing of the Disaster*, trans. Ann Smock (Lincoln: University of Nebraska, 1995),

63 Geoffrey O'Brien, 'Dana Andrews, or the Male Mask', in *Castaways of the Image Planet* (Washington, DC: Counterpoint, 2002), 199.

64 Richard Maltby, *Hollywood Cinema* (London: Blackwell, 2003), 380–9.

65 Similarly, in an early and influential essay on noir performance, Richard de Cordova has noted how noir's frequent use of voice-over 'works to problematise the body by introducing a variety of disjunctions between the bodily image and the voice'. See Richard de Cordova, 'Genre and Performance: An Overview', in *Film Genre Reader III*, 135.

66 del Río, *Deleuze and the Cinemas of Performance*, 4.

67 See W. J. T. Mitchell, *What Do Pictures Want? The Lives and Loves of Images* (Chicago: University of Chicago Press, 2005), 261.

68 References to Bailey's laconic disposition abound in the film, earning him the admiration of the film's sybaritic kingpin, Whit (Kirk Douglas): 'You just sit and stay inside yourself. I like that.'

69 Deleuze, *Cinema II*, xi.

70 See Sobchack, 'Lounge Time', 130.

71 Indeed, part of the image's power resides in the way the neutered serenity of the Swede lying in bed during this scene comes into a sharp contrast with a number of scenes later in the film's flashback narrative where, repeatedly, the Swede is framed lying on a bed in a state of anguish.

72 Michael Walker, 'Robert Siodmak', in *The Movie Book of Film Noir*, ed. Ian Cameron (London: Studio Vista, 1994), 129.

73 Oliver Harris, 'Film Noir Fascination: Outside History, But Historically So', *Cinema Journal*, 43.1 (2003), 3–24.

74 Hirsch, *The Dark Side of the Screen*, 165.

75 Harris, 'Film Noir Fascination', 3.

76 Harris here refers to Blanchot's terminology in *The Space of Literature*, 30.

77 Deleuze, *Cinema II*, 79.

78 As Mary Ann Doane notes, in cinema pathos is more closely aligned with heightened moments and arrested images than with narrative progression.

See Doane, '"Pathos and Pathology": The Cinema of Todd Haynes', *Camera Obscura* 57, 19.3 (2004), 12.

79 *Inception* (Dir. Christopher Nolan, 2010) is another modern noir that hinges on such a 'moment' of rapture/rupture.
80 Harris, 'Film Noir Fascination', 10.
81 It's notable that Siodmak doesn't allow us to see the Swede's death. The Swede's death remains radically *other*: beyond representation, indeterminable.
82 In fact, there can be no question that Siodmak intentionally employs the visual motif of a figure lying in bed throughout the film, as we also observe Kitty strewn seductively across a bed, an image that was also replicated in a number of publicity shots.
83 Blanchot, *The Space of Literature*, 32.
84 Deleuze, 'Immanence: A Life', 25.
85 Deleuze, *Cinema II*, 266.
86 Emmanuel Levinas, 'On Maurice Blanchot', in *Proper Names*, trans. Michael B. Smith (London: Athlone, 1996), 131.
87 Lesley Stern, 'Ghosting: The Performance and Migration of Cinematic Gesture, Focusing on Hou Hsiao-Hsien's *Good Men, Good Women*', in *Migrations of Gesture*, ed. Carrie Nolan and Sally Ann Ness (Minneapolis: University of Minnesota, 2008), 196.
88 Carl Plantinga, 'The Scene of Empathy and the Human Face in Film', in *Passionate Views: Film, Cognition, and Emotion*, ed. Carl Plantinga and Greg M. Smith (Baltimore, MD: John Hopkins University Press, 1999), 239–55. The phenomenon of affective mimicry is one that originates in psychology and cognitive theory and has been influential in Film Studies since Murray Smith introduced it as one element of how 'identification' in its broadest sense occurs between spectators and characters on-screen. While noting that affective mimicry 'does not rely upon narrative context' to function, Smith insists – a little curiously – that, nevertheless, 'the information provided by affective mimicry must be integrated with the spectator's existing knowledge of the narrative context'. See Murray Smith, 'Altered States: Character and Emotional Response in the Cinema', *Cinema Journal*, 33.4 (1994), 47.
89 Thomas Carl Wall, *Radical Passivity: Levinas, Blanchot and Agamben* (New York: State University of New York, 1999).
90 Maurice Blanchot, *The Instant of My Death* / Jacques Derrida, *Demeure: Fiction and Testimony*, trans. Elizabeth Rottenburg (Stanford, CA: Stanford University Press, 2000), 5.
91 Ibid.
92 Ibid., 62.
93 The endurance of this experience for Blanchot, and the strange bliss he retained from it, is evident in a letter he wrote to Jacques Derrida: 'July 20: Fifty years ago, I knew the happiness of nearly being shot to death.' Ibid., 52.

94 Deleuze, 'Immanence: A Life', 25.
95 Ibid., 27.
96 Ibid., 28.
97 Ibid., 29.
98 Ibid.
99 The work I cite from here is *Difference and Repetition*, but we should keep in mind Deleuze's profound debt to Spinoza's own concept of 'beatitude'. See Gilles Deleuze, *Expressionism in Philosophy: Spinoza*, trans. Martin Joughin (New York: Zone, 1990), 303–20.
100 Deleuze, *Difference and Repetition*, trans. Paul Patton (London: Athlone Press, 1994), 74.
101 Ibid., 75.
102 Branka Arsić, 'Active Habits and Passive Events or Bartleby', in *Between Deleuze and Derrida*, ed. Paul Patton and John Protevi (New York: Continuum, 2003), 140.
103 Deleuze, *Difference and Repetition*, 74.

2

The Passion of Ed Crane: Narrative Dissolution, Zero Affect and Beatitude in *The Man Who Wasn't There*

In the last chapter we observed how in *The Killers* the passion of *a life* exceeds narrative attempts to account for it. In short, Reardon's attempt to produce a transparent narrative for the Swede's life fails – unable to account for the fascination and beatitude of the Swede's sensitivity to the dark interval. As J. P. Telotte has observed, the failure of narrative to account for experience is a fundamental feature of much classic noir.[1] And it is invoked much more self-consciously in modern noir. *The Man Who Wasn't There* is the apotheosis of this suspicion of narrative and its inabilities to account for the passion of the intervallic noir figure.

Upon the film's release, many reviewers noted the pronounced 'affectlessness' of its noir protagonist, Ed Crane (Billy Bob Thornton).[2] But I shall argue that, far from being affectless, Ed Crane is actually brimming with affect. In fact, an alternative (and favourably absurdist) title for the film could be 'The Passion of Ed Crane'. It is indeed Ed's essential passion that is the subject of the film, just as it is Joan's affective agency that is observed and magnified in Carl Theodor Dreyer's masterpiece *The Passion of Joan of Arc* (1928). In the Coen brothers' film, Ed's passion is similarly magnified – even if, inevitably, it is delivered with all the arch wit symptomatic of the Coens' filmmaking. Yet, while the Coens would try to convince us – to 'con' us, even – that they are merely presenting us with a 'blank', absent character lacking in passion and feeling, the contrary is true. There have been few characters in cinema who 'feel' as much as Thornton's character does. The character is a veritable feeling machine, and the film is effectively a study of

Ed Crane's essential pathos. Furthermore, this pathos is invoked as a central element of the film's noir stylings. As a protagonist, Ed is continuous with the passive, *acedic* noir figures that we examined in the previous chapter. Ultimately, Ed's enigmatic passivity – his strange, all-consuming absorption in the sustained interval of his own becoming – runs through *The Man Who Wasn't There* in the manner of a second, subliminal 'story': a counter-narrative, and one charged with an anti-narrative force at that. In this, it mirrors the failure of the flashback narrative in *The Killers* to account for the strange passion of the Swede.

In developing this analysis, I will call on various elements in Gilles Deleuze's taxonomy of film, chiefly his conceptions of the affection-image and the interval. Ultimately, I suggest that Ed's experience – at least according to the flashback narrative that he presents to us – is fundamentally *intervallic*. That is to say, it is constituted by his exposure to (and subsequent allegiance with) the 'dark interval', that transient zero horizon on the plane of immanence where the human is exposed to a thought of 'powerlessness' – a thought that is 'intolerable' (Deleuze)[3] – yet a thought that is also conducive to an intuition of 'beatitude', in the Spinozist sense. Howsoever unreliable his flashback narration, Ed's disappearance into the white frame at the film's finale transmits to us an intuition of such beatitude. In part, it does so by prising open Maurice Blanchot's 'space of literature' and exposing therein the enigmatic 'potentiality' resident in the narrative act.

The impossibility of narrative

We should observe how critiques of narrative – the everyday narrative act and its tendency towards occlusion, deception and dissimulation – are central to the Coens' work in general, and especially to their noir films, *Blood Simple* (1984), *The Big Lebowski* (1998), *The Man Who Wasn't There* (2001) and *No Country for Old Men* (2007). Frequently, a Coens' film will centre on the dissonance that arises amidst a network of individuals once their different perceptions of an 'outer' or communal narrative come into conflict, a trope best exemplified by their espionage parody *Burn After Reading* (2008). This dissonance tends to govern the interactions of the characters with one another, as they attempt, and invariably fail, to make sense of events which cannot be comprehended objectively but which can only be filtered through the prism of each character's own limited, partial understanding. Thus, in *Blood Simple* (1984) a taut finale is played out in which each of the protagonists, though interpreting the same events, believes something quite different to be occurring. As James Mottram puts it, despite the fact that the four central characters in *Blood Simple* exist in 'a unified physical world', they 'inhabit a separate mental and emotional space that causes repeated misinterpretations'.[4]

Of all their many films, *The Man Who Wasn't There* lingers most profoundly upon this problem of narrative, exposing not only its essential incoherence, its status as a representation, but also the intractable summons to a narrative identity that the human is faced with as part of communal existence. Narrative – and, by extension, 'narrative identity' – in *The Man Who Wasn't There* is ultimately a pernicious force. It doesn't desire the 'truth' it identifies as its quarry. Instead, it merely obscures human experience by petrifying it, trying to convert it into the order of 'the book'. (References to books abound in *The Man Who Wasn't There*.) Narrative is also a site of extraordinary corruption in the film, with various protagonists manipulating it in order to present false accounts of themselves. Despite the Coens' suspicions of narrative, however, it is also the *act* of storytelling that permits a compelling sense of transcendence at its climax when both the character of Ed Crane and his narrative will together evaporate before us. Thus, the Coens retain a force or a potential within narrative itself. As David Lavery has observed, their films persistently address 'the impossibility of narrative' and yet at the same time '[narrative]'s obsessive need to carry on'.[5] Ultimately, the potential that the Coens extract from the narrative act derives from what Deleuze calls the 'powers of the false'. The latter is an 'artistic, creative power' that can be deployed to present the inconsistent, the conflicting, the imaginary, and to attest to the dense conflux of forces and encounters that inform every event. The false is not simply the opposite of the 'true', but rather brings the system of 'truths' into question, and by doing so it 'resolves the crisis of truth'.[6] In contrast to the forms of 'truthful narration', which 'are developed organically, according to legal connections in space and chronological relations in time', and always imply 'an inquiry or testimonies which connect it to the true', a *false* narration attempts to reveal the incessant, unstable and always transformative forces at work within every connection and relation, and in the process it shatters the judgment-oriented 'truthful' forms of narrative.[7] As Deleuze and Félix Guattari would have it, the representational form of narrative is a creation on 'the plane of organisation', that territory wherein truths, meanings and identities are defined, diminishing the incessant transformation of becomings, which takes place at a more 'molecular' level on a plane of immanence, a plane of Spinozist composition. Aligned with transformation, the 'powers of the false' are an essential affirmative strategy for Deleuze. As David Rodowick has observed, precisely by virtue of their capacity to transport us to an 'outside of thought', the powers of the false are a force by which Deleuze's philosophy creates possibilities for ethical living and for political action: paradoxically by renewing 'a belief in *this* world and *its* powers of transformation'.[8] Deleuze identifies a series of figures uniquely invested with the capacities of the power of the false. These include the con man and the artist, and they include, too, the figure that Deleuze calls 'the forger'. Significantly, this 'forger' protagonist – a variation on the 'unreliable narrator' – recurs in modern noir, and finds one of its most refined articulations in the shape of Ed Crane.

'Yeah, I worked in a barbershop': A narrative synopsis

Set in California in the late 1940s, and shot in a crisp black and white, *The Man Who Wasn't There* centres on Ed Crane (Thornton), a small-town barber who becomes embroiled in a criminal intrigue involving blackmail and murder. In the vein of classic noir, Ed delivers a voice-over narration from – as we will eventually learn – his prison cell on death row. From the outset, Ed appears to be a quiet, laconic individual. He smokes a lot and talks little. His marriage to Doris (Frances McDormand) is not an especially happy one and Ed suspects – quite correctly – that she is having an affair with her employer, Big Dave Brewster (James Gandolfini). In his impassive manner, however, Ed refuses to 'prance' about their tryst, declaring that 'it's a free country'. Fate intervenes, however, when Creighton Tolliver (Jon Polito) – an entrepreneur seeking investors in a new-fangled business opportunity called 'dry cleaning' – enters the barbershop. Seduced by Tolliver's enthusiastic chatter, Ed resolves to invest the necessary $10,000. And to acquire the cash, he sends Big Dave an anonymous blackmail letter threatening to disclose his affair with Doris. Inevitably, the plan goes awry, leading to multiple fatalities before – at last – the machinations of a poetic justice catch up with Ed, who ends up being sentenced to death for a murder he did not commit.

Significantly, throughout the narrative Ed appears to be more a passenger in the events of his life than an active participant, and at the finale he meets his death with a strange calm. Throughout it all, the film's narrative – though littered with intrigue, bloodshed and suffering – has also staged Ed's insistent, unassuming pursuit of 'some kind of peace'. It's a peace he finds in the setting of the church on bingo night, a peace he finds in the piano-playing of local high school girl Birdy Abundas, and a peace that at the last he locates in his ability on death row to stand outside his life and 'see it whole', a quality of experience that we might regard as evoking – however ironically – Spinoza's third form of knowledge: that rare capacity of understanding our life from the vantage point of the eternal (*sub specie aeternitatis*).

Of course, this being the Coen brothers, there are also copious metafictional nods to classic noir texts, as well as a multitude of additional idiosyncrasies woven into the principal narrative. These include threads about family genealogy, UFO abductions and Werner Heisenberg's concept of the 'uncertainty principle'. The latter, famously, queries the scientific assumption that humans can recover 'objective' truths about reality. As such, when the prominence of Heisenberg's theory in the film is wed to the implied unreliability of Ed's voice-over narration, the film's intricate noir narrative can be said only very superficially to account for 'what happens' in *The Man Who Wasn't There*. Something else 'happens' in the film, too, and it occurs on the register not of narrative order but of affective dispersal, as we ultimately witness Ed evaporate before us at the film's close. It is impossible to glean the importance of this affective dispersal, however, if we don't attend first to the critique of narrative practice the film stages.

There is no 'what happened' – The problem of narrative

The very first image in *The Man Who Wasn't There* is one that cautions viewers to be wary of what they think is 'happening'. The film opens with a protracted shot of a barber-pole. Its red-and-white stripes – rendered black and white by the monochrome print – spin in an upward spiralling motion. Yet this upward motion is a deception. The lingering shot of the pole captures the famous visual illusion associated with the barber-pole. This illusion stems from a paradox borne of human perception whereby the diagonal stripes on the barber-pole appear to the eye to be spinning upwards while, in fact, they are actually rotating horizontally along the pole's vertical axis. The long take of the barber-pole, then, with its attendant association of illusion and misperception, indicates from the outset that the narrative of *The Man Who Wasn't There* may not be a reliable one and that the audience should pay attention to the motif of illusion within the film, and to the way in which illusion lays bare the inadequacies of our representational strategies of knowledge.

Indeed, it is a film in which illusion proliferates – and most amusingly in the form of Creighton Tolliver's wig. The illusion of a full head of hair, and the concomitant principle of 'good grooming', is vital for a businessman, Tolliver explains to Ed. 'Grooming', in fact, proves to be a recurrent visual trope in the film. Repeatedly we see Doris arranging herself before her mirror or cleansing herself in the bath. Later, on the morning of the film's first murder trial – a trial that Doris's lawyer, Riedenschneider, calls 'the big show' – we observe this lawyer, too, fastidiously fixing his image in the mirror. In effect, these scenes find the characters 'grooming' their personal projections of themselves.[9] Yet such personal projections – projections not just of 'personality', as Tolliver would have it, but of a narrative identity – are repeatedly exposed as deceptive. Thus, following his death, Big Dave is revealed to have deceived the town with his elaborate war stories, while elsewhere the theme is bolstered by the variety of hucksters that Ed Crane encounters in the film, from Big Dave and Tolliver to an insidious door-to-door macadam salesman and a phoney clairvoyant.

Most notably, the theme of false appearances also extends to Riedenschneider's interest in Heisenberg's famous 'uncertainty principle'. The lawyer reduces the heady theoretical physics of Heisenberg's discovery to what is nevertheless, implicitly, its core tenet: that scientific analysis, in observing its object of inquiry, cannot help but affect the object of inquiry and thus alters both it and the results acquired in the process. Latching on to this fundamental doubt in humanity's ability to know its reality, Riedenschneider reveals that he intends to base Doris's entire defence on this principle of uncertainty, presenting a warped version of Heisenberg's theory in order to bamboozle the jury.

Despite his cynical manipulation of it, however, Riedenschneider's interest in the uncertainty principle *does* underline the key theme in the film: the idea that human perception is unreliable, open to error and manipulation, and, furthermore, that perception cannot be dissociated from the vast affective matrices that inform a person's physical existence in the world. This 'problem of perception' is, of course, a long-standing 'noir hallmark', as J. P. Telotte has observed.[10] And, obviously, if perception is unreliable then human reasoning founded on perception – and the 'narratives' such reasoning fosters, the narrative accounts that are everywhere demanded in *The Man Who Wasn't There* – is also unreliable. Of all the 'illusions' at work in the film's narrative, it is thus narrative itself which is exposed as the most problematic. Principally, the problem arises when we consider the role that narrative plays in shaping and supporting social systems of power while in the process diminishing elements of lived experience that exceed narrativization. Indeed, in his study of 1940s American cinema, Dana Polan suggests that films of the period increasingly interrogate 'the power that narrative structure specifically possesses to write an image of life as coherent, teleological, univocal ... [its] power to convert contingency into human meaning'.[11] In foregrounding its critique of narrative, *The Man Who Wasn't There* thereby makes more overt what was very often a latent principle of noir of the classic period.

In particular, the socio-linguistic mechanism of 'narrative identity' – that mechanism through which intersubjective communal life is governed – becomes the object of a particularly excoriating critique, just as, in the philosophy of Gilles Deleuze and Félix Guattari, it is the orders of representation and their primacy in social life that are fiercely interrogated and contested. Throughout the film, the reserved and enigmatic Ed is constantly harangued to produce a 'narrative identity', and at isolated moments different characters badger him to answer the same probing question: 'What kind of man are you?'

This insistent demand on Ed to assume a transparent identity is an insidious pressure throughout the film. For example, Ed is repeatedly forced to submit his name to people or to remind them of it. And, invariably, he does so with a pronounced expression of discomfort. We might say that his nominal identity is something he suffers or endures rather than inhabits or promotes. When the police call to the barbershop looking for him, he intones 'I'm Crane' as if he has spent his entire life awaiting this Kafkaesque summons. Frequently, the giving of his name is accompanied, too, by a reference to his profession, which is almost always dismissed by others. The most oppressive example of this is when Riedenschneider instructs him: 'I'm an attorney. You're a barber. You don't know anything.'

And yet, Ed's response to Riedenschneider's condescension is also very instructive. While he is constantly discomfited by having to 'produce' a name and a corresponding narrative identity, Ed has also developed a method of mediating this discomfort, a nod of his head which seems almost to constitute an ironic benediction of any troublesome situation in which he finds himself. It's a gesture of equivocation or quiescence that seems to elevate him above the situation itself. Upon Riedenschneider's patronizing diminishment of his profession, Ed briefly averts his gaze while nodding, and then taciturnly says, 'Okay'. It is not the assent of the exploited or the downtrodden, but the assent of someone moving beyond protest, of someone adjusting himself to a narrative situation not of his design.

The nod is thus a gesture that speaks to something exceeding Ed's allotted narrative identity. It alludes to his own sense that he is more than just the terms (his name, his profession) by which this society would summarily assess him. According to Billy Bob Thornton, the nod emerged, auto-affectively, as an unconscious aspect of his performance: 'The "Ed nod" was actually something that we sort of came up with once [the shoot] started, and we started to notice that Ed would always just accept the most horrible things with a tiny little nod ... Everything he sees he just kind of accepts – not that he's genuinely happy every moment.'[12] Ed gives these nods routinely. Sometimes they are more strained than others, as when Ed nods in response to Big Dave's emasculating remarks to him, even while unable to disguise his irritation. But often, too, an implicit note of benediction is quite apparent in the gesture, as when, in a dream sequence at the end of the film, Ed spies a UFO in the night sky and greets it with a nod of cool, detached equanimity.

Despite the detachment such strategies afford him, however, Ed does, somewhat inevitably, find himself responding to the oppressive summons to foster a narrative identity. And, in many respects, at the surface level of the film's narrative, Ed's 'tragedy' lies precisely in this response: his capitulation to the summons of narrative. It is his attempts to adopt a narrative identity – his fantasy of becoming an entrepreneur like Tolliver – that initiates the film's series of tragic deaths and incidents. And even when this narrative imposture collapses around him, Ed moves on to an alternative one: that of becoming the 'talent manager' of Birdy Abundas. This, too, ends badly.

The important point to register is that – at least within the surface narrative, that is, the narrative that Ed's voice-over presents to the audience – Ed is prey throughout to a summons, and then a desire, for narrative identity. That this *has* been his 'tragedy' is very clear at the end when he tells us, 'But I don't regret anything. Not a thing. I used to. I used to regret being the barber.' In the latter remark, there is a poignant acknowledgement of both the oppression that resides in the cultural and ideological orthodoxy of narrative identity, exploited as it is by the oppressive regulatory dictates and class mechanics of advanced capitalism, and the relief that comes in escaping this orthodoxy: in conceiving of the self otherwise.

Of course, this notion of 'narrative identity' has become firmly entrenched in the social sciences in recent decades. Its central tenet – that narrative is a strategy central to situating human life both at the level of the individual and of the community – has been the subject of influential work by a number of prominent thinkers, among them Charles Taylor and Paul Ricoeur.[13] As the latter puts it, 'Between the activity of narrating a story and the temporal character of human experience there exists a correlation that is not merely accidental but that presents a transcultural form of necessity ... *time becomes human to the extent that it is articulated through a narrative mode*'.[14] In a counteractive essay, 'Against Narrativity', Galen Strawson argues that this argument for narrative necessity – and particularly the notion of a 'narrative identity' that it engenders – is too excessively grounded in principles of human psychology and, moreover, is too invested in a concomitant ethics, as Strawson summarizes it, the idea 'that experiencing or conceiving one's life as a narrative is a good thing; a richly Narrative outlook is essential to a well-lived life, to true or full personhood'.[15] Strawson queries these assumptions, insisting that 'there are deeply non-Narrative people and there are good ways to live that are deeply non-Narrative'.[16] In contrast to a conception of identity grounded upon diachronic self-experience, he says, there is a conception of identity that resides in what he terms 'episodic' self-experience, or what I might describe as *intervallic* self-experience. If Strawson's insights are useful for their querying of a concept of 'narrative identity' that has been ubiquitously valorized in our culture, the Coens stage a similar inquiry in *The Man Who Wasn't There*, I would suggest.

Significantly, one of the central problems that Strawson finds with narrative identity is the propensity for 'revision' that such a conception of identity is, inevitably, laid open to. Strawson means revision not solely in the sense of conscious deceits that one might perpetrate about one's 'life story'. Revision would account, too, for a broader tendency in people 'to engage unconsciously in invention, fiction of some sort – falsification, confabulation, revisionism – when it comes to one's apprehension of one's own life'.[17] As he notes, the fact that memory itself is unreliable, and understood at a neurocognitive level not just to record but to 'reconstruct' past events in an individual's life, is a further way in which narrative identities are inevitably doomed to falter.

This revision of personal narratives – conscious and unconscious – is a prevalent motif in *The Man Who Wasn't There*. It informs Tolliver's pretence of a thick head of hair and Big Dave's sham war stories. The insidious lawyer Riedenschneider even encourages Doris to fabricate her own memory of events ahead of her murder trial.[18] But involuntary or unconscious revision of one's personal narrative is also visible in the film. Doris is so committed to her fantasy of becoming comptroller of Big Dave's new store, 'The Annex', that she blinds herself to her lover's blowhard stylings. Doris is the site of yet a further criticism of narrative within the film – its editorial *selectivity*: the way in which it permits occlusion and excision. When Ed first visits Doris in prison she admits that she did help Big Dave embezzle money from the department store. She asks Ed, 'Should I tell you why I changed the books?' Intriguingly, Ed's response is a telling rebuke to the intrusions of narrative 'accounting' upon human relations. 'You don't have to tell me anything,' he says. In this manner, Doris is able to avoid openly admitting her affair to Ed, as well as to herself. In effect, Ed spares her the attendant guilt of that confession – the guilt resident in a narrative account that, no doubt, in Ed's view, could not actually *tell* the whole story anyway. It remains extraneous to their interpersonal narrative and so it is hereby repressed, excised.

This, then, is a further element within the film that challenges the concept of 'narrative identity': the fact that individuals are not simply the *authors* of their own story but are bound up in interpersonal narratives that also presume to inscribe – to co-write (or ghostwrite even) – this story of *theirs*. The upshot is that for each person in a community there comes into existence a full kaleidoscope of diverse narrative identities, distributed to each individual by the perceptions of others around them. As a result, it is inconceivable that any simple unitary 'objective' narrative – a master narrative – could ever square these many perceived identities with one another, let alone with the interior 'personal' narratives pursued discretely, however hazily, by each individual.

A sequence early in the film illustrates the latter very eloquently. It is a sequence in which the radical nature of our mutually exclusive interior narratives is made explicit. It begins with a medium shot in which Ed stands in a doorway inside his home. The space is lit from within the room in which he stands, yet due to the camera's tight perspective we cannot discern which room it is. Behind him, however, there is the hallway – in which he is also partly standing – and it is unlit. There is an essential duality immediately composed via the lighting, then, with Ed traversing two rooms: the one in light, the other in shade. Ed is smoking and, as his voice-over narration makes clear, he is weighing up the temptation of Tolliver's business proposition

FIGURE 11 *Ed Crane in contemplation in* The Man Who Wasn't There.

('Dry cleaning – was I crazy to be thinking about it?'). The camera slowly pulls in close on his face (Figure 11).

He seems to be quite alone, in accordance with the iconography of temptation in film noir. The cigarette, too, in a further adherence to noir iconography, is emblematic of the very thought he is chewing over. The illusion of Ed's solitude is punctured, however, when we cut to the same image viewed from a different angle, this time shot from within the hallway. Now we are looking into the other room that Ed is partially standing in. It turns out to be the bathroom. And behind his silhouette (his profile now shaded) we see Doris reading a magazine in the bath (Figure 12). Rupturing the familiar noir iconography of the lone figure in a state of intervallic seduction, then, we discover that Ed is not alone after all.

Ed's voice-over is interrupted when Doris calls to him from the lighted bathroom: 'Honey, shave my legs, will you?' He enters the room and proceeds to do so. The lighted room, then, becomes the space of an intermeshing 'objective' narrative. (And, interestingly, it is a restrictive space – i.e. in this shared objective territory, Ed is very quickly reduced to his allotted role as 'the barber'.) Even the privacy of his thoughts, meanwhile, is intruded upon metonymically when Doris insists on taking a drag from his cigarette. And yet, though Ed attends to his wife's legs, his voice-over still makes clear that what is on his mind throughout is the business prospect. And so is asserted perhaps the primacy and impregnability of the interior narrative, in which Ed – detached from his present activity, absorbed in the register of the virtual – is now hurling his own story forward upon a fantasy of future entrepreneurial success. At the same time, meanwhile, Doris reads her magazine, oblivious

FIGURE 12 *Intersubjective space poised between light and dark in* The Man Who Wasn't There.

to the machinations playing upon Ed's mind. The narrative situation is not just complex here. It is cacophonous. Doris and Ed's individual perceptions of their narrative situation in this moment could in no way be reconciled. Obviously, there is a tradition in film noir of configuring a fragmented subjectivity via light and shade, yet here the Coens cleverly employ the same visual interplay to address the fragmentary space of the intersubjective. More explicitly, light and shade are used explicitly to address the dark intervals of self-affection that elude, disrupt, multiply or contaminate the bounds of narrative identity. The scene exposes the sense in which each of us can be considered constantly to flit in and out of narratives, both our own and those of others (in whose narratives we may be configured as merely a residual presence: a memory, a fantasy, a projection). In doing so, we also exceed the reach of any consensual outer narrative that would attempt, forlornly, somehow to abridge, absorb and constellate the great multitude of habitual, relational microprocesses that constitute each one of us.

Nevertheless, *The Man Who Wasn't There* is awash with a range of these master narratives that would attempt to perform the latter impossible task.

Family history and the 'commitment' it entails is, arguably, the most prominent master narrative in the film, as when Doris and Ed reluctantly attend a cousin's wedding in the countryside in the name of familial duty. The genealogy hobbyist Walter Abundas is more explicitly the representative of this model of hereditary identity. After Ed becomes fixated on the piano-playing of Walter's teenage daughter, Birdy, he begins to spend evenings at the Abundas's house. There he observes Walter's obsession with tracing his ancestors:

> Maybe Walter found something there in the old county courthouses, hospital file-rooms, city archives, property roles, registries – something maybe like what I found listening to Birdy play, some kind of escape, some kind of peace.

The itinerary of public documentation is not to be missed, however. While Walter Abundas finds solace in dredging through public records, the film itself regards them with more suspicion. As it is in Dreyer's *The Passion of Joan of Arc*, it is the 'public record', the 'public account', the 'historical record' of Ed Crane's life that the film feigns to deliver, in order to subvert. As Walter's engagement with public records indicates, the public documents that delineate 'family lines' and create their by-products (biographical narratives) are bound up in a socio-juridical demand upon all citizens to 'account' for themselves to the state.[19] Intriguingly, references to the keeping of a 'good' record abound in the film. Doris, for instance, suffers immense shame when she is accused of embezzlement. 'My books used to be perfect,' she says. 'Anyone could open them up and make sense of the whole goddamn store.'

More pointedly still, when Ed is sentenced to death ('brought to book', we might say) he tells us,

> [The judge] wasn't buying any of [Riedenschneider's] 'modern man' stuff, or the uncertainty stuff, or any of the mercy stuff either. No, he was going by the book, and the book said I got the chair.

Yet, as Ed's flashback narration has revealed to us, 'the book', the socio-judicial narrative apparatus of the state, is in this instance wide off the mark. Though Ed has been responsible for Big Dave's death, albeit in self-defence, it is the murder of Creighton Tolliver for which, injudiciously, he is convicted. Moreover, Ed is erroneously and spuriously depicted by the district attorney as a 'criminal mastermind' who pressured his wife to embezzle $10,000 and then allowed her to take the fall. Hence, the judicial and historicist imperative to understand events in terms of narrative – specifically, here, the narrative of the law – is itself indicted in the film. It is this wilful hermeneutic enterprise that comprehensively warps the singularity of Ed's existence into a superficial 'life story', a degradation of what Deleuze calls 'a life'.

'This hair ... You ever wonder about it?'

If *The Man Who Wasn't There* is concerned with the ways in which social narratives, and the narrative identities they produce, are always discretely constructed or maintained, it is in the images of hair-cutting and dry cleaning that this critique of narrative 'propriety' also opens on to the film's other chief concern: its fascination with Ed's affectivity and with the *intervallic* experience that it constitutes. As Tolliver's spiel about 'good grooming' establishes early on, 'cleanliness' and presentation become a key metaphor in the film for narrative maintenance. It is notable that Ed's seduction by the prospect of dry cleaning occurs during a scene in which he shaves Doris's legs. Oblivious to the latent irony of his words, he reflects, 'It was clean. No water. Chemicals.' As he does so, we watch the shorn hairs from Doris's leg trail away in the soapy bathwater. Later, in a moving sequence that further underlines the film's metaphor of narrative 'cleansing', this image of the shaven leg will find a poignant echo when, having had 'the book' thrown at him and been consigned to death, the Coens insert an affecting shot of Ed's own leg being shaven as part of the preparations for his electrocution. Ed himself is the waste detritus here: an unseemly specimen to be pared off, sanitized – in effect *dry-cleaned* – from the communal narrative by a dehumanizing, technocratic process.[20]

Indeed, in many respects, what we observe throughout the film is the body being repeatedly 'groomed' or sanitized by extraneous ideological forces that would demand narrative selves oriented upon capitalist production and banal consumerism. On this level *The Man Who Wasn't There* is very much a film about the body and about affect. Indeed, in the world of the film it is 'the bodily' itself that *isn't there*, the bodily that goes unaccounted for. Throughout, the image of shorn human hair is repeatedly offered as a metaphor for an aspect of human experience that eludes narrative ordering, or is expelled from it, yet which constantly dogs it as the uncomfortable residue of an excision. The key scene in this regard occurs early on when Ed, in the middle of cutting a boy's hair, becomes suddenly anxious about the hair he is clipping. The hair, which spirals enigmatically down into a whorl on the boy's scalp, perplexes him to the point where he asks his fellow barber,

> This hair ... Do you ever wonder about it? How it keeps on coming. It just keeps growing. I mean, it keeps growing. It's part of us, and we cut it off and throw it away.

Of course, the episode speaks broadly both to a Sartrean experience of nausea and to a Freudian 'return of the repressed'. Julia Kristeva has provided perhaps the most provocative conception of this latter 'return' by way of her thesis on 'the abject', and Ed's dismay at the discarded hair can certainly be deemed his recognition of abject 'waste' in Kristeva's terms: that which we 'permanently thrust aside in order to live'.[21] As one of a number of sudden shocks – or exposures to the dark interval – that Ed endures in the film, the waste hair triggers an experience of liminality in him. The excised hair, we understand, constitutes the price of narrative identity, of securing a 'clean and proper body' (*le corps propre*) as Kristeva characterizes it.[22] In this regard, it is worth noting, too, Ed's perplexed response to 'dead' hair in another scene – the '100% human hair' that uncannily 'returns' in the form of Creighton Tolliver's wig. Beyond disturbing Ed, the wig indicates how even the abject itself can be sterilized of its force. Absorbed back into a system of order and cleanliness, and reborn as a commodity item, the recuperated abject functions now only as a cosmetic prop to narrative identity and to good business practice.

The image of cast-off hair, then, alludes to something in material existence that remains elusive of the representational register of narrative, or which is expelled from it, while retaining a residual power. Indeed, in *The Man Who Wasn't There*, this residual force of the body comes gradually to convey a more spiritual dimension of human experience, an affective register quite at odds with narrative identity. Towards the movie's end, the significance of this spiritual dimension is underlined when – during the moment of Ed and Birdy's car accident – Ed is moved to reflect,

> Time slows down right before an accident, and I had time to think about things. I thought about what an undertaker had told me one time – that your hair keeps growing, for awhile anyway, after you die. And then it stops. And I thought: What keeps it growing? Is it like a plant in soil? What goes out of the soil? The soul? And when does the hair realise it's gone?

Hair growth is identified here with something elementary and inchoate, the vibrational matter of the universe, as Jane Bennett describes it, in which 'the extent to which human being and thinghood overlap, the extent to which the us and the it slip-slide into each other' is revealed.[23] We might say that it conveys the passive syntheses that occur unheralded every day in our lives as sensate material beings: the habits and microprocesses – our larval selves, as Deleuze would say – that take place on a Spinozist plane of composition, and which thereby underscore our existence, but of which we only ever achieve the faintest glimpse. Ultimately, it points to a register of experience that narrative never absorbs or sufficiently addresses, a register that – as Paul Ricoeur concedes at the close of his influential treatise on narrative – stubbornly eludes narrativization and which only lyrical forms can approximate.[24]

The dissolution of narrative and the affective interval

Of all the many gestures critical of the narrative act in *The Man Who Wasn't There* the most devastating is the film's dissolution of its own narrative when Ed is revealed as an unreliable narrator. Towards the close of his flashback narration, Ed reveals his location to be his prison bunk, upon which he reclines in a sleepy repose, one hand clasped behind his head, much in accordance with the iconography of *acedic* arrest we examined in the last chapter. This, then, is the 'zero point' of Ed's narration, the point from which he has been projecting his version of events. And it is at precisely this point in his voice-over, as this image assumes the screen, that he reveals he has been generating his 'account' for a men's magazine. As he continues his voice-over, we cut to a shot of Ed now sitting at his prison desk and the camera tracks in on a variety of magazines spread across it. Every magazine cover recalls vague elements from the narrative that has just been presented to us, bringing into question the veracity of Ed's own tale. Indeed, Ed even admits that there is something excessive about his story.

> Writing it has helped me sort it all out. They're paying five cents a word, so you'll pardon me if sometimes I've told you more than you wanted to know.

Stanley Orr suggests that at this point in the film there is 'a collapse into textuality'.[25] With its varied inflections of pulp, sci-fi and Atomic Age *ennui*, Ed's narrative appears to be nothing more than a stunning bricolage of itinerant signifiers redeemed from the materials that surround him. Of course, complex reflections on the nature of textuality are very much continuous with a suspicion of narrative and communication in noir. Telotte's exhaustive analysis of the latter points precisely to this: the fact that 'a preoccupation with the conditions and problems of discourse' may even be 'the *noir* film's most consistent generic marking'.[26] Yet, as Telotte points out, invoking Michel Foucault, even in some of the bleakest of noirs, 'a kind of talismanic potential' is often retrieved by a move which pits discourse against itself in a self-reflexive manner.

> For discourse can grant a temporary sanctuary from disaster, hollow out a safe place from which to think and plan. As Foucault notes, it can turn 'back upon itself' where 'it encounters something like a mirror; and to stop this death which would stop it, it possesses but a single power: that of giving birth to its own image in a play of mirrors that has no limits'.[27]

More than a 'collapse' into textuality, then, I would suggest that the meta-narrative playfulness of *The Man Who Wasn't There* induces a productive *lapse* in textuality itself and solicits this 'talismanic potential' – pointing to the potentiality always inherent in narrative. Ed's unreliable narration can be regarded as an exquisite example of the work of a Deleuzian 'forger': that figure who – invested in 'the powers of the false' – dissolves the distinction between the real and the imaginary, the actual and the virtual, the symbolic registers of representation and the more enigmatic registers of affect.

Ultimately, in addition to its surface narrative, *The Man Who Wasn't There* discretely presents a strange counter-narrative – a contrapuntal force rather than a narrative as such – as a subversive retort to Ed's testimonial 'account'. This other 'narrative' (fundamentally a non-narrative) is conveyed via the film's concern with the affective interval.

It is here that my earlier comparison of Dreyer's *The Passion of Joan of Arc* (1928) and *The Man Who Wasn't There* becomes relevant. Deleuze suggests that there are effectively two powers at work in Dreyer's film. One, the power of representation, is that which grounds us in a narrative 'state of things', that is, the trial of Joan of Arc, both as it is depicted in the film and as a historical 'fact'. The other, the power of the affective – that is, 'the Passion' that Joan undergoes – is something which, while it may sometimes be employed to bolster narrative, is of yet another order, that of 'the affect'. Deleuze points out,

> There is a whole historical state of things, social roles and individual or collective characters, real connections between them – Joan, the bishop, the Englishman, the judges, the kingdom, the people: in short, the trial. But there is something else, which is not exactly eternal or suprahistorical … It is the same event but one part of it is profoundly realised in a state of things, whilst the other is all the more irreducible to all realisation … The affect is like the expressed of the state of things, but this expressed does not refer to the state of things, it only refers to the faces which express it and, coming together or separating, gives it its proper moving context. Made up of short close-ups, the film took upon itself that part of the event which does not allow itself to be actualised in a determinate milieu.[28]

I would suggest that we can observe a similar phenomenon at work in *The Man Who Wasn't There*. In its study of the deceptive and compelling 'affectlessness' of Ed Crane, this film, too, attempts to get across the affective relations of force and encounter within which all human life passes but which remain irreducible to a milieu of representation. It primarily achieves this by circumventing the centrality of the narrative via an invocation of noir performance and iconography. The latter occurs by virtue of the film's prominent use of what Deleuze calls 'affection-images'.

In Deleuze's taxonomy, the affection-image is an image uniquely charged with a sense of affective potential. Among other things, it discloses the affective matrices in which the human figure on-screen is participant, and it is also an image which itself *affects* the viewer. In this regard, it has distinct resonances with Aby Warburg's concept of the pathos formula. For Deleuze the close-up is the very paradigm of the 'affection-image', and he classifies *The Passion of Joan of Arc* as 'the affective film *par excellence*'.[29] As is well known, the film is comprised almost entirely of close-ups of Joan (Maria

Falconetti) and of her interlocutors, tormentors and sympathizers. Though *The Man Who Wasn't There* doesn't privilege the close-up to quite the same extent, it too lingers persistently on close-ups and sustained medium shots of its protagonist. Where Falconetti's performance in *The Passion of Joan of Arc* is one that – necessarily – oscillates between expressions of suffering and ecstasy, the austere noir codes that govern Thornton's expressive range in *The Man Who Wasn't There* make this range much more compact. Yet, in depicting this deceptive 'affectlessness' of Ed Crane, Thornton perfects a minimalist scale of expression enriched by nuance and complexity, whereby the most minor variations in facial activity convey his constant suffusion in a series of affective states ranging from awe and suspense to perturbation and contempt.

It is via this micro-expressive activity of his face – that is to say, via *the smallest gestures* – that Thornton delivers a character of boundless feeling, a character whose capacity for feeling is in fact precisely resistant to the bounds of any rigid narrative identity that could condense upon him. At the film's close, the 'story of Ed Crane' may be forestalled by the revelation of its unreliability; yet we have encountered an expression of Ed Crane nevertheless, an expression of 'a life'. A life – 'pure immanence' (as Deleuze says), the potentially at play in any life – has been communicated, and communicated to us *affectively*, by the passion simmering in Thornton's deceptively impassive performance. It is a performance very much steeped in the 'autonomous' performance style of passivity that we examined in the previous chapter.

Notably, Deleuze associates affection-images very closely with another formal concept in his writing on cinema – 'the interval'. While it can be understood technically as the connective space between shots of action and response, the interval is more adequately understood as the site of potential affects, encounters and events of every kind. Affection itself is what 'surges in the centre of indetermination', in the radical openness of the interval. But an 'affection-image' only ever 'occupies' this interval of potential, without neutering or exhausting its radical quality of 'indetermination'.[30]

In the regime of the movement-image, that regime which corresponds to the codes of classical realist cinema and today's mainstream cinema, affection-images occupy the interval in a rational mode focused on facilitating narrative progress, essentially adhering to a cause-and-effect logic. Yet even in this more conventional regime, the interval's radical potential is often to the fore. Indeed, classic film noir was particularly adept at locating affection-images which retained the inchoate, indeterminate force of the interval as pure potential. Some of the most captivating sequences in classic noir are relayed via affection-images whereby time is slowed, made to quiver or submerged in forces of intensive relations. These include the many oneiric sequences (dreams, flashbacks, hypnosis) we associate with noir as well as the explosive eruption of violence and transgression. Examples of the latter, for instance, would include the reciprocal assaults in *The Big Heat* whereby Lee Marvin's mobster first scalds the face of his moll (Gloria Grahame) with hot coffee before she later exacts an identically gruesome revenge on him. The shocking stylization of the violence in such scenes heightens the moment of their taking place, but the Deleuzian concepts of interval and affection-image also play an essential role in their functioning.

For Deleuze, a key point here is that affect in cinema always conveys the pure quality of expression itself. Invoking C. S. Peirce's semiotics, he explains that in sequences committed to a representational order the affection-image appears in a state of 'secondness' – that is to say, in a state of a determined relation – whereby it underwrites a clear, seemingly causal relation between things, ideas and situations. But the affection-image can also engender sequences committed to a purely affective order, when the image is delivered in a state of 'firstness':

> Peirce does not conceal the fact that firstness is difficult to define, because it is felt, rather than conceived: it concerns what is new in experience, what is fresh, fleeting and nevertheless eternal ... these are qualities or powers considered for themselves, without reference to anything else, independently of any question of their actualisation ... It is not a sensation, a feeling, an idea, but the quality of a possible sensation, feeling or idea. Firstness is thus the category of the Possible: it gives a proper consistency to the possible, it expresses the possible without actualising it, whilst making it a complete mode. Now, this is exactly what the affection-image is: it is quality or power, it is potentiality considered for itself as expressed.[31]

Thus, in the regime of the time-image, the affection-image is employed at its most radical: as a power or potentiality. It no longer simply mediates or provides a spur to action. Instead, it exposes both the protagonist and the viewer to an arresting *thought* or *force* ('a profound, vital intuition') that is intolerable.[32]

Very often, Deleuze says, this occurs in moments in a narrative where a human protagonist endures something – a visual ('opsign') or aural phenomenon ('sonsign') – that confounds response. In this instance – this interval – protagonists register the direct force of time itself. As Deleuze puts it, they 'see' in the interval, undergoing a moment of vision that thereafter marks them as *visionary*, a seer.[33] The seer 'sees better and further than he can react, that is think'.[34] Modern cinema, as Deleuze conceives it, 'is a cinema of the seer and no longer of the agent'.[35] If the hero of the movement-image is one who has agency (a will to truth within the systems of representation), the seer of the time-image, by contrast, is one who is exposed to an essential incapacity resident in the human, a powerlessness at the centre of thought.[36] Lest we mistake such an experience of powerlessness as necessarily disengaged or insular, we should recall David Rodowick's suggestion that there is – in this shuddering experience of a 'powerlessness' in thought – a potential to resist social formations of power (Spinoza's *potestas*) that would position all living beings as merely subjects of ideologies or power-systems, diminishing the affective singularity of their existence and the potential (*potentia*) it contains.

If we return, momentarily, to the repeated scenes of the Swede's 'fascination' in *The Killers*, which we examined in the previous chapter, it is not difficult to view these scenes as indicative of Deleuze's interval when it becomes an exposure to an intuition that evades thought, a 'thought from outside' which discloses 'on the one hand the presence of an unthinkable in thought, which would be both its source and barrier; on the other hand the presence to infinity of another thinker in the thinker, who shatters every monologue of a thinking self'.[37] In each of the Swede's transfixion scenes, it is a *sonsign* (the singing Kitty Collins) or an *opsign* (the infinity of the stars) that immerses him in the affective abandon of fascination. And this is especially true of his deathbed sequence in which the door that he stares at so intently is endowed with a peculiar force, a transformative pathos displaced on to the enigmatic light that ghosts between the door and doorframe.

As 'direct presentations of time', opsigns and sonsigns relay the temporal force of the interval itself, the potentiality inherent in it, a potentiality which is – paradoxically – also an essential powerlessness.[38] Though Deleuze identifies the seers of the time-image with modern cinema, we can regard noir protagonists such as the Swede – and his descendants (Walker in Boorman's *Point Blank*, Ed Crane in *The Man Who Wasn't There*) – as 'pure seers' also. They are laid open to the cold radiance of an affective power that rents apart narrative ordering, in the process rendering an enigmatic zero horizon of experience, in which one can plunge through varying thresholds of perception. In essence, such protagonists may inherit from their exposure to the interval both an affective and temporal disposition (as distinct from an identity) that thereafter remains *intervallic*. In *The Man Who Wasn't There*, Ed's *intervallic* status is communicated precisely by the Coens' invocation of a certain vein of noir embodiment – one that 'shows time through its tirednesses and waitings', ingrained in the passivity and affective stillness of Thornton's physical performance. But the film also underlines Ed's own discrete, *intervallic* temporality (his sensitivity to differential intensities of duration) via his exposure to opsigns and sonsigns.

The former include a number of very stylized 'slow motion' sequences in the film. At an iconographic level, these can be seen to convey, too, the condition of Ed's radical self-affection. As Deleuze and Guattari observe repeatedly, discrete affects – arising from the body's capacity for affectivity – are always a function of the intensities inherent in a body's durational and transformational experience of speed and slowness.[39] Importantly, the slow motion sequences are also an example of a 'virtual image', as Deleuze describes it. Here we must recall from the previous chapter Deleuze's engagement with Bergson's notion of *paramnesia*: the idea that the human is always inchoately aware of the present moment at two levels: both as the present-that-passes (the actual) and, residually, as the past-that-it-already-is (the virtual). When virtual images occur in cinema, they disclose a 'pure recollection' of the present as the past-that-it-already-is.

> The virtual image in the pure state is defined ... in accordance with the actual present *of which* it is the past, absolutely and simultaneously.[40]

In noir this involuntary registering of the present as *the past-that-it-already-is* is the very substance of the affective experience endured in the dark interval. Ironically, one of the narratives most trenchantly associated with film noir is, of course, that of a protagonist whose past comes back to haunt him. But when we look at *The Man Who Wasn't There* through a Deleuzian lens we realize that this film's protagonist, Ed Crane, is not a man haunted by his past but rather a *man haunted by the past that his present already is*.

While Ed would recuperate the impassive durational *there*-ness of his existence (his *haecceity*, in Deleuze's terms) within a narrative of functional identity, instead it is the 'counter-narrative' of Ed's affectivity, the potentiality opened to him in his condition of self-affection, that surges to the fore as the film progresses, producing all its strange, tranquil and mesmerizing power. Significantly, it is a *sonsign* – Ed's affinity for the plaintive strains of Beethoven – which is deployed to convey Ed's experience of this self-affection. As Kristi A. Brown has observed, 'Beethoven's music serves as Ed's musical "language" from the outset',[41] and he 'adopts for his inner voice or, more precisely, his *real* voice the slow movements of the piano sonatas'.[42] This adoption of Beethoven's tranquil sonatas by Ed is, in fact, an expression of his self-affection and his means of *falling-in-time* with the affective potentials of his existence more generally. What Ed's '*real* voice', as intimated by the sonatas, conveys is his self-affective immersion in his own essential passion. Indeed, the popular names of the sonatas (the 'Appassionata', the 'Pathétique') even embolden this affective register with which the music is aligned. It induces in Ed a passivity and an affectlessness that is deceptively ablaze with a peculiar passion, that of an exposure to the potentiality at work in any expression of life.

This musical element is thus especially significant for the film's metatextual deployment of noir. As we noted in the previous chapter, in classic noir, the motif of the haunting melody is very often conceived negatively as something daunting, some 'repressed' that is impeding the protagonist's progress and which must be resolved and expiated, as it is in *Shadow of a Doubt* and *The Locket* (Dir. John Brahm, 1946). Yet, on occasion, for example, Preminger's *Laura*, the haunting melody speaks more ambivalently to affective experience and to the potentials inherent in it. In this regard, the haunting melody is resonant with that phenomenon that Deleuze and Guattari term 'the refrain'. The latter is a principle of our affective experience that arises from the phenomenon of music itself, with which it endures an enigmatic and transversal relationship. The refrain is a melodic means of 'territorializing' a relation. One of Deleuze and Guattari's favoured examples is the image of a child singing to himself, creating a mode of affective shelter, a 'calming and stabilising ... centre in the heart of chaos'. If the refrain can be used to territorialize or reterritorialize a relation, then music itself – as capacity, as potential – has a deterritorializing inclination. It is like the background hum from which refrains may emerge and by which they may again be deterritorialized. Fundamentally joyful, and a conduit for 'becomings', music is also marked by a 'thirst for destruction'. It craves dissolution into the molecular. As such, music – as a potential – is what engenders refrains, yet also what threatens to unravel any refrain that emerges from it. Refrains may be implicated in any situation or emotion, joyful, terrifying or banal. And – no more than music itself – refrains are not the privilege of human beings: 'the universe, the cosmos, is made of refrains'.[43]

When the Coens mobilize the trope of the 'haunting melody' in *The Man Who Wasn't There*, they can be regarded as invoking it as an index of the affective register of human experience, then; imbuing the film with a recurrent sonsign of a 'passion' contrapuntal to the workings of the copious narrative orderings within it. Beethoven becomes at once an intimation of a refrain (the melody by which Ed would secure a calm relation to his environment) and an intimation of the potential native to music itself, a potential to dissolve relations, dissolve refrains, change speeds, intensities and ratios of perception.

Indeed, if affective experience in cinema is often relayed and negotiated through the score, then such a principle of 'background music' itself mimics the way that affect, as Eric Shouse has pointed out,

> is what determines the intensity (quantity) of a feeling (quality), as well as the background intensity of our everyday lives (the half-sensed, ongoing hum of quantity/quality that we experience when we are not really attuned to any experience at all).[44]

In *The Man Who Wasn't There*, Beethoven's sonatas – as they fuse with Ed's peculiar passion – come to stand in for this background 'hum', the residual ebbing and flowing sonority of affect in everyday life, always quavering between music and the refrains it engenders. Brian Massumi, too, has repeatedly described the provenance of affect as a 'background' phenomenon. An autonomous feature of our existence, affects exceed the scope of the body they are anchored in; they are 'open', 'virtual' potentials. He points out that it is the inevitable fate of affect to be 'captured and closed' by experience, converted into an array of 'formed, qualified, situated perceptions and cognitions', of which emotion is the most prominent.[45] Yet, emotion always involves a double-articulation, Massumi insists. It becomes both a trace of affect's capture and of its capacity to elude capture. A sense of its escape, then, is also grasped 'alongside the perceptions that are its capture'.[46] This 'side-perception' of affect's escape and its fundamental autonomy can occur as a puncture in our otherwise narrative approach to existence, in which case 'it is usually described in negative terms, typically as a form of shock'.[47] But, Massumi notes, also, that a continuous and lingering sense of affect persists as a 'background perception that accompanies every event, however quotidian'.[48]

Of course, this persistent notion of a background perception or 'background hum' – of a constant yet muted and intangible awareness of affect – is precisely the object of query when the human falls into a state of *acedia*: the dark interval of a radical self-affection. In the grip of this state, in thrall to one's own affectivity, the human's affective register is temporarily exposed to itself like a raw nerve.

Something like beatitude

In counterpoint to its ostensible voice-over narrative, then, *The Man Who Wasn't There* is a film that – in keeping with its suspicion of narrative and its salutation of affect – immerses the viewer within the 'background hum' of the affective. It does so, chiefly, via the strategies of the affection-image and interval (the emphasis on close-ups that relays Ed's self-affection) and its presentation of Beethoven's sonatas as an extra-narrative force within the film. In the film's very accomplished climax, these two strategies coalesce with a third – the subtle dissolution of the film's narrative – to produce a tantalizing sense of the transcendental, an experience not fixed on a 'beyond' exceeding our world, despite Ed's use of this term, but grounded in the order of affective experience itself. This is a Deleuzian condition of transcendence that is figured as an opening on to 'the plane of immanence', that plane of affective forces and encounters where relational compositions take place. Delivered to this plane, where neither the categories of the subjective nor the objective can obtain in any simple sense, Ed Crane and the film itself – as a narrative – are diffused:

> The life of the individual gives way to an impersonal and yet singular life that releases a pure event freed from the accidents of internal and external life, that is, from the subjectivity and objectivity of what happens.[49]

This is the 'giving way' that Ed Crane experiences upon the moment of his execution at the close of *The Man Who Wasn't There*. Like Dickens's

Riderhood, upon the point of his own death, he becomes the very paradigm of Deleuze's 'homo tantum', a man 'who attains a sort of beatitude', the site of 'a haecceity no longer of individuation but of singularisation: a life of pure immanence'.[50]

How does this 'giving way' occur in the film? At the close of his monologue, Ed's accession to a plane of immanence is communicated via the dissolution of his unreliable, forged narrative and his own visual dissolution into the tranquil strains of Beethoven that all along have marked his sustained passage of self-affection. This dissolution is complemented by a visual white-out effect whereby the irreal whiteness of the execution chamber gradually saturates the entire frame. As the image becomes gradually more overexposed, the close-up of Ed's face within the frame dissipates before us, leaving only a white frame humming with the essential quietude of Beethoven's ' "Archduke" Trio'.

Obviously, Ed's giving way accords with the 'peace' – a capacity to 'see it all whole' – that he has sought throughout his voice-over. It is a peace that arises from an intuition of the tumult of forces at work in the world, of the world's irrepressible plenitude, that Ed Crane finds in Beethoven. And it is this intuition which *assumes* him in the finale: a beatitude, or elevated sense of potentiality, that throughout the film has been invoked in Thornton's nuanced performance of affectlessness and impassivity, the pathos formula of 'zero affect'. As such, *New York Times* reviewer A. O. Scott is more perceptive than he realizes when, in his review of the film, he observes that the 'intense stillness of [Thornton's] face,' having become 'the film's centre of gravity', at the end 'begins to glow with something like beatitude'.[51]

This potentiality is, moreover, relayed not simply as *belonging* to Ed Crane but as the space or interval that is opened up by the narrative act itself – its capacity to unlock the powers of the false. The latter have their equivalent in the literary theory of Maurice Blanchot, who distinguishes between a similar space of transformative potential (which Blanchot calls 'narration') and another more conventional space of representation ('narrative'). In producing a final image of the blank but abundant space of potentiality, what *The Man Who Wasn't There* succeeds in doing is 'narrating itself' as Blanchot puts it: 'It becomes the event it is narrating.'[52] At the end of the film, we thus encounter not a melancholy collapse into a textuality, steeped in postmodern parody, as Stanley Orr has suggested, but rather a more experimental exposure of the lapse – the dark interval primed with potentiality – to which 'narration', understood as itself the potential inherent in any narrative act, responds and mimics. In distinction to the testimonial impulse the film's voice-over feigns, we realize that what Ed Crane's 'narration' – and the film itself – has provided us with is a non-narrative, a 'non-testimony', a neutering of narrative under the weight of affect. In this way a narrative can produce its own counter-narrative, pledging allegiance to the forces of passion and pathos rather than to a reductive narrative fixed only on representation and a judgmental or hermeneutical will to truth.

Moreover, in the dissolution of Thornton's presence within an infinite white frame at the film's close we glimpse, too, what Deleuze calls the 'spiritual automaton': the neutral, autonomic capacity for thought and affect that inhabits the camera's own framing of images, including the performative bodies on-screen. An enigmatic concept, the 'spiritual automaton' is the means by which cinema reveals another 'thinker within the thinker'. In *The Man Who Wasn't There*, this automaton – having repeatedly ruptured the film's narrative during the intervallic sequences that disclose a radical 'powerlessness' in thought – should be understood not simply to linger residually within the fictional persona of Ed but within the affective processes of the film's viewer also. In the manner of Jean-Louis Schefer's concept of the 'enigmatic body', by which the viewer of cinema is the one who lends their own capacities for affect to the bodies on-screen and is stimulated reciprocally by these screen bodies too, the 'man' who isn't there in the Coens' film is simply this strange passenger, then: this 'other thinker' ghosting residually within our own thoughts, this disavowable capacity for affect before which we are powerless. In Schefer's terms, this passenger can be associated with the 'inexpressible' which 'grows in the living as it lives',[53] much like the hair that in *The Man Who Wasn't There* goes on living even after the human body which it subtends has deceased.

As Rodowick notes, Schefer's notion of the 'enigmatic body' in cinema and Deleuze's concept of the 'spiritual automaton' are closely related. Deleuze adopted the latter from Antonin Artaud, but – as Rodowick rightly observes – Deleuze's 'spiritual automaton' also owes a clear debt to Spinoza. The 'spiritual automaton' can perhaps usefully be regarded as *a passenger*, the perennial passenger of human experience, the background hum of affect that ghosts along – almost mutedly – in every passage of our lives. It is significant that one of the most daring modern noirs of the 1970s – Michelangelo Antonioni's *The Passenger* – similarly attempts to disclose this automatist or autonomic force at work both in human life and in cinema spectatorship. In the latter, a strangely passive noir protagonist – having assumed the identity of another man – will eventually disappear evocatively from the film itself, leaving us alert to the 'passenger' or spiritual automaton that the cinematic experience has all the while been working through us, the viewers. The film's closing shot famously forces us to turn our gaze on ourselves and thereby to realize that we ourselves are the *passengers*. The 'passenger' is within us. This is consistent with the sleight-of-hand that many modern noirs pursue, repeating the tactic of Boorman's *Point Blank*, which retreats at the close to the strange space of a single instant within which the entire narrative, it seems, has been unfolding. In ways such as this, as Rodowick puts it, parsing Deleuze,

What cinema contributes to the history of thought is a powerlessness – in fact, a dispossession of thought in relation to the image – that is equivalent to the division of the subject by the pure form of time ... Dispossession becomes a primary force.[54]

It is intriguing that such a cinematics of dispossession has become a key feature within modern noir. Yet it should not be surprising. The experience of dispossession is itself a dominant motif within noir of the classical era. Even if most classic noirs do not strive to induce an experience of dispossession on the part of the viewer in the complex way that *The Passenger* or *The Man Who Wasn't There* does, such films nevertheless very frequently depict characters who undergo a strange dispossession of the rational self, a dispossession or 'suspension' that is invariably at the very crux of the narrative. One such depiction of dispossession is to the fore in *Cat People* (Dir. Jacques Tourneur, 1942), where the enigmatic allure of the film's heroine troubles the prescribed social certainties of order and reason as well as the very category of the human itself. Significantly, as we will note in the next chapter, the convention of the 'haunting melody' is once more at work in this film.

Notes

1 J. P. Telotte, *Voices in the Dark: The Narrative Patterns of Noir* (Urbana: University of Illinois, 1989), 12. Žižek, too, has reflected at length on noir's complex conception of narrative. See 'The Thing That Thinks', 202.

2 In a negative critique, Peter Rainer described Crane as 'a monotonous blank'. See Rainer, 'Skin Deep', *New York*, 5 November 2001. Richard Schickel, by contrast, paid tribute to this performance of affectlessness: 'Affectlessness is not a quality much prized in movie protagonists, but Billy Bob Thornton, that splendid actor, does it perfectly as Ed Crane.' See Richard Schickel, 'Short Takes', *TIME*, 29 October 2001.

3 Deleuze, *Cinema II*, 41.

4 James Mottram, *The Coen Brothers: The Life of the Mind* (London: B.T. Batsford, 2000), 20.

5 David Lavery, '"Secret Shit": The Uncertainty Principle, Lying, Deviation, and the Movie Creativity of the Coen Brothers', *Post Script*, 27.2 (2008), 148.

6 Deleuze, *Cinema II*, 131.

7 Ibid., 129.

8 David Rodowick, *Gilles Deleuze's Time Machine* (Durham, NC: Duke University Press, 1997), 192.

9 On the human propensity to perform 'selfhood', see Erving Goffman, *The Presentation of the Self in Everyday Life* (Garden City, NY: Doubleday, 1959).

10 See J. P. Telotte, *Voices in the Dark*, 101. Telotte mounts an incisive analysis of the 'blind spots' and effacements of perception in *Murder, My Sweet* (Dir. Edward Dmytryk, 1944), *The Lady in the Lake* (Dir. Robert Montgomery, 1947) and *Dark Passage* (Dir. Delmer Daves, 1947), 88–133.

11 Dana Polan, *Power and Paranoia: History, Narrative, and the American Cinema 1940–1950* (New York: Columbia University Press, 1986), 12.

12 Billy Bob Thornton, DVD Commentary, *The Man Who Wasn't There*, Eiv, 2002.

13 See Charles Taylor, *Sources of the Self: the Making of the Modern Identity* (Cambridge: Cambridge University Press, 1989), Paul Ricoeur, *Time and Narrative: Volume 1*, trans. Kathleen McLaughlin and David Pellauer (Chicago: University of Chicago Press, 1984) and Paul Ricoeur, *Oneself as Another*, trans. Kathleen Blamey (Chicago: University of Chicago Press, 1992).

14 Ricoeur, *Time and Narrative: Volume 1*, 52. Emphasis in original.

15 Galen Strawson, 'Against Narrativity', *Ratio*, 17 (2004), 428.

16 Ibid., 429.

17 Ibid., 443.

18 Riedenschneider's rhetorical use of narrative in the courtroom is hardly unusual. As narrative theorist Peter Brooks has noted, using the terminology of Russian Formalism, 'The courtroom lawyer's task would seem to be to take an often fragmentary and confusing *fabula* and turn it into a seamless, convincing *sjuzet*.' Peter Brooks, 'The Law as Narrative and Rhetoric', in *Law's Stories: Narrative and Rhetoric in the Law*, ed. Peter Brooks and Paul Gewirtz (New Haven, CT: Yale University Press, 1996), 16.

19 On the 'juridical' origins of archival practice, see Terry Cook, 'Evidence, Memory, Identity, and Community: Four Shifting Archival Paradigms', *Archival Science*, 13 (2013), 95–120.

20 The film's evocation of *Double Indemnity* becomes intriguing here. In Billy Wilder's 1944 film, Walter Neff (Fred MacMurray) dies at the end from a gunshot wound inflicted on him by the film's femme fatale (Barbra Stanwyck). Yet, as is well known, Wilder had originally filmed an alternate ending. In that prior finale, Neff actually survives the gunshot but is then executed for his crimes in the gas chamber. James Naremore has argued that this death, poignantly witnessed by Neff's friend and the film's self-righteous moral adjudicator Barton Keyes (Edward G. Robinson), would have brought to a more adequate crescendo the resounding criticism of a machinic modernity that Wilder had woven into the film. In *The Man Who Wasn't There*, the Coens might be said to restore the lost finale of *Double Indemnity* by having their own antihero, Ed Crane, executed in the electric chair, as inhumane and technocratic a fate as Neff's killing in the gas chamber. See Naremore, *More Than Night*, 81–95.

21 Julia Kristeva, *Powers of Horror: An Essay on Abjection*, trans. Leon S. Roudiez (New York: Columbia University Press, 1982), 3.

22 'The body must bear no trace of its debt to nature: it must be clean and proper in order to be fully symbolic.' Ibid., 102.
23 Jane Bennett, *Vibrant Matter* (Durham, NC: Duke University Press, 2009), 4.
24 Paul Ricoeur, *Time and Narrative: Volume 3*, trans. Kathleen Blamey and David Pellauer (Chicago: University of Chicago Press, 1988), 273.
25 Stanley Orr, 'Razing Cain: Excess Signification in Blood Simple and the Man Who Wasn't There', *Post Script*, 27.2 (2008), 21.
26 Telotte, *Voices in the Dark*, 27.
27 Ibid., 35.
28 Deleuze, *Cinema I*, 106–7.
29 Ibid., 106.
30 Ibid., 65.
31 Ibid., 98.
32 Deleuze, *Cinema II*, 22.
33 Ibid., 21.
34 Ibid., 170.
35 Ibid., 126.
36 'What cinema advances is not the power of thought but its "impower", which is much more important than the dream: this difficulty of being, this powerlessness at the heart of thought.' Ibid., 166.
37 Ibid., 168.
38 Ibid., 43.
39 Deleuze and Guattari, *A Thousand Plateaus*, 254.
40 Deleuze, *Cinema II*, 79.
41 Kristi A. Brown, '*Pathétique* Noir: Beethoven and *The Man Who Wasn't There*', *Beethoven Forum*, 10.2 (2003), 142.
42 Ibid., 160.
43 See *A Thousand Plateaus*, 295–350.
44 Eric Shouse, 'Feeling, Emotion, Affect', *M/C Journal*. http://journal.media-culture.org.au/0512/03-shouse.php, accessed 21 November 2014.
45 Brian Massumi, 'The Autonomy of the Affect', *Cultural Critique* no. 31 (1995), 83–109.
46 Ibid., 96.
47 Ibid., 97.
48 Ibid.
49 Deleuze, 'Immanence: A Life', 28.
50 Ibid., 29.
51 A. O. Scott, 'First Passive and Invisible, Then Ruinous and Glowing', *New York Time*, 31 October 2001.

52 Blanchot, *The Siren's Song: Selected Essays*, ed. Gabriel Josipovici, trans. Sacha Rabinovitch (Brighton: Harvester, 1982), 63.
53 Jean-Louis Schefer, *The Ordinary Man of the Cinema*, trans. Max Cavitch, Noura Wedell and Paul Grant (New York: Semiotexte, 2016) 13.
54 Rodowick, *Gilles Deleuze's Time Machine*, 190.

3

Vesperal Noir: Intervallic Suspension in *Cat People*

Cat People (Dir. Jacques Tourneur, 1942) has long been regarded as a crucial text within the diaphanous gene pool of film noir.[1] The first of producer Val Lewton's moody masterpieces for RKO, the film is frequently understood as bridging a generic divide between noir and horror.[2] Indeed, the manner in which the film straddles genres – horror, fantasy, melodrama and psychological thriller – is indicative of its own mercurial in-betweenness, its resistance to any final categorization. In this regard, of course, it mirrors the elusive semantic status of film noir itself. *Cat People* is noir at its most enigmatic and atmospheric. It is a noir film in which – like many noir films – the narrative seems entirely secondary to the provocative images of intervallic human experience that it hosts, and secondary, too, to the philosophical interrogation of knowledge and identity that these images foster. As such, in this chapter I will examine Tourneur's film primarily in relation to its iconography rather than its narrative per se and the allegory of prohibitive sexual anxiety the narrative nurses. While Anna Powell has rightly identified the film as a Deleuzian site of animal becomings, and while Gilles Deleuze himself regarded the film as exemplary of that aesthetic strategy he names 'lyrical abstraction', in this chapter I will be focusing on *Cat People*'s conception of the interval as a fundamentally indeterminate state and primarily examining this idea via an engagement with the thought of Giorgio Agamben and Martin Heidegger.

Intriguingly, J. P. Telotte has described *Cat People* as a 'vesperal film'.[3] The latter, he says, designates a cinematic form that is distinguished by its 'labyrinthine, indeterminate, and dark perspective on the modern world and its rule of reason'.[4] Lewton's films are paradigmatic of this form, insists Telotte. They 'repeatedly [deconstruct] our normal vision of things and our usual methods of formulating or narrating the complexities of human experience'.[5] Obviously, this latter querying of perception and narration resonates with my own analysis of *The Man Who Wasn't There* in the previous chapter.

Although Telotte never refers to film noir in his study of *Cat People*, his description of the 'vesperal film' corresponds extremely closely with terms that he *does* use in relation to film noir in *Voices in the Dark*, his seminal study of noir's eclectic narrative conventions. Certainly, the epistemological ambiguity that arises when one is confronted with the more ineffable aspects of human experience is clearly, in Telotte's view, a recurrent and pivotal feature of noir films. It is thus not too much of a leap to consider that Telotte's conception of a 'vesperal cinema' might serve to describe not just the idiosyncratic Gothic films made by Lewton's unit at RKO but a certain strain within film noir itself, a strain in which an epistemological – and often ontological – crisis is staged, one whereby the very 'nature' of humanity falls under suspicion.

Telotte draws his use of the term 'vesperal' from the psychoanalytic thought of cultural theorist James Hillman.[6] To adapt the term to my own analysis of *Cat People*, however, I would like to suggest that the 'vesperal' is essentially a gesture (one that is, in part, incantatory) made by the human during twilight, at the onset of night. We might regard it as a gesture or affective exchange which is at once constitutive of – and a response to – an experience of the 'dark interval'. The origins of this concept of the 'vesperal' extend back to the Greek myth of the Hesperides, the nymphs of evening light. The term itself, meanwhile, derives from the Latin *vesper*, which denoted evening or the 'evening star', before – in the fifteenth century – it evolved to signify a Christian service of prayer and song. (In Old French *vespres* denoted 'evensong'.[7]) The difference between the terms 'night' and 'vespers' is thus a subtle one. The night, in the most mundane terms, is the period of darkness between sunset and sunrise. Vespers (and the vesperal), however, would specifically indicate a *relation* of the human to dusk and to the imminence of nightfall. It is an affective relation often channelled through ritual (e.g. song and performance), and this aspect of song is certainly very significant in *Cat People*.

Cat People: The friendly night

As with all of Val Lewton's films at RKO, the ideas for *Cat People* were conceived collaboratively, in this case chiefly between Lewton, director Jacques Tourneur and writer DeWitt Bodeen.[8] Yet, while the film's distinctive lyrical motifs – the work of Lewton and writer Bodeen – strike a suggestive tone, the ethereal visual sensibility produced by Tourneur in conjunction with cinematographer Nicholas Musuraca and designer Albert D'Agostino is crucial to the film's unique and enduring charm. This is significant because, famously, Tourneur, Musuraca and D'Agostino would collaborate again some years later on one of the most iconic of noir films, *Out of the Past* (1947). Indeed, Musuraca is one of the great noir auteurs, and his contribution to its visual legacy has still not been adequately acknowledged. Wheeler Winston Dixon has recently begun to redress this failing.[9]

The narrative of *Cat People* centres on the romance between Irena Dubrovna (Simone Simon), a fashion designer recently immigrated to New York from Serbia, and Oliver Reed (Kent Smith), a draughtsman for an engineering firm. The latter is – in his own words – 'a good, plain Americano', a rather dull, hard-working model of bourgeois mores. Yet what attracts Oliver to Irena is something that exceeds his understanding: something equivalent to the power he finds in her scent – 'something warm, something living', as he puts it. Conceiving his love for her explicitly at the level of affectivity, then, he confesses, 'I'm drawn to her … There's a warmth in her that pulls on me. I have to watch her when she's in the room. I have to touch her when she's near.' Irena's own attraction to Oliver, meanwhile, seems to stem from his being the first person to extend affection to her in America. 'You might be my first real friend,' she says. This seemingly innocuous comment is made more complex, however, when just a few moments later Irena will tell Oliver that she likes the darkness of night because it is 'friendly'. Clearly, Irena's conception of friendship exceeds any mundane understanding of the term. It appears rooted in an intuition of affective relation and resonance between beings, one reminiscent of Spinoza's vision of a world comprised of the ceaseless encounters and compositions of 'modes'. Indeed, Deleuze and Félix Guattari note the relation between an animal's stalking habits and the fall of night, observing that the night, the animal and its behaviour are all components of the same phenomenon: the 'becoming-evening, becoming-night of an animal'. As they stress, 'climate, wind, season, hour are not of another nature than the things, animals, or people that populate them, follow them, sleep and awaken within them'.[10]

In any event, drawn ineluctably to one another, Irena and Oliver marry. Their happiness is obstructed, however, by Irena's conviction that she carries a curse upon her: she believes that if she relents to her sexual passions she will become a cat like the devil-worshipping women of her homeland many centuries before. As a result, Irena and Oliver never consummate their marriage and a divide grows between them. Seeking to expiate what he regards as Irena's superstitious fears, Oliver convinces her to consult a smug psychiatrist, Dr Judd (Tom Conway), who swiftly declares that Irena's fears are merely a product of her mind. Meanwhile, Irena's jealousy erupts as she observes her husband growing closer to Alice, his like-minded, hard-working and assuredly rational colleague at the engineering firm. This jealousy leads to a series of terror scenes in which Irena stalks her love rival, during which the film ambiguously suggests that Irena may indeed have the ability to morph into a panther. When Oliver finally confesses his new-found love for Alice, the heartbroken Irena reacts in a frenzied state, capitulating to the legion of unknown intensities within her. 'There's nothing you can say,' she tells Oliver in delirium. 'There's only silence. But I love that. I love loneliness. And they ... they are in me. Their strength, warmth. They're soft. They're soft.' Frightened by Irena's apparent breakdown, Oliver consents to have her committed to psychiatric care, and this decision sets in motion a tragic finale in which Irena – resisting the carnal attentions of Dr Judd – will succumb to her animal nature, transforming into a panther and killing the psychiatrist, before slinking away into the shadows.[11]

In the film's closing sequence, Irena – perhaps seeking solace – arrives at the public zoo and the panther cage where she had first met Oliver in the film's opening scene. Irena is holding her left shoulder, where she has been wounded by Judd's knife. She opens the cage door and the captive panther, snarling, retreats from her just as many animals have done throughout the film. Her face subtly registers this rejection. She is no less disowned by the animal world, we realize. With an enormous leap, the panther flees the cage, springing upon Irena in the process. The cat's attack is on her right shoulder. We cut to a shot of her on the ground where she lays dying. We can see that the broken blade of Judd's knife is still stuck in her left shoulder. She has thus been jointly dispatched by the animal and the human, renounced as a *chimera* by both. Moments later Alice and Oliver arrive at the zoo to find a sprawled black figure in front of the opened panther cage. Significantly, Tourneur frames their point of view from a distance so that we cannot tell if the black figure is the dead human wrapped in her fur coat or, in fact, the remains of Irena's body in its panther form. She is thus rendered as just a vague dead being: a strange form of life that has come to its end.

'The Open' in *Cat People*

The most telling factor of *Cat People*'s narrative is Irena's rejection by both orders: that of the human and that of the animal. Irena stands as something in-between. Her status is hiatal or intervallic. Insomuch as *Cat People* is a film noir, then, Irena herself can be regarded as actually incarnating the 'dark interval', in this case the indeterminate ontological interval between the human and the animal. She is the dark interval made flesh, which is very often how female protagonists are envisioned in noir. Of course, this latter configuration can be somewhat reductive, reducing feminine experience to the status of 'enigma', as frequently occurs in classic noirs like *The Locket*, *The Lady from Shanghai* and *The Woman in the Window*. But it can be a source of female empowerment, too, as it is for the great many irrepressible femme fatales of the classic era, culminating in a modern noir like *The Last Seduction* (Dir. John Dahl, 1993), where the character's empowerment stems precisely from her ability to command her intervallic status, wilfully reversing the signifiers in play around her.

Significantly, while observing how all of Jacques Tourneur's films dramatize a core 'conflict between the terms A/B', Paul Willemen has shrewdly pointed out that 'it is the "/" which contributes the enigmatic pivot upon which [his] films turn'.[12] Certainly, it is this, the '/', that provides the keener philosophical import of *Cat People*. In the film, the '/' is a figure not simply of a barrier but an interval, a hiatus, in which the ontological properties that might distinguish a concept of the animal (a 'natural' form of life) from the terms that would deliver a concept of the human ('rational' form of life) are suspended. *Cat People* is thus, ironically, the antithesis of a 'creature-feature', those popular Universal films in which an anthropomorphic predator causes terror. Instead, both the film's terror and its elegiac tone stem not from the merging of allegedly distinct categories of life but from its concern with probing the ambiguity of the barrier that separates man and animal in the first place: an intangible division that subsists in the human. Irena, who believes that she is suppressing a beast within, will ultimately die from trying to occupy, without compromise or concession, this impossible hiatus, the '/': that interval which separates man from animal and yet which conjoins them also. As Deleuze and Guattari observe persistently, on the plane of immanence, all that distinguishes beings – or 'singularities' – are the thresholds of intensity or perception to which they can gain access, traverse or 'deterritorialize'.

The film's meditation on a humanity fated to occupy an impossible interval between man and animal can also be usefully approached via the notion of 'the Open': an ontological concept important to the poet Rainer Maria Rilke, to the philosopher Heidegger and, more recently, to Agamben. Notably, Heidegger developed his concept of 'the Open' in direct response to Rilke's *Duino Elegies*, while markedly dissenting from Rilke's original image. It is this dissension, the fundamental difference between these two conceptions of 'the Open' – Rilke's and Heidegger's – which provides the focus for Agamben's fascinating study in *The Open: Man and Animal*.[13] Therein, Agamben reflects upon the Enlightenment project of humanism. The ongoing conceptual division between man and animal, he argues, is an 'anthropological machine', a device for producing the human. By means of suspending the animal and the natural in man, this machine has emboldened the centrality of a world view that validates, for instance, the technological exploitation of our environment for human benefit.[14] (Though Agamben doesn't address it, the latter is actually an example of a human tendency which Heidegger elsewhere calls 'Enframing', a concept which I'll outline further in due course.)

So what are the differences between Rilke's concept of the Open and that of Heidegger?

For Rilke, those who inhabit 'the Open' are the animal, the dead and, for a while at least, the child. It is notable that when one takes into account not just *Cat People* but also its strange sequel, *The Curse of the Cat People* (Dir. Gunther von Fritsch and Robert Wise, 1944), each of these figures (the animal, the ghost and the child) is structurally accounted for and each of them is indeed identified with a rare access to a world of unmediated experience, a 'pure, unguarded space'.[15]

'The Open', for Rilke, is an ontological site of plenitude and primordial immediacy that represents man's existence before the fall into language and history. It has certain parallels with Deleuze's plane of consistency or composition, but differs insomuch as Rilke's concept seems steeped in a transcendentalist metaphysics, while Deleuze's 'open' is one of pure immanence. As far as Heidegger is concerned, Rilke's suggestion that animals have access to a serene undifferentiated world, one unencumbered by the constraints of consciousness, is merely the result of a stubbornly animalist strain of nineteenth-century thought, a strain he observes running through the work of Schopenhauer and Nietzsche, before culminating in Freud. The consequence of this thought, says Heidegger, is 'a monstrous anthropomorphisation of ... the animal and a corresponding animalisation of man'.[16] (It is likely that Heidegger would view Deleuze's own concepts of acceding to 'animal becomings' as informed by a similar principle.)

Heidegger proceeds to reverse the terms of Rilke's 'Open'. Far from being barred from 'the Open', it is the human alone, says Heidegger, who envisions this strange region. It is the human, *Dasein*, who has exclusive access to 'beings in their totality'.[17] In fact, it is this access to 'the Open' which constitutes the very site of *humanity* in the first place, and indeed the site of philosophy. In other words, for Heidegger, the moment of consciousness is the moment of consciousness *of* 'the Open', and not – as in Rilke's prelapsarian contention – the moment when we are forever foreclosed from it. This, of course, is in keeping with Heidegger's fundamental conception of man as one who witnesses the coming-to-presence of beings in a revealing (*aletheia*). The latter is an event that *unconceals* being, even while something of being withdraws and remains concealed. Man is, in effect, the witness of being (or, as Heidegger also puts it, the 'shepherd' of being).[18]

The important distinction Heidegger draws between the animal's relation to 'the Open' and that of the human is that while the human – by virtue of his *ek-sisting* in 'the Open' – has 'a world', the animal, by contrast, has only 'an environment'. And within its environment the animal is subject only to 'captivation'. Captivated, the animal is only 'opened-to' what Heidegger calls its *disinhibitor*, that process or set of processes which stimulate and dictate the animal's behaviour. But the animal remains unaware of this 'opening-to'.[19] Man, on the other hand, as Agamben points out, deciphering Heidegger astutely, is an animal that 'has awakened *from* its own captivation *to* its own captivation'.[20] In other words, man is aware of its own potentiality, its own 'opening-to' the other beings in its environment. As a result, man's environment has the potential to become a world.

Yet the tragic existential dimension of Heidegger's thought also foregrounds that Dasein himself is fated to suffer another kind of captivation, a 'tranquilization' quite different from the captivation of the animal. His glimpsing 'the Open' – the *being* of beings – may allow Dasein to inhabit, create and occupy a world rather than an environment, yet Dasein, tragically, 'falls' into this world, forgetting his 'opening' on to being, and leading to his own alienation.[21] The most dangerous collapse into the world is when Dasein falls prey to the excesses of 'Enframing', an erroneous disposition to existence that Heidegger examines in his essay 'The Question Concerning Technology'.[22] Enframing is a technological disposition (*technē*) to the world, perfectly legitimate of itself, but which, when not controlled, distorts the human's relation to 'the Open' (in other words, to the conditions of its own being). In such an instance, *Dasein* comes to regard all unconcealed beings as 'standing-reserve,' that is to say, as things to be exploited rather than, more benignly, to be used in a cooperation.

> [Man] exalts himself to the posture of lord of the earth. In this way the impression comes to prevail that everything man encounters exists only insofar as it is his construct. This illusion gives rise in turn to one final delusion: It seems as though man everywhere and always encounters only himself ... In truth, however, precisely nowhere does man today any longer encounter himself, i.e., in his essence.[23]

In both of Lewton's *Cat People* films, this is precisely the estrangement from 'himself' that characterizes Oliver, Irena's husband. Whereas Irena is compelled towards an affective state of suspension, one that (heuristically, at least) we might associate with the undifferentiated animal environment of Rilke's 'Open', Oliver – the rational human – has lapsed into the 'everyday' captivation of 'Enframing', whereby 'the Open' is just a submissive domain to be chartered and exploited as man deems fit, to be measured in ways that correspond tautologically to the representative terms that man himself has generated. (As we will see in later chapters, critiques of the alienating effect of technology were an endemic feature of many classic noirs.) Oliver's immersion in such thinking is symbolized by his occupation as a draughtsman, and the latter metaphor is made to resonate strongly for us in one of the seminal sequences in *Cat People* where Oliver, in mortal terror, latches dearly to a symbol of instrumental reason, a T-square, which he converts into a makeshift crucifix to protect himself and Alice from Irena in panther form (Figures 13–16).

Obviously, Oliver's superstitious act conflates the orders of the rational and the religious in order to quell the irruption of something entirely *other* to both, a more inchoate phenomenon borne of the terror of encountering one's own 'essence' (to employ Heidegger's problematic term). Notably, when Irena ceases to threaten them, the world of rational order is restored – albeit,

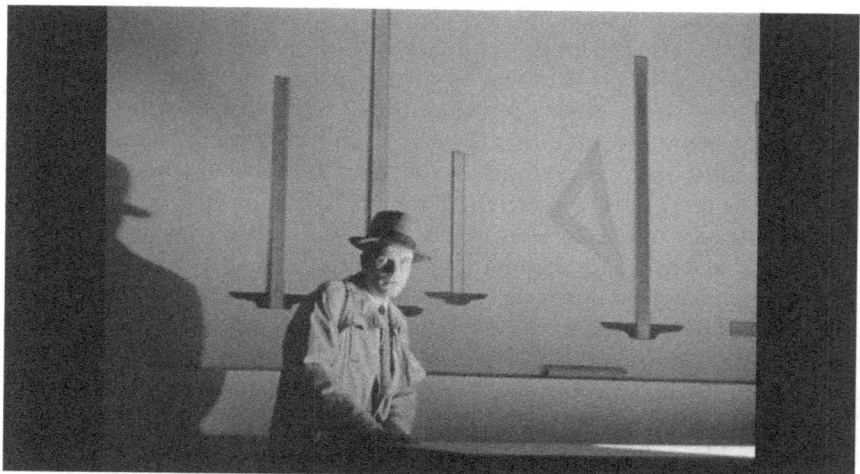

FIGURE 13 *Attack on the space of reason and order in* Cat People.

FIGURE 14 *Oliver uses an instrument of reason (a T-square) for protection.* Cat People.

not without some irony – as is indicated by the camera's framing of Oliver and Alice, now released from the terror of the uncanny, against a numerical backdrop that runs 1–10 (Figure 16).

Significantly, if Oliver, as an agent of 'Enframing', has lost sight of 'the Open' – and, for Heidegger, what is most characteristic of the human is 'the forgottenness of being'[24] – then 'the Open', for all that, is not forever

FIGURE 15 *The instrument of reason takes on religious qualities.* Cat People.

FIGURE 16 *A return to reason and order in* Cat People.

foreclosed from him. 'The Open', for Heidegger, is uniquely accessible during times when man finds himself in a certain mood, a mood the philosopher terms 'profound boredom'.[25] In such a moment as this, man's everyday absorption in the world (his fallenness) evaporates and another captivation comes to the fore. Importantly, it is an experience that comes into 'close proximity' with the animal's own captivation by the stimuli of its environment. In such a state, as Agamben puts it, the human – like the animal that responds only to its stimulus (the disinhibitor) – is 'delivered over to something that obstinately refuses itself'.[26] For Heidegger, this affective state ('being-left-empty') that profound boredom induces in man is then succeeded by a second affective state, 'being-held-in-suspense', where what man glimpses is what Agamben glosses as the condition of being's pure 'potentiality-for-being': the possibility that underscores being itself, the possibility beneath all the 'concrete and specific possibilities' of worldly life.[27] As Agamben explains, this 'being-held-in-suspense', this opening-to or awareness of potentiality is precisely what constitutes the human condition, for Heidegger.

> Profound boredom then appears as the metaphysical operator in which the passage from … animal environment to human world, is realized; at issue here is nothing less than anthropogenesis, the becoming Dasein of living man.[28]

But, as Agamben is keen to underline, this 'becoming Dasein', this awakening of 'the human', 'does not open on to a further, wider, and brighter space, achieved beyond the limits of the animal environment, and unrelated to it'.[29] What distinguishes the human is not the ability to see some realm 'beyond' what the animal sees. All that the human sees is the same 'closedness' to which the animal responds, and by which, ultimately, it is no less bound. This is why Agamben, with considerable subtlety, describes the human as merely an animal 'awakened *from* its own captivation *to* its own captivation'.[30]

This awakening *from* captivation *to* captivation carries a considerable resonance with the state of fascination in noir that I looked at in the first chapter, the fascination that surges up in the 'dark interval'. It is also worth noting that one of the most recurrent and striking conceptualizations of the transfixing force of affective experience – and, in particular, self-affection – arises in affect's power to trigger a state of 'suspension' or 'passion'. As Brian Massumi puts it, this is precisely a Spinozist principle: 'affect as a suspension of action-reaction circuits and linear temporality in a sink of what might be called "passion"'.[31] Obviously, the iconography of *acedic* arrest carries resonances, too, with such suspension, and with Heidegger's experience of 'profound boredom' and 'being left-empty'. Indeed, this sense of awakening from captivation to captivation also resonates with Deleuze's own Spinozist conception of a 'transcendental' experience, howsoever qualified: that intuition of pure immanence; the condition of an immanence that has become immanent to itself, which at its apex may result in an experience of beatitude for the being who endures it.

In *Cat People*, Oliver, the 'good ole Americano', is exposed to just such a fascination in his very attraction to Irena. Intriguingly, in addition to invoking qualities and intensities of affect (her warmth, her scent) the film underlines Oliver's fascination with her by mobilizing a trope now familiar to us – that of the haunting melody. The trope is used in the film in a manner that illustrates perfectly the captivation that occurs in Heidegger's state of profound boredom, in Massumi's affective state of suspension, or – in yet another philosophical cognate for this experience – the state of paradoxically *empty attentiveness* that Maurice Blanchot describes as central to the experience of 'waiting'.

> Attention is the emptiness of thought oriented by a gentle force and maintained in an accord with the empty intimacy of time.
>
> Attention is impersonal. It is not the self that is attentive in attention; rather, with an extreme delicacy and through insensible, constant contacts, attention has always already detached me from myself, freeing me for the attention that I for an instant become.[32]

The 'haunting melody' sequence occurs early in the film, at the outset of Oliver and Irena's romance, and it is notable, too, for participating in the pathos formulae of 'zero affect' that we find recurring across noir iconography (Figure 17).

Oliver lies idly on a sofa in Irena's apartment. With his back to camera his gaze is fixed intently upon Irena who stands by the window while humming a lilting melody – a French lullaby that will become her leitmotif. The centrality of the window should not be overlooked. It is continuous with iconographic renderings of a radical 'outside' that we examined earlier – in particular in the paintings of Edward Hopper – and continuous, too, with the prevalence of window sequences in film noir. Windows in noir

FIGURE 17 *Irena and Oliver in the dark interval.* Cat People.

are, as Dana Polan puts it, 'invested with ambivalent possibilities'.[33] They can articulate everything from anxious contemplation (*Double Indemnity*) and desire (*Gilda* (Dir. Charles Vidor, 1946)) to fatalistic impermanence (*Criss Cross* (Dir. Robert Siodmak, 1949)) and dangerous observations (*The Window* (Dir. Ted Tetzlaff, 1949), *Shock* (Dir. Alfred Werker, 1946)). In this key window scene in *Cat People*, night is falling outside and, with little interior lighting, the room is almost completely dark. Yet these two serenely idle figures seem untroubled by the darkness, contented by one another's company in a strange interval that has arrested or transformed temporal experience. A sudden roaring of animals nearby threatens their aimless joy, however. A surprised Oliver asks, 'What's that?' Irena, well-used to the sound, explains that it is the lions in the zoo. She admits an affection for their roaring: 'To me it's like the sound of the sea is to others. Soothing and natural.' (The lions prompt her to think of the panther, however, and how it 'screams like a woman'. 'I don't like that,' she tells Oliver, revealing a hint of the psychosexual trouble that lies down the line for them, the film here forfeiting the scene's iconographic charge and subsiding into the rather clunky metaphysical and psychological allegories that drive the narrative.)

The important thing for our purposes here is that we observe Oliver's reduction to a strange, almost blissful passivity and idleness during the scene, as he is transfixed by Irena's humming. Irena, too, is evocatively passive, and her humming can be regarded as a vesperal gesture, an affective adjustment to the arrival of night, a 'becoming-night'. Moreover, in its own way, her humming indicates the 'autonomy of affect', as Massumi describes it. The scene, then, finds Oliver opening on to the 'dark interval', here articulated in the suspension of the ontological distinction between animal and human existence, a suspension that carries a vaguely redemptive quality. It is the intervallic figure of Irena herself that embodies that very possibility of redemption, yet by the end of the film Oliver will have turned his back on her. With considerable subtlety, in a scene late in the film, the cost of this rejection – Oliver's dismissal of the potentiality that can be glimpsed in intervallic states – is staged as a poignantly ironic echo of the earlier scene. Now it is Oliver, Alice and Dr Judd who wait at night in Irena's apartment, with the objective of ambushing Irena and committing her to a psychiatric institution. As they wait for her, Judd lies in a louche posture on the couch, smoking his cigarette, while a distracted Alice fumbles with some music records. On the film's soundtrack, Irena's leitmotif has been accompanying the scene and both Judd and Alice seem in languid thrall to it. In short, they appear in a state of 'captivation'. By contrast, Oliver – now no longer the 'profoundly bored' figure of the earlier scene – paces the room in anxiety and frustration. He walks to the record player and, abruptly lifting up the needle, intradiegetically halts the film's score. 'Let's not play that,' he says. This is the same song that earlier in the film had so captivated him. As such, his rejection of Irena – a rejection of the '/', the condition of suspension – is now complete.

Intriguingly, in a wonderful intertextual move, in *The Curse of the Cat People* Oliver will once again be exposed to 'the Open' by the same haunting melody. In the latter film Oliver is still the nice but rigidly empirical rationalist. His distress in this film stems from his daughter's propensity for daydreaming and her conjuring of an imaginary friend. In a telling scene, Oliver's attention wanders during a card game with his friends, and it does so at precisely the moment when upstairs in the house (the ghost of) Irena has begun singing to his daughter Amy (Ann Carter). She sings her signature tune from the earlier *Cat People* and it results in a strange scenario where, aroused by his uncanny attunement to the song, Oliver drifts into a strange trance. Alice (now his wife) shakes him back to the present, and Oliver apologizes, saying, 'Sorry. I was somewhere else.' 'The Open', then, remains a ground that the human, though fallen into the world, can regain access to. And, even if, ultimately, it is an access only to the stubborn 'closedness' of being itself, for Heidegger this access can foster an approach to life that he calls 'authentic' existence.[34]

'The Open' is an elegiac figure of both loss and hope, then. Yet, in *Cat People*, the experience of the 'dark interval', the wandering off into 'the Open', is configured as predominantly tragic – a source of terror even – given the fascination or bewitchment it can cast upon the human. It is notable that during the penultimate sequence where Dr Judd ambushes Irena in her apartment, leading to his own death, he is again playing her song on the record player. This fascination with the mystery of 'the Open' – configured in his obsession with Irena and his falling spellbound to her haunting melody – ultimately proves Judd's undoing. Oliver, by contrast, survives because, like most of the people in the film, he pointedly extricates himself from 'the Open'. Meanwhile, because the sensitive Irena tries to occupy it, this twilight or vesperal world, it leads promptly to her demise.

And yet, nevertheless, the film projects positivity and hope on to this paradoxical figure of the '/', the interval, the condition of ontological suspension. And it does so by suggesting that the human's intervallic status can be retrieved and safeguarded by the intervention of art. This, too, corresponds with Heidegger's own understanding of art, as outlined in his essays 'The Question Concerning Technology' and 'The Origin of the Work of Art'. For Heidegger, art – like technology – is a strategy of revealing, a process that the ancient Greeks termed *poiēsis*, a 'bringing-forth'. Indeed, technology (*technē*), too, is a kind of *poiēsis*. When it is corrupted, however, technology forgets its role of revealing, collapses into its own order of representation and treats the world as a set of objects standing in reserve for man's exploitation. Art, however, strives to retain the dignity of the fundamental human project of revealing – even if this revealing only 'unconceals' being as something that remains stubbornly concealed. In *Cat*

People the artist, Irena, is the agent of this project of *poiēsis*, one who is open to the disclosure of being, in which the human, Dasein, discovers its potentiality and its freedom. For Heidegger, the 'freedom' that results from exposure to 'the Open' is like a veil that 'shimmers' while nevertheless retaining the power of the veil to appear as 'what veils'.[35] For all her troubles, Irena, as an artist, is at ease with this shimmering and veiled nature of being – its simultaneous unconcealment as that which remains stubbornly concealed. She recognizes in it the 'placeless place' opened up by melancholy, a home to phantasms but also a cradle of creativity as well as sorrow. Those around her are not at ease in 'the Open', however. They find in it only a source of irrational terror or a 'secret' to be exposed. Thus, Oliver and Alice dismiss (i.e. forget) being in favour of their more narcissistic 'Enframing' of the world. Meanwhile, though he acknowledges the greater affective depths of human experience, Dr Judd does so only in order to decipher and explain these affects as symptoms: as a 'canker' of the mind. His psychoanalysis is thus merely another mode of Enframing. By contrast, art, for Irena, is a vesperal mediation of the human's intervallic exposure to its own residual affective intensities. Her sketches are part of that mediation, as are the copious ornaments, paintings and various artistic artefacts that she surrounds herself with in her apartment.

Of course, the 'bringing-forth', or revealing, that *Cat People* – as itself a work of art – specifically centres on is the ontological hiatus in which the human exists by suspending its animal nature. Within the narrative, art becomes a means of negotiating this suspension, which is made clear in one of the most moving scenes in American cinema, in which Irena – having lost balance and succumbed to the animal within – returns to her apartment and sits crying in her bathtub. In the sequence prior to this shot, Irena has stalked Alice and, sublimating her desires to kill her, has destroyed a lamb in a city farm. As she cleanses herself of this act, the shot of Irena in the bath commences with the framing of a metal 'leg' fixture at the foot of the tub. The fixture is moulded in the shape of a predatory bird's talon clutched tightly to a sphere. The camera then tilts upward, framing the white ceramic tub. It halts again once Irena comes into view. Irena, her back to camera, is crying. Her human skin is uncannily accentuated by the drops of water that sit on her shoulders while her disavowed animal nature is alluded to by the ornamental talon at the foot of the bath. Here, then, we find distilled, in perhaps the most brilliant and economic composition in a visually dense film, the force of the narrative's wonderful tension between the human and the animal, and its meditation, too, upon the one thing that is capable of mediating and 'containing' this tension: the work of art. It is through such objects as this ornamented bathtub, such works of art, that the human negotiates the terms of its intervallic nature. In short, the sequence captures something of the 'eternal duration of the interval', 'the meanwhile, never finished, still enduring – something inhuman and monstrous', that

Emmanuel Levinas insists is precisely the quality that humanity invests in the work of art.³⁶

The dense use of art-objects in the mise en scène in *Cat People* everywhere attests to this mediation that art performs in human life, its mediation of the force of the interval and the potentiality it exposes. It is perhaps worth noting here, in passing, the frequency with which artworks centrally inform the plots of noir films of the classic era. *Phantom Lady* (Dir. Robert Siodmak, 1944), *Scarlet Street*, *The Dark Corner* (Dir. Henry Hathaway, 1946) and *Crack-Up* (Dir. Irving Reis, 1946) are just a few of the prominent noirs that centre on artists and artworks.

The saved night

To complete my study of *Cat People*, I must begin by pointing out a subtle distinction that Agamben draws in relation to the experience of profound boredom: that experience which I have identified as an iteration of the 'dark interval'. For Heidegger profound boredom has the capacity – much like Nietzsche's 'eternal return', it should be stressed – to awaken the human to its own possibility. And, for Agamben, profound boredom discloses such potentiality, too. But he dissents from Heidegger in an important way. Where Heidegger regards the suspension borne of profound boredom as being the site of the human, Agamben suggests that, while disclosing potentiality, this suspension brings animal and human, the being of animal and human, into 'indistinction'. As Paolo Bartoloni parses it,

> The difference between Heidegger and Agamben is that for the latter these moments of suspension are precisely the moments when humans and animals become suspended in indistinction, and when animality and humanity are momentarily reconciled. These are the moments at which the anthropological machine (*la macchina antropologica*) comes to a halt.³⁷

In terms of how the dark interval recurs as a trope in noir, the significance of Agamben's conception of this halting of the anthropological machine is important. And I will examine a range of elements that are resonant with this 'halting' – this recession of the human into a zone of indistinction – in films such as *Alphaville*, *The Long Goodbye* and *The Missing Person* in the chapters that follow. Before then, with specific regard to *Cat People*, we might ask: if such a zone of indistinction is ushered into view by the dark interval, what benefit can this intervallic experience offer to the human? Agamben is quite clear. It is not simply the awakening to potentiality in the interval that is important. It is the realization that what distinguishes man is his ability to suspend potentiality itself – to do or not to do, or, to put it another way, to conceive of being and also to conceive of *not* being. It is the realization, then, that a fundamental 'impotentiality' is the originary intuition that always subtends the human's sense of potentiality. As Agamben delineates it,

> Aristotle offers the most explicit consideration of the originary figure of potentiality, which we may ... define with his own words as the *potential-not-to-be*. What is potential is capable (*endekhetai*), Aristotle says, both of being and of not being ... The potential welcomes non-Being, and this welcoming of non-Being *is* potentiality, fundamental passivity. It is passive potentiality, but not a passive potentiality that undergoes something other than itself, rather, it undergoes and suffers its own non-Being.³⁸

We are returned here, I would suggest, to that quality of passive arrest borne of *acedia*, that experience of self-affection which Agamben examines in *Stanzas*, and which I earlier employed to reflect upon the persistent iconography of the dark interval in film noir. In fact, as Agamben's analysis of the figure of (im)potentiality in Aristotle proceeds, his analysis takes on terms that carry a distinctive significance for that unique drama of humanity fallen into crisis that seems ever to be at stake in noir films.

> The greatness – and also the abyss – of human potentiality is that it is first of all potential not to act, potential for darkness ... What is at issue here is nothing abstract. What, for example, is boredom, if not the experience of the potentiality-not-to-act? This is why it is such a terrible experience, which borders on both good and evil.
>
> To be capable of good and evil is not simply to be capable of doing this or that good or bad action (every particular good or bad action is, in this sense, banal). Radical evil is not this or that bad deed but the potentiality for darkness. And yet this potentiality is also the potentiality for light.³⁹

This 'abyss of potentiality', then, is something the human is irrevocably exposed to, and in film noir, via the trope of the dark interval, we repeatedly witness the staging of this exposure. (Recall the image of Walter Neff absently chewing his cigarette in temptation in *Double Indemnity* or his modern counterpart Ed Crane in *The Man Who Wasn't There*.) Agamben's imagery here – 'potentiality for darkness', 'potentiality for light' – should not be mistaken as inviting a simplistic moralism. Certainly, it does solicit the ethical, provided ethics is understood, accurately, as the adoption of a 'manner', a way of being, in direct response to a sense of one's own potentiality. Ethics, like metaphysics, is a category of thought that cannot but emerge from the human's originary exposure to its own potentiality. What Agamben is alerting us to, via this difficult concept of potentiality, is the very vitality that exists in the experience of exposure itself and in the suspension that such exposure can induce in our relation to the ideologies and structures that would subsume us, all the discursive 'Enframings', we might say, in Heidegger's terms. At an aesthetic level, whether through expressionist lighting and mise en scène, iconography, performance or other means, one of film noir's great innovations is precisely this tendency to stage a vision of a passivity and suspension that is wrought of the human's exposure to the dark interval: that is, the human's exposure to its own impotentiality and to the potentiality the latter shelters. What noir rescues, however dimly, from this recurrent trope of the dark interval is a conception of redemption that is far removed from traditional religious conceptions of salvation. It's a more earthy idea of redemption that Agamben meditates upon at the end of *The Open* via a turn to the thought of Walter Benjamin and the figure of 'the saved night'. Via the latter image, Benjamin invokes a Gnostic distinction between nature and history, and considers the relevance of this distinction to the fate of the human. Nature (which also accounts for man's ideas and for art) is a 'world of closedness', quite distinct from history (the 'sphere of revelation'). The latter – the historical – seeks a classical redemption, an accounting for all things. The natural, however, would seek a contrary salvation, one grounded in the human's capacity for resting within itself, by way of 'the saved night'.

> The 'saved night' is the name of this nature that has been given back to itself, whose character, according to another of Benjamin's fragments, is transience and whose rhythm is beatitude. The salvation that is at issue here does not concern something that has been lost and must be found again, something that has been forgotten and must be remembered; it concerns, rather, the lost and the forgotten as such – that is, something unsavable. The saved night is a relationship with something unsavable.[40]

We might describe such a relationship as 'vesperal', a gestural communication with the night that does not attempt to diminish the inchoate mysteries of time or becoming nor to resolve the crisis of 'the human' but rather to savour them.

Obviously, we should be attentive to Agamben's use of the term 'beatitude' here. 'Beatitude', though used sparingly, and wearing its debt to Spinoza on its sleeve, is a term that recurs in the work of both Agamben and Deleuze, and which comes to refer to a sort of benediction of life as a field or plane of pure potential. While Ian Buchanan has pointed to the dangers of conflating Deleuze's philosophical project with that of Agamben's, particularly in relation to their respective and very distinct concepts of 'a life' and 'bare life',[41] I tend to agree with William Watkin, who – while also incisively identifying the differences between both thinkers – notes 'the incredible consonance' between many of their principal ideas.[42] In his work in *The Open*, Agamben suggests a condition of beatitude emerges when the distinction between man and animal is suspended, and 'in the reciprocal suspension of the two terms, something for which we perhaps have no name and which is neither animal nor man settles in between nature and humanity and holds itself in the mastered relation, in the saved night'.[43] Deleuze would likely suggest terms like 'affect' or 'becoming' as placeholders for this 'something for which we perhaps have no name'. In any event, the saved night becomes yet another synonym for the dark interval, the hiatus, 'the Open': that zone of indistinction which – in exposing potentiality – proffers a redemption founded on opening oneself to a certain alluring and radical passivity with which *a life* (impersonal, purely immanent life) can but respond to time's passing.

Such radical passivity, to revisit Thomas Carl Wall's term, is very vividly demonstrated in *Cat People*. Despite its tragic narrative and pessimistic depiction of human relations, two of its most enchanting elements are nevertheless its subtle meditation on friendship and its depiction of the human when lost to a strange passivity. We have already noted the latter in that scene where Oliver and Irena are transported by their own inertia and the fascination it evokes in them. In that scene we find some of the 'atmosphere of both exhausted sensuality and subdued melancholy' that Agamben, in providing a visual model of 'the saved night', discovers in Titian's painting *Nymph and Shepherd* (1575).[44]

For Agamben, the latter image of sensual, melancholic lovers, who lie in repose against a landscape that is very much a slowly perishing idyll, dramatizes the strange, elegiac redemption available to the human in 'the saved night'.

> In their fulfilment the lovers learn something of each other that they should not have known – they have lost their mystery – and yet have not become any less impenetrable. But in this mutual disenchantment from their secret, they enter, just as in Benjamin's aphorism, a new and more blessed life, one that is neither animal nor human. It is not nature that is reached in their fulfilment, but rather ... a higher stage beyond both nature and knowledge, beyond concealment and disconcealment. These lovers have initiated each other into their own lack of mystery as their most intimate secret ... their condition is *otium*, it is workless {*senz'opera*} ... In their fulfilment, the lovers who have lost their mystery contemplate a human nature rendered perfectly inoperative – the inactivity {*inoperosità*} and *desœuvrement* of the human and of the animal as the supreme and unsavable figure of life.[45]

While I find Agamben's description of this 'new and more blessed life, that is neither animal nor human' perfectly applicable to the scene in *Cat People*, we should acknowledge that one major distinction between the two scenes resides in Agamben's suggestion that the nymph and the shepherd are exposed to one another's lack of mystery in part *as a result of* their sexual intimacy. In *Cat People*, by contrast, as the narrative makes clear, such intimacy between Irena and Oliver has been rendered impossible. Nevertheless, I feel the resonances between these two images are strong and suggestive, and the film's iconography, moreover, can be regarded as independent of its narrative and exceeding its scope. Indeed, at the level of iconography we can even observe a direct continuity between Tourneur's film and Titian's painting. In the latter, the nymph lies languidly upon a leopard skin, a long-standing visual convention by which cats are associated with female sexuality, one we can also find in Dürer's famous *Adam and Eve* (1504).

Agamben stresses that what emerges as redemptive in Titian's scene are an essential 'inoperativity' (*desœuvrement*) and also a sense of the 'great ignorance' that the lovers abide in and seem unperturbed by.[46] These two elements together bestow upon the human pair a peculiar 'blessedness'. Titian's painting also carries connotations of friendship, I would suggest. This would be a conception of friendship as a mutual exposure to the vulnerability of existence itself, a conception of friendship (affinity) as something fundamentally intervallic. This is precisely the terms in which Blanchot conceives friendship. For Blanchot, a 'friend' can only be greeted in a mutual relation with 'the unknown', in a mutual 'estrangement'.[47] The friend, for Blanchot, is one who 'reserve[s], even on the most familiar terms, an infinite distance, the fundamental separation on the basis of which what separates becomes relation'.[48] Such a friendship is founded in the 'pure interval that, from me to this other who is a friend, measures all that is between us, the interruption of being that ... far from preventing all communication, brings us together in the difference and sometimes the silence of speech'.[49] There is an elegiac quality here that should not be missed. Where Deleuze may stress connection and relation, singularities also experience disconnection and distinction, howsoever it may be a function of a representational (or molar) understanding. Friendship is a hinge that conjoins the separate.

If we consider the theme of 'the friend' that runs through both *Cat People* and its strange sequel *The Curse of the Cat People*, we realize that friendship is the symbol that the film employs to denote the kind of intervallic relationship that Blanchot has in mind here. Friendship in *Cat People* effectively attests to the redemption of the human in 'the saved night', as Agamben sees it. This is the very night that Irena finds 'friendly', of course. This friendship that Oliver and Irena initially share is one whereby their 'great ignorance' – their frailty as humans, their lack of mystery – is laid bare. Moreover, it is one that renders them idle, inert, passive and 'inoperative'. With the latter in mind we should reflect on the degree to which the figure of work is so overdetermined in the film. (Oliver and Alice are constantly working and tend to sublimate their gathering strife in work.) Once we do, we realize how significant this brief allusion to inoperativity, inscribed affectively in the liminal space of Irena's apartment, really is. It is a depiction of romantic connection, of course, but also of a friendship in the dark interval of 'the saved night', and an expression of the beatitude that comes of opening oneself to one's own affectivity and to the affectivity of the other. The tragedy in *Cat People* is that this saved or vesperal night is ultimately made derelict, no longer a home to humans who – under the weight of a far too positivistic materialism (Oliver, Alice and Judd) or else burdened by a deviated, superstitious mythology (Irena) – cannot abide in it. The 'saved night', the strange affective potentials resident in the vesperal, thus give way to an 'endless night': that same 'endless night' that is alluded to in the film's final frame, a title card featuring a slightly altered couplet from one of John Donne's Holy Sonnets: 'But black sin hath betray'd to endless night / My world, both parts, and both parts must die.'

Within the narrative of *Cat People* the potentiality that flares up in the interval is squandered. But the film itself, as a work of art, nevertheless, captures and relays the irreducible force of the dark interval, and thus – like *The Man Who Wasn't There* – succeeds in delivering a redeeming sense of potentiality to its viewers.[50]

Notes

1 See Andrew Spicer, *Historical Dictionary of Film Noir*, ed. Andrew Spicer (Lanham, MD: Scarecrow Press, 2010), 402. James Naremore uses *Cat People* as a conceptual bookend, a boundary-text that helps to delineate the outer reaches of classic film noir. (His other mooted bookend is *Invasion of the Body Snatchers*.) See Naremore, *More Than Night*, 9.

2 See E. Ann Kaplan, 'The "Dark Continent" of Film Noir: Race, Displacement and Metaphor in Tourneur's *Cat People* (1942) and Welles's *The Lady from Shanghai* (1948)', in *Women in Film Noir* (London: BFI, 1998), 183–201. On *Cat People* as a genre hybrid, meanwhile, see Eric Somer, 'The Noir-Horror of *Cat People* (1942)', in *Film Noir Reader 4*, ed. Alain Silver and James Ursini (New York: Limelight, 2004), 191–206 and Paul Meehan, *Horror Noir: Where Cinema's Dark Sisters Meet* (Jefferson, NC: McFarland, 2011), 43–72.

3 J. P. Telotte, *Dreams of Darkness: Fantasy and the Films of Val Lewton* (Urbana: University of Illinois, 1985), 39.

4 Ibid., 186.

5 Ibid.

6 Ibid., 5.

7 'vesper, n.' *OED Online*. Oxford University Press. Web. 26 May 2014.

8 Famously, though Lewton took co-writing credits on only two of his films at RKO (*The Body Snatcher* and *Bedlam*), the producer had a hand in the writing of all the projects under his guidance, and on every project it was he who edited the final shooting script. (It's worth noting that *Cat People* shares some affinities with a short story, 'The Bagheeta', written by Lewton earlier in his career.) See Edmund Bansak, *Fearing the Dark: The Val Lewton Career* (McFarland, 1995), 19–20.
9 Wheeler Winston Dixon, *Black and White Cinema: A Short History* (New Brunswick, NJ: Rutgers, 2015), 101–11.
10 Deleuze and Guattari, *A Thousand Plateaus*, 263.
11 Much to the chagrin of Lewton and Tourneur, RKO's front office demanded that the footage of a real panther be inserted. See Telotte, *Dreams of Darkness*, 21.
12 Paul Willemen, 'Notes towards the Construction of Readings of Tourneur', in *Jacques Tourneur*, ed. Claire Johnson and Paul Willemen (Edinburgh: Edinburgh Film Festival, 1975), 23.
13 Giorgio Agamben, *The Open: Man and Animal*, trans. Kevin Attell (Stanford, CA: Stanford University Press, 2004).
14 Ibid., 33–8.
15 Rainer Maria Rilke, *The Duino Elegies and the Sonnets to Orpheus*, trans. A. Poulin Jr. (New York: First Mariner, 2005), 55.
16 Agamben, *The Open*, 58.
17 Ibid., 62–7. *Dasein* is Heidegger's term for human being.
18 See Martin Heidegger, 'Letter on Humanism', in *Basic Writings*, trans. David Farrell Krell (London: Routledge, 1993), 234–45.
19 See Agamben, *The Open*, 49–56.
20 Ibid., 70.
21 On the 'tranquilization' of fallen Dasein, see Martin Heidegger, *Being and Time*, trans. John Macquarrie and Edward Robinson (London: Blackwell, 1962), 178.
22 Martin Heidegger, *The Question Concerning Technology and Other Essays*, trans. William Lovitt (New York: Harper and Row, 1977), 3–49.
23 Ibid., 27.
24 Martin Heidegger, *Contributions to Philosophy*, trans. Parvis Emad and Kenneth Maly (Bloomington: Indiana University Press, 1999), 79–82.
25 Agamben, *The Open*, 63–70.
26 Ibid., 65.
27 Ibid., 66–7.
28 Ibid., 68.
29 Ibid.
30 Ibid., 70.

31 Massumi, *Parables*, 28.
32 Blanchot, *The Infinite Conversation*, 121.
33 Polan, *Power and Paranoia*, 275.
34 Agamben, *The Open*, 67.
35 Heidegger, 'The Question Concerning Technology', 25.
36 Emmanuel Levinas, 'Reality and Its Shadow', in *The Levinas Reader*, ed. Seán Hand (Cambridge: Blackwell, 1989), 141. Importantly, for Levinas, the 'empty interval' that art is capable of configuring produces an ethical relation to reality rather than one of 'evasion' or disengagement.
37 Paolo Bartoloni, 'The Open and the Suspension of Being', *CLCWeb: Comparative Literature and Culture*, 7.3 (2005), 4.
38 Agamben, *Potentialities*, 182.
39 Ibid., 181.
40 Agamben, *The Open*, 82.
41 See Ian Buchanan, 'Deleuze's "Life" Sentences', *Polygraph*, 18 (2006), 129–47.
42 William Watkin, *Agamben and Indifference* (London: Rowman and Littlefield, 2014), 137–78.
43 Agamben, *The Open*, 83.
44 Ibid., 85.
45 Ibid., 87.
46 This concept of 'inoperativity' owes obvious debts to Jean-Luc Nancy. See *The Inoperative Community*, trans. Peter Connor, Lisa Garbus, Michael Holland and Simona Sawhney (Minneapolis: University of Minnesota, 1991), 1–42. Agamben employs variations on the concept of the 'inoperative' in a number of texts.
47 Blanchot, *Friendship*, 291.
48 Ibid.
49 Ibid.
50 In a Deleuzian reading of the film Anna Powell notes something similar: The closing imagery of the film, she says, 'leave[s] us with a sense of indetermination. This uncertainty exceeds narrative closure and continues to alternate, working its potential through our mind/body.' Anna Powell, *Deleuze and Horror Film* (Edinburgh: Edinburgh University Press, 2005), 71.

4

Saving Those Who Weep: The Interval of Affective Rupture in *Alphaville*

Cat People rehearses a strange myth of 'the fall', reimagined as a Heideggerian existential tragedy of the human's captivation by its own representation, the world the human has itself constructed, only to lose sight of that constructedness. In the vast diversity of films that loosely constitute the classic cycle of film noir it is remarkable how many touch on this notion of the fall. The epitome of these noirs of 'the fall' is *Force of Evil* (Dir. Abraham Polonsky, 1948) which traces the fall of corrupted humanity in vertical terms. Joe Morse (John Garfield) begins the film as a high-flying lawyer for a crooked racketeer, and he has the executive office in a skyscraper to prove it. But by the end – in a tragic but also transformative and hopeful passage – he will have to climb down to the very bottom of the city, beneath its foundations, to its amorphous riverbanks, to retrieve the body of his dead brother.

Very often, this counterfeit, fallen world is signified simply as the city itself. Making precisely this point about the oppressive spatial confinement of the city in noir, Nicholas Christopher has cited the German historian Oswald Spengler on the fate of twentieth-century man who 'is seized and possessed by his own creation, the City, and is made into its creation, its executive organ, and finally its victim'.[1] Given the prominence of this theme in noir it is hardly surprising that, in one of his many engagements with film noir in the 1960s, Jean-Luc Godard, too, employed noir to examine this idea of the human's lapse into an alienating world of its own design.[2]

In *Alphaville: A Strange Adventure of Lemmy Caution* (1965) Godard stages a thematic confrontation between reason and sentiment, science and romance. The film's dystopic city-state of Alphaville is a 'world' where the

'Enframing' tendencies of *technē* have run amok, absorbing the human within a reductive reverence for logic and a dispassionate materiality. Art emerges here once more as a redemptive principle, however, just as it did in *Cat People*. In *Alphaville*, lyrical art forms such as poetry and photography provide a means of evoking and soliciting the dark interval, in order to retrieve the potentiality resident in the human's affective capacities.

Godard's film centres on a hard-boiled secret agent, Lemmy Caution (Eddie Constantine), who is dispatched to the cosmic outpost of Alphaville on a vague mission to capture or kill a rogue scientist. In his costume, his terse patois and his gruff attitude, Caution is a knowing appropriation of the noir detective.[3] Yet Godard's keen understanding of noir is such that the power Caution is invested with in *Alphaville* is not a brute physical force or a deductive cunning but rather *poiēsis* itself, the power of 'bringing-forth', the force of light. Professor Von Braun – the film's representative of technocracy – tells Caution that Alphaville is becoming a 'civilisation of light', and it is true that everywhere in the serpentine, nocturnal city of Alphaville electric light abounds. But the noir detective is identified with a more incipient, if also more evanescent, light still: the flame of potentiality. The latter is rendered metaphorically in the vivid flicker of the detective's cigarette lighter in our very first glimpse of him. Thus, Godard specifically brings two forms of light into discursive conflict in *Alphaville*, the light of instrumental reason versus the more mercurial fire which Caution safeguards, the power of *poiēsis*, epitomized in the film by the Surrealist poetry of Paul Eluard. Such poetry illuminates – however dimly – the uncertainties and ambivalences of night. Moreover, and to continue a theme from the last chapter, it illuminates this night while 'saving' it, savouring its uncertainties and affective potentials.[4] Caution's objective is to summon the memory of this saving power in the inhabitants of Alphaville. In a world lit up by blinding electricity, they have, in Kaja Silverman's words, 'forgotten the sacred origins of light',[5] and thus Caution will become for them a modern-day Prometheus, the modern-day herald of fire, *poiēsis* and potentiality.

It is important to note, too, that in *Alphaville* this saving light is specifically equated with affect (and with the intervallic temporality it solicits). Above all else, it is the affective register of their own existence from which the residents of Alphaville have been divorced. Caution's mission is to reacquaint them with it. Although his official objective is to locate and arrest Von Braun, the elusive architect of Alphaville, he is more inchoately charged with a second task and a greater responsibility still: 'to save those who weep'. The latter instruction is the dying sentiment of his fellow detective, Henry Dickson, a hard-boiled aesthete overwhelmed by the oppressive rationality of Alphaville and its omniscient mainframe computer, Alpha 60. In a bathetic parody of romantic agony, Dickson dies during a sterile sexual tryst with one of Alpha 60's robotized human 'seductresses'. But upon his death he passes a book of poetry to Caution and reveals to his detective comrade the task that constitutes his true mission: to redeem the affective potential of human beings.

> Henry: Lemmy ... conscience ... conscience ... make Alpha 60 destroy itself. Tenderness ... Tenderness ... Save those who weep.

Dickson's reference to 'weeping' should not be mistaken as determining human affectivity as purely a melancholic condition. Certainly, the film is charged with the elegiac sensibility which so predominates in noir, but weeping here stands not just for the capacity to experience sadness and loss but functions metonymically: that is, to weep *is* the capacity to feel, to undergo emotion, to be affected. The denizens of Alphaville are robotized humans, 'slave of probabilities' as Lemmy describes them, who have been divested of such affective capacities. Those who resist the programming of Alpha 60 – artists, aesthetes and lovers – are executed. 'Their crime', as Harun Farocki has noted, 'is behaving illogically, or – in a word – affect'.[6]

It becomes Caution's mission, then, to alert the inhabitants of Alphaville to their affective potential. Against the automation of Alpha 60's programming he will raise the autonomous force of affect. He will do so, intriguingly, by beckoning the power of the 'dark interval', exposing this enigmatic force to both the film's inverted femme fatale, Natacha (Anna Karina), and to his arch-nemesis, the despotic Alpha 60. (The dark interval's power is, of course, that it is an affective interval, an *affecting* interval.) *Alphaville* thus treats the now familiar noir motif of the dark interval as akin to a cinematic 'myth',[7] one in which self-affection – whether configured as a Heideggerian 'coming-to-presence' or as a Deleuzian lapse across thresholds of becoming – is a vital component. Yet, it's important to point out, too, that the film also critiques any attempt to inhabit the 'zero horizon' of the dark interval, to linger in, or to reify, any heightened 'presence' such a moment might disclose. Lemmy at one point dismisses Alphaville as a 'Zeroville' precisely because, under the thumb of Alpha 60, the city has come dogmatically to reify the present, converting time into a barren series of discrete, successive, regimental *nows*. 'The present is the form of all life,' Alpha 60 tells Lemmy. The detective, however, equates the human not just with affect and the powers of *poiēsis* but with the ecstatic, distended and discordant qualities of temporality itself. Affect, potentiality and temporality are thus inextricably linked in the film. (Lemmy's motto becomes 'We must advance to live', a line from Eluard's poetry.) As such, *Alphaville* is an exemplary site upon which to examine the motif of the 'dark interval' in film noir, as the film examines not just the shimmering quasi-redemptive quality (beatitude) of this intervallic experience but also warns against the recklessness inherent in any attempt to disjoin the force of intervallic experience from the necessity of temporal progression or becoming. (As we will see in the following chapter on *2046*, Wong Kar-Wai specifically invokes both film noir and *Alphaville* itself in a narrative that depicts the melancholic predicament of just such a lingering in the interval.)

Noir as a myth of the dark interval

Alphaville opens with imagery of the architecturally dense skyscape of Alphaville at night, before – abruptly – introducing us to the film's protagonist, Lemmy Caution, as he lights his cigarette in his Ford Galaxy. Instructively, though Caution will eventually assume the film's voice-over duties, at the outset it is the banally oppressive supercomputer Alpha 60 that commences the voice-over narration. This move points to an easily missed dimension of the film. Alpha 60 is not just Caution's nemesis. He is his alter ego: the technocratic tendency of the human. Hence, the two antagonists, in effect, *share* voice-over duties. The film's opening words – voiced by Alpha 60 – are amusingly self-reflexive, referring directly to the film's mobilization of noir aesthetics: 'Sometimes, reality becomes too complex for oral communication. But legend embodies it in a form which enables it to spread all over the world.' At this, the camera tilts downward to frame an evocative American car slowing to a halt in the city night. (The images relayed to us are no doubt the work of Alpha 60's surveillance cameras.) We then cut to the interior darkness of the car where – with the flash of his cigarette lighter – Caution (legend and archetype) almost supernaturally comes into view.[8]

Here, appropriately, it is Alpha 60, the *structuring*, computational component of the human, that recognizes the representational value of 'form', in this case the form of noir itself and the 'legendary' figure of the noir detective. Thus, it is with a playful irony that Godard uses the oppressive computer to validate the director's own mobilization of the cinematic aesthetic of noir. Yet, while Godard may appropriate the noir aesthetic as a 'form', the voice-over also alerts us that this form has been chosen because it uniquely manages to convey the sense of an elementary *formlessness*, a zone of indistinction, subtending our complex reality, a formlessness which resists 'oral communication'. Noir is thus identified as a contradictory 'form' which endeavours to capture aspects of human life that are beyond structure, codification and verbal articulation: aspects that Godard's film will ultimately characterize as 'affective'. As such, noir is conceived as a lyrical form that addresses itself primarily to feeling rather than to reason. As *Alphaville* progresses, it is the human's capacity for gesture – allied to the lyrical word that in itself approximates the force of gesture – that is valorized as the human's proper medium of communication. Gesture is the medium that might save those who weep. And noir is thus summoned as a cinema of gestures – of specific pathos formulae or 'surviving images' and the powers they nurture. Lemmy's lighting of his cigarette at the moment of his introduction is the first of these gestures.

Metaphors of light and exposure

As *Alphaville*'s narrative emerges, Natacha Von Braun becomes the crux of Lemmy's redemptive project, the point upon which it will succeed or fail. The daughter of Alphaville's fascistic scientific engineer, Professor Von Braun, Natacha has been hardwired with the extreme rationality of Alpha 60. (Among other things, her past has been bleached from her memory and she no longer knows that she was born in the 'Outlands' beyond Alphaville.) Like the other inhabitants of Alphaville, she has also been steadily cleansed of any knowledge of her affective agency as an embodied form-of-life, chiefly by the erosion from her memory of all words associated with affect. However, sensing the vitality in Natacha, Lemmy will bring about what Andrew Utterson has called her 'emotional salvation'[9] by exposing her to the power of affectivity itself. This affectivity is transmitted by lyric poetry, on the one hand, and is incarnated in Lemmy's own amorous attraction to her, on the other.

Nor is it any accident that Caution 'senses' Natacha's potential. Caution is not just a 'secret' agent. He is the agent of all that is secret, an agent of passion and of affect. As such, one of Caution's most significant powers is to recognize the potentiality proper to the human being as a quality arising in its affective capabilities. Mirroring Alpha 60's own surveillance cameras, which coldly observe everything in the dystopic city-state, Caution, too, employs a camera in his registering of the world. But what the noir detective's own instrument of light exposes is the affective potential within the human. We divine this early on when – having brusquely slapped Beatrice, the automatized seductress who persistently trails him around his hotel room – Lemmy promptly takes a photograph of her (the first of many photographs he will take of Alphaville's inhabitants). Simultaneously, in his voice-over, he remarks, 'I was struck by the sadness and durability of her face.' Though the scene carries an unsettling undertone of misogyny, within the narrative Lemmy's action is consistent with his mission to reawaken the senses of the robotized humans he encounters, and thereafter – with his camera – to document any fluctuating stirrings of emotion.

This ability to 'capture' affect via his camera is, moreover, internal to Caution himself, being merely an extension of the perceptive 'power' of the human eye to register affect, a power that Caution instinctively exerts, and which Natacha, despite her programming, clearly retains, however confusingly. The detective's camera is but a prosthetic, a technical amplifier for the eye's power to scan affect. As such, it points to the positive, redemptive possibilities inherent in *technē* (which Martin Heidegger is always at pains to observe). Registering affect is a risky business, however. Artists and aesthetes have been executed in Alphaville precisely because of this activity – that is, because of the renegade way in which they dare to 'see' things. The resonances that Godard draws between Alpha 60 and Lemmy Caution, the rational and the aesthetic applications of *technē*, are once again underlined here. If the excessive, circuit-board rationality of Alpha 60 is 'inhuman', the artistic seeing of Lemmy Caution, too, is itself a kind of inhumanity, insomuch as it dares to hover in the intervallic space where the concept of the human comes into crisis. In this respect, Godard retains a wonderful ambivalence in relation to Lemmy and his camera, an ambivalence that, inevitably, must also be seen as self-reflexive comment on his own status as a filmmaker and artist.[10] Lemmy's inhumanity comes into view in the scene in which his fellow detective Henry Dickson dies. As Dickson, desperate for human intimacy, fumbles forlornly with a seductress on his bed, a voyeuristic Caution – stationed out of view – trains his camera on what is unfolding. When Dickson's failed sexual encounter leads to his death, the stoic Caution remains remarkably detached and dispassionate, and when Dickson manages at last to utter his gnomic dying words ('Save those who weep') to Caution, the camera strangely lingers upon the dying man. During this lingering, the viewer can only assume that Caution – who has indeed departed the frame in a generic movement suggesting urgency – is already rushing back out into the city to pursue his battle with Alpha 60. However, at the very moment that Dickson expires, the flash of a light – the flash of Lemmy's camera – suddenly illuminates the frame.

The implication here is somewhat disturbing. It suggests that, out of frame, Caution has been observing Dickson's death at a remove all along, just as the viewer and Godard have been, of course. In doing so, Caution's chief concern is apparently to capture the very second of the man's passing – thereby maintaining his role as a 'documenter' of affect. The effect of this information would perhaps be less unnerving had Godard chosen to intersperse shots of Lemmy as he looks on. But no such shots are offered to us. In the end, we realize that where he might have chosen to comfort Dickson in his final moments, Caution – as an artist-detective – seems strangely inured to the human capacity for empathy, and this despite his being an 'agent' of affect in the film. Instead, he seems motivated only to photograph the moment of death itself, and the affective transition that occurs in such a moment.

Caution, then, as an artist-detective, is an ambivalent figure: as inhuman in his own way as the 'mutants' of Alphaville. His 'inhumanity' resides in his curiosity and his fascination with the intervallic thresholds of human experience. Indeed, far from some rhetorical tirade against technology, Godard's film depicts *both* technology and art as each hosting the ability to approach the apex of what it means to be human, and yet also to broach the enigma of the human's strange intervallic status, its essential 'inhumanity': its irrevocable encapsulation within circuits of affect that exceed human representations of self-identity and systems of knowledge. In this respect, the film can be said to demonstrate Jean-François Lyotard's reflections on the two quite distinct forms of inhumanity that essentially mark human life. The first he associates with rational 'development' and with structures of order that often come to govern and oppress us, the other with a more inchoate experience that Lyotard identifies, in part, with our acquisition of humanity during a 'pre-human' phase of infancy when mystery and secrecy reign. 'It is indispensable to keep [the two forms] dissociated,' says Lyotard. 'The inhumanity of the system which is currently being consolidated under the name of development (among others) must not be confused with the infinitely secret one of which the soul is hostage.'[11]

This other, secreted inhumanity, borne of the human's intervallic condition – its liminal status as something located between man and animal, between life and death, chaos and order, infancy and history, affect and reason – emerges from the same principles (*poiēsis*, *technē*) as the inhumanity of the machine-consciousness of Alpha 60. Both the computer and the camera-wielding Caution are invested in acts of 'Enframing', then, as Heidegger describes it. But 'Enframing' is, of itself, not necessarily negative or simply machinic. '[Enframing] is nothing technological, nothing on the order of a machine. It is the way in which the real reveals itself as standing-reserve,' insists Heidegger.[12] The problem is that the Enframing of modern, industrial-scale technology *challenges* 'the real', *challenges* 'nature', rather than simply revealing it. And, as such, it threatens to deny to man 'a more original revealing and hence to experience the call of a more primal truth'.[13] This is why Heidegger regards 'Enframing' as fundamentally dangerous. Nevertheless, he closes his essay on technology on a hopeful note. Quoting Hölderlin ('But where danger is, grows / The saving power also'), he reflects on the meaning of 'saving':

> 'To save' is to fetch something home into its essence, in order to bring the essence for the first time into its genuine appearing. If the essence of technology, Enframing, is the extreme danger, and if there is truth in Hölderlin's words, then the rule of Enframing cannot exhaust itself solely in blocking all lighting-up of every revealing, all appearing of truth. Rather, precisely the essence of technology must harbour in itself the growth of the saving power.[14]

In this way, though Godard astutely renders it with ambivalence, Lemmy Caution's own employment of *technē*, and the inevitable 'Enframing' it serves, are ablaze with Heidegger's 'saving power'. Technology as such is not the enemy in Alphaville, then. Technocracy is. As such, Caution – like the filmmaker Godard – will employ not just poetry but also technology (i.e. his camera) to expose the human's essential suffusion within the matrices of affect, which far exceeds the fixity foisted upon it by the insidious regimes of data management and ordering: structures that would traffic under the name 'development', as Lyotard calls it. A contemporary noir that similarly explores the destructive qualities of these latter structures – in a way quite continuous with *Alphaville* – is Richard Linklater's *A Scanner Darkly*, which similarly features an undercover detective at odds with a control society that reduces the singularity of a human life to a mere field of data, a 'dividual', as Gilles Deleuze terms it.[15]

At the close of *Alphaville*, as Alpha 60 malfunctions, having been forced by Lemmy to experience affective agency and the temporal ecstasies of human consciousness, Godard employs intermittent shots printed in reverse-negative to indicate the computer's new-found perception of the amorphous affective flux in which the human – and all of life – is suffused. As Chris Darke has noted, these sudden, apparently random snatches of photo-negative have 'flummoxed more than a few commentators'.[16] Robin Wood, in an early and influential analysis, dismissed them as misguided, 'facile' attempts at a Brechtian distanciation.[17] As Darke points out, however, the device is actually a 'quotation' from two films that heavily influence *Alphaville* thematically and visually: *Nosferatu* (Dir. F. W. Murneau, 1922) and *Orphée* (Dir. Jean Cocteau, 1949). As in those films, I would suggest, the device of the reverse-negative indicates a transition in perception: the transition between one mode of seeing and another, which is the very transition that Alpha 60 undergoes. In keeping with the central metaphor of the photographic that Godard has employed throughout, the shots in reverse-negative are glimpses of Alpha 60's own surveillance cameras which earlier, in the opening images of the film, had coldly scanned the city. Now, having been dramatically recalibrated by Caution's interaction with the computer, these surveillance cameras suddenly register the more protean force of life itself, as opposed to the defined structures that it had earlier recognized, and had too excessively 'enframed'. In effect, what the device of the photo-negative indicates is that Alpha 60 has been compromised by its exposure to affect. Following on from references to Einstein's theory of relativity earlier in the film, and resonating with the film's broader themes about light and optics, Godard's use of reverse-negative printing here essentially imagines the affective realm as interchangeable with what the quantum physicist David Bohm controversially called 'the implicate order' of the universe. (As Timothy S. Murphy has noted, the correspondences between Bohm's 'implicate order' and Deleuze's conception of an affective flux of restless becoming are provocative.)[18]

Natacha's exposure to affect

If *poiēsis*, the bringing-to-light incarnated in the noir icon of Caution, is the subject of *Alphaville*, it is not simply art or technology that registers this force, this potential. The human organism is more constituently still the site of its registration. As Marshall McLuhan has observed, the human is a far more primary medium than art or technology.[19] Beyond the symbol of the camera as a tool for registering the elementary force of light, the master-symbol within the film is the idea of the human as a 'pure medium', a pure registrar of affect. As is commonly observed in commentaries on the film, lyric poetry and romantic love are the obvious allusions to this centrality of human experience. However, what has largely gone unnoticed, in this regard, is the role Godard assigns to gesture in relaying this experience.

When Caution 'saves' Natacha – that is to say, alerts her to the register of affect – he does so by exposing her to a volume of Paul Eluard's poetry, *The Capital of Pain*. One of the poems he prompts Natacha to read is 'La mort dans la conversation' (Death in Conversation). Natacha reads, 'Your eyes have returned from a despotic land / Where no-one has known the meaning of a glance.' Obviously, Alphaville itself is this despotic land. As the reference to 'a glance' in the couplet makes clear, however, what this land has made alien in its inhabitants is not simply affect but their means of negotiating it, that is, the gestural capacities of the human. In addition to censoring all words pertaining to affect from the minds of its denizens, Alpha 60 has also corrupted human gesture – gesture being the most immediate index of the human's immersion in affect.[20] The chief image of this corruption of gesture in the film is that of Natacha's paradoxical shaking of her head whenever she says 'Yes'. Transculturally, the gesture of the headshake is generally understood to indicate rejection, yet here in Alphaville it misfires, becoming bonded to its contrary meaning. Gesture is not simply dysfunctional in Alphaville, however. It is entirely *suspect*. One of the public executions that Caution witnesses is that of a man who, illogically (and thus, criminally), has shed tears upon his wife's death. This gesture of weeping – as was already established in Dickson's instruction to 'save those who weep' – is perhaps the major motif within the film. By the end, this gesture of weeping will be redeemed as not exclusively an experience of the human but as a potentiality of the machine also. 'Those who are not born do not weep and do not regret,' Alpha 60 too over-confidently tells Caution in their final showdown, but Caution ultimately triumphs by forcing the computer to experience regret, the poignant confusion wrought in any creature that suffers temporality. In the end, Alpha 60, with his 'central memory' banks, and a language so embroiled in tenses, cannot but succumb to consciousness, duration and regret.

Yet, for as long as Alpha 60 is in the ascendant, weeping – as perhaps the human gesture par excellence – is strictly outlawed. When Natacha weeps at the sight of Caution's beaten body as he is hauled away by Professor Von Braun's 'heavies', a bystander brusquely asks her, 'Are you crying?' With impeccable logic, Natacha replies, 'No, because it is forbidden.' And yet at the same time, undermining her words, her face conveys distress as a tear rolls down her cheek. Words here, contrary to Alpha 60's earlier dictum, *have* lost their meaning, then. For Natacha, merely reciting the logical reason not to cry – that is, that it is forbidden – means paradoxically that she is not crying, even while her eyes shed tears. In this way, Godard suggests that any ethical potential in language is made defunct once it is disconnected from the more primary gestures that it complements, from the body it is rooted in and from the affective experience it negotiates.

Intriguingly, Giorgio Agamben has in fact characterized modernity as 'an age that that lost its gestures' and, because of this loss, has become unconsciously 'obsessed by them'.[21] In Agamben's view, cinema speaks above all else to this essential loss of gesture and to the obsession with gesture that it has fostered. 'In the cinema, a society that has lost its gestures tries at once to reclaim what it has lost and to record its loss,' he says. 'Cinema leads images back to the homeland of gesture.'[22] We might complement Agamben's observation here by adding that such transmissions of gesture – or the very possibility of transmissibility of affective states and temporal experience – are precisely what Aby Warburg's own conceptions of surviving images and pathos formulae serve to address.

What characterizes gesture, for Agamben, is that 'in it nothing is being produced or acted, but rather something is being endured and supported'.[23] The originary force of gesture is not as a 'means' towards an objective or an end but resides more ambiguously in the way in which it finds the human exhibiting its own ontological status as a 'means'. '*The gesture is the exhibition of a mediality: it is the process of making a means visible as such.* It allows the emergence of the being-in-a-medium of human beings and thus it opens the ethical dimension for them.'[24] As we saw in the previous chapter on *Cat People*, this ethical dimension, for Agamben, resides in an essential exposure of the human, a laying bare of its frailty, before the intractable mystery of its own condition. Importantly, Agamben argues that not alone does such an articulation of 'exposure' open up the proper sphere for an ethics; it opens up the proper sphere of the political also. (We will examine this in my final chapter, in relation to *The Big Lebowski*.) The gesture's redemptive capacity resides ultimately not in some specific communication but rather in the way it is a 'communication of a communicability', a zero degree of communication. It would call on the human to recognize and reassert its powers as a mediating being, which would involve, concomitantly, a reflection upon the limitations of language itself.

> [The gesture] has precisely nothing to say because what it shows is the being-in-language of human beings as pure mediality. However, because being-in-language is not something that could be said in sentences, the gesture is essentially always a gesture of not being able to figure something out in language; it is always a gag in the proper meaning of the term ... From this point derives not only the proximity between gesture and

philosophy, but also the one between philosophy and cinema. Cinema's essential 'silence' (which has nothing to do with the presence or absence of a sound track) is, just like the silence of philosophy, exposure of the being-in-language of human beings: pure gesturality.[25]

Gesture, then, for Agamben, is 'always the gesture of being at a loss in language'.[26] In many respects, this is true even of the corrupted gestures in *Alphaville*, which, in their contrary relation to the verbal information they accompany, carry a subversive power, a suggestion of the insufficiency of this verbal information. Nevertheless, the reconciliation of verbal and gestural communication is also very much at stake in the film, as is indicated during Dickson's exchange with Caution. Asked if Dick Tracy is dead, Dickson gives a headshake, the contrary sign of affirmation in Alphaville. Caution then asks if Flash Gordon (Guy Léclair) is dead too. This time – just as he is about to give the same wayward headshake – Dickson physically resists the false gesture, forcefully pushing his head with his fist, to gesture with the more conventional nod of the head to indicate 'Yes'. Hereby, word and gesture are brought briefly into accord once more. Notably, his struggle to control his own gestures even appears to cause Dickson pain.

Reasserting the originary force of human gesture will thus become key to Caution's task but also key to Godard's project in the film itself. Indeed, at an extra-diegetic level, the persona of Lemmy Caution, the film's noir antihero, is itself nothing other than an articulation of the pure power of gesture. Epitomizing the strange (im)passivity inscribed in the body of a certain noir protagonist, it is the gestural force of this figure's intervallic status – its particular *pathosformel*, in Aby Warburg's terms – that Godard clearly mobilizes in *Alphaville*. Indeed, for Godard, Constantine's virtues as an actor were clearly bound up with the sense of dense embodiment that the actor emitted, much as Mitchum and Lancaster had done in the classic cycle of American noir. As Darke notes, the director repeatedly referred to Constantine as a 'block', a term he also used in relation to Jean-Paul Belmondo's performance in his earlier noir, 1960s *À Bout de souffle* (*Breathless*).[27] His earlier casting of Constantine in the short film *La Paresse* (*Sloth*), too, reveals a kind of Eisensteinian 'typage' at work in Godard's perception of the actor.[28] In the latter, Constantine plays a spellbindingly jaded celebrity who has grown tired of everything. Notably, his extraordinary passivity is rendered throughout the film via a range of pronounced gestures: the most banal and superlative of which occurs when Constantine raises his hand coolly to a petrol pump attendant to indicate how much gas he requires, saving him from having to expend even the meagre energy required for verbal interaction. Of course, such laconic or 'cool' gestures are symptomatic of the 'purely gestural vocabulary' that came to be fetishized in the noir films of the 1940s and 1950s, as Roland Barthes has observed.[29] Indeed, there is in Constantine's screen persona the very lassitude that

Barthes salutes in another essay, 'Dare to Be Lazy'. Therein Barthes notes how in such a transformative laziness, one is potentially 'dispossessed' even of the consistency of one's subjectivity. 'That would be true idleness,' notes Barthes. 'To be able, at certain moments, to no longer have to say "I".'[30]

If this idleness, this gestural dispossession of subjectivity, is inscribed in the very noir persona of Constantine, it is one that, within the narrative of *Alphaville*, is also eventually commuted from Lemmy Caution to the character of Natacha Von Braun in the scene of the latter's ecstatic awakening. As mentioned earlier, this epiphanic quality resident in the dark interval is triggered in Natacha by the combination of lyric poetry and Lemmy's love for her. (Indeed, the 'subject in love', in Barthes's view, is precisely the one who most desires access to a state of 'true idleness', this disavowal of subjectivity.)[31] For our purposes, what is most important to note here is that Natacha's flash of insight is rendered in a sudden cascade of gestures, the latter accompanied by passages of Eluard's poetry delivered in voice-over by Natacha herself. 'Light that goes,' her monologue begins. 'Light that returns. A single smile between us both.' Here, we may note how, in a lyrical gambit, an equivalence is drawn between gesture ('a single smile') and light, each conceived as an autonomous transmission of affect. As Natacha's elliptical quotation of Eluard's poetry continues, a startling montage relates her suffusion in a volley of elegant gestures, ranging from demure glances off-screen to a self-conscious exchange of caresses with Lemmy. In fact, the entire sequence is articulated via a host of Deleuzian affection-images. But what the montage principally attests to is the force of gesture: the latter laying bare, in Agamben's words, 'the sphere of a pure and endless mediality' to which the human is bound.[32] Significantly, in keeping with the iconography of the dark interval, Natacha's awakening is depicted as an expansive moment outside of time, a strange, atemporal and seismic event in which chronological time seems insufficient to the affective experience she endures. Adrian Martin describes this atemporal sequence as 'a magical "fold"', 'perfectly "out of time" with the narrative', during which Natacha enters 'a whole new, hitherto unimagined state of being'.[33] Of course, this notion of a moment in which time folds in on itself is precisely one of the strategies by which the modern noir tends to configure the dark interval, as exemplified in Boorman's *Point Blank*.

For Darke, the importance of the strange atemporal sequence in *Alphaville* is that it seems to suggest, 'Natacha and Lemmy have together created love's time, which can exist, vulnerable but autonomous, according to its own law beyond Alphaville's time'.[34]

This notion of 'love's time', beyond the law of Alphaville, is intriguing, given the sequence's final image in which Natacha and Lemmy, now only vague silhouettes, stand at the window in the unlit environs of the hotel room. Facing out upon the bright skyscape of Alphaville, they are seemingly immune to its oppressive electrical omniscience, while alive to the affective pulsation of the light it produces. It is worth pointing out that the whole sequence of 'Natacha's awakening' opens and closes with an image of a gaze through the window: the first that of Natacha on her own, the closing image that of Natacha and Lemmy together. The sequence is thus continuous with a certain noir iconography of the dark interval that we have examined earlier, and certainly shares resonances with the scene of 'the saved night' from *Cat People* in which Irena and Oliver lounge idly in their own unlit dwelling in a radical state of temporal and ontological suspension. In *Alphaville*, too, the image of the lovers by a window connotes the same 'atmosphere of both exhausted sensuality and subdued melancholy' that Agamben observes in Titian's painting of the nymph and shepherd.[35] Like those classical lovers, and like all lovers, in fact, Natacha and Lemmy – who Godard explicitly codifies as modern-day inflections of Eurydice and Orpheus – initiate each other into 'their own lack of mystery as their most intimate secret'.[36] And it is through such a 'pure gesture', which alone can mediate the affective power of the dark interval, that this initiation takes place. As Agamben puts it elsewhere, in his work on gesture, a scene such as this one stages 'a wholly profane mystery in which human beings, liberating themselves from all sacredness, communicate to each other their lack of secrets as their most proper gesture'.[37] This gesture, moreover, is one 'that felicitously establishes itself in [the] emptiness of language and, without filling it, makes it into humankind's most proper dwelling'.[38]

Here, gesture – working as a complement to Deleuze's affection-image, and emerging in romantic love – is heralded not just as redemptive but as a genuine ethos, the mode of being most proper to the human. It is the incipient force of gesture, then, by which – in addition to the human's 'profane mystery' – the human's status as a 'pure means', its affective mediality, is foregrounded. And it is gesture, then, that Lemmy Caution ultimately salvages from Alphaville.

The interval: A question of time

While it illuminates the ontological thresholds that are productive of the human, there remains in *Alphaville* a seeming paradox in its treatment of temporality. The film reflects on the atemporal or extra-temporal force of affect, gesture, and lyrical modes of expression. Yet at the same time, it also puts Lemmy Caution (as well as lyric poetry), both of which can be seen to epitomize these qualities, in the service of a linear temporality whereby the human is one who must, by necessity, 'advance' to live. This is a problem. Pure gesture, as Agamben would have it, is akin to the power he finds in Warburg's *pathosformel* and in medieval images of *acedic* arrest. Its power resides in a certain atemporal force that *the image* can potentially usher into view. Indeed, as Asbjørn Grønstad and Henrik Gustafsson note, Agamben's long engagement with images has invariably centred on asserting the force of the visual 'to interrupt the continuum of homogenous historical time in order to recover an original space in the present'.[39] How do we reconcile this with *Alphaville*'s concern with the necessity of temporal progression, and specifically its invocation of noir to imply that necessity? The paradox is perhaps beyond resolution, and yet, at the same time, there is no paradox. Godard employs gesture – as well as editing principles of repetition and stoppage that express the mediality of the subject – to make explicit the very contradictions of human temporality (and experience). The 'moment' of the interval is one that cannot be reified as an eternal present. Godard insists instead that temporality is in essence lyrical: that is to say, all at once intervallic, durational and ecstatic. Human beings must progress in time, accede to the necessary passing of time, without either capitulating to the excessive mechanistic rationale of a chronological 'clock-time' or attempting to inhabit a reified present, a fanciful 't zero' in Calvino's terms. The philosophical model of temporality that Godard at least partially salutes in this regard is that of Henri Bergson's *durée*. (In the film Caution even quotes Bergson. When asked about his religious beliefs by Alpha 60, the detective replies with a play on Bergson: 'I believe in the immediate data of conscience.')[40] Indeed, as Alan Woolfolk has observed, in *Alphaville* 'Godard seems to operate from the Bergsonian premise that it is our reduction of the single, indivisible quality of time, the *durée*, to a series of discrete units in space that disrupts our genuine experience of time and memory.'[41] Woolfolk quotes Bergson: 'Pure duration is the form which the succession of our conscious states assumes when our ego lets itself live, when it refrains from separating its present state from its former states.'[42] The latter image of duration captures its temporal-ontological aspect effectively. For our purposes, we will complement it only with the observation that Bergson's intuition of the *durée* emerges first from what he describes as the 'cerebral interval', the gap between perception and response, in which the human is exposed to emotion, that which mercurially presents itself in the interval. As Gregg Lambert has observed, Deleuze's affection-images are explicitly bound up in this same Bergsonian notion of the gap or interval, and the emotion that appears within it.[43] It is emotion – and, in broader terms still, affect – that 'allows the human being to become open to a duration that remains "outside" its own plane, to transform the limited and 'closed' present of habit or instinctive reaction into the openness of creative intuition'.[44] This, then, is the temporality that Lemmy Caution protects in *Alphaville*: the redemptive affective temporality – at once human and yet also inhuman – to which he exposes both Natacha and Alpha 60, shaking them from their own temporal and affective enclosures. Ultimately, the *durée* dissolves the distinction between linear, narrative time and the time of atemporal rupture, collapsing together the categories of past, present and future, and locating instead a temporality and an intuitive consciousness of ecstatic fluidity, ecstatic duration. As *Alphaville* illustrates, this recognition of human time as duration is dependent on an interval of rupture for its emergence – presented in the film as the interval of Natacha's awakening. And the latter is articulated, too, as an instance of Nietzschean 'eternal return'.

As I pointed out in the introductory chapter, Nietzsche's doctrine of the Eternal Return of the Same can be considered an inflection of the 'dark interval' as I have termed it, and perhaps even the grand model for the various articulations of the interval that emerge in twentieth-century continental thought. Certainly, Deleuze conceives of the interval and the moment of eternal return as largely interchangeable. For Deleuze, as for Pierre Klossowski,[45] what returns in the moment when one undergoes eternal return is not 'the Same' (construed as the regressive, stubborn presence – the site – of being) but rather *difference-from-itself*, where difference is understood as the tumult and flow of affective encounters, impersonal becomings, in which each one of us is always irredeemably suffused.[46] In short, the 'same' of the eternal return is that it is always the *same return to difference*, triggering a dispersal of all certainties, values and identities, and a sudden awakening to one's immersion in the affective flux of durational becoming as the only intuitive certainty. In relation to Deleuze, Claire Colebrook captures this conception of eternal return well:

> This is how Deleuze refers to the idea of 'eternal return' ... Time is eternal only in its power to always produce the new, over and over again – with no origin and no end. The only constant in time, the only 'Same', is the power of not remaining the same. Affect is the expression of this impersonal becoming, precisely because affect is an event that is not grounded in any agent or subject. It is not the becoming *of* some being but a becoming that is nothing more than its own distinct difference and flow.[47]

For Nietzsche, this experience of eternal return, when it ruptures forth, is something that has to be affirmed, and like Spinoza – as well as Maurice Blanchot, Deleuze and Agamben – he describes it as being conducive to a state of joy, a state that is inherently *beatific*. Indeed, Clement Rosset has suggested that the condition of beatitude is 'the central and constant theme of Nietzsche's thought – I would willingly say the *only* theme'.[48] Natacha's transformation in *Alphaville* indicates precisely such an awakening to an 'impersonal becoming' steeped in affect (which, in a manner of speaking, might also be called a passageway into the intuitive temporality of Bergson's *durée*). Natacha's awakening is, then, a moment of eternal return. Here, it is worth noting that, in their analysis of *Alphaville*, Harun Farocki and Kaja Silverman appear to miss this element of the film, with Farocki instead identifying the model of 'now' temporality instigated by the computer Alpha 60 as being an articulation of the eternal return:

[The computer] is always associated with the present tense. In Alphaville, it is altogether forbidden to dwell in the past, and every effort is made to plan for and predict the future in ways which subordinate it to the present. Temporality is banished in the name of the eternal return of the same.[49]

This is a common misappropriation of Nietzsche's concept, which understands *the same* as a reference to some irreducible, stable temporal 'presence', a banal, always self-evacuating progression of 'nows'. But if we follow Klossowski and Deleuze, as we should, we grasp the more accurate and pressing meaning of the eternal return of the same: the irruptive shock wave of difference, of becoming, of affective flux. Like the quality of 'background hum' associated with affect, it is precisely the reverberation of this affective flux to which Natacha is exposed in her experience of eternal return. This affective hum is moreover the very 'echo that runs through the day' that she reads about in Eluard's *The Capital of Pain*, and which she intuitively recognizes as the truth of her own existence. Indeed, the echo manages to double as an image of her affective exposure and as an image of her agency as a creature endowed with consciousness (*conscience*), marking the two (affect and consciousness) as interdependent. The Eluard lines she reads aloud run as follows:

> We live in the void of metamorphoses.
> But the echo that runs through the day ...
> ...that echo beyond time, anguish or caress ...
> Are we near to our conscience, or far from it?

The echo is thus the echo not just of affect but also of *conscience* (consciousness). We might consider it as the echo of 'conscience' in Heideggerian terms, too: as something subsisting beneath the world of inauthentic human existence and its misguided Enframings, something that has the capacity to 'call' to us.[50] It is the *enframed* world which props up the 'void of metamorphoses', a world of timid historicized transitions that actually mask our more original constituency in affective flux and becoming. As such, Silverman is clearly mistaken in her interpretation of the echo as 'the voice of Alpha 60, which has seized possession of the psyches of the inhabitants of Alphaville, and rendered "consciousness" unconscious'.[51] The insidious auto-suggestive programming of Alpha 60 may perhaps constitute something of a degenerate, technological analogue of the echo of affect, but it is certainly *not* the echo of affect, the echo of *conscience* to which Eluard's poem refers. The 'echo' signifies that which subtends the apparent 'void' of our metamorphoses through time: that is, the sole constant of flux and becoming which underlies the transience of thingly existence. The echo is the processual affective hiss of an eternally recurring potential – not a reified 'presence' but the present as difference and flux. What Caution rescues from eternal return, then, is a sense of open-ended possibility (potentiality) resident in it. This is a divination of an electric present, the interval of authentic 'presencing' as Heidegger might put it, that is always liberating. By contrast, Alpha 60 views the present solely as *use*-related, functional; the present as self-evident, banal, merely something to be enumerated and calculated as the site of an instrumental reason. Lemmy helps to awaken the automatized Natacha to the autonomous echo of affect humming beneath everything, and awakens her, too, to the potential for affirmation incipient in the 'dark interval' of the eternal return. That the eternal return is dramatized as a retrieval of gesture should not be overlooked either. As Agamben has noted, 'the eternal return is intelligible only as a gesture (and hence solely as theatre) in which potentiality and actuality, authenticity and mannerism, contingency and necessity have become indistinguishable'.[52] I would suggest that here, in Agamben's conception of eternal return as gesture, we have a suggestive resonance with the 'time-image' that Deleuze discovers operative in modern cinema. What is the 'powerlessness' of 'the seer' before 'the image of thought' in Deleuze's terms, if not a description of a certain iconography, a certain *pathosformel*, a certain gestural intimation of the eternal return?

In the next chapter, I will examine a kind of misappropriation of the gesture of eternal return, a misfiring – or perhaps, in its own way, simply another *possibility* – of the dark interval, as it occurs in Wong Kar-Wai's elegiac noir rhapsody, *2046*.

Notes

1 Christopher, *Somewhere in the Night*, 16.

2 *Alphaville* anticipates the later rise of 'future noir' or 'tech-noir'. Such films (and literature) foreground futuristic noir-inflected dystopias characterized by an all-pervading dehumanizing technology: for example, *Blade Runner*, *Brazil* (Dir. Terry Gilliam, 1985), e*XistenZ* (Dir. David Cronenberg, 1999), *Dark City* (Dir. Alex Proyas, 1998) and *Inception* (Dir. Christopher Nolan, 2010).

3 In fact, the film was a rekindling of a popular French series of B-movies about the detective Lemmy Caution in which Eddie Constantine had starred. For more, see Chris Darke, *Alphaville* (London: I.B. Tauris, 2005), 19. Notably, Godard reanimated Caution for another outing in *Germany Year 90 Nine Zero* (1991).

4 During his interrogation by the supercomputer Alpha 60, Caution is asked, 'Do you know what illuminates the night?' He replies, 'Poetry'.

5 Kaja Silverman and Harun Farocki, 'Words Like Love', *Speaking about Godard* (New York: New York University Press, 1998), 60.

6 Ibid., 72.

7   The film's opening emphasizes that it mobilizes noir (and specifically the figure of the noir detective) because the latter is a 'legend' or 'form', one that communicates non-verbally the essential disenchantment of a modernity in which the dehumanization by technology, and an excess of reason, is the norm. Noir, then, is a myth that responds to this disenchantment.

8   With regard to Lemmy's emergence in a flash of fire, we should note that it further underlines his correspondence with Alpha 60. The film's very first image has been that of an electric lamp – the metonymic symbol of Alpha 60 throughout the film – flashing on and off in an otherwise black frame. Our introduction to Caution, too, identifies him with a flickering of light. Alpha 60 and Lemmy Caution are, then, merely different inflections of the same principle – illumination in the midst of darkness. As the film progresses, we realize that whereas Alpha 60's 'Enframing' has skewered the human gift of *poiēsis*, bringing forth only a monstrous and oppressive technocracy, the melancholy but hopeful detective is still in touch with a more fundamental power of bringing-forth.

9   Andrew Utterson, 'Tarzan vs. IBM: Humans and Computers in Jean-Luc Godard's *Alphaville*', *Film Criticism*, 33.1 (2008), 47.

10 As Utterson puts it, Godard is 'necessarily implicated in technics by virtue of his profession'. Ibid., 61.

11 Jean-François Lyotard, *The Inhuman: Reflections on Time*, trans. Geoffrey Bennington and Rachel Bowlby (Cambridge: Polity Press, 1991), 2. Lyotard also describes the necessary politico-cultural antinomy between these two conceptions of our inhumanity. 'What else remains as "politics" except resistance to this inhuman? And what else is left to resist with but the debt which each soul has contracted with the miserable and admirable indetermination from which it was born and does not cease to be born? – which is to say, the other inhuman?' 7.

12 Heidegger, *The Question Concerning Technology*, 23.

13 Ibid., 28.

14 Ibid.

15 Gilles Deleuze, 'Postscript on the Societies of Control', *October* 59 (1992), 3–7.

16 Darke, *Alphaville*, 58.

17 Ibid., 58.

18 Timothy S. Murphy, 'Quantum Ontology: A Virtual Mechanics of Becoming', in *Deleuze and Guattari: New Mappings in Politics, Philosophy, and Culture*, ed. Eleanor Kaufman and Kevin Jon Heller (Minneapolis: University of Minnesota Press, 1998), 211–29. See also Murphy's essay on the resonances between Bohm's quantum mechanics and Henri Bergson's own engagement with Einstein's theory of relativity. 'Beneath Relativity: Bergson and Bohm on Absolute Time', in *The New Bergson*, ed. John Mullarkey (Manchester: Manchester University Press, 1999), 66–81.

19 Indeed, art and technology evolved as merely extensions of the human body, whether as artistic transmutation (dress, painting, piercing) or technical prosthesis (hand tools, weapons). The latter, for Marshall McLuhan, are classified as 'extensions' of human bodily appendages: 'The arrow is an extension of the hand and the arm, the rifle is an extension of the eye and teeth.' Marshall McLuhan, *Understanding Media: The Extensions of Man* (Cambridge, MA: MIT Press, 1994), 341.

20 This primacy of gesture is, of course, precisely what Warburg's study of the *pathosformel* – which we looked at in the first chapter – addresses.

21 Giorgio Agamben, 'Notes on Gesture', in *Means without End*, trans. Vincenzo Binetti and Cesare Casarino (Minneapolis: University of Minnesota Press), 53.

22 Ibid., 56.

23 Ibid., 57.

24 Ibid., 58. Emphasis in original.

25 Ibid., 59–60.

26 Giorgio Agamben, 'Kommerell, or on Gesture', in, *Potentialities*, 78.

27 Darke, *Alphaville*, 20.

28 *La Paresse* was Godard's contribution to *Les Sept Péchés Capitaux* (1961), an anthology film also featuring shorts by Jacques Demy and Roger Vadim.

29 Roland Barthes, 'Power and "Cool"' in *The Eiffel Tower and Other Mythologies*, trans. Richard Howard (Berkeley: University of California Press, 1997), 43–5. The essay is an analysis of what he calls the 'gangster film'. But the essay was written at a time before 'film noir' had become the lexical commonplace for the very films that Barthes has in mind. For instance, he specifically cites Jacques Becker's 1954 noir, *Touchez pas au Grisbi*.

30 Roland Barthes, 'Dare to Be Lazy', in *The Grain of the Voice: Interviews 1962–1980*, trans. Linda Coverdale (Berkeley: University of California Press, 1985), 342.

31 Ibid.

32 Agamben, 'Notes on Gesture', 59.

33 Adrian Martin, 'Recital: Three Lyrical Interludes in Godard', in *Forever Godard*, ed. Michael Temple, James S. Williams and Michael Witt (London: Black Dog, 2004), 263.

34 Darke, *Alphaville*, 50.

35 Agamben, *The Open*, 85.

36 Ibid., 87.

37 Agamben, 'Kommerell, or on Gesture', 85.

38 Ibid., 78.

39 Asbjørn Grønstad and Henrik Gustafsson, 'Giorgio Agamben and the Shape of Cinema to Come', in *Cinema and Agamben* (New York: Bloomsbury Academic, 2014), 3.

40   See Henri Bergson, *Time and Free Will: An Essay on the Immediate Data of Consciousness* (London: Dover Press, 2001).

41   Alan Woolfolk, 'Disenchantment and Rebellion in Alphaville', in *The Philosophy of Science Fiction Film*, ed. Mark T. Conard (Lexington: University Press of Kentucky, 2008), 195.

42   Ibid.

43   Gregg Lambert, 'Cinema and the Outside', in *The Brain Is the Screen: Deleuze and the Philosophy of Cinema*, ed. Gregory Flaxman (Minneapolis: University of Minnesota Press, 2000), 264.

44   Ibid., 284.

45   Pierre Klossowski, 'The Experience of the Eternal Return', in *Nietzsche and the Vicious Circle*, trans. Daniel W. Smith (London: Athlone Press, 1997), 55–73.

46   The return to this difference-from-itself is, moreover, what Deleuze's time-image in every instance produces:

> If there is no self-identical subject who can speak for the image or interpret it as whole, if the complexity of the image itself can be neither reduced nor represented as a whole that can be contained in memory, then what does the time-image represent or communicate? Only time, the impersonal form of time that divides the ego from the I and disjoins all forms of identity, in the subject or in the image, as a force of becoming. This is the ineluctable return of that which differs – difference in itself that returns from beyond any absolute horizon or from deeper than any interiority.

Cinema II, 188. For more on this, see David Rodowick in *Gilles Deleuze's Time Machine* (Durham, NC: Duke University Press, 1997), 131–7.

47   Claire Colebrook, *Gilles Deleuze* (London: Routledge, 2002), 60.

48   Clement Rosset, 'Notes on Nietzsche', in *Joyful Cruelty*, trans. and ed. David F. Bell (Oxford: Oxford University Press, 1993), 26. In examining the theme of beatitude in Nietzsche, Rosset takes as his starting point the insights of Henri Birault. Birault examined the theme of beatitude in Nietzsche at an influential conference on Nietzsche in 1972, one which was attended by many of the most significant figures in contemporary continental philosophy, among them Deleuze, Jacques Derrida and Michel Foucault. In an essay based on his conference presentation, Birault describes what is at stake in Nietzsche's conception of beatitude.

> There is a will to establish distance from all the traditional philosophies, and, at the same time, the still unspoken elaboration of a new philosophy, or rather of a new manner of philosophising: the joyous knowing – no longer the ascending knowing, but the declining knowing; no longer the knowing that rises from unhappiness toward happiness, but the knowing that descends, that overflows, that pours out of the over-full cup, the over-ripe cluster, the over-rich star: a primal abundance and superabundance, joyous and painful, of a Dionysian wisdom and beatitude!

Henri Birault, 'Beatitude in Nietzsche', in *The New Nietzsche: Contemporary Styles of Interpretation*, ed. David B. Allison (Cambridge, MA: MIT Press, 1994), 226.
49 Farocki and Silverman, 'Words Like Love', 61.
50 See Heidegger, *Being and Time*, 312–48.
51 Farocki and Silverman, 'Words Like Love', 76.
52 Agamben, *Potentialities*, 83.

5

2046: Orphic Lingering in the Dark Interval (or, What 'Becomes' of Lemmy's Cigarettes)

As we observed at the close of the previous chapter, the contradictory condition of human temporality – the pull between diachronic succession and synchronous arrest, between time (in the everyday sense) and atemporal rupture (the ecstatic 'present') – is brought to a kind of syncretic fusion in *Alphaville* through the temporal model of Henri Bergson's *durée*. Though it occasions a rupture of the extra-temporal, a giving way to the eternal return, the dark interval of ecstatic awareness that Natacha undergoes does not 'freeze' time indefinitely but opens her to duration and specifically to the human necessity of advancing in time. Human temporality in *Alphaville* is thus understood to involve both an exposure to the necessity of time's progression and to its restorative capacity for arrest. As such, the film risks a 'happy ending', one that ironically turns the Orpheus myth on its head, insomuch as Orpheus now successfully makes off with 'the girl', neither of them *looking back*. (As they flee the self-destructing city behind them, Caution specifically warns Natacha: 'Don't look back'.) This self-conscious happy ending is founded upon Natacha's awakening to the autonomy of affect, her retrieval of the mediality of gesture and, ultimately, her discovery of love. Indeed, in many respects, the film suggests that love is the most appropriate response to the enigma of time. Love itself is borne of the contradictions that are native to temporality: it imbues a moment, an affective interval of time that has become disentangled from banal continuous time, with significance, and thereafter redefines the human experience of duration in terms of this interval and its affective charge. In doing so, love thus dwarfs time's enigmatic force, traduces it even. The film's closing exclamation – Natacha's 'I love you', uttered as much to the universe as to Lemmy – solves the 'problem' of time in an amusing, self-reflexive, almost pataphysical manner, by diminishing the agonies of temporality and celebrating instead the simple, immediate joy of persistence that time-as-becoming affords to living creatures. This is 'love's time', *love-as-durée*, time now retuned to affect.

Nevertheless, the tensions between progressive 'clock-time' and atemporal rupture remain stubbornly extant. They are not resolved by the affirmation of love so much as they are eased or obscured by it.

Indeed, it should be noted that the original Orphic myth treats love with far more complexity. The myth is well known. In his grief, Orpheus ventures into the underworld to retrieve his dead lover, Eurydice, and this show of love, aligned with his gifts for music, charms Hades and Persephone, the gods of the underworld. The latter allow Orpheus to lead Eurydice back up to the mortal world, but with the caveat that he must not look upon her until they reach the realm of living things. In his desire for her, however, Orpheus ignores the interdiction of the gods. He glances back upon Eurydice, and, upon doing so, she recedes once more to the underworld. And so Orpheus loses her yet again.

Clearly, the myth concerns the same agonies of time that *Alphaville* will later take as its own theme, but in the original Orphic myth love is not redemptive but complicit in these agonies. In the wake of her death, it is precisely Orpheus's love for Eurydice that fosters in him a rejection of the necessities of chronological succession and of the impermanence of mortal existence. In short, *the lover*, Orpheus, is one who rejects time's passing and particularly resents the temporal category of 'the past'. He craves the presence of Eurydice here and now in a timeless condition of permanence. Ironically, when he does succeed in winning her back it is this same desire for (her) presence that betrays him once more. This time it is his impulsive disregard for the future – the fact that Orpheus lacks the patience to wait for Eurydice – that causes his anguish. In his haste to force the present, he loses her once more. Thus, the myth of Orpheus is ultimately one about acquiring an appropriate disposition to time and its passing. And so, contrary to its revision in *Alphaville*, in the original myth love does not conquer time, precisely because Orpheus's love of Eurydice is one that attempts to stem the tide of time's passing. In Godard's reworking, however, Natacha's love of Caution is not in conflict with time but rather finds a deeper affinity with it. Natacha's love is as much a love of time's passing, the duration to which she has just awoken, as it is an amorous passion for the object of her affection. Love, then, in *Alphaville*, is an inflection of a specific kind of adjustment to temporality. In effect, it becomes a weird synonym for Bergson's *durée*. And, in the film, it is love-as-duration, as an affirmative submission to affective becoming, that is salvaged from the experience of the dark interval.

However, there is another possible response to the affective interval, and to the force of love – or potentiality – that nestles within it. And that is to attempt to reify, or calcify, the interval, to arrest and occupy it: the transgression of Orpheus. This, in part, is the theme of Wong Kar-Wai's noir-inflected *2046* (2004), a film that makes subtle references to Godard's *Alphaville*, revisiting the latter film's engagement with temporality but in a more complex, mannered and melancholy manner. Notably, Wong is unable to take solace in the joyful *faux-naiveté* that Godard opts for at the conclusion of his film. Instead, as we will see, what *2046* demonstrates is the human propensity for lingering in the interval.

2046: 'Avant-noir' all over again

Significantly, like *Alphaville*, Wong's film engages with noir tropes and particularly with the iconography of the interval. Upon the film's release, many reviewers could sense noir at work in the film: in *Time* magazine Richard Corliss described the film rather obscurely as an 'avant-noir',[1] while in the *San Francisco Chronicle* G. Allen Johnson made the claim that, with *2046*, Wong had perfected something he calls the 'romance noir' genre.[2] However ad hoc such categorizations may appear, their coinage speaks not just to the semantic drift we observed at the outset of this study but to the powerful yet intangible ways in which Wong mobilizes noir in his films. In *2046*, the director invokes noir as a sensuous cinematic form, one oriented towards expressions of temporality and affect, and, in fact, throughout his *œuvre*, this 'poet of time'[3] has repeatedly engaged with noir in terms of its distinctive treatment of temporality. Wong, then, clearly conceives of noir as not so much a genre as a mood, a texture or a tonality that addresses the complexities of time and duration. Prior to *2046* there had been numerous articulations of noir in earlier Wong films like *As Tears Go By* (1988), *Days of Being Wild* (1990), *Chungking Express* (1994), *Fallen Angels* (1995) and *In the Mood for Love* (2000). It's notable, however, that *2046* is the first of his films openly to take the theme of temporality as its principal subject, and in this its noir stylings are quite pivotal. Intriguingly, in studying time and invoking noir, *2046* also makes some subtle but very resonant allusions to *Alphaville*, and I would suggest that the film should be regarded as a thematic companion-piece to the latter. Where the earlier film attempts a harmonizing of the contrary temporalities that tug on the human, *2046* articulates a more ambivalent response to time, a more melancholic inflection of the temporality at work in *Alphaville*.

Alphaville and *2046*: Echoes beyond time, anguish or caress

Because of his formal experimentation and his supreme interest in time, Wong is frequently compared with Godard. Indeed, Janice Tong locates Wong in a direct lineage to the French director precisely because, like Godard, he 'toy[s] with and challenge[s] our experience of time as a linear succession of moments, as well as the rudimentary notion that time's trajectory is that of past, present and future'.[4] The influence of Godard is one that Wong moreover has made explicit. His contribution to the French anthology film *To Each His Own Cinema* (2007), for example, stands as a clear tribute to his New Wave predecessor.[5] Bearing the knowing title *I Travelled 9,000 km to Give It to You*, the lyrical short is set in a cinema, wherein a couple succumb to their passions while – out-of-frame – *Alphaville* plays on-screen. (The film takes its title from one of Caution's lines in the film.) While it is far less overt, I would suggest that *2046*, too, can be considered to pay direct homage to *Alphaville*. This homage occurs at a number of levels. Notably, both films make a meta-cinematic investment in film noir and in sci-fi. (Wong's film includes a fiction-within-the-fiction interlude, a futuristic story of lovers travelling to a spatiotemporal utopia called '2046' in order to recover lost memories. Noir elements, meanwhile, are iterated in the iconography and narrative.) Both films also share a formal emphasis on facial close-ups and gesture and on affection-images more generally. At the level of narrative, both films involve protagonists – Natacha in *Alphaville*, Chow Mo-Wan in *2046* – who are alienated from their affective capacities, albeit in quite distinct ways, and both narratives close with images of these protagonists being driven away to an unknowable future. At the level of iconography, Wong pointedly mirrors elements from Godard's film, principally the robotized seductresses, which, in Wong's film, are no longer humans bleached of affect but are now literally androids, devoid of affect in the first place. Most importantly, as already mentioned, both films also mobilize the noir iconography of the interval. The predominant noir trope in *2046* is the visual of the contemplative, cigarette smoking figure, often cast against a vesperal light: a visual which – as we shall discuss in due course – takes on an insistent and mesmerizing lyrical power within the film. Finally, at the level of theme, we should observe the way in which both films meditate upon time and affect: the paradoxes and contingencies of temporality, and its essential underwriting of human affective experience.

Intriguingly, in engaging with *Alphaville*, *2046* also becomes in the process one more pleat in the enduring fabric of the Orpheus myth. Indeed, Wong's film can be seen as but the latest chapter in a subtle lineage of cinematic treatments of the myth that stretches back through *Alphaville* to one of the films that influenced Godard: Jean Cocteau's *Orphée* (1949).

FIGURE 18 *As Lemmy and Natacha escape Alphaville, Natacha clings to the walls that house the supercomputer.* Alphaville.

The connections between *Orphée* and *Alphaville* have been explored in some depth by Chris Darke.[6] *Orphée* itself, of course, is a text very much imbricated in the poetics of film noir. As Phillipe Azoury and Jean-Marc Lalanne have put it, Cocteau's film resembles a kind of 'dream of film noir'.[7] Elsewhere, Glenn Erickson has observed the suggestive similarities between the nocturnal London underworld in Jules Dassin's landmark noir *Night and the City* (1950) and Cocteau's own reimagining of the underworld in *Orphée*: 'La Zone'.[8]

As Darke points out, one of the references that Godard makes to Cocteau's film is the repeated shot of 'inhabitants stagger[ing] through the corridors of Alphaville as the city self-destructs, clinging to the walls like the deathly denizens of *Orphée*'s "Zone"'.[9] Natacha herself is one such sufferer (Figure 18).

If we look closely at *2046*, we will see that this visual is in its turn quoted by Wong, who depicts one of his own robot seductresses – the android attendant 'wjw1967' – in the same gesture: clinging passionately to the corridor walls of the fantastical train destined for 2046.[10] Like Natacha in *Alphaville*, wjw1967 makes this strange gesture after having been exposed to the force of affect (Figure 19).

Indeed, while Darke is correct that the images of 'clinging' in *Alphaville* recall those of Orphée's navigation through 'the Zone' in *Orphée*, I would argue that they are actually more resonant still with the famous image of Orphée (Jean Marais) gripping his bedroom mirror sensually, trying to commune with the other realm that he senses beyond it, a 'realm' that the mirrored image connotes as being equivalent to the intervallic condition of self-affection itself (Figure 20).

FIGURE 19 *In 2046, the android wjw1967 (Faye Wong) grips the walls of the train corridor passionately, having been exposed to temporality and affect by her romantic encounter with a passenger.*

FIGURE 20 *Interval of self-affection: Orphée sensually grips the mirror, gateway to 'the Zone', the underworld.* Orphée.

In any event, as I have suggested elsewhere,[11] the way in which these images speak to one another across the three films – Orphée, Alphaville and 2046 – suggests that we can regard Wong's film, too, as a knowing cinematic invocation of the Orpheus myth.[12] Indeed, though the actual framing of the shot produces only a vague resemblance, the gesture of Orphée's communion with the mirror (above) is one that Wong effectively repeats at the end of *In the Mood for Love* when his hero, Chow Mo-Wan, places his hands around a hole in the ruined façade of the Angkor Wat temple and whispers a secret therein. Chow might be regarded, then, as another cinematic iteration of Orpheus. In the Greek myth, it is his dead wife that Orpheus wishes to retrieve from the underworld. In the case of Chow, it is his stillborn romance with Su Li-Zhen (Maggie Cheung) – the narrative 'black hole' at the centre of *In the Mood for Love* – that he refuses to let recede into the past. This love, the interval of its occurrence, the potential resident in it, the passion it has opened him to and his refusal to let it expire, *his rebuke of time*, in other words, is the secret he entrusts to the walls of Angkor Wat. In a fascinating move, *2046*, the 'sequel' to *In the Mood for Love*, comes to incarnate this passion. Rather than developing a straightforward narrative continuity, the entire film can be regarded as a crypt and an encryption of the secreted passion of the earlier film.[13] It is an encryption that the viewer can only partially decipher at best. And, indeed, though it is the crypt of his very own secret, Chow himself is reduced to attempts at deciphering it. A recurrent image in *2046* is Chow's peeping into room '2046' in the hotel where he lodges.[14]

This number '2046', this number of the encrypted secret, actually comes to connote numerous elements within the film. It is the number of the hotel room that adjoins Chow's own (his room being 2047). It also exists as a memory; insomuch as it is the number of a prior hotel room, the one that Chow shared with Su Li-Zhen during *In the Mood for Love*. In addition, it is the title of his science-fiction novella, '2046'. (This novella is itself an artistic transmutation of Chow's secret passion, a further encryption still.) Finally, at an extra-diegetic level, the number '2046' connotes the final year in the guarantee of '50 years without change' that China promised to Hong Kong following the city-state's transition from British sovereignty in 1997. (A promise that China has since reneged on.) It was this latter idea of a time-without-change – what we might describe as a suspended time, where temporal succession has been halted and rendered intervallic – that provided Wong with the inspiration to make *2046*. In effect, then, at an intra- and extra-diegetic level the numerical sign '2046' is a cipher. It functions as a code within (and without) the film: a 'time-code' in as much as it is a code for time itself and for the enigmatic passion of its passing.

Orphic noir

Instructively, the film engages the iconography of noir to transmit this secret code, while deepening also the enduring myth of Orpheus, and indeed there is something that could be described as fundamentally 'Orphic' about many noirs of the classic era. The noir antihero is often an Orphic figure desiring to retrieve something lost or forbidden from a hostile or eerie underworld. Often, this 'underworld' is a criminal milieu, of course. Yet, at a phenomenological level, it might be understood as 'the earth' that juts through 'the world', as Henrik Gustafsson – referencing Martin Heidegger – has described the 'under-world' of noir.[15] Such an underworld, as configured in 'Orphic noir', might be regarded as an affective and temporal registry of experience that lingers beneath our representations of reality and orderings of life. Meanwhile, in relation to the myth's lost or unobtainable object of affection, this loss, too, is frequently configured in a modern 'Eurydice', as it is, for instance, in *Laura*, *The Killers*, *Out of the Past*, *The File on Thelma Jordan* (Dir. Robert Siodmak, 1950), *Vertigo* (Dir. Alfred Hitchcock, 1958) and many other films. Adrian Martin, for example, describes *Vertigo*'s forlorn protagonist as an 'Orphic anti-hero who wanders among the shades and the shadows, between the realms of the living and the dead'.[16]

Laura is perhaps the foundation and apotheosis of this Orphic motif in noir. (It was, of course, one of the five films that Nino Frank originally anointed 'film noir' in his influential study.[17]) It is precisely as a vanished and ambivalent erotic object – lost to him before he has ever encountered her – that police detective Mark McPherson (Dana Andrews) relates to Laura Hunt (Gene Tierney), the victim in the murder case he is investigating. Exceeding any sense of professional duty, the typically passive and impassive detective finds himself drawn towards the dead girl's room wherein he fumbles through her personal items, inspects her diary, inhales her perfume and stares obsessively at the large portrait of her. In this growing infatuation with the deceased, he comes to echo the film's other dominant male protagonist, the cultured intellectual Waldo Lydecker (Clifton Webb), who – prior to Laura's death – had similarly pined for her as an unattainable object of desire. Indeed, due to his own Orphic afflictions, it is not surprising that it is Lydecker who best understands McPherson's strange plight. 'You'd better watch out, McPherson, or you'll finish up in a psychiatric ward,' he tells him. 'I doubt they've ever had a patient who fell in love with a corpse.'

It may not be quite so much Laura's corpse, however, that McPherson has developed a passion for as much as the empty space she leaves in her wake – the absence, gap or interval that, in her death, she has come to signify. McPherson's exposure to this interval of Laura's absence is, tellingly, emboldened by Preminger's use of the noir convention of the 'haunting melody'. As has often been noted, composer David Raskin's theme – eruptive yet ephemeral and elusive – is used in an extraordinary way throughout the film, always foregrounding Laura's essential absence.[18] McPherson's desire for the *absent-yet-perversely-present* figure of Laura ultimately finds him converting her room into a mausoleum, a reliquary, a crypt. In effect, for McPherson, Laura becomes a cipher for the twinned enigmas of being and time, of desire and impermanence, and her room becomes the space of McPherson's own self-affection. Anticipating Chow's encryption of his own passion in the cipher '2046' (which is at once a physical space (the hotel room) *and* an abstract one (the novella)),[19] McPherson encrypts his own existential ecstasies in the space of Laura's room, making it an essentially intervallic space where he can *possess* that which is unobtainable (Eurydice). He inhabits it the way the melancholy angel inhabits Giorgio Agamben's 'space of the unreal' in Dürer's engraving.

McPherson's capitulation to the fascination of this intervallic space, this enigmatic locus of his own encryption, is exemplified in the famous scene where midway through the film, the intoxicated detective sits in an armchair and falls asleep gazing at her portrait. It is at this juncture that the film's famous narrative gambit occurs, when McPherson awakens from his slumber to find Laura, whom he had presumed dead, returned (*to him*). It is frequently observed that the sequence has an ethereal dream quality to it and, as Kristin Thompson has argued, it is entirely feasible that McPherson actually remains asleep and that the rest of the narrative is merely the content of his dream, a 'fantasy fulfilment'.[20] Insomuch as McPherson, in the grip of a Blanchotian fascination, fetishizes Laura's room, this space in which time has been arrested, we can perceive his own instinctive resistance to the transience of temporal experience in his attempt to inhabit the dark interval. And if we view the second half of the film's narrative as in fact a dream, as Thompson suggests, then we can regard this dream as itself the very interval that he inhabits thereafter. (Moreover, it is one which we, the viewers, inhabit with him, and thus cinema itself becomes an encrypted space, the very space of intervallic temporality.) Instructively, the final image in *Laura* is that of the face of a great clock in Laura's room that has been shattered by a gun blast. Together the film's romantic heroes, McPherson and Laura (Orpheus and Eurydice), succeed in departing the crypt of her room, this space of temporal arrest, but the final image is an ominous one: time remains fundamentally dysfunctional.

This 'Orphic' motif in noir has persisted within the modern noir also, with David Lynch's *Lost Highway* (1997) bringing the model to perhaps its most hyperbolic extreme. Indeed, the film's writer, Barry Gifford, originally conceived (somewhat drolly) of the film's narrative as 'Orpheus and Eurydice Meet *Double Indemnity*'.[21] Where *Lost Highway* chiefly engages with noir's Orphic qualities in order to examine the tortuous forces of desire and fractured psychology, *2046*, by contrast, channels it in order to meditate upon temporality, affect and the human's exposure to an intrinsic condition of impermanence.

The complex narrative background of 2046

As already noted, *2046* is a conceptual 'sequel' to *In the Mood for Love*.[22] (Like *2046*, *In the Mood*, too, has been viewed as infused with a distinctive debt to noir.[23]) As a sequel, the film works via a tangential logic. The narrative of the first film had centred on an impassioned but stifled romance between Chow Mo-Wan (Tony Leung) and Su Li-Zhen (Maggie Cheung), two neighbours in a Hong Kong tenement building in the early 1960s. Having discovered that their respective partners are having an affair with one another, Chow and Su are allied in suffering. But as they spend increasing amounts of time together they soon realize that they, too, are falling in love. Under the weight of social decorum, however, they resolve 'not to be like' their unfaithful partners. Instead, they repress their desires for one another, sublimating their passions in a mutual love of martial arts novels, in an endless array of meals and, most evocatively, in imaginative re-enactments of scenes from their partners' affair. When Chow's marriage eventually breaks down, he moves to a hotel room (number 2046), and it is here that he and Su begin to write martial arts fiction together. Everything appears to be building to the physical consummation of their mutual desire, but if they are sexually intimate it is not revealed in the film, and the viewer is left only to speculate.[24] Unable to withstand his intense love for Su any longer, Chow takes a newspaper job in Singapore. Su considers accompanying him, but in her indecision she acts too slowly and, in an emotional scene, she arrives at the hotel room after Chow has already departed. In the film's closing sequence, we observe Chow in the ruins of the Buddhist temple of Angkor Wat in Cambodia, where he has been sent on a newspaper assignment. He whispers something – a secret, a promise – into the ancient walls of Angkor Wat and the film ends. The audience is never made privy to the content of this whisper, but as a gesture it is specifically tied to an anecdote that Chow tells a friend earlier in the film:

> In the old days, if someone had a secret they didn't want to share ... do you know what they did? ... They went up a mountain, found a tree, carved a hole in it, and whispered the secret into the hole. Then they covered it with mud and left the secret there forever.

Chow's gesture – his inaudible whisper – at the end of *Mood* can thus be considered a 'pure gesture' in Agamben's terms, a gesture that indicates at once the fundamental *mediality* of the human while also simultaneously attesting to something that is beyond communication, an expression of what Agamben elsewhere calls 'pure passion'.[25] Indeed, the film itself can be considered as operating with the same logic. While it is enigmatic and intriguing, the narrative of *Mood* is secondary to the film's sensibility, its own mood; the latter wrought of gesture, texture, music, movement and repetition, into which the viewer is immersed with comparatively little regard for narrative clarity, coherence or resolution. It is these sensuous or affective qualities of *Mood*, supplemented by its penchant for sly narrative intrigues, which bind the film to *2046*.

A baroque and stylized romance, *2046* is not so much a narrative as a riddle at the centre of which nestles the very secret that Chow imparted to the hollow in Angkor Wat at the end of *Mood*. This hollow itself returns in the very opening shot of *2046*, where it is now transfigured as a black hole at the centre of a weird, exotic piece of décor (or perhaps it is even an engine) on a high-speed train that travels through time in the year 2046. The camera's initial tracking movement actually takes us into the centre of this hole. As Stephen Teo observes, the image is 'a strikingly feminine symbol that Wong invokes with a hint of immodesty and voyeurism'.[26] However, it is worth pointing out that the strange object on-screen also very suggestively resembles an eye and that, in its initial framing, moreover, it even looks like an eye poised in the centre of a film strip. It is therefore quite a self-reflexive image, one that asserts that the film – in addition to exploring love, desire, affect and temporality – is also about cinema itself.

Notably, the opening sequence of the film imagines Hong Kong in the year 2046. CGI effects conjure an image of a frantic futuristic cityscape in which bullet trains fly past rapidly like thoughts along neural pathways. The imagery at this juncture is very much in the style of 'tech-noir', a popular hybrid genre that has gathered apace since the 1980s when it originated in *Blade Runner* and William Gibson's novel *Neuromancer*. (Indeed, with its subplot involving androids who become exposed to affect and to temporality, *2046* carries suggestive resonances with *Blade Runner*.) Accompanying these opening tech-noir images in *2046* is the voice-over of train traveller Tak (Takuya Kimura), who explains that in the year 2046 it is possible to journey to a strange topos (named 2046) where one can retrieve lost memories. This seductive tech-noir setting abruptly gives way, however, and the narrative proper takes hold. We are returned to 1960s Hong Kong and to the classic noir milieu of *Mood*. The sci-fi imagery, it transpires, has been but a visualization of the novella '2046', a work that the film's protagonist, Chow, will write during the course of the film's narrative. (He also writes a sequel, '2047', and later in the film there is an extended visualization of this novella too.)

Though it is elliptical and non-linear, the narrative that thereafter emerges in *2046* is a reasonably unproblematic one. At the outset, we observe Chow's return to Hong Kong from Singapore, where he is leaving behind an unresolved relationship with Black Spider (Gong Li). The latter is a sensitive but secretive femme fatale, an artful gambler who happens to share the same proper name (Su Li-Zhen) as Chow's 'love interest' in *Mood*. (This is but one of a great many doublings in *2046*.) Upon his return to Hong Kong, Chow eventually settles in room '2047' of the Oriental Hotel. Viewers familiar with *Mood* quickly realize that he is no longer the same acquiescent and tender soul from the earlier film, however. He is now more passionate, more temperamental and more cynical, having reinvented himself as a playboy-gambler-aesthete, complete with pencil-line moustache and slick suit. Shortly into his stay at the hotel, Chow commences a torrid affair with his neighbour in room '2046', Bai Ling (Zhang Ziyi), a glamorous call girl. For Chow, it seems, this relationship – which he explicitly describes as merely a means of passing time – is motivated only by sexual desire. Bai Ling initially plays along with his indifference, but his non-committal disposition ultimately takes a destructive toll on her, and she pines for him long after their fractious parting.

As time wears on, Chow himself suffers a muted, unreciprocated infatuation with another woman, Wang Jing-Wen (Faye Wong), daughter of the hotel's owner. Striking up a friendship, they begin to pen martial arts novels together (just as he had done with Su Li-Zhen in *Mood*). Meanwhile, Chow helps to smuggle letters to her from her Japanese lover, a man her bigoted father has rejected as unsuitable. Having earlier in the film written the popular novella, '2046', Chow now writes its sequel, '2047'. The story tells of a man attempting to return from 2046 on one of the time-travelling trains, and of his falling in love with an android whose affective responses are hindered by temporal delay. In this, the story clearly mirrors Chow's unrequited relationship with Jing-Wen, while also invoking his unfulfilled love of Su Li-Zhen in *Mood*. When Jing-Wen suddenly moves to Japan to wed her Japanese lover she requests that Chow's sad ending for '2047', in which a despairing Tak now flees once more to the atemporal haven of 2046, be altered. Chow attempts to revise the novella, but he cannot manage even to write a single word. A series of shots linger upon his fountain pen as it hovers, unmoved, above a blank page, as if vacillating in Maurice Blanchot's space of literature.

Nevertheless, it seems that Wang Jing-Wen's critique of his ending for '2047' has pierced the armoury of Chow's supreme resignation, and so he attempts to alter the drift that has come to mark his own life. Chow now returns to Singapore to look for Black Spider. He fails to locate her. Yet here in the gambling dens of Singapore (so evocative of his past) he nevertheless makes a breakthrough. He realizes that Black Spider's rejection of him years earlier was not because of secrets in *her* past, as he had presumed, but rather because she could perceive how debilitated Chow was by his own buried secrets, that is, his love for the original Su Li-Zhen and his fascination with the passion this love had wrought in him.

In *2046*'s climactic sequence, Chow has now returned to Hong Kong. Bai Ling has contacted him in order to ask a favour: that he will recommend her to a potential employer in Singapore, where she is moving. We come to suspect however, that she is, in fact, making a final, forlorn attempt to rekindle their relationship. On the eve of her departure, Chow walks Bai Ling to her lodgings but he resists her suggestion that they spend the night together. Making her desperate love for him obvious, she pleads with him: 'Why can't it be like it was before? Please don't go. Stay with me tonight. Let me borrow you.' Chow responds impassively, but not entirely without sympathy: 'Do you remember? You once asked me ... if there was anything I wouldn't lend. I've given it a lot of thought. And now I know ... there is one thing ... I'll never lend to anyone.' Rather than explicitly tell her – and tell us – what this 'one thing' is, however, Chow merely clasps her hand briefly, then breaks away from her and descends the stairs of the hotel. Bai Ling remains behind him at her door, heartbroken. As he walks off through the city streets Chow's face wears a sentimental, resilient smile and we cut to a title card bearing the following caption: 'He didn't turn back. It was as if he'd boarded a very long train heading for a drowsy future through the unfathomable night.'[27]

The film's final image appears directly after this caption. Finding Chow alone in the rear seat of a taxi, distinctly adrift, it is a delirious, meta-cinematic invocation of images from earlier in the film and, indeed, of images from previous Wong films that had also starred Leung (*In the Mood, Happy Together* (1997)). In those earlier scenes Chow/Leung had shared taxi rides home with lovers, his head rested on their shoulders, or else their head on his.[28] But now the shot is repeated with a key difference – Chow is alone, united only with the memories and the passion which sustains him, his head rested against the car window, melancholically contented in the interval of his own passing, his own passion.

The 'pure passion' of eternal return

The repetition of the taxi ride image is but one of countless repetitions in *2046*. The latter could, of course, be regarded as pointing to a Freudian dynamic of 'repetition compulsion' at work in Chow's character.[29] Such a reading is certainly available, if in my view a little too trite. I would argue that the repetitions are far more suggestive of the significance of Nietzsche's eternal return to the film's examination of temporality and affect. Notably, Stephen Teo has observed the motif of eternal return in *2046* and in Wong's films more generally, and does so while invoking Gilles Deleuze's conception of the 'return' as a return not to 'the same' but to the flux of *difference*, an articulation of becoming.[30] I would add to that observation, however, that there is a joy, a quality of beatitude, in the experience of eternal return, the shuddering experience of exposure to the eternal *difference* of affective becoming. In it, we might say, there resides a 'mood for love'. This is the quality – the beatitude, the mood for love – that Natacha harnesses in *Alphaville*, the potentiality that allows her to embrace time as duration and as a submission to affective becoming. In *2046*, however, it is the very *mood* of potentiality itself, the feeling of beatitude, rather than the potentiality ('to advance to live') that it discloses, which comes to fascinate Chow. Ultimately, we realize, the cipher '2046' is throughout the film nothing other than an encryption of this very mood, this *passion* of self-affection. Passion *is* the secret of *2046*.

Significantly, Agamben has reflected upon Nietzsche's cardinal idea of the eternal return specifically in terms of such a passion. (It should be said that Agamben has engaged with eternal return in a number of works, and not always consistently.[31]) In an early essay, 'Eternal Return and the Paradox of Passion', he explicitly identifies the doctrine with a certain 'paradox of potency', the conception of which he sees stretching back to the very origins of Western metaphysics.[32] This paradox is particularly visible, says Agamben, in Aristotle's distinction between the two kinds of potentiality at the root of human subjectivity: '*potentia passiva*, passivity, receptivity, and *potentia activa*, tension towards action, spontaneity'.[33] The two potentialities coincide in what he calls 'pure passion' – a term which, of course, resonates with the use of expressions such as 'pure gesture' and 'pure means' elsewhere in his corpus. Wherever terminology of this order occurs within Agamben, what he invariably has in mind is the passion of the human in a profound condition of self-affection: the human as nothing other than the site of this 'pure passion'.

Agamben contends that, despite its centrality to Nietzsche, the 'will to power' is not the only response to eternal return that Nietzsche conceives. He suggests that although we are used to seeing Nietzsche's concept of the return as providing the platform for an active potentiality ('will to power'), in fact, 'what Nietzsche tried to do in the concept of eternal return is precisely to conceive the final identity of the two *potentiae*, the will to power as a pure passion affecting itself'.[34] In this, he would find agreement with Deleuze, who – as we observed earlier – points out that the will to power is constituted precisely by the human's apparently passive capacity to be affected; it is therefore not a passivity but 'an affectivity, a sensibility, a sensation ... a *feeling of power*', a formative pathos.[35] For Agamben, therefore, eternal return occasions and is occasioned by an interval of supreme passivity, a passion of fascinated receptivity and self-reflexion, in short, self-affection. As we observed in relation to *acedia* in the opening chapter, Agamben continually returns to this image of self-affection, of a 'pure passion affecting itself', throughout his work. Always, it involves a vision of a temporal suspension that challenges history, tradition and structures of control, opening us to a pure potentiality at the very heart of the human. He sees in this passion a quiet (but not necessarily *quietist*), quasi-anarchistic hope: the hope that harnessing the potentiality it produces may be the first move in a recuperative ethics or politics. This hope can only emerge from the recognition that, as he says, 'power, *potentia*, is first and foremost *potentia passiva*, passivity and passion'.[36]

The passionate passivity involved here may indeed nurse such a transformative possibility, and, indeed, Natacha's awakening in *Alphaville* is very much versed in just such a conception of the eternal return. In *2046*, however, as is very often the case in noir of the dark interval, it is this radical passivity – as a sort of terminus in itself – that comes to dominate. It discloses a passion not necessarily connected to any redemptive project. Instead, characters become fascinated by this 'passivity and passion', by the condition of temporal arrest it fosters and by the seductive sense of *beatitude* sheltering within it. In other words, they become fascinated with the melancholy condition of their own self-affection. In *2046* the chief means by which this passion of self-affection is communicated to the viewer is via the iconography of the dark interval – here invoked by imagery of languid detachment and, in particular, by scenes that render the enigmatic passivity involved in the smoking of a cigarette.

Iconography of the dark interval in *2046*

The iconic noir image of the passive *acedic* figure alone in a laconic repose is found a number of times in *2046*. Notably, our first shot of a human character in the film is that of Tak, the lone passenger aboard the train making the impossible journey back from 2046. In keeping with the openings of so many noir films, we find Tak here laid up in a passive, withdrawn repose, framed in a medium shot, his legs hunched up before him.

The temporal suspension inscribed in his repose is emboldened by a curious gesture he makes with his hand, which repeatedly reveals and obscures the electric light on the wall before him. As it does so, Tak absently counts backwards (998, 997), the numbers charting his melancholic flight from '2046'. Importantly, the symbolic use of the light fixture here recalls Natacha's words ('light that goes, light that returns') during her redemptive reverie in *Alphaville*. It also recalls the way that Godard's film repeatedly presents electric light – as an image of potentiality – as at once entrancing and alienating for the film's characters. The latter is best exemplified in a scene where Lemmy Caution and Henry Dickson are distinctly troubled by a swinging light bulb on the landing of Dickson's dingy lodgings.

Later on in *2046*, meanwhile, a more familiar noir image of the dark interval is rendered in a depiction of a jaded Chow lying in bed, caught in a condition of *acedic* self-absorption. Instructively, Wong suggestively plays with this visual convention. The shot in question occurs during the romance between Chow and Bai Ling when, in the aftermath of intercourse, Chow is framed more or less explicitly in the noir iconography of the interval, his body in slouched repose upon the bed, his gaze fixed out of frame, his mouth drawing on a cigarette. Yet protruding into the frame there is also the leg of Bai Ling, a decisive intrusion into Chow's *acedic* detachment.

Even though the scene quickly develops into a bout of further lovemaking, the initial framing in this shot accentuates Chow's essential disinterest in Bai

Ling as a romantic partner and his more thorough absorption in his own self-affection. Notably, this image has its predecessor in *Days of Being Wild*. There, too, Wong mobilizes the conventional iconography of the interval of *acedic* self-affection but undercuts the male protagonist's detachment by placing an unwanted lover in a peripheral but stubbornly intrusive position in the frame.

The most telling element of Wong's invocation of noir iconography in *2046*, however, and it is alluded to in the shot above, resides in the constant cigarette smoking of both Chow and the other protagonists. Cigarette smoke is the most overdetermined signifier in the film, coming to stand for the impersonal force of time itself. The tendency reaches its apotheosis in a shot where a frame featuring only a cloud of cigarette smoke facilitates a cerebral transition from archival news footage of political turbulence in Hong Kong in 1967 (the virtual register of the past) to the imaginative, interior projections of Chow's sci-fi story (the virtual register of literature). The image suggests that ultimately everything that occurs in human duration – the passing of events in the 'actual', historical world as well as all the virtual and untimely potentials of our imagining – carries an equivalent status within time itself. In addition to being an image for the ephemeral charge of time and the mystery of temporality, however, cigarette smoke is also Wong's key image for the experience of eternal return in *2046*. Wong appears to regard cigarettes as totemic divining rods that mysteriously conjure an experience of eternal return. Indeed, as Richard Klein has pointed out in his influential cultural study *Cigarettes Are Sublime*, this is a common conception of cigarettes. According to Klein, cigarettes are 'objects of reflection' that by their very nature 'invite the return of the same'.[37] In *2046* the repeated shots of protagonists drawing on their cigarettes, often taking time to gaze at the amorphous clouds engendered by their own exhalations, underline an experience of eternal return that denotes enrapture in self-affection, a relishing of the potentiality, the beatitude, which trembles seductively in the dark interval, but without any urgency to integrate it into a future-oriented project of self-articulation. Instead, what we find is absorption in the passivity of one's own taking place. This is very much in keeping with the metaphysical associations of temporal arrest that have become inextricably linked with cigarette smoking, as Klein describes it:

> The cigarette kills time, chronometric time, the stark mechanical measure of mortality ... The series of moments the clock records is not only a succession of 'nows' but a *memento mori* diminishing the number of seconds that remain before death. But the cigarette interrupts and reverses the decline, accomplishes a little revolution in time by seeming to install, however briefly, a time outside itself ... Smoking cigarettes ... is permanently linked to the idea of suspending the passage of ordinary time and instituting some other, more penetrating one, in conditions of

luxuriating indifference and resignation toward which a poetic sensibility feels irresistible attraction.[38]

Of course, a sophisticated poetics of cigarette smoking is itself one of the visual codes that we have come to associate with film noir. As Rashna Wadia Richards very keenly observes, one of the upshots of this exalted manner with which Humphrey Bogart 'transform[ed] the simple act of lighting a cigarette into an aesthetic performance' was the creation of a 'gesture [which] stalls the narrative'.[39] Of course, this image or gesture with the potential to stall the narrative is precisely the sort of 'arresting image' we have been associating with the dark interval in noir.[40] Indeed, this poetic transformation of time that Bogart's screen persona achieves is inscribed not just in his cigarette smoking but works in conjunction with a certain seductive stillness in his performance also: the 'contemplative' and 'sedentary' attributes that Thomas Schatz finds in the Bogart figure in repose.[41]

Cigarettes in noir are invested with a temporal metaphor, then, and classic noir is quite self-conscious about this. Nowhere is this better exemplified than in *Out of the Past* in a scene where Whit (Kirk Douglas) offers his nemesis, Bailey (Robert Mitchum), a cigarette, only for Bailey to hold aloft a cigarette already in his hand and reply, laconically: 'Smoking'.[42] Of course, Bogart's profuse smoking was, for Godard, emblematic of film noir, and in both *Breathless* and *Alphaville* the French director employed several very overt visual quotes of Bogart's smoking. As I noted in the last chapter, Caution's very power as an agent of *poiēsis*, potentiality, is symbolized in the film by his cigarette lighter. In his very first exchange with Natacha the latter asks the detective, 'Got a light?' Caution fires up his lighter and replies knowingly, 'I've travelled 9,000 km to give it to you.' The scene is an affectionate nod to a similar exchange between Bogart and Lauren Bacall in the 1944 noir *To Have and Have Not* (Howard Hawks), where the cigarette's 'power' is of the more reductive phallic variety. In *Alphaville* the exchange establishes all of Caution's poetic powers in the totemic emblem of the cigarette and it lays the ground for his eventual exposure of Natacha to affect. In this way, the cigarette as a metaphor for temporality, but also for duration and affective becoming, is central to *Alphaville*. In *2046*, however, the cigarette means something similar and yet something quite different. It denotes a stalling in self-affection, not a 'will to power' but a passive, desistant lingering in the experience of eternal return.

Visuals of characters alone with their cigarettes abound in *2046*. Invariably, these cigarettes connote a state of fascinated self-affection. Frequently, characters even stop to behold the images of their own smoking, responding to their cigarettes precisely as exaggerated 'objects of reflection', in Klein's terms. Wang Jing-Wen does so early in the narrative, during the period when her father has banned her from seeing her Japanese boyfriend. Clearly mobilizing the noir visual aesthetic of the dark interval, the shot is rendered in ethereal slow motion and captures Wang dragging on her cigarette before then glancing at it strangely, her eyes tracing the smoke as it dissipates above her. The image is later replicated during a visualization of Chow's tech-noir novella in which Wang Jing-Wen has now been reimagined as an android, wjw1967. Here the image intones the self-awareness of temporality and affect, to which the android has been irrevocably exposed by her romantic liaisons with Tak. Unlike Natacha's exposure to affect in *Alphaville*, however, wjw1967 becomes self-destructively fascinated instead with her own affective capabilities, immersed in and stalled by self-affection. Just as for Tak (and his author, Chow), this immersion in affect becomes all-consuming and distinctly melancholy.

Elsewhere in the film there is a repeated visual motif which captures solitary figures on the roof of the Oriental Hotel, framed against an evocative vesperal skyline in a condition of affective reverie, often melancholically tinged. This figure against a dusky skyline is, of course, an iconographic composition with a rich noir heritage, one of many variations on the contemplative noir figure. Chow, Bai Ling, Wang Jing-Wen and the latter's sister, Wang Jie-Wen (Jie Dong), are all captured in such shots. In each case these figures on the roof are smoking, with one notable exception – that of the precocious younger sister, who instead is depicted savouring an ice cream. The latter image may be regarded as conveying the innocence, urgency and youthful insouciance that is native to the experience of self-affection before, with age, a worldlier and more melancholic disposition towards the experience comes to prevail. As such, subtle as it is, the distinct and discrete connotations of these two signifiers of self-affection and duration – the cigarette and the ice cream – suggest, on the part of the protagonists, alternative attitudes to time and its passing.

Intriguingly, in these shots the 'O' in the neon-lit signage of the Oriental Hotel is lit in a different colour from the remaining letters, a vivid red that draws the eye. The 'O' here, I would suggest, carries overtones of both the number zero and of circularity: the rapture of eternal return.[43] And it corresponds with the many other iterations of 'O' in the film, too, including the enigmatic hole into which the camera drifts at the outset of the film and the 'O' gesture that the android wjw1967 creates with her thumb and forefinger for Tak, when – slowly bringing her hand to her mouth – she tries to lure him into a kiss. Of course, the 'O' could also be understood to allude to what Maurice Merleau-Ponty calls the 'nullpunkt', that point of orientation unique to each of us, which is rooted in our physical embodiment.[44] Ultimately, what these images on the rooftop connote is an elegiac affective experience, that of a 'self' wavering between containment and dispersal in the eternal return. It is vital, too, to observe in these images the perverse satisfaction that they denote, the lure of self-affection as Agamben describes it, whereby one relishes the passivity of undergoing the 'pure passion' that one is.

This, ultimately, is Chow's condition in *2046*: a wilful lingering in the interval of his own passion, and it is this – his passion – which is the secreted 'one thing' that he insists he will never 'lend' to anyone. As Jacques Derrida suggests, passion and 'the secret' are actually the same phenomenon: 'The secret impassions us.'[45] Passion *is* the secret that hides in plain sight.[46] It is therefore this, the secret of *his* passion, the promise or potential of it, that Wong confides to the hole in Angkor Wat, and which he encrypts in his novellas '2046' and '2047'. Moreover, as we will observe, he encrypts it, too, in his own person, in the form of the character that he adopts in *2046*: that of the gambler/seducer.

The 'recurrence of one's passion', I would suggest, is the proper connotation of the term 'the same' in Nietzsche's expression 'the eternal return of the same'. The same of the eternal return is that it is always the *same* passion – ultimately an impersonal passion, the passion inherent in potentiality – that one returns to. In returning to it, one always experiences it anew, the repetition altered by the different affective intensities at work in each specific occurrence of the return. Passion, on these terms, is one way of understanding Deleuze's concept of *difference-from-itself*.[47] Moreover, the passion of one's immersion in affective becoming can thus be understood as at once a sign of difference *and* of identity, however attenuated the latter may be. Importantly, the 'joy' that Nietzsche associates with awakening to this passion in the eternal return is closely connected to another of his grand concepts, *the will to power*. In Nietzsche's view, affirmation of the eternal return is only complete when one recognizes and forges in oneself *the will to power*, the will to orient one's being to the force of becoming itself. The means of doing so are principally artistic: in short, one must become a 'character'.[48] While Nietzsche shares with Aristotle and Paul Ricoeur a conviction in the human necessity of building a 'character', this necessity is, in his design, rooted more intuitively in the impulses of the 'will to power', the very pathos of affectivity, than in any overarching ethics of narrative identity. The assumption of character is nothing but a demonstration of the will to power, and in Nietzsche's view it cannot be pursued merely in the service of 'identity', narrative constancy or any ethics concomitant with these. Instead, character must be achieved 'artistically', worked into being from the intangible fabrics of 'style'. Such character is only oriented upon 'attaining' satisfaction with oneself:

> *One thing is needful.* – To 'give style' to one's character – a great and rare art! It is practiced by those who survey all the strengths and weaknesses of their nature and then fit them into an artistic plan until every one of them appears as art and reason and even weaknesses delight the eye. Here a large mass of second nature has been added; there a piece of original nature has been removed – both times through long practice and daily work at it. Here the ugly that could not be removed is concealed; there it

has been reinterpreted and made sublime ... In the end, when the work is finished, it becomes evident how the constraint of a single taste governed and formed everything large and small. Whether this taste was good or bad is less important than one might suppose, if only it was a single taste! ... For one thing is needful: that a human being should *attain* satisfaction with himself, whether it be by means of this or that poetry and art; only then is a human being at all tolerable to behold.[49]

It is precisely this kind of 'character', this style, an attenuated identity, that Chow pursues in *2046*. Moreover, he does so in a condition of passivity that is quite deceptive, for Chow's will to power is, in fact, a will to powerlessness – a submission to the passivity and passion of the return. Furthermore, this will to powerlessness should not be regarded as a betrayal of the Nietzschean 'active' will to power but as actually conversant with its keener meaning, that which Nietzsche calls 'amor fati': a love of fate, an affirmation of one's fate. As Pierre Klossowski points out, it is the will to power itself that 'projects its powerlessness on time, and in this way gives time its irreversible character: the will cannot reverse the flow of time – the non-willed that time establishes as an accomplished fact'.[50] The will to power thus involves a distinct powerlessness.[51]

Let us look closer, then, at the 'character' that Chow adopts in *2046*. Re-booted from the more docile figure of *In the Mood*, the Chow of *2046* is, as Paul Arthur describes him, 'alternately tender, aggressive, blasé, compassionate, and unfailingly forlorn'.[52] This latter quality, his forlornness, is most significant. For one thing, it illustrates that Chow is implicated in one of Søren Kierkegaard's 'stages' of life: that of infinite resignation.[53] The important point, however, is that, in the stylization of his new 'character', Chow takes this forlornness, this resignation – a quality that the doggedly life-affirming Nietzsche would certainly regard as 'ugly' – and, reinterpreting it, makes it sublime. His principal means of doing this is via the noir persona he assumes – that of the gambler/playboy. The ludic gambler in classic noir – again, one thinks of Bogart – is someone who intuitively grasps his own powerlessness and yet somehow locates a mercurial power within it.[54] Chow's reinvention as a gambler/playboy follows the episode of romantic heartbreak he suffered in *Mood*, and the reinvention is a way of adjusting to his 'powerlessness' over time's passing. He is fascinated by the temporality that gambling and seducing involve, which we might describe as a pronounced state of suspension, as well as a suffusion in the ecstasy of perpetual loss. Indeed, he is the very model of Walter Benjamin's gambler, one for whom 'time spills from every pore'.[55] What Chow achieves by means of his gambler persona is a means of inhabiting the interval, the moment of eternal recurrence, of a heightened, vertiginous presence.[56] As such, Chow's gambling is not restricted to the gambling dens – of which we see very little in *2046*, in fact – but it more broadly informs every facet of his existence.

Intriguingly, in his analysis of Dostoyevsky's novels, Mikhail Bakhtin has compared the time of gambling to the final moments of consciousness before execution, which he describes as 'time on the threshold', 'life taken out of life'.[57] The parallel that Bakhtin draws here may conveniently unite for us the 'time of gambling' with that experience of beatitude that Blanchot uncovers in his (biographical) story 'The Instant of My Death',[58] and with the very similar experience that Deleuze perceives in Riderhood's near demise in Dickens's *Our Mutual Friend*. As I argued earlier, both are resonant with the Swede's fascinated gaze and exalted state on the threshold of death in *The Killers*. However, whereas each of the latter scenarios describes a 'moment' of heightened awareness, a sudden and ephemeral flaring up of 'pure immanence' in Deleuze's terms, in *2046* Chow attempts to remain in this moment, to reside passively in the dark interval of his self-affection, in short, to reify the experience of eternal return. That it leads to the film closing with a bittersweet melancholic image – the resigned, forlorn, yet strangely contented Chow adrift alone in the rear seat of a taxi – is perhaps inevitable. Chow embraces powerlessness, the passivity of his own passion, as a power in itself. In effect, this 'pure passion affecting itself', as Agamben describes the eternal return, radically conflates Orpheus and Eurydice. By way of such auto-affection, Orpheus discovers that he is also Eurydice, the object of his own passion. But it is a melancholic image – an image of *acedic*, atemporal arrest as well as interminable temporal drift. It invites inevitable associations with the Freudian conceptions of the 'drive' and repetition compulsion, of course, and as such Chow can certainly be read as continuous with the masochistic noir hero as Žižek defines it.[59]

At the end of *Alphaville*, Natacha and Lemmy Caution – Godard's own Orpheus and Eurydice – depart together, placing their faith in Bergson's duration, an impersonal becoming that nevertheless requires their lyrical appropriation of potentiality, and solicits, too, a commitment to advancing in time. Such an end is not possible for Chow in *2046*. The maudlin topos of '2046', this mysterious space which is not simply the repository of lost memories but is also ultimately a cipher for loss itself, is located nowhere other than within Chow, we realize. It *is* Chow. '2046' merely becomes the code, the conduit, for his accessing and acceding to his own passion, the 'pure passion' that he is. But in opting to inhabit the dark interval of self-affection rather than progressing onward from it, as Natacha does, Chow can but remain in a time that is undone, *adrift*, out of joint. The character he has adopted, the gambler/seducer, can obtain effectively in such a time, because – while the gambler/seducer is attentive and attuned to the present – he truly regards it as something already past. The interval for the gambler is always only the interval of time's passing, of a passion's own passing. The potentiality the interval shelters is savoured only for itself, not the potentiality to act, the potentiality to embrace one's gestural powers, one's scope for communication, but only the passive joy of potentiality itself, the

FIGURE 21 *Natacha asleep on Lemmy's shoulder.* Alphaville.

beatitude of self-affection, the beatitude inherent in constituting a passion and its joyful suffering of time. To illustrate the distinction between Chow's capitulation to self-affection and Natacha's more active opening on to potentiality, we can examine the two closing images of each film, which again seem to speak peculiarly to one another.

At the close of *Alphaville* Lemmy and Natacha flee the technocratic city in the detective's Ford Galaxy. Lemmy pushes the drowsy Natacha – disoriented by her tumultuous awakening to affect – into the car and drives off. We watch the car careening down the motorway and then we cut to a shot in the car's interior as it speeds away from Alphaville. Lemmy is driving. Natacha is passed out on his shoulder (Figure 21).

Natacha promptly awakens, however, and Lemmy slowly assists her to adjust to her new circumstances, her new allegiance with affective becoming, with her own passion. As we noted earlier, this allegiance is ultimately facilitated by her words, directed at the world as much as to Lemmy: 'I love you.' She smiles upon uttering them, and then we cut to the film's closing shot. Offering us Natacha's point of view, the frame vibrates ever so slightly, indicating the car's motion (her motion). And what is framed is nothing but the motorway that extends far before her. She is thus enacting the film's mantra, a line from Paul Eluard's poetry; she is 'advancing to live'.

By contrast, *2046* closes with a visual that carries strange echoes of this one, but its graphical content suggests an entirely different fate for Chow. Earlier in the film we have observed images of cab rides that Chow has taken with Bai Ling and Su Li-Zhen respectfully (Figures 22 and 23).

As a 'memory' from *In the Mood*, the latter has the status of the virtual in Deleuze's terms. It is a 'crystal image'.[60] In each of these images, his head rests on his partner's shoulder as he sleeps (or feigns sleep).[61] In the final shot of *2046*, however, Chow is again framed in the back seat of a cab, but this time he is alone, his head rested on the car's interior. And now his eyes are

FIGURE 22 *Chow asleep on Bai Ling's shoulder. 2046.*

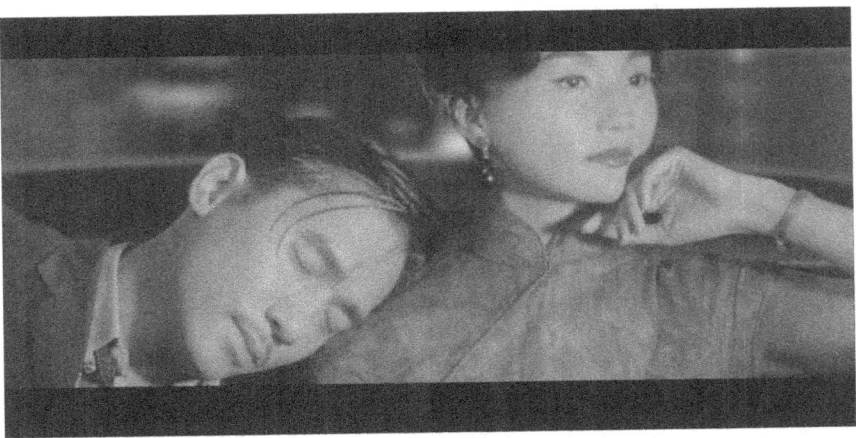

FIGURE 23 *Chow asleep on Su Li-Zhen's shoulder. 2046.*

open, his face distinctly solemn and melancholy as he is consumed with his thoughts and memories, bound by his elegiac self-consignment to the dark interval of his own passion (Figure 24).

And when we cut to the film's closing image it is not to a POV shot of the road lying open before Chow but rather to a shot of the vortex ('2046') that is about to engulf him (Figure 25).

The image connotes Chow's interminable lingering in the interval of his own passion and this idling, detached waiting, or even simple dissolution[62]

FIGURE 24 *Chow alone, resting his head on the cab door. 2046.*

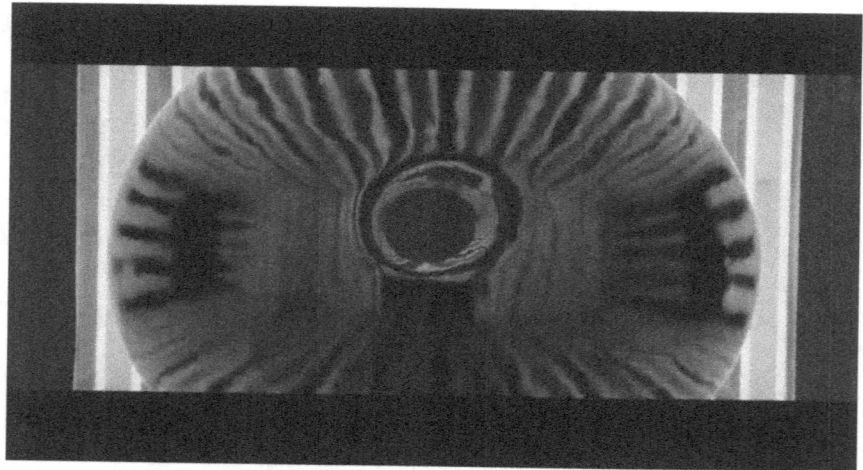

FIGURE 25 *Into the vortex. 2046.*

is a fate that affects many noir protagonists in the era of the modern noir, from the 1960s onwards. In *2046* it accounts for the 'aesthetic of non-identity' that Allan Cameron perceives to be at work in the film.[63] Of course, an elegiac dispersal of self, 'infinite resignation', *is* inevitably a possible outcome of exposure to the dark interval, to the potentiality and beatitude it renders, and perhaps even the outcome most often foregrounded in noir. In the following chapters I will examine this trope of dispersal in the interval as it emerges recurrently in modern noir as a breakdown in 'the law' and in the arrested time of a 'community' of missing persons.

Notes

1. Richard Corliss, '2046: A Face Odyssey', *Time*, 1 August 2005.
2. G. Allen Johnson, 'Frustrated Romantic Trapped in the Past, with Hope for the Future', *San Francisco Chronicle*, 19 August 2005.
3. Wong was popularly anointed the 'poet of time' by Tony Rayns in an influential article in *Sight and Sound*, 5.9 (1995), 12–16.
4. Janice Tong, 'Chungking Express: Time and Its Dislocation', in *Chinese Films in Focus*, ed. Chris Berry (London: BFI, 2003), 47.
5. *To Each His Own Cinema* (Various, 2007).
6. Darke, *Alphaville*, 94–9.
7. Phillipe Azoury and Jean-Marc Lalanne, *Cocteau et le cinema: Désordres* (Paris: Cahiers du Cinema, 2003), 80. My translation.
8. Glenn Erickson, 'Expressionist Doom in *Night and the City*', in *Film Noir Reader*, 204.
9. Darke, *Alphaville*, 95. Jonathan Rosenbaum has also reflected on the images of 'clinging' in *Alphaville*, pointing to their resonance with the images of the sleepwalking Cesare crawling along the wall in *The Cabinet of Dr Caligari* (Dir. Robert Wiene, 1919). See Darke, *Alphaville*, 57.
10. With its circular overhead lamps and narrow passageway, this image also clearly invokes the image of the hotel corridor in *2046*'s predecessor, *In the Mood for Love*.
11. See my video essay 'Echoes Beyond Time, Language or Caress: *Orphée, Alphaville, 2046*', *[in]Transition: Journal of Videographic Film and Moving Image Studies*, 6.2 (2019).
12. If, as Jacques Aumont has suggested, Godard treats the film text of *Orphée*, and the ancient myth of Orpheus itself, as a metaphor for cinema throughout his work, then in *2046* Wong can be regarded as extending this metaphor. For a summary of Aumont's perspective in this regard, see Darke, *Alphaville*, 96.
13. Indeed, as Rayns notes, the film itself is 'a giant "hole" into which everyone – including, of course, [Wong] himself – can whisper their secrets'. See Tony Rayns, 'The Long Goodbye', *Sight and Sound*, 15.1 (2005), 22.
14. As Kelly Oliver and Benigno Trigo point out, the 'fortified room, its locked door, and the self-constitutive function of both are common tropes of film noir and neo-noir.' See *Noir Anxiety* (Minneapolis: University of Minnesota Press, 2003), 216.

15 Henrik Gustafsson, 'A Wet Emptiness: The Phenomenology of Film Noir', in *A Companion to Film Noir*, ed. Andrew Spicer and Helen Hanson (London: Wiley Blackwell, 2013), 55.
16 Adrian Martin, *Last Day Every Day: Figural Thinking from Auerbach and Kracauer to Agamben and Brenez* (New York: Punctum, 2012), 20.
17 Nino Frank, 'A New Kind of Police Drama: The Criminal Adventure', trans. Alain Silver, in *Film Noir Reader 2*, ed. Alain Silver and James Ursini (New York: Limelight, 1999), 15–19.
18 Ness, 'A Lotta Night Music', 59–63.
19 As Leland de la Durantaye observes, in *Stanzas* Agamben invokes the meaning of the Italian word 'stanza' as 'room'. See Leland de la Durantaye, *Giorgio Agamben: A Critical Introduction* (Stanford, CA: Stanford University Press, 2009), 156. This association between the space of poetry and the physical space of a room informs Agamben's argument throughout *Stanzas* that the poetic act divides time and space; it creates a room – a third intermediary space, a phantasm, an abstraction – for the approach of the enigmatic object of desire. The relevance of this to the dynamics of *2046* is self-evident.
20 Kristin Thompson, *Breaking the Glass Armour: Neoformalist Film Analysis* (Princeton, NJ: Princeton University Press, 1988), 163.
21 Barry Gifford, 'Foreword', in *The Complete Lynch*, ed. David Hughes (London: Virgin Books, 2001), x. Another modern noir that clearly has an Orphic dimension is *Inception* (Dir. Christopher Nolan, 2010).
22 In fact, the films were initially shot concurrently. The latter was completed much earlier, however, and released to critical acclaim in 2000, winning the Palme D'Or at Cannes. *2046* was not released until four years later, following a difficult production beset by delays.
23 See Gary Bettinson, 'Happy Together? Generic Hybridity in *2046* and *In the Mood for Love*', in *Puzzle Films: Complex Storytelling in Contemporary Cinema*, ed. Warren Buckland (London: Wiley-Blackwell, 2009), 167–86. Bettinson says of *In the Mood for Love*: 'Noir iconography invades the *mise-en-scène*: ringing telephones and doorbells remain discomfitingly unanswered; cigarettes are obsessively smoked and function as ubiquitous markers of anxiety; and at night a perpetual rainfall pounds the lamp-lined streets of Hong Kong.' 'Happy Together?', 175.
24 A deleted scene would seem to make explicit the fact that they did make their relationship intimate. Moreover, at the close of the film itself, it is vaguely suggested that Su Li-Zhen may even have borne Chow's son. However, bolstering the theme of deferral that runs through the film, we can never know for certain if they were intimates or not.
25 See Agamben, *Potentialities*, 79.
26 Stephen Teo, *Wong Kar-Wai: Auteur of Time* (London: BFI, 2005), 138.
27 The caption, like earlier intertitles in the film and in *Mood*, is a quote from the Hong Kong novelist Liu Yichang. For more on Wong's use of Liu Yichang throughout the film, see Teo, *Wong Kar-Wai*, 151–2.

28 In *Mood* it is Su who rests her head upon Chow's shoulder. In *Happy Together*, it is not Chow but the actor playing him, Tony Leung, who is the point of continuity: in that film the head of his lover, Ho Po-wing (Leslie Cheung), rests on his shoulder.

29 Freud discusses repetition compulsion in detail, ultimately associating it with the death drive. See Sigmund Freud, *Beyond the Pleasure Principle*, trans. and ed. James Strachey, *The Standard Edition of the Complete Works of Sigmund Freud, Vol. 18* (London: Hogarth, 1953–74), 3–64. For an analysis of *2046* largely focused on repetition compulsion, see Todd McGowan, *Timeless in Space: Desire in Atemporal Cinema* (Minneapolis: University of Minnesota Press, 2011), 157–80. For McGowan, 'Chow exists as a being of the drive – continually sustaining a failed relation with his lost object' (170).

30 See Teo, *Wong Kar-Wai*, 84.

31 For an overview of Agamben's repeated engagements with the eternal return and the conflict in his different articulations of it, see de la Durantaye, *Giorgio Agamben*, 319–23.

32 Agamben, 'Eternal Return and the Paradox of Passion', 9–17.

33 Ibid., 15.

34 Ibid., 17.

35 Deleuze, *Nietzsche and Philosophy*, 77.

36 Agamben, 'Eternal Return and the Paradox of Passion', 17.

37 Richard Klein, *Cigarettes Are Sublime* (Durham, NC: Duke University Press, 1993), xiii.

38 Ibid., 8.

39 Rashna Wadia Richards, 'Loose Ends: The Stuff That Movies Are Made of', *Arizona Quarterly*, 63.4 (2007), 101.

40 On the cinematic function of 'arresting images', see Barbara Klinger, 'The Art Film, Affect, and the Female Viewer: *The Piano* Revisited', *Screen*, 47.1 (2006), 19–41.

41 Thomas Schatz, *Boom and Bust: American Cinema in the 1940s* (Berkeley: University of California Press, 1999), 221.

42 *The Man Who Wasn't There* explicitly quotes this scene when the chain smoking Ed Crane responds with a similarly laconic gesture to an offer from a police officer.

43 Of course, as Edward Said pointed out in his influential study *Orientalism*, the word 'orient' carries other more chauvinistic connotations. Western audiences are often guilty of exoticizing Eastern cinema and this is a tendency that Wong Kar-Wai may be slyly satirizing.

44 Invoking Merleau-Ponty's work, J. P. Telotte has explored the nature of this zero horizon of embodiment in a number of classical noirs, among them *Murder, My Sweet*, *Dark Passage* and *The Lady in the Lake*. As Telotte points out, Merleau-Ponty also understood that the 'nullpunkt' of embodiment implies that there exists for each person an ineluctable blind spot of perception

when it comes to themselves. As Telotte puts it, 'Haunted by something that always escapes or effaces itself before our gaze, we constantly struggle to confront and understand our real selves and the world in which we seem to be meaningful figures.' See Telotte, *Voices in the Dark*, 89. Telotte's application of Merleau-Ponty to noir is generally steeped in epistemological rather than ontological concerns. But the two categories are hardly discrete or non-related, and certainly a consciousness of the 'nullpunkt' is reasonably analogous to that state of self-affection we have been examining.

45 See Jacques Derrida, 'Passions – An Oblique View', in Jacques Derrida, *On the Name*, ed. Thomas Dutoit, trans. David Wood (Stanford, CA: Stanford University Press, 1995), 29.

46 Ibid., 26.

47 This is how Deleuze conceives of eternal return. Though he doesn't put it in these terms, eternal return discloses the impersonal nature of 'the passion that one is caught up in'. Of course, it excludes the 'one' – the subject or agent – from experiencing it as a stable unity, as an identity. Passion is a more rarefied experience, an experience of difference as 'difference-from-itself'. 'The eternal return does not cause the same and the similar to return, but is itself derived from a world of pure difference.' *Difference and Repetition*, 125. Nevertheless, the eternal return may be regarded as engendering identity, albeit as an illusion 'retrojected' on to the experience of 'pure difference'. 'The same and the similar are only an effect of the operation of systems subject to eternal return. By this means, an identity would be found to be necessarily projected, or rather retrojected, on to the originary difference and a resemblance interiorised within the divergent series. We should say of this identity and this resemblance that they are "simulated"' (126).

48 Since Aristotle the development of a person's 'character' has been understood as a means – and, moreover, the ethical means – of negotiating the intractable mysteries of existence: time, consciousness, identity and community. This idea of character is indeed the 'narrative identity' that Paul Ricoeur theorizes, which – in *Oneself as Another* – he explicitly describes in terms of the keeping of a promise: the promise to remain recognizably the 'same' over time, even while not immune to change. Ricoeur conceives of 'character' as a kind of bridging of two registers of identity to which the human belongs: *ipse* and *idem* identities. While character allows one to present the narrative constancy of what he calls *idem*-identity, the historical 'person', it also absorbs something of *ipse*-identity, that quality of the 'self', the singular, unrepeatable entity that each of us discretely is. However, though he grants an element of the 'ineffable' to the *ipseity* of human beings, Ricoeur's interest in character and narrative identity is at its core grounded in ethics rather than metaphysics. Ricoeur's conception of narrative identity is thus continuous with the Aristotelian conception of character and the virtuous life, centred upon ethics and community, the way in which one's identity is bound up narratively, historically, with 'the other'. See Paul Ricoeur, 'Utterance and the Speaking Subject', in *Oneself as Another*, 40–55. (This motif of 'the promise' is not irrelevant to *2046*, which Wong has described as 'a film about promises'.)

49 Friedrich Nietzsche, *The Gay Science*, trans. Walter Kaufmann (New York: Vantage Books, 1974), 232–3.
50 Klossowski, 'The Experience of the Eternal Return', 67.
51 Of course, the elegiac charge of such a will to powerlessness would seem, for many, to undermine the 'affirmative' and joyful force that Nietzsche, and Deleuze after him, locates in an affective becoming. Yet this is to overlook the fact that eternal return is not simply some venerable experience one affirms but also a dispersive experience to which one accedes. However 'unbecoming' it may be in the eyes of many Deleuzians to associate eternal return with elegiac dispersal, a sense of powerlessness is nevertheless pivotal to eternal return. Moreover, a quality of the elegiac itself is something that Deleuze acknowledged at work within his own character. As Deleuze admitted in his famous video interviews with Claire Parnet, one valid and recurrent expression of Deleuze (generally diminished in the work of most Deleuze enthusiasts) is a tendency towards the elegiac. Parnet even describes him as 'the great advocate of the complaint and the elegy', to which Deleuze responds in laughter before detailing the power of the elegiac itself. See *Gilles Deleuze from A to Z*, with Claire Parnet and Pierre-André Boutang, trans. Charles J. Stivale (Los Angeles, CA: Semiotexte, 2011).
52 Paul Arthur, 'Philosophy in the Bedroom', *Cineaste*, 30.4 (2005), 7.
53 Under the alias of one of his many pseudonyms, 'Johannes Climacus', Kierkegaard develops the figure of the knight of infinite resignation. See *Fear and Trembling*, ed. and trans. Howard V. Hong and Edna H. Hong (Princeton, NJ Princeton University Press, 1983), 34–52. The knight of infinite resignation is one who, having concentrated 'the whole substance of his life and the meaning of actuality into one single desire' (43), suddenly divines that its attainment is not possible in this world. (Kierkegaard's example is a romantic one: a young man's impossible love of a princess.) As a result of this painful reckoning with impossibility, and in a no less concentrated 'act of consciousness', the man now makes the movement of infinity that will make him a 'knight of infinite resignation'. Entering into the eternal, which diminishes this world and its finite possibilities, he renounces finitude, even while reconciling himself with it. Hereafter, he retains his love for the princess but seeks no 'finite occasion' for its realization. 'He has grasped the deep secret that even in loving another person one ought to be sufficient to oneself' (44). Despite the pain it involves, Kierkegaard insists that there is 'peace and rest' in the 'spiritual' movement of infinite resignation (55). Nevertheless, it is surpassed by a final stage, a further movement – the movement of faith – which, 'by virtue of the absurd', permits the 'knight of faith' to similarly renounce everything infinitely and yet to remain in finitude, to place his faith in it again. His example is Abraham who – by virtue of the absurd – can obey God's command to sacrifice Isaac while retaining an absurd faith in this world, a faith that Isaac would not be taken from him. Though Climacus says he has yet to encounter an authentic 'knight of faith', he says he would appear as no different than a bourgeois man, but one who relishes life, works assiduously at his every task and generally lives with the 'freedom from care of a reckless

good-for-nothing' (40). Chow can very much be regarded as a knight of infinite resignation, one who has 'peace and rest', yet who is resigned only to his own 'infinite' passion, unable to invest it any longer in the finitude of an everyday world and its everyday relations.

54   The gambling milieu was a fixture of classic noir, to the fore in films such as *Body and Soul*, *Force of Evil*, *The Asphalt Jungle* and *The Killing* (Dir. Stanley Kubrick, 1956). Of course, given noir's preponderant concern with themes of chance and fate, gambling was a fertile symbol. Most often, the subject was treated with a sombre tone as something intrinsically destructive. Nevertheless, a subversive model of the gambler also arises in noir: that of the gambler who really cares little about whether he wins or loses but instead cares only for the game: for the heightened temporality, the thrill of the game. This persona reached its apotheosis, again, in the form of Bogart. The actor washes up in gambling joints in *The Big Sleep* and *Dead Reckoning*, always with an effervescent disregard for the stakes (usually, his own life).

55   Walter Benjamin, *The Arcades Project*, trans. Howard Eiland and Kevin McLaughlin (Cambridge, MA: Harvard University Press, 2002), 107.

56   Eva Mazierska and Laura Rascaroli argue that a desire to live in the present is characteristic of Wong's protagonists. See 'Trapped in the Present: Time in the Films of Wong Kar Wai', *Film Criticism*, 25.2 (2000), 2–20.

57   Mikhail Bakhtin, *Problems of Dostoevsky's Poetics*, ed. and trans. Caryl Emerson (Minneapolis: University of Minnesota Press, 1984), 172.

58   The resonance is further emboldened by the fact that Dostoyevsky had withstood a similar incident to the one Blanchot recounts in *The Instant of My Death*. He, too, had been placed before a firing line for execution before being spared. In *Demeure*, Derrida examines this resonance, 74–5.

59   As noted earlier, Todd McGowan provides an analysis along these lines.

60   On the crystal image see Deleuze, *Cinema II*, 55–82.

61   Notably, the cab images are visual quotes from earlier Wong films, *In the Mood for Love* and *Happy Together*. See note 27.

62   In *Point Blank* Walker literally vanishes from the diegesis, as does David Locke (Jack Nicholson) in Antonioni's *The Passenger* (1975).

63   Allan Cameron, 'Trajectories of Identification: Travel and Global Culture in the Films of Wong Kar-Wai', *Jump Cut: A Review of Contemporary Media*, 49 (2007). https://www.ejumpcut.org/archive/jc49.2007/wongKarWai/text.html, accessed 1 June 2014.

6

Outside the Law: *The Long Goodbye*, Temporal Lapse and Force-of-Law

In this chapter I examine a tradition in noir that dramatizes capitulation to the interval as a form of socio-juridical lapse whereupon 'the law' is suspended and time comes off its hinges. A number of tropes, motifs and iconographical gestures are repeated in the noir films which evince this tendency. One of these is a concern with a chronological time, a communal time – the time of the polis, of the law; a narrative time – that is malfunctioning and must be repaired. I begin by examining a number of classic noirs (*The Big Clock*, *The Stranger* and *The Unknown Man*) in which the central theme of a temporal lapse is mobilized. In the latter, in particular, the lapse is conceived as a discrepancy between justice and law. This lapse constitutes a rupture in which potentiality is exposed, in this instance as the extra-juridical force of pure violence that founds and thereafter haunts the figure of 'the law'. I illustrate how *The Unknown Man* works to contain this force, even while exposing it. I then turn to *The Long Goodbye* in order to show how this modern noir instead harvests the anarchic force of violence, of potentiality, as an ethical act – albeit a deeply problematic one – capable of serving a contrary sense of community to that of sovereign state power.

The spectral time of justice: Big clocks and temporal lapses

In the films of the classic noir era the image of the clock, the 'timepiece', is often mobilized to convey psychological, social and juridico-political dysfunction.

Of course, given the fact that so many of the classic noirs rehearse the idea of a deterministic fate closing in on a cornered protagonist, it is inevitable that images of clocks and references to time abound in the films of the 1940s and 1950s.[1] In fact, the 'timepiece' in noir can connote a concern with any number of themes, among them the notion of a predetermined fate, the return of the repressed and the terror of finitude. But perhaps the most potent use of the image has been as a means of critiquing the broader juridico-political narrative of 'the law' and interrogating the concept of justice that 'the law' is supposed to uphold. In what follows I examine a number of films in which the 'keeping' of time is made analogous with the keeping of 'the law', and where the failure to keep time, and hence to keep law, becomes a central motif.

Two well-known noirs of the classic era – *The Big Clock* (Dir. John Farrow, 1948) and *The Stranger* (Dir. Orson Welles, 1946) – centralize the spectacle of a grand and imposing communal clock. In the former, the immense and incredibly accurate timepiece of the title literally presides over the city on the summit of the Janoth Publications building. The film's hero, George Stroud (Ray Milland), works for imperial media mogul Earl Janoth (Charles Laughton) and rails against being treated like 'a clock with springs and gears instead of flesh and blood'. Yet when he revolts against the impingement of industrialized 'clock-time' – quitting his job in order to spend more time with his family – it is as if time itself warps every new circumstance to take vengeance on him and he finds himself the unwarranted suspect of murder. Notably, as J. P. Telotte has observed, Stroud's flashback narration can be regarded as occurring within a temporal lacuna – *l'espace littéraire*, we might say, invoking Blanchot – that is opened up by Stroud's accidental halting of the big clock.[2] Throughout the film, timepieces are depicted as oppressive and lethal instruments, and in the film's most grandstanding sequence Stroud is even pursued through the alienating interior mechanism of the 'big clock' itself. Ultimately, the film's clock imagery affects an unambivalent, if somewhat timid critique of a socio-industrial 'public' time that has come to occlude 'personal' time – and thus the liberty – of the individual.

In contrast to *The Big Clock*, where a city is dominated by an omniscient and fastidiously accurate timepiece, in *The Stranger* the setting is a sleepy hamlet, the pleasant Connecticut town of Harper, in which the enormous Strasbourg clock in the town's church tower has never been known to run in the first place. That changes when Franz Kindler (Orson Welles) – a Nazi fugitive living in Harper under an assumed identity – undertakes to repair the clock. This activity deepens the suspicions of the Nazi-hunter who has pursued him to the town, 'Mr. Wilson' (Edward G. Robinson). The latter knows that Kindler is a man for whom the study of clocks 'amounts to a mania'. As the narrative progresses, and Kindler's phoney alias begins to unravel, the fugitive comes to stake everything on the clock tower, using it first as a weapon – a trap for his unsuspecting wife – and, finally, as a refuge from an outraged community. Significantly, in the film's dramatic conclusion, Kindler falls to his death after he is pierced by the sword of one of the clock's metal ornaments, an automaton of an avenging angel.

Where in *The Big Clock* the communal clock – as an emblem of social order – is characterized as a straightforward pernicious force, in *The Stranger* the clock is a far more ambivalent specimen. On the one hand, the clock is indicative of the fascistic Kindler's 'mania' for public order and control. (Indeed, as Jennifer Lynda Barker has noted, in an early draft of the script Kindler describes the 'ideal social system' in terms of a clock, 'comparing the teeth of the mechanism to individuals'.[3]) Yet, on the other hand, despite his reverence for the object, it is the clock itself that rejects Kindler and, in effect, ultimately brings him to justice. Meanwhile, even as the clock dispenses this justice, a subtle but distinctive stress is laid upon the impotence of the film's purported custodian of the law, Wilson. Injured, and armed only with an empty gun, the latter is reduced to a spectator as, first, the villain's wronged wife, Mary (Loretta Young), representative of the community, and then the clock itself as some form of sublime avenger, finally dispatch Kindler. (Notably, during this intense finale the giant clock has become deranged, its hands revolving in a frenzy of motion.)

Though I cannot pursue it much further here, the extravagant, baroque melodrama of *The Stranger* is most noteworthy for the suggestive associations it draws between time, law and justice.[4] At the film's climax, the blunt, stubborn force of the narrative attempts to reconcile these three distinct elements – 'the law', justice and the question of an appropriate disposition to time's passing – in the clock's eradication of Kindler. Yet any reconciliation between the three is spurious and unstable, and the film ends on a note of macabre irresolution.

While a schism between justice and 'the law' is hinted at in *The Stranger*, before being spuriously reconciled, the pivotal disjunction between the two is allowed to resonate more intriguingly in *The Unknown Man* (Dir. Richard Thorpe, 1951), a less ambient, somewhat more procedural noir that examines both the human's compunction towards justice and the inherent failings of the juridico-political system. Significantly, it does so while again mobilizing the metaphor of the 'timepiece', thus underlining justice's incipient relation to the human's conception of time.

The film's intricate narrative centres on a successful civic lawyer Brad Masen (Walter Pidgeon) who hubristically defends a hoodlum, Wallchek (Keefe Brasselle), against a murder charge. Masen wins the case but is later disturbed when he discovers that Wallchek – an enforcer in a brutal extortion ring – is indeed guilty. When he subsequently learns that the elusive kingpin running organized crime in the city is actually his friend, Andy Layford (Eduard Franz), the head of the Crime Commission, Masen impulsively plunges a knife into the latter's back, slaying him. In a twist of fate, however, it is the thug Wallchek who is wrongly accused of Layford's murder, and this time the young thug *is* found guilty and swiftly sentenced to death. Troubled by this development, Masen – setting himself against the letter of the law, and proclaiming his allegiance to justice as a form of 'religion' – contrives to bring about a poetic justice both for himself (the actual killer) and Wallchek (the violent criminal). What Masen seeks, in short, is some median between the letter of the law and the spirit of justice. Inveigling his way into Wallchek's cell, he reveals to the hoodlum that it was he, Masen, who killed Layford, and – throwing the murder weapon provocatively upon the prison bunk – taunts him: 'I'm not sorry I killed him, and I can't say I'm sorry you're going to die for it.' Then, picking up a Bible and, turning his back to Wallchek, he reads aloud: 'It's in the Old Testament, isn't it? An eye for an eye. A tooth for a tooth.' Goaded and enraged, the delinquent young bruiser sinks the knife into Masen's back and the latter collapses dead. In this way, Masen manages, in one fell swoop, to atone for murdering Layford, while Wallchek, having killed Masen, will at last be held to account, indirectly, for his earlier, unpunished homicide.

While the narrative of *The Unknown Man* is formulaic and its aesthetic values fairly dull, the film is noteworthy for its earnest treatment of the disparity between justice and the mechanism of the law. The thematic significance of time to society's conception of justice is also established early on during a sequence where Masen and other city dignitaries converse at a dinner party. When a venerable old judge (Lewis Stone) grandiosely quotes Cicero – 'Justice is even more important than law' – Masen shows the judge his watch, which bears an inscription of the same Cicero proverb. The watch had belonged to Masen's father, also a lawyer, we learn. What is most important to note here is the way in which, as in *The Stranger*, the vague sense of a justice that overrides the law is inscribed upon a timepiece. Of course, the function of a timepiece is to calibrate chronological time and, in effect, to facilitate a human 'construction' of objective time along the lines of a linear, progressive temporality. In this regard, chronological time is equivalent to 'the law', itself a construction: an approximation of the human exigency towards justice but also one that is never entirely sufficient to experience, as we observed in the chapter on *The Man Who Wasn't There*. In *The Unknown Man*, this discrepancy or insufficiency is underlined by the judge's observation about Masen's watch: 'You're ten minutes slow.' Instructively, the judge observes this discrepancy precisely at the juncture that Masen arrogantly decides to take on the fateful case that – while leaving him on the right side of the law – will leave him on the wrong side of justice, prompting him to sacrifice his own life to make amends.

This suggestion of a delay, a lag or interval between justice and the law, is the pivotal thematic feature of the film's narrative, then. From the moment Masen is ensnared in the elusive temporal lapse between justice and the law, he becomes transformed from a too self-assured executor of 'the law' to a humble but righteous agent of justice. Notably, before he gives up his life for the sake of justice, he passes on the watch to his son who is soon to graduate from law school. The watch has now become the emblem of Masen's commitment to an exertion of the law that defers to justice, but which also tries to make the two – law and justice – chime together. In his vanity, Brad Masen had earlier come to view the two concepts as being interchangeable, but the film documents his correction of that error. In passing on the watch to his son he instructs him to bring it to a watchmaker to be repaired. 'It loses ten minutes,' he warns him.

This fixing of the watch mirrors Masen's own re-tuning of the law so that it now corresponds more closely to justice and not to the vulnerable narrative orders of the justice system, which, as the film makes clear, are routinely corrupted. However, the more emphatic re-tuning of the law takes place in the body of Masen himself. In sacrificing his life, he makes himself at once a ritualistic offering that purifies and reinstates the law, and, at the same time, by virtue of his act's extra-juridical power, he makes himself the sovereign agent of a justice that exceeds the framework of the law. In committing this action, Masen enters an interval of time that might be considered 'sacred', a time founded not on chronological order but on the repetitions of ritual sacrifice, a time of suspension that Victor Turner has very influentially described as 'liminal'.[5]

As a vessel of justice, then, and yet also as the renewed 'covenant' of the law, Masen comes to embody this fundamentally intervallic space between justice and law, where the latter is presented as a juridical framework to which justice itself is not reducible. And yet, even though Masen – who proclaims at one point that man may be 'reaching for something higher [than law], something that's probably beyond his reach' – understands that justice is not reducible to the law, his final effort is nevertheless to attempt to bridge the interval between the two concepts and to produce a harmony between them. Such bridgings, such attempts at reconciliation, are the very function of sacred rites, of course, and of the recursive temporality that they invest in. Here, Masen's cleansing acts of violence – his slaying of Layford, his luring of Wallchek to murder – invest violence with a sacral quality.[6] Moreover, this 'healing' of the law in a temporal lacuna that brings one *outside* the law is a characteristic narrative gambit in film noir, where a legal transgression – what Giorgio Agamben would term an 'extra-juridical act' – is undertaken precisely in order to remedy a perceived fissure between justice and law. Thus, in *The Big Heat* detective Dave Bannion (Glenn Ford) – like Masen in *The Unknown Man* – steps outside the law and adopts an extra-juridical agency, but does so, too, in order that 'the law' can be purified and restored. A similar resolution occurs in *Where the Sidewalk Ends* (Dir. Otto Preminger, 1950). In the latter, hardened detective Mark Dixon (Dana Andrews) oversteps the bounds of law, killing one criminal and trying to frame another for his murder. Yet he confesses to his own culpability at the end of the film, in order that the system of law which he serves can remain intact.

Of course, these classic noirs established a lasting trope within crime cinema thereafter: the figure of the vigilante cop, the officer of the law prepared at all times to transgress the law in order, paradoxically, to enforce it. In Hollywood cinema the 'Dirty Harry' movies and, later still, the *Lethal Weapon* franchise are perhaps the most hyperbolic inheritors of this trope. Curiously, at roughly the same time as these 'rogue cop' films began to gain traction, a quite contrary articulation of the same noir tradition was also coming to prominence in American cinema: that of the detective or (agent of detection) who is, by contrast, rendered impotent by the interval that erupts between justice and the law. Prominent films in this vein include *Chinatown* (Dir. Roman Polanski, 1974), *The Conversation* (Dir. Francis Ford Coppola, 1974) and *Night Moves* (Dir. Arthur Penn, 1975). Intriguingly, one film that stands apart from, and yet is also continuous with, both of these noir offshoots is *The Long Goodbye* (Dir. Robert Altman, 1973). *The Long Goodbye* is a film about a supreme powerlessness before the corrupt forces of the law and an apathetic, dysfunctional culture. Yet it is also about the mercurial power of a justice – borne of potentiality – that surges up in the dark interval. That the latter, this mercurial power of the interval, is delivered through Altman's weird concoction of satire and tragedy does not diminish its significance. While *The Long Goodbye* is certainly both a parody of Hollywood's noir conventions and a satire on the complacent values underlying those conventions, its final sequence – in which Philip Marlowe (Elliott Gould) suddenly, and shockingly, executes his contemptible best friend – is arguably modern noir's most provocative and devastating expression of the dark interval and the force it lays open. I will examine that final sequence shortly. Before then, I will offer a brief summary of the film, noting its continuity with a noir tradition that explores law and justice in relation to the metaphor of a fundamental scission in time.

'There's a long goodbye and it happens every day'

The Long Goodbye updates Raymond Chandler's 1953 novel of the same name to the contemporary Los Angeles of 1973.[7] Against a suggestive backdrop of hippie burnout and sociopolitical degeneration, Philip Marlowe is a man much more adrift than any protagonist of classic noir. The film's detective plot centres on Marlowe's best friend, Terry Lennox (Jim Bouton), who arrives at Marlowe's apartment in the middle of the night, asking to be driven immediately to Tijuana. Marlowe duly obliges. It will later emerge, however, that Lennox's wife, Sylvia, has been brutally murdered this same night. Just a few days later, Lennox, too, turns up dead. The latter, it transpires, has committed suicide in a Mexican village, having left behind him a confession to his wife's murder. As Marlowe attempts to figure out what 'really happened' to his friend, he encounters an unhinged gangster Marty Augustine (Mark Rydell) and becomes embroiled, also, in the lives of the alluring Rebecca Wade (Nina van Pallandt) and her gruff, alcoholic writer husband Roger (Sterling Hayden). The Wades live in a beachside home nearby the Lennox's former residence. Roger, we discover, is prone to dipsomaniacal episodes of rage and violence; he eventually drowns one night after wading into the ocean in a fit of drunken, suicidal abandon. In the moments after his death, Rebecca then leads the befuddled Marlowe to believe that it was, in fact, her husband who killed Sylvia Lennox.

At this point, however, Marlowe deduces that something entirely different has been going on all along. He goes to Mexico and discovers that Terry Lennox had bribed authorities there to falsely document his death. The detective promptly tracks down his old friend in the courtyard of his idyllic retreat, where Lennox lazes in a hammock. Diffident and unrepentant, Lennox tries to cajole Marlowe into overlooking his deceit and overlooking, too, the hideous murder of his wife. But Marlowe is intent on justice. In a manner that utterly confounds audience expectation, the detective suddenly pulls out a gun and clinically executes Lennox. Spitting contemptuously on the ground, he then walks away from the scene, ignoring the arrival of Lennox's co-conspirator, Rebecca Wade, who drives past him in her jeep, anxiety deepening on her face.

The film concludes with a long shot of Marlowe as he gradually disappears from view on the horizon. Significantly, despite the brutality of the act he has just carried out, a range of quirky visual and audio markers underline his strange ease and contentment with the outcome; Marlowe plays a tune on a harmonica and performs an impromptu dance step with an elderly Mexican woman. As if this conclusion were not strange enough, meanwhile, Altman further stifles conventional narrative pleasure via the satiric eruption of 'Hooray for Hollywood' on the soundtrack. The latter draws attention to the film's status as representation, of course, and queries the satisfying (if shocking) narrative 'resolution' of Marlowe's action, while underlining, too, the film's own complicity with mass media and pop culture.

'Nobody cares but me'

The Long Goodbye has gained significant analysis over the years. Generally, the film is understood as both a quirky satire of noir narrative and a subversion of Hollywood and the American culture it subtends.[8] While Altman's film certainly undertakes both objectives, it is a gross error to regard its relation to film noir as simply one of satire or subversion. Robert Kolker is correct in acknowledging that, if the film is a parody, it is 'a deeply felt, intellectually and emotionally rigorous' one.⁹ Though many commentators see Elliott Gould's Marlowe as a straightforward caricature of this prototypical noir hero, Altman himself always regarded Gould's depiction of Marlowe as being much closer in spirit to Chandler's creation than the famous classic-era versions by Humphrey Bogart, Robert Montgomery and Dick Powell.[10] Certainly, Gould imbues the character with a distinctive languor and jadedness that – while consistent with the literary Marlowe's outsider status – *seems* antithetical to the character's irrepressible sense of agency. Yet the pursuit of truth and justice by Gould's Marlowe is in its own way no less relentless; it is his definitive characteristic throughout the film. Moreover, Marlowe's outward detachment and pronounced weariness is, in fact, extremely deceptive; throughout the film, Marlowe is – like the restive camera itself – ever so nonchalantly in a condition of flow: always quietly probing, always shape-shifting. He is a model of transparency and yet, by virtue of the very blankness that this transparency conjures, he is also a figure that persistently eludes us. As such, Kolker's assessment that Marlowe at the film's end remains little more than 'a jerk, still unconnected to his world' is far too short-sighted.[11] Gould's Marlowe is, in fact, deeply connected to his world. It's what forges in him his compulsion towards justice – a compulsion, moreover, that has taken him *outside* the confines of the law.

If he is disconnected from anything, it is from his culture – the morass of apathy, banal zeitgeist spirituality, deranged violence, therapeutic quackery and socio-juridical breakdown that threatens to engulf him. The film's vision of Los Angeles captures what Garrett Stewart has wryly described as 'a society suffering from terminal modernity'.[12] We might observe, in addition, that this is a society which – in hock to the invasive oversight of the modern State, the vagaries of a rampant capitalism, and the oppressive pseudo-liberating ideologies tethered to each – too thoroughly circumscribes the possibilities for living native to any individual's affective constituency (*potentia*). Thus, Marlowe's memorable catchphrase, 'It's okay with me' – which, like so much of Gould's dialogue in the film, is merely mumbled forlornly at the world – is an indication not of lethargic complacence but rather of a resigned adjustment to a time and a culture that is wholly dysfunctional. Moreover, the underlying narrative intrigue in *The Long Goodbye* resides in Marlowe's inability to make this adjustment complete. The truth is *it's not okay with him*. The time is 'out of joint' and Marlowe feels a supreme weight upon him to make it right. In this, he could not be closer to Chandler's original character. At the climax, and in marked contrast to his mantra, he responds to his treacherous friend's grim evasion of responsibility ('What the hell? Nobody cares!') with the pained, resilient retort, 'Yeah, nobody cares but me', before shooting him dead.

The shocking nature of this final sequence can only be understood when placed in conjunction with the film's opening.

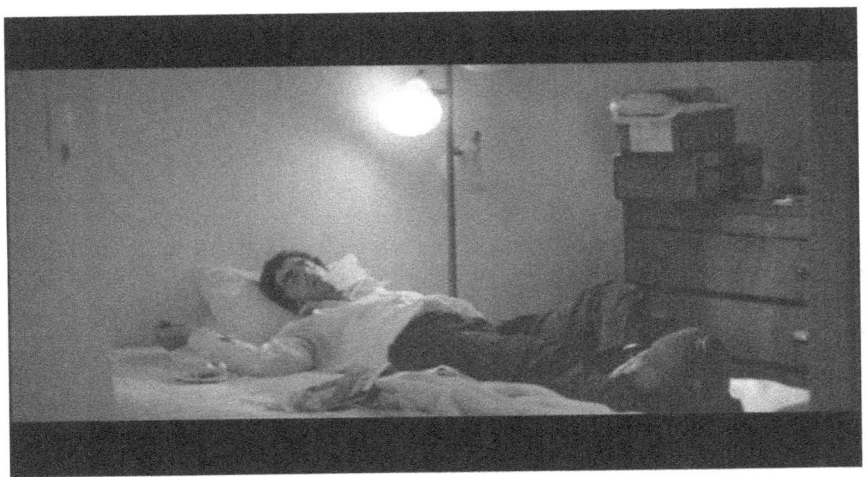

FIGURE 26 *Opening shot of Marlowe (Elliott Gould) in* The Long Goodbye.

In the opening shot of *The Long Goodbye* the camera pans through the interior of Marlowe's apartment before locating the detective fast asleep on his dishevelled bed. Obviously, the image is continuous with that iconographic tableau we identified at the beginning of this study, whereby the opening shot in noir so often frames the protagonist in a condition of recumbent repose. In this specific instance, as Marlowe is asleep, the shot may not be immediately connotative of *acedic* absorption, but his posture certainly carries overtones of drift and withdrawal (Figure 26).

Marlowe lies there, fully clothed, his shoes still on. Incongruously, he is soundly asleep despite the fact that there is a searing hot lamp shining starkly above his head. Nevertheless, Marlowe's sleep, it will transpire, is a sound one: the sleep of a righteous man. And in the narrative that develops, and against the dismal snapshot of 1970s America that emerges, Marlowe will gradually be revealed as a rare (if problematic) agent of righteousness.

Altman's satiric drive asserts itself at the very outset of the film when Marlowe's sleep is promptly broken by, of all things, the attention of his pet cat. Marlowe sits up, looks at his wristwatch and intones drowsily, 'Oh, right, yeah.' It's as if the cat wakes him in order to instigate the 'time of the narrative', to self-consciously rehearse the myth or 'legend' of noir dynamics, just as Godard's *Alphaville* had done before it. And, if so, Marlowe's weary, vague response to his watch reveals his profound disinterest in doing so. But just the same, the cat – like the audience – demands to be fed. Rousing himself from his slumber, Marlowe spends the opening ten minutes of the film trying, dismally, to satisfy the animal's cravings, a mission that even takes him on an early-hours-of-the-morning excursion to the supermarket.

Notably, this mission ends with failure, the cat refusing to eat any cat food other than his preferred brand, despite Marlowe's last-ditch ruse of swapping the brand labels. The sequence provides novelty and self-reflexive comedy, of course. Like Marlowe's cat, the audience is also soon to realize that this mumbling, shabby Marlowe is not the preferred noir brand (which is to say, he is not Humphrey Bogart).

But the cat sequence also fulfils certain narrative functions, the chief of which is to reveal character. Marlowe, we gather, is a loner, a man who – when not talking absently to his cat – mutters absently to himself. The latter impression, when wedded to the opening shot of him asleep, as well as to the shots of his alienating environment – the coterie of wasted, meditating hippie-chicks who live beside him, the supermarket that resembles a profane cathedral of mass consumption – all point to Marlowe being a man 'out of time'. Indeed, Altman's nickname for the character was Rip Van Marlowe.[13] In effect, Marlowe is – to use Chris Darke's term – a 'revenant', someone who has come back from the dead, or, at any rate, from a 'dead time': the noir milieu of 1940s and 1950s cinema. In this regard, as Darke notes, he is peculiarly resonant with Lemmy Caution in Godard's *Alphaville* and Walker in John Boorman's modernist noir *Point Blank* (1967).[14] In making this connection, Darke follows Larry Gross who had earlier noted the correspondence between the three characters, each of whom, in his view, exists solely as a 'formal anachronism': that is, the anachronism of the noir hero relocated to an alien time and space.[15] Thus, says Gross, a sense of 'temporal discontinuity' is the overriding principle that defines these characters:

> Linguistically, behaviourally, and in terms of the gratuitous and excessive principle of violence they unleash, they are always seen in terms of their temporal uprootedness. This uprootedness has about it no psychological interior. Space – not character – has become destiny. The existence of this special figural hero creates a collision between two incommensurable time-schemes, an environment stylised toward the future with a spurious notion of progress, and a figure oriented in equally formal terms to the past. The collision is between two kinds of emptiness.[16]

Gross's insights here are considerable. His attention to the principle of excessive violence, for instance, will have a resonance for us later in this chapter. Moreover, his attention to the disruptive temporal status of these protagonists underlines the way in which – replacing the figure of the dysfunctional timepiece in classic noir – the noir 'hero' is now invested with a similar metaphorical quality. They come to embody the schismatic temporality that the metaphor of the broken timepiece had originally alluded to. Nevertheless, I believe Gross fails to recognize the most pressing 'temporal discontinuity' that agitates these figures, and which agitates Marlowe and Caution, in particular. The temporal discontinuity these characters embody is ultimately not between an 'empty' past and an 'empty', alienating future.[17] The more insistent 'temporal discontinuity' that motivates these figures is between two inflections of 'the present'. Each protagonist is aligned to an intuition of the present that brims with potentiality, the present as *duration* or becoming, but this alertness to potentiality also brings them into conflict with their 'present-day' surroundings, a world that takes its own mundane 'presence' to be something concrete, stable, progressive and self-evident. Upon such illusory 'presence' there has been erected a far too rigid and systematic determination of 'the law' and its various mechanisms, many of which are corrupted by their implication in repressive ideologies. Because of his peculiar alertness to, and yet his paradoxical division from, his present moment, Marlowe in *The Long Goodbye* embodies an inexpiable and irreconcilable tension between order and disorder and between progress and regression. This is ultimately a tension that continuously troubles the very 'presence' upon which rests the presumed sovereignty of state power, its legal mechanisms and the culture it generates.[18]

With regard to the narrative ploy of the noir anachronism, we should also note, if only in passing, that the motif of the revenant or the 'man-out-of-time' emerges for the first time not in these self-reflexive modern noirs which treat their protagonists as 'formal anachronisms'. In fact, this narrative motif is already implicit in classic noir, as is clear from our earlier analysis of *The Unknown Man*. There, it is the disjunction between Masen's allegiance to 'the law' and his allegiance to justice that makes him a man 'out of time', a man-*become*-intervallic. Indeed, a great many classic noir protagonists occupy precisely this liminal status, an ejection from the 'common time' of everyday linear chronology, the most famous being Frank Bigelow in *D.O.A.* A veritable 'dead man walking', the fatally poisoned Bigelow – the clear predecessor to Walker in *Point Blank* – is explicitly a revenant: a living spectre seeking justice for his own murder.

At any rate, the key point to observe is that this spectral 'time outside of time' in noir's narratives of justice is only a further expression of 'the intervallic' as we have been pursuing it in this study. Indeed, Jacques Derrida, in an analysis of *Hamlet*, explicitly equates the figure of the revenant with 'the spectre' of justice and conceives the revenant, moreover, as a fundamentally *intervallic* figure. 'To be just', according to Derrida, is to be 'beyond the living present in general.'[19] Justice splits the present, splits *presence*, against itself in a 'spectral moment', 'a moment that no longer belongs to time', a moment that compels the human to be receptive to justice.[20] This spectral moment is, moreover, an affective moment, consistent with the force of madness that Derrida assigns to the instant when the Cartesian cogito presents itself: 'the instant of intuition, the instant of thought being attentive to itself',[21] a 'silent and specific moment [that] could be called *pathetic*.'[22]

In *Spectres of Marx* Derrida takes up the notion of jointure/disjointure that Martin Heidegger relates to justice in his essay 'The Anaximander Fragment'. Derrida suggests – *contra* Heidegger – that the human is not simply one who, when acting appropriately, uncovers a temporality of presence, a temporality of harmonious jointure. Instead, he insists, the fundamental experience of 'dis-jointure' is itself the great, unreckonable anomaly at the core of human existence, the spectral quality that splits presence from itself, infinitely deferring it. Our phantasmatic and pressing sense of the necessity of justice emerges precisely from our exposure to this disjointure. In a 'spectral moment' we are exposed to the other – as well as to those past others who have preceded us in time, and those yet to come. To be just, then, is not to produce a jointure in time but rather, in effect, to remain open to one's exposure to this fundamental, ineluctable and irredeemable experience of disjointure and to the urgency of a justice always 'to come'. Derrida coins the neologism 'hauntology' to underscore the way in which the condition of disjointure, and the justice it demands, always haunts our ontological status as beings. In other words, the spectre of justice, *the essential spectrality of justice*, is bound to the fundamental problem of ontology itself: the fact and manner of our existence. Ontology is always ghosted by a justice 'to come', by some impossible demand to account for our tenuous presence and its passing. Significantly, Derrida insists that it also necessitates that we account, too, for our being implicated in the presence and the passing of the other.[23]

If *The Long Goodbye* positions Marlowe as a revenant, then, we might perceive it to position him as 'a spectre of justice' in Derrida's sense. His agency, such as it is, belongs not to everyday time, the time of 'the law', but to a more elusive and urgent time still: the intervallic time ablaze with potentiality, whereupon an impulse towards justice *presents* itself. The film's narrative is really only a vehicle to stage a moment in which Marlowe's spectrality, his intervallic status and the profound allegiance to an extralegal justice it nurtures in him, is made evident. This is the moment that closes the film, of course; the moment when he executes Lennox. What determines Marlowe's action here is the fact that he is exposed to the full force of potentiality: that force which flares up in the dark interval.

It's vital to point out here that, like Chow in *2046*, Marlowe no longer experiences the rapture of the interval as an isolated event. As the film's opening imagery suggests, he has – like one of Gilles Deleuze's 'pure seers' of the time-image – already come to personify the interval such that his temporality, his being, his beleaguered existential condition is fundamentally and perpetually *intervallic*. Thus, though it is certainly a moment that Altman italicizes in the film, it is not the case that the moment when Marlowe discovers Lennox still alive is for him a particularly transformative one. Yes, it is ripe with a peculiar form of agency – an agency divested of any sense of self and located instead in a dissolution of self. But the key point to understand about Marlowe is that – as the opening image of his bed-bound detachment underlines – he is one who has already been irrevocably marked by such moments as this. As such, and on these terms, he has become an agent of the dark interval, the agent of the potentiality it discloses and of the acts of justice it may compel.

However, it's important to note that, concurrent with his intervallic status, and in spite of the force of potentiality that it has nursed in him, Marlowe has adopted an outer armour of world-weary detachment. This is the function of his personal mantra, 'It's okay with me', muttered archly and stoically in every situation, no matter how ludicrous, distressing or vicious. In this respect, Marlowe mutes somewhat the full force of the interval and its workings upon him. Like Chow – who commits himself to savouring the passion resident in the feeling of potentiality, the 'mood' of it, so to speak – Marlowe in *The Long Goodbye* seems content enough, too, to rest idiosyncratically within the melancholy confines of his own deep passion, while presenting to the world a playful solemnity. This is a significant break with the protagonist of Chandler's novels. In the novels, Marlowe's beleaguered code of honour pitches him always as a modern 'knight', and no matter how flawed or disillusioned he becomes, the literary Marlowe remains invested in a commitment to certain chivalric ideals.[24] The noir adaptations of the classic period all retain to varying degrees this sense of Marlowe as 'knight-errant'. Yet, in Altman's film, we might say that Marlowe has acquired properties of another knight altogether: Kierkegaard's 'knight of infinite resignation', to whom we alluded in the previous chapter.[25] The latter is a figure that Kierkegaard employs in *Fear and Trembling* to account for an adjustment to existence that is inherently elegiac, which is to say melancholic and solemn, and yet not without peace, wisdom, solace and contentment. Kierkegaard contrasts this condition with a further and final 'movement' of the spirit, that by which one would become a 'knight of faith'. For Kierkegaard the knight of infinite resignation is one who, renouncing the finite world and finitude, is alienated from his world, even while he continues profoundly to experience his exposure to this world. In a manner that resonates with Nietzsche's experience of eternal return, as well as Spinoza's viewpoint *sub specie aeternitatis*, the knight of infinite resignation steps ecstatically outside his own finitude and attains in that moment his 'eternal validity'. But for this hapless figure, the intuition of the 'infinite' leaves the finite world pointless, impossible and absurd; it divorces him thereafter from his own finitude, rather than joyfully bonding him to the world. By contrast, the knight of faith – exemplified by Abraham, who was willing to sacrifice his beloved son Isaac on God's instruction – makes the same 'infinite movement' as his counterpart, the knight of infinite resignation, but, in stepping ecstatically outside his own finitude, embraces the absurd and places his faith in the act, in the world and *in* his own finitude. His act, his sacrifice, is one that retains and renews a belief in the world, and it is for this reason, according to Kierkegaard, and later Deleuze, that Isaac/the world is ultimately restored to him.[26]

Though Kierkegaard (rather conservatively) estimates that there have been perhaps only two knights of faith in all of human history, we might risk describing Marlowe's trajectory in *The Long Goodbye* as an ascent from an intervallic disposition of infinite resignation to one of faith. His resolution to take vengeance on Terry Lennox, and to do so in contravention of both the law and the broader ethical frameworks of his community, aligns him with Abraham who 'has the passion to concentrate in one single point the whole of the ethical that he violates'.[27] Importantly, this act – an act of passion which reasserts the ethical even while dissolving it – is akin also to the 'extra-juridical' acts that Agamben reflects upon in *State of Exception*, those acts that respond to, and channel, an originary force-of-law; as Walter Benjamin had characterized them, acts of 'pure' or 'divine violence'.[28]

As Agamben points out, it is this ability to assume this force-of-law that founds and underwrites the sovereignty of state power and its legal mechanisms in the first place. Yet, paradoxically, this force-of-law, precisely because of its extra-juridical status, can also be claimed by the revolutionary (or revolutionary organization) that would revolt against state authority. Whether it is assumed by the state or by one in revolt, however, any assumption of the force-of-law is always an act that inaugurates a 'state of exception'. The latter, says Agamben, constitutes 'an anomic space in which what is at stake is a force of law without law'.[29] Marlowe's act at the finale of *The Long Goodbye* is an appropriation of just this force, one motivated by his compulsion towards justice. It is, moreover, conceivably a 'pure gesture' of revolt against the domineering and dysfunctional culture that he finds all around him. The police force and legal systems of both the United States and Mexico are depicted in *The Long Goodbye* as inherently corrupt, inept, slovenly and petty. As such, they are symptomatic of the breakdown of 'the law', its suspension, in the era of the modern state, whereby every citizen is subject only to an ever more invasive juridico-political authority, a 'biopolitical machine', as Agamben calls it. (This is a machine that acts in accordance not with law but with the originary force-of-law that is fundamentally extra-juridical: a system that acts, in other words, not under the sign of *nomos* [the law] but under the constant anomic authority of the 'state of exception'.) The grim reach of this biopolitical machine is demonstrated early in *The Long Goodbye* when two police officers jostle Marlowe around, falsely arrest him for assault and then are hypocritical enough to read him his 'rights' afterwards as they escort him to the police station. 'Yeah, I got a lot of rights,' says Marlowe, dryly. 'It's okay with me.' It is precisely because his rights 'under the law' are so traduced that Marlowe, in turn, refuses to adopt a stable identity before the police. In the interrogation room, he repeatedly deflects questions about his identity, calling himself first 'Sidney Jenkins' and then – after smearing finger-print ink all over his face – horses around at being first a quarterback, then Al Jolson. Marlowe's whole routine in this scene is designed to travesty the law's own perverse, insuperable and controlling logic of identity construction.[30]

This is, of course, what is at stake in Agamben's political philosophy – the impulse to query, disrupt and, indeed, halt the 'biopolitical machine' of the sovereign authority (in our case, the modern state): this machine which produces, politicizes and vigilantly marshals the 'bare life' of the human.[31] This is why, though it lasts hardly a minute, the scene in which Marlowe's cellmate, 'Socrates' (David Carradine), discusses his arrest is one of the most incisive scenes in *The Long Goodbye*. From what we can gather, Socrates has been arrested for driving while intoxicated, and there is a suggestion, too, that he may have been charged with possession of marijuana. So he is certainly in contravention of the law. (Indeed, Marlowe's demeanour of inattention during Socrates's story perhaps indicates condemnation on the detective's part.) Nevertheless, Socrates highlights something about prison that is significant to the film's critique of 'the law', and all the more so when we learn that, at this point, Marlowe himself has been detained for three days on a trumped-up charge. 'They don't have burglars and thieves in here anymore, you know, and rapists,' says Socrates. 'You know what they got in here now? They got people who smoke marijuana. "Possession" – "Possession" is what you get in here right now. "Possession" of, eh, noses. "Possession" of gonads. "Possession" of life.' Socrates' wry intuition here – that 'possession of life' is indeed deemed a crime – while droll and hyperbolic, captures a fundamental tenet of the film's depiction of the forces of the law. Moreover, it chimes precisely with Agamben's critique of the modern state's biopolitical control of human life. Alison Ross summarizes well the essential thrust of this critique:

> Like Foucault, Agamben thinks that modernity is characterised by an increasingly more radical tendency to take control of 'life'. For Agamben, the significance of this tendency can be measured against the distinction that classical political philosophy (Aristotle) maintains between *zoē*, bare or naked life, and *bios*, the life constituted in the *polis* ... [H]e wishes to foreground the dire consequences of the *zoē-bios* distinction for the life that is naked or bare, the latter understood in terms of its complete exposure to sovereign action.[32]

It is their mere living – the mere 'possession of life' – that exposes Marlowe and Socrates before the biopolitical machine of the law. That the law routinely abuses its power over life is thus inevitable, as human life is perpetually produced, detained by and controlled within, the model of the sovereign state itself. What is forfeited, or certainly compromised, as a result, is the potentiality that each singular existence 'possesses'. As Claire Colebrook has observed, in her own analysis of Agamben, 'what is lost in [the] increasing normalisation of biopolitics is the life that is neither human nor inhuman: the open potentiality from which the speaking, self-constituting human will emerge.'[33]

While it is without question a gesture that courts anarchy, Marlowe's own extra-juridical act at the film's close is a channelling of that potentiality, one that retrieves the force-of-law, Benjamin's 'pure violence' and re-grounds it in the human's experience of its own potentiality and the irresistible impulse towards justice that such an experience can condition. Though it represents a different articulation of it, the power of this gesture is also, in essence, the same power resident in Natacha's transformative awakening to self-affection in *Alphaville*. And, indeed, Marlowe's exertion of the 'force-of-law' ultimately summons for him a similar affective quality of 'beatitude' to that which Natacha experiences, one similar to the experience of beatitude that we have noted in the various articulations of the 'dark interval' that we have examined already.

In the film's closing image, after his summary dispatching of Terry Lennox, Marlowe walks away through an idyllic grove. As Rebecca Wade passes him in her jeep, the detective's features still exude contempt for Lennox's betrayal, and he ignores her presence entirely. But, unexpectedly, Marlowe's mood then lifts. As Wade speeds away, the detective pulls a miniature harmonica from his pocket and starts playing a breezy melody. We then cut to a long shot of Marlowe, his back to camera, receding from us as he ambles gaily down through the grove. Now the empty grove suddenly becomes peopled with anonymous strangers, who emerge from among the trees. Marlowe dallies with one of them, an old lady, with whom he performs a quick twirl. At this, his up-tempo harmonica is drowned out by the striking up of the title music, the same ironic blast of 'Hooray for Hollywood' that had opened the film. It calls attention to the film's status as representation, of course, but it in no way diminishes Marlowe's sudden expression of joy. As the tune plays on, Marlowe's ever-receding figure now seems to have become a vehicle for communicating only the vibrancy of life itself. He kicks out a foot-shuffle and repeatedly claps his arms over his head, continuing in this expression of unbridled joy as he disappears from our view.

The key to understanding this strange closing imagery and the condition of serenity or beatitude that it appears to imbue upon Marlowe is to be found in the sequence prior to the detective's hunting down of Lennox. This is a short sequence set in a hospital room where Marlowe, having been knocked down by a car, awakens to find himself sharing a ward with another patient, a man attired entirely in bandages (Figure 27).

As Marlowe prepares to abscond from the room, he makes his customary wisecracks to this other patient, deadpanning that he has seen all his films. The reference is likely to *The Mummy* pictures of the 1930s and 1940s, and that's certainly how most commentators read it.[34] Moreover, the mummy image certainly fits in with the theme of the 'revenant' that the film elsewhere

FIGURE 27 *Marlowe's strange exchange with a bandaged man, an impersonal figure of life*. The Long Goodbye.

elicits. William Luhr identifies another possible meta-cinematic reference here, too, however: a nod to *The Invisible Man* films.[35] And this, too, is a useful observation, given its invocation – similar to 'the mummy' – of a liminal condition of human life and identity. In any event, this other patient, evidently in discomfort, calls Marlowe over to him and entrusts a miniature harmonica to him.

As Jonathan Rosenbaum has noted, in light of the role that this harmonica comes to play in the film's enigmatic closing sequence, Marlowe's adoption of it here is a 'cryptic' one, not the least because Marlowe is hereafter doubled with this other man.[36] (As he exits the room he even tells a nurse: 'I'm not Mr. Marlowe, this is Mr. Marlowe here.') Of course, what the bandaged man ultimately signifies – both as a mummy that refuses to die and as a cipher for an 'invisible' form of life (a cipher for '*a* life', as Deleuze might say) – is life itself, bare life and the potentiality it shelters. This is the same elemental life, 'pure immanence', which, as the jailbird Socrates notes, is deemed a threat by 'the law'. And, at the close, it is this expression of an impersonal life, a *man who is not there*, potentiality, that Marlowe remains in supreme and sole allegiance with. (Moreover, it is *a life* which Lennox – in beating his wife to death and in staging his own death – has, in Marlowe's view, demeaned and diminished.) As an extra-juridical act, Marlowe's execution of Lennox thus occurs as a gesture of 'pure violence' in Benjamin's terms. This is a violent act which, as Agamben parses it, determines violence as a 'pure medium' that expresses only itself, that is, the human's own mediality, its being-in-language, or what we might regard as the human's potentiality:

> Pure language is that which is not an instrument for the purpose of communication, but communicates itself immediately, that is, a pure and simple communicability; likewise, pure violence is that which does not stand in a relation of means toward an end, but holds itself in relation to its own mediality ... so pure violence is attested to only as the exposure and deposition of the relation between violence and law ... pure violence exposes and severs the nexus between law and violence and can thus appear in the end not as violence that governs and executes ... but as violence that purely acts and manifests.[37]

Marlowe's execution of Lennox is an impulsive appropriation of just such a 'pure violence'. What it communicates, however bleakly, is Marlowe's extreme exposure to life *itself*, his exposure to potentiality.[38] In this, the violent act, as a moment of pure mediality that arises from an irrepressible intuition of injustice, is equivocal to his eccentric performance of mediality in the final frame as he skips away out of view, joyously playing the harmonica and dancing. Helene Keyssar spies something similar at work in this scene. Rejecting readings that would perceive Marlowe's violent act as one of 'callousness', she insists that the conclusion conveys only Marlowe's inherent 'dignity', and for her the harmonica is the emblem of this dignity. Noting that it is 'a gift from a fellow-sufferer', she suggests that the harmonica 'declares his survival and reminds us that [despite the film's grim narrative] gestures of human relationship are not entirely obliterated'.[39] Though she may not couch it in such terms, Keyssar effectively recognizes here, in the encounter between the bandaged man and Marlowe, a gesture which Agamben would call a 'pure' gesture – the gesture that exposes the human as itself only a medium for the pursuit of its own potential.

The impact of this pure gesture continues to resonate in Marlowe's impromptu dance with the Mexican lady and, indeed, informs his suffusion into the exalted community of anonymous humanity that the film closes on. Marlowe – who Lennox dismisses as a 'born loser' – accepts his fate: 'to lose' and, fundamentally, to *lose time*, to open himself to an intervallic temporality.[40] As a knight of faith he accepts his exposure to the enigmas of time, temporality and finitude. And he resolves to live in this world that may not be saved, yet which remains a place wherein a communication of 'pure language' – the human's status defined as pure being-in-language, as 'mediality' – nevertheless offers some redeeming light and might even foster some hope of an alternative community to that produced and marshalled by the biopolitical machine of state power and the law. In contrast to those contemporaneous 'pessimistic' noir films – *Chinatown*, *Night Moves*, *The Conversation* – with which it appears to share so much, *The Long Goodbye* finds power in the very frailty of life, power in our exposure and, in its final image, places a strange hope, a 'faith', in a community grounded only upon this communication of *a life* that is irredeemably exposed.

What is important about this is the alternative time of the community that it discloses – a time that I would once more characterize as 'intervallic', but which in contemporary thought is often called 'messianic' – and the conception of community that this time engenders. We will return to this in the final chapter. Before then I wish to reflect upon how, despite the articulation of a strange, bittersweet hope in the act of violence that closes *The Long Goodbye*, the overriding tendency in noir has been to stress the dangers of the anarchy that such an accession to the dark interval of potentiality involves.

At the close of *The Long Goodbye* we are far from those attempts to 'bridge' the disjunction between 'the law' and justice that recurs in classic noir. Where *The Unknown Man* attests to the force of the interval (to potentiality and the force-of-law) and depicts Masen's allegiance to justice above law, it nevertheless attempts to contain the force-of-law, its channelling of potentiality, and thus to limit the inherent critique of the law that the narrative's climax constitutes. In stark contrast to Masen's action in *The Unknown Man*, Marlowe's extra-juridical act at the close of *The Long Goodbye* is not diluted of its power. Its force shakes the ground from beneath us. It is a response to the potentiality of the interval that marks him, a potentiality that remains fundamentally anarchic and neutral.

It is vital that we acknowledge this underlying neutrality of the force-of-law or 'pure violence'. Certainly, Altman doesn't shy away from it in *The Long Goodbye*. One of Altman's major additions to Chandler's source material is a notorious scene in which pretentious gangster Marty Augustine smashes a Coke bottle across the face of his girlfriend (Jo Ann Brody), a gruesome act entirely unprovoked and excessively violent. Augustine commits this heinous act in a moment of deranged fury with Marlowe, in a meta-communicative exposure of his anger and power. 'That's someone I love,' he tells Marlowe. 'You, I don't even like.' Robert Kolker is correct in observing here an equivalence between Augustine's brutal act and Marlowe's later execution of Lennox, although his moralizing view that the two acts are equally 'repulsive' is misplaced.[41] The latter seems an entirely subjective judgement that takes no stock of Marlowe's compulsion towards justice as opposed to Augustine's seething psychosis. From a more objective standpoint, however, we should agree that the two acts – pure gestures of power, acts of 'pure violence' – while not 'equally repulsive', are certainly equally anarchic.

The fact is the force of the dark interval *is* anarchic. It sunders the ground (in Greek, the *arche*) of the law and deracinates the very reason and rationality (in Latin, the *ratio*) that human communities have historically valorized. (What is more, it is hardly a surprise that such principles are valorized, given the constant threat of such an anarchic force freely discharging itself.) In an earlier chapter we noted a notorious example of this intervallic moment of anarchic abandon, this expression of 'pure violence', as it occurs in the hideous hot coffee disfigurements of *The Big Heat*. A scene in a less well-known noir, *The Sound of Fury* (Dir. Cy Endfield, 1950) is notable for visually presenting the anarchic moment as a very literal 'giving way of ground'. The film's narrative centres on the criminal abduction and killing of a young man, the heir to a wealthy tycoon. One of the two killers is simply a man down on his luck, Howard Tyler (Frank Lovejoy), who stupidly falls in with a psychotic criminal, Jerry Slocum (Lloyd Bridges), and by the end, both men will pay a terrifying price. While the film is marked by a melancholy humanism that at times collapses into pithy moralizing, there remains an incredibly raw power in its pessimistic climax, which – in shocking scenes – depicts a community utterly disregarding the procedures of law and lynching the two murderers themselves.[42] This sequence, which commences with an unsettling mob assault on the prison, is a vivid one, but, in fact, the film's key moment – staging a first reckless irruption of anarchy – occurs earlier at an old gravel pit. The young man is to be robbed there, then left behind bound and gagged. However, the psychotic Slocum impulsively decides to kill his captive rather than risk being caught. And so, despite Tyler's protests, Slocum suddenly flings the victim into the pit, pursues him downhill and bludgeons him to death. Tyler looks on, helpless and dismayed.

What is significant is how the film relays visually the abyssal temporality of the anarchic moment. A low-angle long shot places the protagonists at the top of the frame, on the summit of the gravel pile. This framing accentuates the terrifying power of Slocum's psychosis, but it also permits the audience a penetrating visual of time itself becoming at once viscous and deranged. We observe the abducted man being rolled down the hill, and then the murderous Slocum following after him with malign intent. A moment later, Tyler follows too, emitting his anguished, futile protests. The two men descend the shifting stone surface beneath them in large, distorted steps, their feet enveloped in loose gravel and rising dust. The stones giving way beneath them shuffle downwards past the camera frame. It's a dramatic visual that captures perfectly the disruption of the ground, the *arche*, of the law, and it heralds a time that is suddenly rent apart and delirious. As if by contagion, this act – and the interval it prises open – then drives the whole community to anarchy as, fired up by sensational media reportage, an amorphous and vengeful mob invades the prison, overwhelms the forces of law and order, and finally lynches the two men. By the end, as James Naremore observes,

> Justice and civil order collapse utterly. The stunned newspaperman and the helpless police chief sit in an overturned office, listening all night to savage, carnivalistic whoops from a crowd in the distance.[43]

The stakes, then, in noir's treatment of this dark, anarchic interval which disturbs the ground of the law are complex and sensitive, relaying, as they do, the human's exposure to the shuddering force – for good and for ill – of potentiality. In this regard, Walter Neff's reference in *Double Indemnity* to his sudden inability to hear his own footsteps (a losing of ground) is just as apt an image as the disturbed rock of the gravel pit in *The Sound of Fury*. This 'losing of ground', as a metaphor for the rupture and possible collapse of the law, is in fact one of noir's most vivid signifiers. Among other things, it certainly informs what Edward Dimendberg has noted as noir's 'proclivity ... for urban topoi on the verge of destruction'.[44] And though I don't have time to pursue it here further, we might observe that this metaphor of groundlessness has informed a distinct tradition in noir, one whereby the dark interval is rendered spatially in the form of a conceptually 'blank' space, a terrain beyond the codifications of 'the law'. Key films in this tradition would include *The Naked City* (Dir. Jules Dassin, 1948), *On Dangerous Ground* (Dir. Nicholas Ray, 1951) and *The Hitch-Hiker* (Dir. Ida Lupino, 1953). In short, in noir, the ground giving way is a spatial metaphor complimenting the disorienting temporal force unleashed during iterations of the dark interval, particularly when the latter addresses a fundamental discrepancy between the system of law and some force of justice that exceeds its scope.

Notes

1. Indeed, references to time-keeping and temporality frequently inform the titles of noir films (e.g. *Johnny O'Clock* (Dir. Robert Rossen, 1947), *Time Table* (Dir. Mark Stevens, 1956)), or else explicitly motivate the narrative action as in *Panic in the Streets* (Dir. Elia Kazan, 1950). At other times a preponderant use of clock imagery underlines the theme of the temporal. The image of a clock, for instance, provides the opening images in *Johnny O'Clock*, *The Big Clock* (Dir. John Farrow, 1948) and *The Stranger* (Dir. Orson Welles, 1946). One of the most famous 'clock images' in noir is that of the closing frame of *Laura*: the image of a large clock that has been shattered by a gun blast. At the close of the narrative the accent on a 'broken time' invites an array of meanings. J. P. Telotte has attended to the significance of the object of the clock in both *Laura* and *The Big Clock*. See J. P. Telotte, 'The Big Clock of Film Noir', *Film Criticism*, 14.2 (1989–90), 1–11.
2. Telotte, 'The Big Clock of Film Noir', 5.
3. Jennifer Lynda Barker, *The Aesthetics of Antifascist Film: Radical Projection* (London: Routledge, 2013), 248.
4. The concepts of time and justice are inextricably implicated in one another in Western thinking. Indeed, they are two of the core concerns in the oldest surviving artefact of Western thought – the 'Anaximander Fragment'. The latter is a short segment of the philosophy of Anaximander (610–546 BC) which was quoted, and thereby salvaged for posterity, in the work of a later

writer, Simplicius. Nietzsche, Heidegger and Derrida have each, respectively, engaged with the Anaximander Fragment to pursue disquisitions on time and justice.

5   A distinction between profane time and sacred time is one that recurs in contemporary thought, informing the work of Mircea Eliade, Georges Bataille, Victor Turner, Rene Girard and Giorgio Agamben, among others. In *The Sacred and the Profane*, Eliade argues that primitive, religious men employed a concept of sacred time (e.g. times of religious festival) to re-engage with myths of social foundation. See Eliade, *The Sacred and the Profane*, trans. Willard R. Trask (New York: Harvest, 1968), 68–113. Articulating a similar idea, Girard stresses that what is re-enacted in the recursive temporality of sacrificial rites is a very specific foundational myth – that of an originary act of violence (scapegoating) upon which the community and the law has been constituted: 'The rite is therefore a repetition of the original, spontaneous "lynching" that restored order in the community by re-establishing, around the figure of the surrogate victim, that sentiment of social accord that had been destroyed in the onslaught of reciprocal violence.' Rene Girard, *Violence and the Sacred*, trans. Patrick Gregory (London: Continuum, 2005), 100. Turner's influential conception of liminality as a temporal state is outlined in the chapter 'Liminality and Communitas', in *The Ritual Process: Structure and Anti-Structure* (Chicago: Aldine, 1969), 94–130. Notably, R. Barton Palmer has applied Turner's concept of liminality to noir. See 'The Divided Self and the Dark City: Film Noir and Liminality', *symploke*, 15.1–2 (2007), 66–79.

6   We should note that *Act of Violence* (Dir. Fred Zinnemann, 1948) produces a similar narrative outcome, with the poetic justice of a man, Frank Enley (Van Heflin), sacrificing himself in retribution for a past transgression.

7   The script was written by Leigh Brackett, who – alongside William Faulkner and Jules Furthman – had adapted Chandler's *The Big Sleep* for the famous 1946 version by Howard Hawks. Brackett's ending, in which Philip Marlowe executes his corrupt friend Terry Lennox, departs entirely from Chandler's original, and it was this intervention, Brackett's revised ending, that convinced Robert Altman to direct the film:

> I said, 'I'll do the picture, but you cannot change that ending! It must be in the contract' … If she hadn't written that ending, I guarantee I wouldn't have done it. It said, 'This is just a movie'. After that, we had him do his funny little dance down the road and you hear 'Hooray for Hollywood', and that's what it's really about – 'Hooray for Hollywood'.

See *Altman on Altman*, ed. David Thompson (London: Faber and Faber, 2006), 75.

8   Naremore, for instance, says the film 'subjects the Chandleresque detective film to offbeat casting and a certain amount of derisive parody, all the while making Brechtian jokes about Hollywood.' *More Than Night*, 203.

9   Robert Kolker, *A Cinema of Loneliness* (Oxford: Oxford University Press, 2011), 398.

10 Altman later reflected: 'Everyone said Elliott's not Philip Marlowe and I wasn't being true to the author, but what they really were saying was that Elliott Gould wasn't Humphrey Bogart. In fact, I believe we were closer to Chandler's character than any of the other renditions, where they made him a kind of movie superhero.' *Altman on Altman*, 81.

11 Kolker, *A Cinema of Loneliness*, 397.

12 Garrett Stewart, 'The Long Goodbye from Chinatown', *Film Quarterly*, 28.2 (1974), 26–7.

13 Altman:

> I decided we were going to call him Rip Van Marlowe, as if he'd been asleep for twenty years, had woken up and was wandering through this landscape of the early 1970s but trying to invoke the morals of a previous era … So we just satirised the whole time. And that's why that line of Elliott's – 'It's OK with me' – became his key line throughout the film.

See *Altman on Altman*, 76. We should not overlook Marlowe's response to the cop in the interrogation scene when asked where he is from. 'I'm from a long time ago,' says the detective drolly.

14 At the time of *Alphaville*'s release, Godard described Caution as 'a man from twenty years ago who discovers the world today and can't believe it'. Quoted in Darke, *Alphaville*, 27. In *Point Blank*, meanwhile, Walker's surreal back-from-the-dead revenge narrative is famously revealed to be nothing other than the fantastical fever-dream of a man on the point of quietus.

15 Larry Gross, 'Film Après Noir', *Film Comment*, 12.2 (1976), 44.

16 Ibid., 45.

17 Though, in the case of both *Alphaville* and *The Long Goodbye*, the films' directors certainly play with this juxtaposition.

18 The idea that Marlowe is peculiarly attuned to his present moment is one that is supported by the title for its long mooted sequel, *It's Always Now*, for which Alan Rudolph, assistant director on *The Long Goodbye*, has written the script. See James Mottram, 'Elliott Gould: I didn't have a drug problem. I had a problem with reality'. *The Independent*, 22 July 2012.

19 Jacques Derrida, *Spectres of Marx: The State of the Debt, the Work of Mourning, and the New International*, trans. Peggy Kamuf (London: Routledge, 2006), xix.

20 Ibid.

21 Jacques Derrida, 'Cogito and the History of Madness', in Jacques Derrida, *Writing and Difference*, trans. and intro. Alan Bass (London: Routledge, 2005), 70.

22 Ibid., 72.

23 See Derrida, *Spectres of Marx*, 20–56.

24 Chandler invokes imagery of the chivalric knight repeatedly in the Marlowe books. The metaphor is established in the opening pages of *The Big Sleep*, the first Marlowe novel, wherein the detective reflects upon the picture of a knight

in a stained-glass window, ultimately aligning himself with it. See Raymond Chandler, *The Big Sleep* (London: Penguin, 2005), 1.

25 It should be noted that this resignation is not entirely out of step with Chandler's use of the knight imagery. In the novels Marlowe's modest knightly conceits are always diluted by consciousness of his falling short of the mark. For instance, in *The High Window* he is described as little more than 'a shop-soiled Galahad'. See Chandler, *The High Window* (London: Penguin, 2005), 214. In *The Big Sleep*, meanwhile, the image of the knight is ambiguous. Marlowe identifies himself with the knight in the stained-glass window, yet later – while meditating on a chessboard – he interrogates the knight image once more and this time pronounces it to be an irrelevant one, making the loaded remark, 'Knights had no meaning in this game. It wasn't a game for knights'. See *The Big Sleep*, 170.

26 See Kierkegaard, *Fear and Trembling*, especially 34–53. Also, see note 51 in the previous chapter.

27 Kierkegaard, *Fear and Trembling*, 78.

28 Agamben, *State of Exception*, trans. Kevin Attell (Chicago: University of Chicago Press, 2005), 52–64.

29 Ibid., 39.

30 References to the unreliability of identity recur in the film. Terry Lennox, we learn, was originally Lenny Potts, before trading that name in for a 'fancier' one. Roger Wade, too, traffics under an assumed name, his publishers having advised him that 'Billy-Joe Smith lacked something for the kind of book he writes'. Meanwhile, the pressure exerted on identity by popular culture – and especially by Hollywood – is epitomized by the security guard at the entrance to the Wades' home who impersonates Barbara Stanwyck (in *Double Indemnity*), Jimmy Stewart and Cary Grant. As I later note, Marlowe himself even suggestively trades identities with a bandaged man in his hospital room at the end of the film.

31 Agamben develops his influential concept of 'bare life' in *Homo Sacer: Sovereign Power and Bare Life*, wherein he explains how the production of 'biopolitical' life is the self-founding act of sovereign power. The sovereign is ultimately that entity which assumes control over biopolitical life. The biopolitical 'citizen' constituted by sovereign power is vulnerable at all times to an extreme force of juridico-political 'abandonment', one which reduces him or her to the status of 'bare life'. It is this power to decide what – or, rather, who – constitutes 'bare life' which is the defining structural act of sovereignty itself. Agamben's paradigm for this 'bare life', cast out from the shelter of the law and left utterly exposed, is the *homo sacer*, a figure from Roman law who, as an outcast, could be killed without legal consequence but could not be sacrificed in communal rites. Ominously, in the era of the modern state – when, as Agamben claims, the 'state of exception' which dissolves the law has become 'the rule' – 'all citizens can be said, in a specific but extremely real sense, to appear virtually as *hominess sacri*'. Giorgio Agamben, *Homo Sacer: Sovereign Power and Bare Life*, trans. Daniel Heller-Roazen (Stanford, CA: Stanford University Press, 1998), 111.

32 Alison Ross, 'Introduction', *Agamben Effect*, *South Atlantic Quarterly*, 107.1 (2008), 2.
33 Claire Colebrook, 'Aesthetics, Potentiality, and Life', *Agamben Effect*, *South Atlantic Quarterly*, 107.1 (2008), 11.
34 See Kolker, *A Cinema of Loneliness*, 396; Jonathan Rosenbaum, *Essential Cinema: On the Necessity of Film Canons* (Baltimore, MD: John Hopkins University Press, 2008), 91; Helene Keyssar, *Robert Altman's America* (Oxford: Oxford University Press, 1991), 108.
35 William Luhr, *Film Noir* (London: Wiley-Blackwell, 2012), 161.
36 Rosenbaum, *Essential Cinema*, 91.
37 Agamben, *State of Exception*, 62.
38 It might also be considered the articulation of an ethics, in Agamben terms. 'Ethics begins only when the good is revealed to consist in nothing other than a grasping of evil and when the authentic and the proper have no other content than the inauthentic and the improper.' Agamben, *The Coming Community*, 13.
39 Keyssar, *Robert Altman's America*, 107–8.
40 Marlowe's disappearance at the climax is intriguing. Of the myriad modes of becoming that Deleuze and Guattari address in *A Thousand Plateaus*, 'becoming-imperceptible' is described as the ultimate mode, 'the immanent end of becoming', to which all becomings rush. In developing this concept, Deleuze and Guattari notably invoke the Kierkegaardian figure of the 'knight of faith', who they regard as the very 'man of becoming'. In effect, this man of becoming is one who – having been exposed to the beatitude of 'a life' – accedes to the plane of immanence (the plane of faith) and inherits all of the finite. In so doing, the knight of faith is one who 'becomes imperceptible'. This *becoming-imperceptible* means in the end 'to be like everybody else'. 'To go unnoticed is by no means easy,' insist Deleuze and Guattari. 'If it is so difficult to be "like" everybody else, it is because it is an affair of becoming. Not everybody becomes everybody.' See *A Thousand Plateaus*, 279.
41 Kolker, *A Cinema of Loneliness*, 396.
42 The film, widely released at the time under an alternate title, *Come and Get Me!*, is based on a factual event in 1933 when the suspects of the murder of a young man in San Jose, California, were lynched by a mob. The proto-noir *Fury* (Dir. Fritz Lang, 1936) is also based on this real-life case. Borde and Chaumeton identify the scene in *The Sound of Fury* where a prison is assaulted by a mob as 'one of the most brutal sequences in postwar American cinema'. *A Panorama of American Film Noir*, 118.
43 Naremore, *More Than Night*, 127.
44 Edward Dimendberg, *Film Noir and the Spaces of Modernity* (London: Harvard University Press, 2004), 64.

7

Missing Persons and Deadbeats: 'Abiding' in the Dark Interval

The closing imagery of *The Long Goodbye* brought us to an end that is commonly staged in modern noir: an end that is not an end, an end that is intervallic.[1] And it brings a question into view: How does noir end? How does this cinema so steeped in an aesthetics of the intervallic *end*? This final chapter responds to that question. I shall look at two distinctive 'ends' in the modern noir, those of *The Missing Person* and *The Big Lebowski*, and reflect upon the way that they mobilize the themes that I have been examining throughout this study – themes of the intervallic, of the potentiality (*potentia*) it exposes and of related imagery of passivity, passion and affect in noir.

The ends of noir

The endings of noir films – like their openings – are far too heterogeneous to be accounted for under a single overarching formula. We can note, of course, that – despite the general impression of noir as a pessimistic 'genre' – many classic noirs actually end 'happily', with the resolution of the narrative 'problem' and the guy getting the girl. Needless to say, we can also note the converse: that a great many noirs culminate in the death or destruction of the film's protagonist(s), the narrative problem left unresolved or only vaguely resolved, and with the guy annihilating the girl, and the girl doing likewise. Notably, in the latter case, this fatal outcome is frequently qualified by a sense that these dead or destroyed characters are nevertheless somehow redeemed by virtue of the passion that they have borne, no matter how detrimental this passion may have been. In short, the film's viewers are left with the insight that these lives were not merely the sum of narrative events but that they bore a singular being quite in excess of such narrativization. That insight is certainly one of the endings of noir, then: one of the ways that it 'ends' – with this sense of what we might call 'the supremacy of passion'. Indeed, it is on such terms that passion and 'noir' are inextricably bound together. That is to say that noir deals with this quality of the singular individual, Derrida's 'secret passion', this quality that eludes any ultimate determination and which eludes narrative identity. This is also to say that, if noir deals with anything, it deals with 'missing persons'. Noir is, effectively, a cinema of missing persons. Exposing the *missingness* of these persons – this is one of the 'ends' to which noir is driven. Perhaps it is even its most proper 'end'.

This essential missingness, I would suggest, imbues noir with a sensibility that is inherently 'fugal'. This term, 'fugue', denotes a basic sensibility of flight – of fleeing, of the fugitive – that we so often encounter in noir. But it also puts us in mind of a psychological condition, the 'fugue state' – a disorder of the mind in which a person suddenly, if only briefly, departs themselves, adopting another identity entirely.[2] The term 'fugue' also summons rich musical associations, of course. The compositional structure of a fugue relies on multiple recurrences of the same theme but also on the 'response' of a counterpoint. As we observed in the previous chapter, the constant parrying of the law-abiding citizen, the biopolitical subject, against a contrapuntal element that one might describe simply as the condition of its own 'passion' clearly produces a fugal sensibility in many noir films.

Certainly, a conception of noir narratives as inherently 'fugal' resonates especially well with those films in which the protagonist is tasked with tracking down a fugitive that they already know, or later discover, to be none other than themselves. The latter motif – the man charged with pursuing himself – is central to the narratives of *The Unknown Man*, *Black Angel*, *Where the Sidewalk Ends*, *The File on Thelma Jordan*, *The Big Clock* and *Somewhere in the Night*, among others. In the era of the modern noir, meanwhile, it is taken up, often with playful or subversive variations, by films such as *Angel Heart* (Dir. Alan Parker, 1987), *Lost Highway*, *Memento*, *The Departed* (Dir. Martin Scorsese, 2006), *A Scanner Darkly* and *Shutter Island* (Dir. Martin Scorsese, 2010).

This essential missingness has become such a self-conscious feature of the modern noir that the film titles often explicitly allude to it, as is the case in *The Man Who Wasn't There*, *The Missing Person* (Dir. Noah Buschel, 2010) and *You Were Never Really Here* (Dir. Lynne Ramsay, 2018). Notably, these films treat this missingness, this intangible or attenuated quality of presence poised on the brink of absence, not merely as a narrative ploy but as the film's core philosophical intrigue.

The missing person and the condition of 'being missing'

Although it is a less accomplished film than *The Man Who Wasn't There*, *The Missing Person* nevertheless is notable for the way in which it invokes the intervallic as the decisive condition of a certain noir protagonist. The film's narrative is set almost a decade on from the 9/11 attacks on the World Trade Centre, and its protagonist, John Rosow (Michael Shannon), is a former NYPD officer who now works as a private detective in Chicago. As the narrative progresses we gradually learn that Rosow's wife was killed in the World Trade Centre and that, in the wake of this disaster, his relocation to Chicago marks a melancholy withdrawal from his 'past life'. He is another of noir's revenants, then, living on after he has already died. Recalling Gould's Marlowe, Rosow's revenant status is denoted by his anachronistic suit and tie. But Rosow goes further, adopting even the archaic patois of the hard-boiled detective, in an attempt to remove himself from his world, to retreat beneath the shelter of an assumed noir persona, an identity (or *non-identity* even) associated, contrarily, with both resilience and resignation.[3]

As mentioned in the first chapter, the opening of *The Missing Person* clearly mobilizes the noir iconography of the dark interval, introducing us to Rosow as he lies in bed in an austere room, lost in a strange extra-temporal torpor (Figure 3).

His physical presence throughout the film, meanwhile, is similarly marked as intervallic. Like Mitchum, Lancaster and Dana Andrews in their languid, lumbering stillness, Shannon pushes his body slowly through each frame, his noir persona engulfed in an aura of dense passivity. 'You have a sad disposition', an FBI agent tells him. '"Sit still and let 'em examine you", that's what I always say,' Rosow replies dryly. His droll response at once attests to his unavoidable exposure before the law and yet to his spirit of non-compliance: his disregard for, or resistance to, the law. Indeed, the law in *The Missing Person* is depicted as unreliable and corrupt, with Rosow eventually finding himself double-crossed both by the lawyer who hires him and his old friend in the NYPD.

The film's noir narrative is itself clever, if somewhat conventional, its 'noirisms' at times a little tiresome. Rosow is hired to track down a man who, having survived the World Trade Centre attacks, has allowed everyone to believe he is dead rather than return to his old life. Rosow's ethical dilemma is whether or not to bring this 'missing person' back to his grieving wife in New York. The narrative, however, is only a platform for a character study of Rosow, this man who – in the wake of a traumatic loss – has become *intervallic*. Notably, the detective is rendered as a typically impotent noir figure, caught up in machinations beyond his control, and yet nevertheless a figure attuned, too, to a redemptive potentiality. The latter is captured in a number of sequences in the film but most evocatively in a scene where Rosow sneaks into the trunk of a taxi cab in order to trail his target. The frame goes black for a prolonged interval and, on the audio track, a moody version of 'Pearl's Lullaby' from *Night of the Hunter* (Dir. Charles Laughton, 1955) strikes up.[4] The darkness is then suddenly punctured by the appearance of a pair of glow-in-the-dark sunglasses that Rosow has donned. In this way, all of a sudden, Rosow becomes only the very vaguest trace of human presence – at once melancholy and joyful – in the midst of all-consuming darkness (Figure 28).

As Massumi might describe Rosow's state of being during this scene, he is a 'body without an image' (akin to Deleuze and Félix Guattari's BwO, the body without organs),[5] merely a set of coordinates moving processually across a plane of immanence. Occupying 'a gap in space that is also a suspension of the normal unfolding of time,' Rosow enters – through processes of visceral sensitivity and proprioception – a passive state of 'utter receptivity', wherein his current 'actual' movement (in the dark of the car trunk) fuses with the 'virtual' movements of memory and anticipation ingrained in the singularity of his existence.[6] This is the very quintessence of an experience of the dark interval.

This lyrical and economic image notably approximates the characteristics of Deleuze's 'direct time-image', whereby, in 'a pure optical and sound situation',[7] there is relayed a 'direct presentation of time' itself: 'a little time in its pure state'.[8] The song here is important, too. In Laughton's famous Gothic noir, Pearl (Sally Jane Bruce) hums the lullaby to herself as she and

FIGURE 28 *Figuring the dark interval*. The Missing Person.

her little brother boat down a river at night in the midst of an eerie and ineffable natural landscape. In *Night of the Hunter*, then, the song is a 'refrain' in Deleuze and Guattari's sense, a shelter within which the hunted children take haven, and it becomes also a figure of transition: a rite of passage from innocence to experience. In *The Missing Person*, however, the scene testifies not simply to a quality of transition but to something similar and yet very different: Rosow's 'suspension' in the interval or *passage* of his own becoming. Rosow is stalled, perpetually in transit. And yet, while Rosow cannot move on from his loss, his intervallic suspension is not simply melancholic. The scene conveys also the strange joy he finds in this suspension, the sheer affective potential inherent in the 'passage' of a life's taking place.

Rosow will eventually come to realize that this bittersweet joy of intervallic suspension is also the experience of Harold Fullmer (Frank Wood), the man he is escorting back to his wife, against his wishes. (Fullmer – himself a revenant – is obviously Rosow's double.) When Rosow chides Fullmer that he 'can't just drop out' of the world, the fugitive – who spends his life now as an anonymous saviour of endangered children – replies,

> The life I lead now is the very contrary of dropping out. Most people can't wait to get home to their house, their apartment, shut the door and turn on the TV. To me that's dropping out. I never felt myself as a civilian. This kind of life, *being missing*, it suits me. It all changed so fast. One day I was one person, then came the explosions, and then I was another person.[9]

At the narrative's close Rosow ultimately decides to let Fullmer escape and to continue savouring this experience of 'being missing'. Significantly, his decision is prompted by a child's picture, a recreation of Edward Hopper's 1939 painting, *New York Movie* (Figure 29).

Hopper's painting captures an usherette in a condition of acedic arrest. Her hand clasping her head, she is oblivious to the cinema screen that compels the audience. We discover that Fullmer's young daughter – the victim of a botched kidnapping – had painted her recreation of the picture before her death. Rosow is incredibly moved by the image, and not without cause. Throughout the film he has been having enigmatic dreams about his dead wife, dreams in which she is depicted in a similar pose and in a similar setting to the usherette in Hopper's painting (Figure 30).

Thus, disturbed by this paranormal coincidence, he opts at the close to let Fullmer flee into his preferred state of 'being missing'.

Clearly, Hopper's image, in its two replications – the one by a girl who is dead, the other of a woman who is dead – is invoked as a cipher for a form of ontological suspension in life itself, for this fundamentally *acedic* condition of 'being missing' that the film depicts: Hopper's state of 'intermission'. The

FIGURE 29 *The child's replication of Hopper's painting* New York Movie *(1939) in* The Missing Person.

FIGURE 30 *The detective's dream also replicates Hopper's painting*. The Missing Person.

painting can thus be said to present an image of 'arrest' in the terms that Giorgio Agamben applies to Albrecht Dürer's *Melencolia I*. As we noted in the opening chapter, Agamben glimpses in the latter image 'an atemporal dimension, as though something, interrupting the continuum of history, had frozen the surrounding reality in a kind of messianic arrest'.[10]

Famously, the melancholic figure in Dürer's engraving is an angel and – intriguingly – *The Missing Person*, too, pointedly mobilizes Hopper's painting as an invocation of the angelic. The mistake here, however, would be to regard the usherette as 'the angel' in question, although it is perhaps even the mistake that Buschel himself makes. Rather, it is the painting that is the angel, just as it is Rosow's dream that is angelic. In human culture the angel and the image (imago) are abstractions that function identically.[11] They are 'mediators' of something with which the human comes into contact that is beyond its comprehension. But, at a more incipient level still, the angel – like the image – is emblematic of the human's auto-affective relation to itself. The angel is thus not solely a mediator between the eternal and the temporal but embodies the principle of affective mediation itself, just as the image is not simply a 'projection' or 'transmutation' of reality but a mediation of one's own affectivity. (This principle of affective mediation is precisely what Aby Warburg attempts to grapple with via his notion of the 'pathos formula'.) Of course, within the painting the usherette is also conferred with the status of 'angel' insomuch as her gesture of *acedic* self-absorption, that is, the hand holding the head in contemplation, is itself a pure gesture of mediation, of self-affection, of a life opening on to its own immanence, during an irruption of the 'dark interval'.

Rosow, we realize, has himself been ejected to this intervallic 'angelic' realm, in which he remains suspended. This accounts for his frustration with his detainee, Fullmer, when the latter at one point begins rambling about angels. 'Tomorrow morning you go back to her,' Rosow tells him. 'This is the old reality, Harold. You're in New York. You ain't dead. There aren't any "angels". And the missus wants to see you.' Fullmer, however, informs Rosow that he observed how deeply moved the detective was while listening to a jazz saxophonist play during their meal, and he concludes adroitly, 'You know about angels, Rosow.' At the film's climax, when the silhouetted Rosow, cigarette in hand, is framed against a city skyline at night (in an image that itself belongs to the iconography of the interval in noir), we understand that his intervallic condition can indeed be equated with the in-between ontological status and the strangely suspended temporality of the angelic (Figure 31).

This latter temporality, I would suggest, is not simply a time without time. Nor is it human progressive time or the perfect endlessness of eternity. Rather, following Frank Kermode, we can understand this time as the category of the 'sempiternal', a third intermediate order of temporal duration devised by St Thomas Aquinas to account for the 'peculiar betwixt-and-between position of angels'.[12] As Kermode notes, though supposedly exclusive to the angel order, this perplexing temporal category was gradually 'humanized', precisely because it served as a means of addressing a certain indeterminable aspect of human experience:

FIGURE 31 *Close of* The Missing Person: *the iconography of the dark interval.*

[The sempiternal] helped one to think about the sense men sometimes have of participating in some order of duration other than that of the *nunc movens* [progressive chronological time] – of being able, as it were, to do all that angels can. Such are those moments which Augustine calls the moments of the soul's attentiveness.[13]

Kermode employs this category of the sempiternal to address the temporality of characters in literary fiction, but he notes, in passing, that both Spinoza's concept of *duratio* and Henri Bergson's concept of *durée* appear to be direct appropriations of this temporal category.[14] For our purposes here, we can consider this temporality to be 'intervallic' – the quality of time that is disclosed in the 'dark interval'. The experience of acceding to the interval and the temporality it heralds is also, as we have seen, resonant with the experience that Bergson and Deleuze call *paramnesia*. And it is a temporality that is uniquely to the fore in film noir. Importantly, it is a temporality that also forges in the human a distinctive passivity.

Bearing this passivity in mind, and, in closing our analysis of *The Missing Person*, we should be attentive to the significance of the 9/11 attacks as the occasion of communal 'disaster'. As Kermode has noted, narratives of impending catastrophe and apocalypse have always been endemic to human culture.[15] One of the curiosities of the World Trade Centre attacks – as both Slavoj Žižek and Jean Baudrillard promptly observed – was that, for decades prior to its occurrence, cinema had been fantasizing about just such an event, or at least a catastrophe equivalent to it.[16] In *The Missing Person*, however, the disaster of 9/11 collides with another disaster – 'the disaster' of the interval, as Maurice Blanchot describes it. For Blanchot, this disaster – an epistemological and ontological disaster – is a fundamentally enigmatic experience, beyond simple affirmation or negation, involving an erasure of the possibility to respond to it and yet at the same time necessitating some response. Blanchot's meditations on this figure of 'the disaster' feature the French thinker at his most cryptic:

> The disaster is unknown; it is the unknown name for that in thought itself which dissuades us from thinking of it, leaving us, by its proximity, alone. Alone, and thus exposed to the thought of the disaster which disrupts solitude and overflows every variety of thought, as the intense, silent and disastrous affirmation of the outside.[17]

This is Blanchot's mercurial 'thought from outside', then: the same perversely 'affirmative' force of power/powerlessness with which Deleuze explicitly associates the time-image at its keenest.[18] Indeed, we will note here, in order to develop the motif very shortly, that Deleuze specifically identifies this irruptive force of the time-image, that is, the disaster, as arising in the 'postures' – what Agamben might call the 'pure gestures' – of the body, and specifically the weary, passive body:

> The body is never in the present, it contains the before and the after, tiredness and waiting. Tiredness and waiting, even despair are the attitudes of the body. No one has gone further than Antonioni in this direction. His method: the interior *through* behaviour, no longer experience, but 'what remains of past experiences', 'what comes afterwards, when everything has been said', such a method necessarily proceeds via the attitudes or postures of the body. This is a time-image, the series of time. The daily attitude is what puts the before and after into the body, time into the body, the body as a revealer of the deadline. The attitude of the body relates thought to time as to that outside which is infinitely further than the outside world. Perhaps tiredness is the first and last attitude, because it simultaneously contains the before and the after: what Blanchot says is also what Antonioni shows, *not* the drama of communication, but the immense tiredness of the body ... and which suggests to thought 'something to incommunicate', the 'unthought' life.[19]

Deleuze here may as well be describing the image of pronounced lassitude which, throughout this study, I have been associating with a certain noir protagonist – the protagonist exposed to the 'dark interval'. It is these bodily gestures of 'immense tiredness', this tiredness that incommunicates the 'unthought' life of the affective body, its passivity and its passion, that Shannon's performance in *The Missing Person* – just like that of Billy Bob Thornton's in *The Man Who Wasn't There* – invokes in the name of noir. This is a passivity that is not the spurious opposite of activity, but which, rejecting such a reductive binary schema, merely indicates an intervallic attentiveness to the affective register of one's own being/becoming. Indeed, as Deleuze and Guattari repeatedly point out via one of their favoured images, that of the catatonic knight, the affective spectrum of speeds and intensities must always be understood as a continuum. For this reason, the knight resting on his mount can suddenly depart like an arrow; the knight's 'absolute immobility, pure catatonia, is a part of the speed vector'.[20] It is this sense of a potentially resident in the lumbering physicality of a certain noir icon that imbues the performative passivity of Mitchum, Lancaster, Andrews and their inheritors with such a residual affective charge. Moreover, the qualities in play here, which are visual and affective associations that function explicitly at the level of iconography and surviving images, account for the way in which this most modern icon – the passive noir antihero – is so closely entwined with images of knights, a link that originates with Chandler, and samurai, the latter a link that runs through Melville's *Le Samouraï*, Sydney Pollack's *The Yakuza* (1974) and Jim Jarmusch's *Ghost Dog: The Way of the Samurai* (1999), all of which feature somnolent antiheroes. As Deleuze and Guattari observe, martial arts such as those of the knight or samurai 'have always subordinated weapons to speed, and above all to mental (absolute) speed; for this reason, they are also the arts of suspense and immobility. The affect passes through both extremes.'[21]

To return to Blanchot, the disaster involves the revelation of this 'certain passivity' of the body, and of the human's passivity before its own body.[22] It denotes the passion wrought of self-affection, that *acedic* or elegiac experience that nurtures melancholy but harbours, too, an experience of beatitude. In *The Missing Person*, the sociopolitical disaster of losing his wife triggers in Rosow the experience of this Blanchotian disaster, an irruption of the dark interval that imbues him with immense passivity and yet also a passion, this passion of a life bristling with potentiality (*potentia*). In the aftermath of this more mercurial disaster, Rosow is consumed by 'the passion of patience, the passivity of a time without present', and it becomes his 'sole identity'.[23] In other words, the disaster, the dark interval, is what exposes the noir detective to the experience of 'being missing' and the peculiar temporality it inaugurates (the sense of 'a time without present'). The latter temporality is human time rendered intervallic – or sempiternal.

Among other things, such a temporality is equivalent to the condition that time takes on during the juridico-political 'state of exception', that is, that indeterminate situation that Agamben describes as inherently 'devoid of law', a situation whereby 'all legal determinations ... are deactivated'.[24] And, significantly, the two disasters in *The Missing Person* – the historical, sociopolitical disaster of 9/11 and the ontological, spiritual disaster that Rosow undergoes – thus mirror one another in their production of precisely this intervallic time. In the wake of the 9/11 bombings the US government promptly implemented a 'state of emergency', enabling the establishment of the paralegal detainment camp of Guantanamo Bay, myriad extra-juridical martial practices (extraordinary rendition, torture) and the sanctioning of the invasive biopolitical mechanism of the 'Patriot Act' (2001). At the level of 'community', such measures instigate a sense of time that is fundamentally intervallic – relying as they do on the spurious idea that the community has entered a 'temporary' period of instability between periods of alleged stability and juridico-political order (the past 'pre-emergency' and future 'post-emergency' periods). This social dimension of time, however, also has its double in the temporality that assumes one who is exposed to the dark interval, as Rosow is. The latter opens on to a 'messianic' time, in Agamben's terms, 'the time that remains between time and its end'.[25] This is a time that has been radically de-historicized, a time when the juridico-political machine overseeing the 'human' is perceived as deactivated, suspended: when the law is rendered 'inoperative'.[26] What this inoperativity inherently reveals is a temporality of potentiality, of 'passion'. As Agamben puts it, this is 'the time that we ourselves are, and for this very reason, is the only real time, the only time we have'.[27] It is in order to withstand this other temporality, then, to adapt to its power, that Rosow transforms himself into the noir detective. In *The Missing Person* noir is, paradoxically, at once a shelter from and a shelter for the force of the intervallic. At the film's climax, Rosow is not reintegrated with his past life nor realigned with the apparatus of 'the law'. Instead, like Gould's Marlowe, he merely walks out of the frame, adrift and yet strangely at ease, a human fallen into the betwixt-and-between temporality of the angelic order. In short, he embraces *the missing being* that he is.

'Whatever' noir in *The Big Lebowski*

Agamben has developed a concept that speaks very well to the noir experience of 'being missing' and the intervallic temporality associated with it. The concept is 'whatever-being': 'being such as it is' or 'being-such'.[28] In Agamben's view, under the aegis of this 'whatever-being' there exists not defined individuals, and certainly not coherent identities, but rather 'whatever-singularities'. These are humans shorn of all predicates (i.e. the 'qualities' that would consign them to given categories – e.g. nationality, gender, colour, political orientation, etc.). They are beings that are restored to a more originary condition of belonging itself, a belonging grounded in their 'being in common'. Such beings are not 'identified' as what they are called but instead are 'exposed' by the very property of their being-in-language, the linguistic relation that determines their *being-called* in the first place.[29] Significantly, for Agamben this *being-such* or *whatever-being* necessarily involves an acknowledgment of what we might call the elegiac, as living in cognizance of our *being-such* means living in awareness of what Agamben calls 'the Irreparable':

> The Irreparable is that things are just as they are, in this or that mode, consigned without remedy to their way of being. States of things are irreparable, whatever they may be: sad or happy, atrocious or blessed. How you are, how the world is – this is the Irreparable.[30]

Agamben's aim in mobilizing this elegiac figure of 'the Irreparable' is not to valorize an attitude of sociopolitical acquiescence or apathetic disengagement, however. Rather, he perceives in the originary ontological category of 'being-such' the enduring promise of an alternative community – a community *to come* that is, by implication, also the community to which we always already *belong*: a community of whatever-singularities. And, despite its denoting a condition beyond-remedy, the Irreparable is nevertheless leavened by a salvation of sorts, the salvation resident in the human being's exposure to its own taking place ('the coming of the place to itself', as Agamben calls it).[31] This, of course, is precisely what occurs in that experience which we have termed the 'dark interval' in noir and the condition it occasions: the fostering of a being/becoming that is hereafter intervallic.

A paradigmatic vision – and an appropriately ludic one at that – of this coming community, this community of 'whatever-singularities', is staged in the Coen brothers' delirious meta-noir, *The Big Lebowski* (1998). The film exhibits a stunning array of characters, all of them indices of vastly different predicates (principles, modalities and belief systems), and yet all of them members also – albeit unbeknown to themselves – of a community of *being-as-such*. Moreover, as my analysis will show, the film's protagonist, the Dude (Jeff Bridges), can be regarded as someone who, in Agamben's terms, consciously 'appropriates his being-such', and does so in contrast to almost all of the other characters, all of whom attempt to ground themselves in elaborate and superficial narrative identities. Notably, the film attests to all of the guiding elements I have been pursuing throughout this study – that is, the intervallic, the elegiac, passivity, passion, 'zero affect', potentiality and beatitude.

The Dude: Embodying the interval

Although the iconography of the dark interval is invoked only very subtly in *The Big Lebowski* we can consider its force to have been transposed into the very lassitude and pronounced passivity of the Dude himself. In the preamble delivered by the film's idiosyncratic narrator, the Stranger (Sam Elliott), we are informed that the Dude is 'a lazy man ... quite possibly the laziest in Los Angeles County, which would place him high in the runnin' for laziest worldwide'. The latter description accompanies visuals of the Dude as he ambles leadenly (and yet gracefully) through a supermarket, his bathrobe dangling around his plump belly as he opens – and then samples – a carton of milk from the dairy section. Erik Dussere has noted the significance of this supermarket scene in its forging a connection with prior noir visuals of the supermarket in Wilder's *Double Indemnity* and Altman's *The Long Goodbye*.[32] Indeed, as Jenny M. Jones conceives it, Gould's Marlowe is even explicitly 'the precursor' for the Dude.[33] Certainly, there are a number of suggestive resonances between the two films and this continuity between Gould's Marlowe and the Dude is especially important.

As the film's narrative makes clear, the Dude is configured as an offbeat articulation of the jaded and laconic noir hero.[34] In driving this archetype to its hyperbolic and humorous extreme the Coens also simultaneously penetrate the archetype's very core. For what the Dude reveals about the archetype is that one of its most constitutive characteristics has always been an enigmatic passivity and detachment that involves a strange but potent sense of beatitude. In this regard, we would have to dispute Olivier Bohler's suggestion that Alain Delon's hitman in *Le Samouraï* provides the conclusive 'telotype' (or ultimate articulation) of the archetypal noir hero.[35] A 'telotype', as Bohler conceives it, is an archetype brought to its final state. In fact, the Dude, rather than Delon's Jef Costello, would be this ultimate noir 'telotype': the Dude is a distillation of the archetype down to its very core; in this case, to the spirit of profound lassitude, detachment and perversely contented withdrawal that has, from the icon's inception, recurrently marked the noir hero. Moreover, this lassitude – the Dude's splendid commitment to a detached easy-goingness bordering on total inertia – is precisely how, in Agamben's terms, he appropriates his 'being-such'.

Unlike virtually all of the other characters in the film – the nihilist abductors of Bunny Lebowski, the hedonistic Bunny herself (Tara Reid), the phony 'go-getting', capitalist achiever Jeffrey Lebowski (David Huddleston), the smug experimental artist Maud Lebowski (Julianne Moore) and the war veteran Walter Sobchak (John Goodman) who immerses himself, irreconcilably, in a strident Judaism and a deranged politico-militarism – the Dude appropriates few defining characteristics to himself. Those that he does assume (his nickname, his love of bowling, his affection for Credence Clearwater Revival) are blatantly contingent and arbitrary, rather than definitive and essential. They are idiosyncratic elements of a passion rather than fundamental facets of a committed narrative identity. The only thing the Dude seems committed to doing is *the doing of very little*; merely living; and doing that as comfortably as he can while expending as minimal an effort as possible. But this 'merely living' – the Dude's intuitive adjustment to his own taking place, to his life, *a life* and its potentiality – is his salvation.

This salvation occurs at the level of the body.

The Dude, as Jonathan Elmer puts it, is 'an exuberantly embodied character'.[36] If the body (the site of a singularity, of a passion) can be identified, at the level of affect, with the 'missingness' of the noir persona, then the Dude is someone closely in touch with this missingness: pivotally aware of – if not in control of, nor in a desire *to* control – his own inescapable status as *a missing person*.[37] Instructively, while reflecting upon the extraordinary cult status that has evolved around the film, and particularly around the Dude's 'way of life',[38] Jeff Bridges has said that the character's 'philosophy', so to speak, is grounded precisely in a concept of 'the bodily':

> For me, the Dude has a certain type of wisdom. I like to call it the 'Wisdom of Fingernails': the wisdom that gives you the ability to make your hair and fingernails grow, your heart beat, your bowels move. These are things that we know how to do, but we don't necessarily know *how* we know how to do them, yet still we do them very well. And that to me is very Dude.[39]

Of course, the wisdom that Bridges salutes here is precisely those physiological contractions of the body that Deleuze describes as the processes of 'passive syntheses'. This is the immanent realm of 'larval selves', as Deleuze proposes it, wherein an impersonal, affective becoming (which subtends the existence of every human being) takes place. Finding a resonance with Bridges's own words, Deleuze says passive synthesis 'constitutes our habit of living, our expectation that "it" will continue'.[40] Inevitably, this continuance of 'it', of life, borne of the habitual 'becomings' of our bodies, also carries very suggestive resonances with the tiredness and the waiting of the body that Deleuze associates with the 'time-image'.

Though he spends much of the film 'stressed out' due to the incursions of others into his existence, the Dude's fundamental disposition is one that attempts to access and harness the beatitude that is sheltered in the mere living of life itself. The film repeatedly stages quiet moments before others intrude on his privacy (always in the most violent or invasive manner): in each of these moments the Dude seeks out a quotidian serenity, whether it's the minor bliss of smoking a joint in the bath or the gestural meditations of his tai chi practice.

The Dude, then, is always attempting to achieve 'transcendence' in Agamben or Deleuze's terms – not a supernatural or mystical transcendence beyond physical, mortal existence but a transcendence of 'the thing' towards itself, its own taking place: 'toward its own being such as it is'.[41] What the Dude attempts to 'incommunicate' with, via such practices, is 'the unthought life' of the body, the very *incommunication* that Deleuze perceives at work in the time-image. Or, to put it another way, he wishes to channel that impersonal 'beatitude' that Deleuze regards as obtaining in passive synthesis.[42] This is illustrated in an unassuming scene where the

FIGURE 32 *The Dude's channelling of the 'dark interval'*. The Big Lebowski.

Dude – laying supine in meditation upon his new rug, his head rested in the centre of what vaguely resembles a Buddhist mandala – listens to a recording of past bowling strikes and allows his hands to channel the muscle memory of these previous 'strikes' (Figure 32).

Moreover, it is in this very seeking of the beatitude that resides in self-affection that the Dude acquires his ethos – the ultimate ethos, as Agamben sees it. This is an ethos steeped in the immanence of one's own habitual being/becoming: an ethos which, according to Agamben, discloses perhaps the 'only happiness' available to human life:

> Being engendered from one's own manner of being is, in effect, the very definition of habit (this is why the Greeks spoke of a second nature): That manner is ethical that does not befall us and does not found us but engenders us. And this being engendered from one's own manner is the only happiness really possible for humans.[43]

Abiding

Of course, in The Big Lebowski this 'ethos' has a name: abiding. As the Dude attests in his final words in the film, 'The Dude abides'. Significantly, he then dissipates into the soft-focus humanity of his beloved bowling alley, just as Marlowe before him dissipates among a horizon of anonymous humanity at the close of *The Long Goodbye*. Unsurprisingly, many commentators have reflected on the Dude's 'abiding'. Indeed, the motif of 'abiding' is central to the extraordinary cult following that has condensed upon the film. However, the concept of 'abiding' itself is not defined in *The Big Lebowski*.[44] In his reflections on the concept, Jonathan Elmer notes the semantic differences in the 'big' Lebowski's use of the word ('I will not abide another toe') and the use that the Dude later makes of it. The first, says Elmer, means 'endure': 'to maintain an identity, to withstand external assaults'. By contrast, the Dude's preferred iteration of 'abide' means, '"To remain in expectation, wait" ... "To remain in residence; to sojourn, reside, dwell".'[45]

We might note here in such a meaning of 'abiding' the resonances with the patience, passivity and passion that Blanchot suggests marks the one exposed to 'the disaster'.[46] While Blanchot's disaster is principally an affective concept and does not strictly require a cause or correlate in social life, we can nevertheless perceive in the Dude's life a disaster in the community that would rhyme with the more existential quality of 'disaster' at work in his life (i.e. his passionate receptivity to time and affect). Suggestively, like the war veterans of classic noir,[47] and like Rosow in *The Missing Person*, the Dude's socio-ideological positioning is underpinned by his fractious relationship to the sovereign authority of the state and to the extra-juridical 'state of exception' that the sovereign authority increasingly consecrates as the norm. The film's opening sequence establishes this with the Dude glancing intently at TV imagery of President George Bush during the First Gulf War (1990–1) while he pays for his milk in the supermarket. Over the course of the film we learn that the Dude has been a political activist (a signatory to the Port Huron Statement and a member of the 'Seattle Seven') and that he is also a 'pacifist'. What we can surmise from the film's own narrative events, however, is that – even if he has evidently withdrawn from activism – the Dude harbours a spirit of disregard for, and non-compliance with, the sovereign authority of the state and its mechanisms. This is most evident in the sequence where he is interrogated by a fascistic police chief in Malibu. The chief badgers him: 'I don't like you sucking around bothering our citizens, Lebowski. I don't like your jerk-off name, I don't like your jerk-off face, I don't like your jerk-off behaviour, and I don't like you. Jerk-off. Do I make myself clear?' Displaying his open contempt for the barrage of obscene epithets sent his way, however, the Dude replies, 'I'm sorry, I wasn't listening.' It may prompt a violent reprisal from the chief, but the Dude's retort nevertheless succeeds in subverting the violent rhetoric of 'the law'. In essence, the scene provides a contest between the Spinozist categories of potential: the diminished possibilities for action circumscribed by the state and other hegemonic forces (*potestas*) versus the more open condition of potentiality (*potentia*) resident in each person's more fundamental affective relations.

The scene is also notable for foregrounding the Dude's refusal – like Marlowe's in *The Long Goodbye* – to take on a stable identity before the juridico-political apparatus of the state. As the chief peruses the Dude's wallet for evidence of his identity all he can find is a 'Ralph's Shopper's Club Card'. This is, as Dussere correctly points out, 'an instance of the Dude slipping between the cracks of official ordering systems'.[48] It is interesting to note that in our current age – an era of invasive data gathering and 'surveillance capitalism', as Shoshana Zuboff has termed it, and which Linklater's *A Scanner Darkly* presciently envisioned – opportunities to curtail the markers of one's identity to such a minimum as this, so that a person might inhabit the cracks or intervals, are becoming increasingly difficult. In any event, what the Dude's slipping between the cracks underlines is that – whether it is as a result of a socio-ideological disaster (perhaps borne of disillusionment with political protest) or it has materialized simply as a spirit of *acedic* disruption borne of self-affection – the Dude is marked as fundamentally *intervallic*.[49]

In such a state of suspension, then, the Dude abides.

The outer manifestation of this abiding occurs on an affective register, at the level of the body. The Dude abides through his allegiance to 'pure gesture', a strategy of pure communication that communicates only itself and the affective potential of the human. Edward P. Comentale has observed how such a reflection upon gesture is, in fact, key to understanding *The Big Lebowski*, observing that, throughout the film, 'manic gesturalism competes with a certain wordless grace. Bodies are put on display, exhibited in their mediality, and, at these moments, they communicate nothing but their own communicability.'[50] Manic gesturalism certainly abounds in the film. But while the Dude is the originator of a share of it, he is also the most intensive site of 'wordless grace' upon which the film lingers. This grace is fundamentally gestural. It presents itself in the Dude's slow, densely embodied gait, in his amusingly ad hoc meditative practice and – most

FIGURE 33 *The Dude a-slouches.*

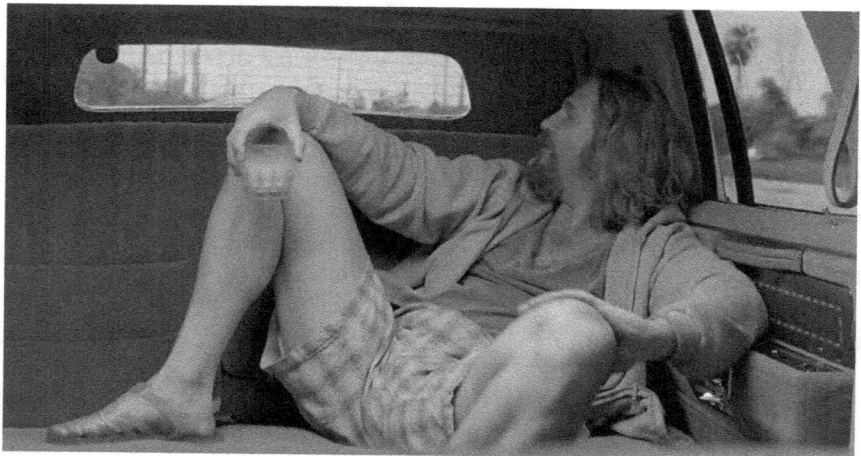

FIGURE 34 ... *And a-slouches.*

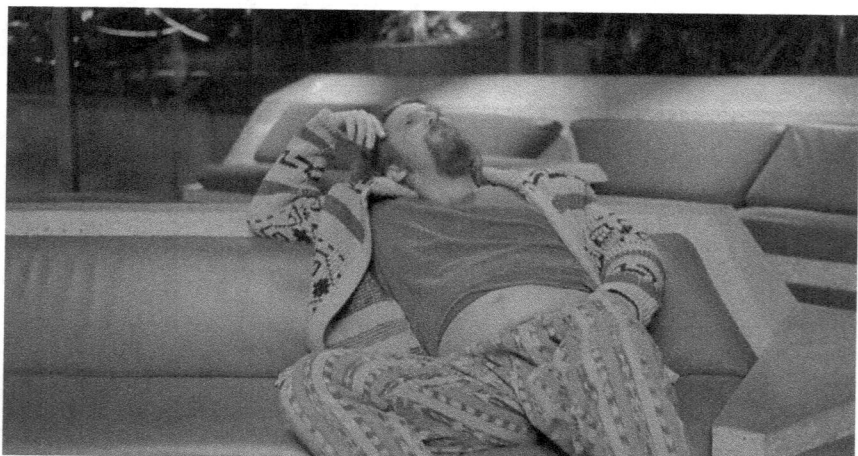

FIGURE 35 ... *And still a-slouches.*

evocatively – in the exorbitant slouching posture he assumes everywhere: on Jackie Treehorn's sofa, in the police chief's office, on the toilet, in the funeral home and especially in the bowling lane (Figures 33–35).

This slouching is mesmerizing in its curious elegance. It attests only to the Dude's 'taking place', his constant immersion in a benign *self-affection*, and, as such, it is the pivotal demonstration of his ethos. Significantly, this slouching gesture, as an index of the Dude's ethos, also unites him with an American countercultural tradition that is implicitly alluded to in the film via the repeated references to the Dude as a 'deadbeat'.[51] The Dude is indeed 'beat' – 'beat' in the sense that Jack Kerouac ascribed to a celebrated generation of countercultural writers and artists that emerged in the United States in the immediate post-war era.[52] Though the term 'deadbeat' emerged in American colloquy in the mid-nineteenth century as a term for an idler or a scoundrel, Kerouac specifically remediated it as being pivotal, conceptually, to 'the beat' identity. Moreover, in the process of doing so he specifically isolated the significance of classic noir personae to his conception of all things *beat*:

> The word 'beat' originally meant poor, down and out, deadbeat, on the bum, sad, sleeping in subways. Now that the word is belonging officially it is being made to stretch to include people who do not sleep in subways but have a certain new gesture, or attitude, which I can only describe as a new *more*. 'Beat Generation' has simply become the slogan or label for a revolution in manners in America. Marlon Brando was not really first to portray it on the screen. Dane Clark with his pinched Dostoievskyan face and Brooklyn accent, and of course Garfield, were first. The private eyes were Beat, if you will recall. Bogart. Lorre was Beat. In *M*. Peter Lorre started a whole revival. I mean the slouchy street walk.[53]

Although Kerouac's itemization of the origins of 'beat' is somewhat scattershot, it is instructive how models of the noir persona (Bogart, John Garfield, Peter Lorre) are identified here, in their very *beat-ness*, as harbouring a gestural quality that, in Kerouac's array of terms, seems suggestively *acedic*. If the beats are credited with bringing 'a certain new gesture' into the light, for Kerouac, it seems, this gesture is also inextricably bound to a certain noir persona – that of the intervallic, strangely passive figure we have been pursuing throughout this study. As such, if *The Big Lebowski* can be regarded as making explicit this enigmatic connection between the beatnik and the noir persona, then the film is also notable for locating this connection in an ethos that is founded upon a distinctive gestural quality somehow encapsulated in Lorre's 'slouchy street walk' or in the Dude's own slouched repose. A slouch is a gesture that would seem to connote a profound, and not always melancholy, sense of self-affection. Such 'slouching' would thus be continuous with the iconography of the 'dark interval' and with the classic imagery of *acedia* that we earlier examined. When we observe, finally, that Kerouac ultimately resolves that 'beat' means nothing other than 'beatific',[54] we can see how *The Big Lebowski* brings noir to an 'end' that it has always deceptively been *gesturing* towards: the beatitude of a potentiality that emerges in self-affection. What the Dude does in 'abiding' is precisely to remain alert to this beatitude, to accede to the affective force of the dark interval and to channel it thereafter through gesture.[55]

Why gesture? Because gesture betokens life, makes manifest 'a life'.[56] Abiding is a remaining in life that is, also, a mode of attesting to life. This attesting is incidental, virtually epiphenomenal, however. Abiding attests only to the taking place of 'something', but it is not a 'testimony' in the juridico-political sense. That is to say, it doesn't narrativize life. As with the 'passion' of Ed Crane, the Dude's abiding attests to life merely by 'demonstrating' it. If we wish to tie this 'demonstrative' or 'gestural' logic back to the Dude's time as a countercultural activist, then we can observe that this is indeed what a mass 'demonstration' means, of course: a passive yet radical demonstration of life, a life that resists being disregarded, trammelled upon or diminished. The latter is one of the ways in which Žižek's suggestion that the experience of Spinozist 'beatitude' inhibits activism or protest is a little short-sighted. The tremulous experience of pure immanence can be a prod towards civil protest. Indeed, in his description of this 'coming' community of 'whatever-singularities' Agamben specifically identifies the famous student protests in Tiananmen Square, Beijing, in 1989 as an instance of *whatever-singularities* peacefully demonstrating their fundamental 'being in common' before a hostile state power.[57]

In his *abidance* the Dude reckons with and attempts constantly to harness the potentiality of a life, the singular, affective and impersonal power that underlies the contingent factors of his existence. In rejecting a conventional name and 'self-applying' the name 'Dude', he even identifies himself only as an example of life itself. Yet, far from sequestering him from life or community, it is his identification with life, *a life*, which vigorously forges his sense of community. The latter may seem somewhat beleaguered at times, yet one of the Dude's distinctive characteristics is that he generally withholds judgement on others, irrespective of how stressed and 'un-Dude'[58] he gets in fraught situations. The Dude remains receptive to life in all its articulations – that is, in the countless ways it manifests itself in those others around him. It is because the Dude accedes to such a conception of community that he remains the friend of Walter Sobchack, his antithesis, an aggressive, fascistic know-it-all. And it is why he retains a spirit of bemused equanimity before the grandstanding bluster of the 'big' Lebowski and the urbane condescension of Maud Lebowski.

The man for his time and place

Ultimately, the Dude serves as a radically passive register of life (of life *as* time). Early in the film, his fellow bowler, Donny, instructs him to record a successful strike ('Mark it, Dude') and this is what he does – *he marks it*.[59] He registers the taking place of things in time, but this registering is nevertheless distinct from the narrative and historical recording of time. He registers

FIGURE 36 *The Dude: 'the man for his time and place'*. The Big Lebowski.

time 'pathetically', or affectively, we might say. He *suffers* time. He abides in time. This is why the scene where he catches his reflection in a novelty mirror bearing the imprint of TIME magazine is important. It identifies the Dude as 'time', or as a passive register of time (Figure 36).⁶⁰ The Dude is not uncomfortable with this – he embraces his radical passivity before time, even if it releases him from, rather than binds him to, his historical moment. He is thus duly flummoxed by a reference to orderly *time-keeping* when his spiritual contrary, the 'big' Lebowski, deduces his unemployment from his casual dress. 'You don't go out and make a living dressed like that in the middle of a weekday', the blowhard snarls at him. A confused Dude replies, 'Is this a ... What day is this?'

The Dude, of course, does not make 'a living'.⁶¹ *He lives*. He abides in time. And this is the import of The Stranger's description of the Dude: 'Sometimes there's a man – and I'm talking about the Dude here. Sometimes there's a man and, well, he's the man for his time and place. He fits right in there.' Where in *The Missing Person* Rosow is left disoriented by the irruption of messianic time, this *intervallic* existence that the Blanchotian disaster has exposed him to, the Dude has already adjusted himself to such a temporality. He abides in the interval. Where Rosow adopts the 'style' of the noir icon largely in order to shelter from everyday narrative dissolution and social breakdown, the Dude's style is an evolution of noir iconicity itself. It is one, moreover, that distils the ethos of the original noir icon down to an affective sensitivity to potentiality, a disposition towards one's own being/becoming, one's own taking place. The Dude's style is 'being-such', *whatever-being*. He styles himself as '*a* dude', an example of life's taking place. As Elmer points out, the Dude holds 'some special germ of exemplarity in him that turned one way can open out onto the abstractions of role, function, and ideological identity ... and turned another way remains essentially unformed, prior to the divisions and individuations that produce the identities we track with pronouns and proper names'.[62] The Dude, in other words, embraces the interval. Like Rosow he has lapsed into this intervallic condition, into a messianic time. But while one of them can be considered to have 'fallen' into *sempiternality*, the other glides within it.

Notes

1. As we observed in an earlier chapter, *The Man Who Wasn't There* is the very apotheosis of the way in which modern noir 'ends' by evacuating or erasing itself, evaporating – like its protagonists – in the dark interval of its own taking place.

2. This latter phenomenon – clinically known as 'dissociative fugue' or 'psychogenic fugue' – was an occasional theme in the classical era of noir, found in the narratives of *Black Angel*, *Somewhere in the Night* and *Crack-Up* (Dir. Irving Reis), for example. The trope was radicalized by David Lynch in his modern noir, *Lost Highway* (1997). The term 'psychogenic fugue' was used in press kits for the film and was frequently referenced by Lynch during interviews. See *Lost Highway* press kit. http://www.lynchnet.com/lh/lhpress.html, accessed 24 April 2010. In a psychoanalytic reading of *Lost Highway*, Bernd Herzogenrath allies the film's metaphor of the fugal state to its other chief metaphor, that of the 'lost highway'. He points out that Jacques Lacan, too, employs the image of the highway and goes on to suggest that the titular 'lost highway' of Lynch's film is, in fact, the protagonist's rejected *law of the father*. See Bernd Herzogenrath, 'On the Lost Highway: Lynch and Lacan, Cinema and Cultural Pathology', *Other Voices*, 1.3 (1999). www.othervoices.org/1.3/bh/highway, accessed 12 October 2014.

3. Catching sight of his revenant stylings, Nick Pinkerton describes him as 'a culture-shocked noir refugee'. See Nick Pinkerton, 'Buschel's *Missing Person* Gestures towards Missing Profundity', *Village Voice*, 17 November 2009. www.villagevoice.com/2009-11-17/film/buschel-s-missing-person-gestures-towards-missing-profundity/full/, accessed 23 November 2010.

4. The cover version is by American rock band, Young People.

5. Deleuze and Guattari, *A Thousand Plateaus*, 150.

6. Massumi, *Parables*, 57.

7. Deleuze, *Cinema II*, 43.

8. Ibid., xi.

9. Fullmer's epiphany and subsequent abandonment of his identity recalls a parable Sam Spade tells in Dashiell Hammett's novel *The Maltese Falcon*, a story which was not used in John Huston's film adaptation. The parable

involves a man who – surviving a near brush with death from a falling beam – suddenly leaves his old stable and secure life, including a wife and children, behind. 'What disturbed him was the discovery that in sensibly ordering his affairs he had got out of step, and not into step, with life. He said he knew before he had gone twenty feet from the fallen beam that he would never know peace again until he had adjusted himself to this new glimpse of life.' See Dashiell Hammett, *The Maltese Falcon* (New York: Vintage, 1992), 64.

10 Agamben, *The Man without Content*, 110.
11 For an absorbing analysis of a religious and mystical tradition of conceiving of 'the angel' as equivalent to 'the image', see Giorgio Agamben, 'Walter Benjamin and the Demonic: Happiness and Historical Redemption', in *Potentialities*, 138–59.
12 Frank Kermode, *The Sense of an Ending* (Oxford: Oxford University Press, 2000), 71.
13 Ibid., 72.
14 Ibid.
15 Ibid., 98.
16 See Slavoj Žižek, 'Passions of the Real, Passions of Semblance', in *Welcome to the Desert of the Real: Five Essays on September 11 and Related Dates* (London: Verso, 2002), 11; and Jean Baudrillard, 'Requiem for the Twin Towers', in *The Spirit of Terrorism and Other Essays* (Verso, 2003), 45.
17 Blanchot, *The Writing of the Disaster*, trans. Ann Smock (Lincoln: University of Nebraska, 1995), 5.
18 'What forces us to think is "the inpower [*impouvoir*] of thought" … What Blanchot diagnoses everywhere in literature is particularly clear in cinema.' See Deleuze, *Cinema II*, 168. The 'thought from outside' is the characteristic motif that Michel Foucault recognizes at work in Blanchot's work and is the title of his study of Blanchot. See Michel Foucault, 'The Thought from Outside', in *Foucault / Blanchot*, trans. Jeffrey Mehlman and Brian Massumi (New York: Zone Books, 1987), 7–60.
19 Deleuze, *Cinema II*, 189.
20 Deleuze and Guattari, *A Thousand Plateaus*, 400.
21 Ibid.
22 Blanchot, *The Writing of the Disaster*, 3.
23 Ibid., 14.
24 Agamben, *State of Exception*, 50.
25 Agamben, *The Time That Remains*, trans. Patricia Dailey (Stanford, CA: Stanford University Press, 2005), 62.
26 Ibid., 109–12.
27 Ibid., 68.
28 Agamben, *The Coming Community*, 1–2.

29 Agamben: 'Exposure is pure relationship with language itself, with its taking-place. It is what happens to something (or more precisely, to the taking-place of something) by the very fact of being in relation to language, the fact of being-called.' Ibid., 97. In other words, 'whatever-being' marks an ontological exposure that is also, fundamentally, the human's exposure to language/communication.
30 Ibid., 90.
31 Ibid., 15.
32 Erik Dussere, *America Is Elsewhere* (Oxford: Oxford University Press, 2013), 40–2.
33 Jenny M. Jones, *The Big Lebowski: An Illustrated, Annotated History of the Greatest Cult Film of all Time* (Minneapolis, MN: Voyageur Press, 2012), 158.
34 The film's parodic noir stylings are self-evident throughout and indicated by the title itself, a goofy take on a number of classic noir titles: *The Big Sleep*, *The Big Heat*, *The Big Knife* (Dir. Robert Aldrich, 1955) and *The Big Combo* (Dir. Joseph H. Lewis, 1955).
35 Bohler's application of the term 'telotype' to Delon's character is discussed by Ginette Vincendeau in *Jean-Pierre Melville: 'An American in Paris'* (London: BFI, 2003), 185.
36 Jonathan Elmer, 'Enduring and Abiding', in *The Year's Work in Lebowski Studies*, ed. Edward P. Comentale and Aaron Jaffe (Bloomington: Indiana University Press, 2009), 449.
37 This familiar noir motif of the human 'subject' in an irresolvable fugal counterpoint with his own 'singularity', his *missingness*, is rendered in a number of ways in the film, one of the most pointed being the use of two songs that stand as the Dude's signature leitmotifs: Bob Dylan's 'The Man In Me' and the anthemic 'Just Dropped In (To See What Condition My Condition Was In)' by Kenny Rogers & the First Edition. Each title ironically foregrounds the essential existential split or disjunction that is generative of the Dude's whole disposition.
38 Despite a mixed reception upon its release in 1998, *The Big Lebowski* very rapidly gained a huge cult following. Its growing popularity led to the establishment in 2002 of the annual Lebowski Fest in Louisville, Kentucky. The festival has since been staged at locations throughout the United States. Attendees dress as characters from the film and the festival has been attended by most of the principal cast members, including Bridges, Goodman and Moore. The perception that the Dude embodies a 'way of life', one generally termed 'dudeism', has become virulent in popular culture and the idea has been explored in an ever-growing array of literature, including monographs such as *The Year's Work in Lebowski Studies*, *The Big Lebowski and Philosophy: Keeping Your Mind Limber with Abiding Wisdom*, ed. Peter S. Fosl (London: Wiley, 2012), and Oliver Benjamin's *The Abide Guide: Living Like Lebowski* (Berkeley, CA: Ulysses, 2011). Benjamin is, notably, the author of a number of Lebowski books. He is also the founder of 'The Church of

the Latter Day Dude'. Jeff Bridges has even written his own book with Bernie Glassman, *The Dude and the Zen Master* (New York: Plume, 2012).

39 Jeff Bridges, 'Foreword' to *I'm A Lebowski, You're a Lebowski: Life, the Big Lebowski and What Have You*, ed. Scott Shuffitt and Will Russell (Edinburgh: Canongate, 2013), xiv. Shuffitt and Russell are also the founders of Lebowski Fest.

40 Deleuze, *Difference and Repetition*, 74.

41 Agamben, *The Coming Community*, 96. It's worth noting here that this attempt at a transcendence towards one's own being carries affinities with the practice of meditation in Zen Buddhism. The aim of such meditation is *satori*, an 'illuminatory moment' of 'sudden dislocation', as Georges Bataille has described it. See Georges Bataille, *On Nietzsche*, trans. Bruce Boone (London: Continuum, 2004), 167. Intriguingly, Bataille observes suggestive resonances between Nietzsche's doctrine of eternal return and the Zen illumination of *satori* (134–5). In fact, I would suggest that a study of the interaction between film noir and Zen would itself prove 'illuminating'. There have been a number of articulations of Zen in the modern noir. The most notable is Jean-Pierre Melville's allusion in *Le Samouraï* to 'the Bushido', the ethos of the samurai warrior which is heavily indebted to Zen. Elsewhere, the figure of Gorodish in *Diva* (Dir. Jean-Jacques Beineix, 1981) is conceived as a cross between the withdrawn noir hero and a Zen master. (At one point, he instructs the film's protagonist in the Zen art of buttering bread.) The Dude, too, seems inflected with a distinctive Zen quality, hence the book that Bridges wrote with Zen master Bernie Glassman. The affinities between Zen and a certain kind of noir protagonist – detached, passive, yet also passionate and joyful – thus greatly undermine the dichotomy that director Marc Rosenbush creates in his 2004 film *Zen Noir*. With a narrative centred on a gruff hard-boiled detective who is baffled by the mystical detachment he encounters in a Buddhist temple, Rosenbush sets up the two modalities – noir and Zen – as antinomical. As I have been suggesting, however, 'Zen' and noir – or at least a certain strain of noir – are in fact peculiarly resonant.

42 Deleuze, *Difference and Repetition*, 74.

43 Agamben, *The Coming Community*, 29.

44 As 'philosophical' concepts go, 'abiding' is not carefully developed but, instead, merely tossed out arbitrarily at the film's finale as if it were some kind of ludic incantation that might provide the key to deciphering the pataphysical riddle of the film. (Of course, that's only if you're 'into' what the Dude would describe as *the whole deciphering thing*. And, the Dude, you suspect – despite his successful 'cracking' of the case in *The Big Lebowski* – is probably not.)

45 Elmer, 'Enduring and Abiding', 453.

46 Indeed, in *The Instant of My Death* Blanchot plays with the concepts of 'abiding' (*demeure*), as Derrida has observed. See Derrida, *Demeure*, 69, 77–8.

47 See Mark Osteen, 'Vet Noir: Masculinity, Memory, and Trauma', in *Nightmare Alley: Film Noir and the American Dream* (Baltimore, MD: John Hopkins University Press, 2013), 77–105.

48 Dussere, *America Is Elsewhere*, 42.

49 Indeed, in very Agamben-esque language, Elmer describes him as 'ideologically and socially interstitial. The Dude is like a socio-symbolic stem cell – pure potentiality in suspension'. See Elmer, 'Enduring and Abiding', 452.

50 Edward P. Comentale, 'I'll Keep Rolling Along': Some Notes on Singing Cowboys and Bowling Alleys in *The Big Lebowski*', in *The Year's Work in Lebowski Studies*, 245–6.

51 One of Jackie Treehorn's goons calls him a 'deadbeat' on separate occasions. On one occasion he pisses on the Dude's rug, pronouncing 'Ever thus to deadbeats'. (This is the act that motivates the entire narrative.) The Malibu police chief also calls the Dude a deadbeat. On another occasion, it is the Dude who describes himself as 'a deadbeat, a loser, someone the square community won't give a shit about', while summarizing the way in which his rival, the big Lebowski, no doubt views him. (The big Lebowski replies, 'Well, aren't you?' and the Dude responds 'Well … Yeah.')

52 Kerouac coined the term 'beat generation' in an interview with John Clellon Holmes in 1948, but it only came to prominence as the name for a cultural movement in the late 1950s, following the publication of Allen Ginsberg's poem 'Howl' and Kerouac's novel *On the Road*. See Jack Kerouac, 'Beatific: On the Origins of the Beat Generation', *Playboy*, June (1959), 31–2, 42, 79.

53 Ibid., 42.

54 Ibid.

55 The idea of the Dude's receptivity to beatitude would find resonance in Morgan Rempel's analysis of the character in Epicurean terms, whereby the Dude attempts to live 'blessedly'. See Morgan Rempel, 'Epicurus and "Contented Poverty"', in *The Big Lebowski and Philosophy*, 69.

56 This is the value of the brief scene showing the esoteric contemporary dance performance of Marty (Jack Kehler), the Dude's landlord. The latter – poignant in its tragicomic elements – speaks to the human's attempts to channel the affective intensities underlying its own being. Inevitably, the few audience members in attendance disregard Marty's performance. The Dude and Walter, in particular, pay scant attention, whispering to one another about the latest setback in the Bunny Lebowski case and deciding to instigate the next step once Marty's performance is completed.

57 Agamben: 'What the State cannot tolerate in any way … is that … singularities form a community without affirming an identity, that humans co-belong without any representable condition of belonging … Wherever these singularities peacefully demonstrate their being in common there will be a Tiananmen, and, sooner or later, the tanks will appear.' *The Coming Community*, 85–7.

58 At one point in the film Walter tells the stressed protagonist, 'You're behaving very un-Dude.'

59 Later, in what will eventually escalate into a violent confrontation with Walter, another bowler, Smokey, tells him, 'Mark it eight, Dude.'

60 Intriguingly, in the original draft of the screenplay the mirror was to bear the emblem of 'Life' magazine, an alternative that would have been perhaps even more apt.

61 Interestingly, in relation to the Dude's studious unemployment, Agamben describes messianic time as an *intervallic* time when the law is rendered inoperative and one is called to no vocation. '*The messianic vocation is the revocation of every vocation.* In this way, it defines what to me seems to be the only acceptable vocation. What is a vocation, but the revocation of each and every concrete factical vocation?' See *The Time That Remains*, 23. The messianic vocation is, by contrast, simply a calling to 'a generic potentiality' resident in one's own taking place, a potentiality that can be 'used' without being 'owned'. Ibid., 27.

62 Elmer, 'Enduring and Abiding', 452.

8

Coda: Passion at the Impasse – Noir in Transit

As the Dude might say, film noir is a 'complicated case' with 'a lot of strands', and in this study, too, we have been pursuing a lot of strands. We have examined and traced an iconography of passivity specific to film noir, and we have identified the frequency with which noir films stage an irruption of a 'dark interval'. This is an experience by which the noir protagonist is overtaken by a sense of his or her own passion: their own taking place, their own potentiality. In doing so, we have examined various articulations of this dark interval as it occurs in noir, including the interval of fascination with a radical 'outside'; the interval between narrative identity and the passions that subtend, elude, and disrupt it; the ontological interval between man and animal; the poetic interval between technologically conditioned cognition and a sense of affective agency; and that temporally charged extra-juridical interval in which the biopolitical distinction between 'the law' and 'life' comes into a sharp and anarchic focus.

The dark interval is an ambivalent phenomenon, and it is marked by something no less ambivalent: it induces in the noir protagonist a 'radical passivity', to recall Thomas Carl Wall's term from an earlier chapter, as well as an atemporal (or extra-temporal) sensibility. It may disclose, too, a quasi-redemptive sense of beatitude. As we have observed, this potentiality that the dark interval shelters – this sense of the mercurial possibility that is proper to the human – may even suggest to us the site for a new ethics and a new community: a 'coming community', in Giorgio Agamben's terms. This would be a community that valorizes life itself: *bare life*, our being-*such*, as Agamben puts it; the beatitude that inheres quietly in the passive syntheses of 'a life', in the conception of Gilles Deleuze. Sloping towards this latter end, and in a perhaps unlikely progression, we have charted the development of a certain noir archetype of melancholic detachment and enraptured fascination through many eclectic articulations to its terminus (or, at least, to one of its terminals): that of 'The Dude' Lebowski.

The Dude is the at once quotidian and exotic telotype towards which the specific noir figure of the passive, intervallic antihero has perhaps always inclined. He is a *whatever-singularity* who – resisting the socio-juridical mechanisms of narrative identity – submits only to a community of 'being in common' and to the potentiality immanent in the passion of his own becoming. And yet, even while the Dude embodies a nomadic wakefulness to potentiality, one that many passive protagonists of film noir have always nurtured, we have noted, too, that this potentiality is not a reductively benign principle but an affective experience that at heart is fundamentally anarchic, and as such entirely threatening to human categories of order and rationality. The potentiality that might forge a new community is also the same potentiality (force-of-~~law~~) that forges the sovereign law of the state and the narrative orders tied to it. For this reason, among others, our charting of the passionate passivity that characterizes the intervallic noir protagonist has also underlined the irreducibly elegiac dimensions of this figure's fate, which is the fate of the human itself: to be torn between the sometimes oppressive phantasms of order, on the one hand, and the sundering force of anarchy, on the other, thus becoming the *subject* of a 'ravaged site' or a 'double bind', as Reiner Schürmann has put it.[1] Though we have retrieved from within the dark webs of film noir the quasi-redemptive motif of *beatitude*, it would be a mistake to place noir too strenuously under the star of some impassive 'Zen' contentment. Noir of the 'dark interval' may harbour degrees of grace and beatitude, but it harbours melancholy and anarchy just as profoundly.

Nevertheless, it is hoped that my study has helped to cast in a new light the significance of passivity in film noir, the way in which this passivity survives in a certain noir iconography and the manner in which this iconography itself centres on capturing a mercurial affective quality inherent to the human: the potentiality that flares up in an experience of suspension or 'indeterminacy' that is constitutive of a body in a state of 'passage', as Massumi might put it.[2] The dominant critical perception of the noir antihero (so often a man, of course, but not exclusively so) has tended to drift towards either of two poles: a protagonist who is an austere, resilient figure, and who struggles to maintain a stable subjectivity borne upon the attainment of a hard-fought existential freedom, or, by contrast, a fundamentally melancholic or masochistic figure, bound to the destructive Freudian workings of the drive. My work here has attempted to tease into view another inflection of passivity in noir – one that attests to the potentiality resident in self-affection, that condition transmitted in the pathos formula of 'zero affect', whereby one is overcome and possibly transformed by the experience of one's own taking place. This is a potentiality that *slouches* unassumingly in the shadows of noir. We should resist attempts to lock it down to a stable 'meaning'.

Noir in *Transit*

What, for instance, does the sustained imagery of the dark interval in Christian Petzold's *Transit* (2018) ultimately 'mean'? The latter is a captivating noir narrative of arrest, drift and repetition, but what does its self-aware deployment of an enduring noir iconography of passivity communicate? *Transit* can be interpreted in any number of ways. The film is a slow-burning thriller. It's a ghost story. It's an art house flick steeped in European mythology. It is also an incisive commentary on the parallels between refugee experience during the Second World War and the horrific refugee crisis unfolding in Europe in recent decades. However, while these summaries may glean something of the film's thematic investments, Petzold's use of a certain noir iconography of the dark interval pursues strategies that are more elusive still. Primarily, it suffuses the film with an affecting sense of temporal experience – a charged tempo of quavering duration – that is not simply a function of the film's narrative as such but which emerges instead from its array of images of waiting, detachment and suspended passage. Olivia Landry has noted in the film an 'aesthetics of stretched out time' that – while not marginalizing or aestheticizing the terror and degrading toll of waiting inherent in the contemporary refugee experience of detention – nevertheless locates a quality of the 'possible' in the film's depiction of its hero's own strange and mercurial passivity.[3] Such an aesthetics of waiting is, of course, very much a trait of noir iconography and performance. As I have noted throughout this study, noir images of suspended temporality can be understood as 'surviving images': iconographic configurations of waiting that reverberate across multiple artworks of every age, ricocheting through diverse epochs and temporalities, none of which are therefore historically discrete but which instead resonate together, bringing history itself into a suggestive condition of lapse or 'standstill', as Walter Benjamin famously insisted was the radical capacity native to every powerful image.[4]

Very often, what survives in these images of passive withdrawal, waiting and detachment – from the figure idling in the terrain beyond the city in Giulio Campagnola's sixteenth-century engraving of Saturn that we discussed in an earlier chapter to the images of arrest in *Transit* – is a mood or sensation of 'impasse'. This sense of impasse may emerge at a phenomenological level when a passion is confounded by an intuition of the inscrutable thereness of material existence, what Maurice Blanchot calls 'the inertia of being'. However, at a sociopolitical, cultural or historical level, such a sense of impasse may emerge, too, when a human being feels the tremulous urgency of its own potential – its constituency in passion – circumscribed by social forces that would marshal its existence in the name of sovereign power structures. In our own era – when, as Agamben and others suggest, such power structures are ferociously 'biopolitical' – Lauren Berlant has suggested that just such a principle of 'impasse' has come to mark everyday social life, a by-product of the teeming inequities produced by oppressive state systems entrenched in the imperatives of 'neoliberal' capitalism. (It should be said that Berlant uses the latter term heuristically, acknowledging its limitations: that is, the way the term 'neoliberalism' tends to suggest a far too totalizing sense of social determinism and homogenization that overlooks the immensity and indeterminacy of affective relations and encounters – the cracks, fissures and potentials that actually mark the social field.)[5] Petzold's *Transit* seems to speak to Berlant's concept of 'impasse' and to a Blanchotian quality of impasse, too: fusing the two together, while funnelling its use of noir iconography into an acute critique of social forces that diminish or traduce the potential of the singular life and a more equitable community of 'being in common' to which such a singular being could aspire.[6]

Petzold's film is an adaptation of Anna Seghers's celebrated 1942 novel of the same name, inspired by the author's own flight from France in the 1940s as the Nazis occupied the country. Notably, this was a flight that her friend and fellow exile Walter Benjamin did not manage to complete. Stalled on the border between France and Spain, and unable to secure a visa to ensure passage to Lisbon and on to the United States, the latter took his own life rather than face deportation back to occupied France. In some strange way, Benjamin's fate lingers around the edges of both the novel and Petzold's film adaptation; Benjamin is one of the figures constellated within the images of waiting and detachment that *Transit* summons.

The film centres on a young man Georg (Franz Rogowski) who – like many other fleeing refugees – desperately needs to secure safe passage from the port city of Marseille to Mexico as the occupying forces close in. To do so, he assumes the identity of a dead writer whose papers and final unfinished story have fallen into his possession. As such, he is yet another of noir's 'missing persons'. By the film's end, however, when his 'transit' visas finally arrive, it is his suspended condition of statelessness, the more fundamental ontological experience of transit itself – radical passivity, self-affection – with which the impassive Georg ultimately finds himself aligned.

Consistent with the pathos formula of 'zero affect' that I have charted throughout this study, the film's visual strategy repeatedly frames Georg (and his fellow refugees) in Blanchotian states of 'infinite' waiting. These are melancholy and sometimes very saddening images, but they are marked in many instances by a conspicuous residual quality of power and potential. Moreover, the film is shot entirely in the spaces of transience that Vivian Sobchack associates with the spatiotemporal zones unique to noir: its 'lounge time'. Thus, the film opens with an image of Georg waiting absently in a café in one city and closes with him in a similar suspended state of waiting in another city still, the closing shot notably echoing the Swede's ambiguous, strangely elated gaze into the 'Outside' in *The Killers*. All of the spaces in the film – hotels, consulates, cafés – are sites of transition, iterations of a vague 'placeless place'. Meanwhile, in one of the film's most impressive formal conceits, time itself is out of joint, with characters from Seghers's 1940 setting circuiting the environs of contemporary Marseilles like lost ghosts, brushing shoulders with North African refugees from our contemporary moment. Notably, in developing this experimental 'untimely' quality of the film, Petzold drew inspiration from Altman's *The Long Goodbye* and its own depiction of Los Angeles (and the noir imaginary itself) as a palimpsestuous space shimmering with multiple times and temporalities.[7]

Indeed, before we move on to a short analysis of the film's imagery, we should note that *Transit* – functioning like a digest of the many strands that have informed this study – also fulfils many other conventions associated with the 'dark interval' in noir. The film's narrative folds back on itself at the finale, when the narrator's voice-over repeats almost verbatim the text of a story – in actuality, the closing section of Seghers's original novel – that we have observed Georg reading earlier in the film. Like *The Man Who Wasn't There*, then, this is a noir film invested in inducing an experience of *lapse*, by raising the possibilities of Blanchotian 'narration' above the surface 'narrative' itself. In effect, it opts to channel the force of potential resident in the space or fissure of the creative act by effacing or short-circuiting the narrative and embracing instead the dispersive aesthetic of a mise en abyme. Elsewhere, the film can also be seen to channel the imagery of 'Orphic noir' that we earlier examined, with Petzold muting slightly the Kafkaesque dimensions of Seghers's original narrative, and amplifying its investment in Greek mythology. Both Georg and the object of his affection, the elusive Marie (Paula Beer), oscillate between the poles of Orpheus and Eurydice throughout the film, with countless scenes specifically evoking an Orphic iconography, in particular an inventive relay of fateful backward glances at the film's climax. And we should note, too, that Georg is also a kind of Hermes, as a scene which finds him repairing a young refugee's radio suggests. Thereby, the film completes the triad of figures – Orpheus, Eurydice, Hermes – that fascinated Rainer Maria Rilke and later Jean Cocteau. Hermes, messenger between worlds, can only be understood as an intervallic figure. Indeed, to re-pitch McLuhan's famous formula, we could say that Hermes is his own message. And that message is *relation*: the force, power and potential inherent in every relation and in our affective capacities for relation. In Orphic noir, where self-affection becomes the counterpoint to the surface storyline, the antihero – whether a detective, an outlaw or a drifter – is always at once a triptych configuration of Orpheus, Eurydice and Hermes.[8]

Insomuch as *Transit* employs an iconography of the dark interval and even specifically a pathos formula of 'zero affect', we can observe it in numerous elements, whether it is in the sense of languid embodiment that underlines Rogowski's performance as Georg, the recurring images of figures framed at windows or the repeated tableau of a human figure strewn

FIGURE 37 *Georg (Franz Rogowski) in one of many moments of suspension.* Transit.

across a bed in a state of torpor that – in the case of Georg, at least – seems propitious to a radical passivity far beyond mere listlessness or disaffection. Georg is repeatedly framed recumbent on a floor or in bed, or else reclining in chairs, somewhat agitated in his inertia, and yet also somehow at peace with it (Figure 37).

Meanwhile, in a key scene that transmits Georg's gathering attraction to Marie, we share his point of view as he observes her lying prone across a bed in a melancholy detachment (Figure 38).

Petzold's composition of this scene is reminiscent of the framing of similar bed-bound figures in the paintings of Edward Hopper, and the prominence of the open windows, through which the region's mistral breeze suffuses the room, similarly evokes a sense of Hopperian intermission. That both Georg and Marie at different points in the film forego an opportunity to escape Marseille indicates, too, a strange submission to the force of this intervallic state they have found there.

Inevitably, states of boredom – the more prosaic kind, but also those consistent with Martin Heidegger's 'profound boredom' – are prevalently articulated in the film, as Georg and the broader community of the displaced await confirmation of their transit visas. Boredom is a strong theme in Seghers's novel, too, where it is the experience of 'a *cafard*' – a French concept for the sensation of a restless, dispiriting listlessness – that moves her protagonist to read the dead writer's unfinished manuscript.[9] This 'cafard', an experience of 'a Godless emptiness', as Seghers's narrator describes it, could be regarded as a more negatively primed expression of existential

FIGURE 38 *Marie (Paula Beer) in a state of Hopperian lethargy and intermission.* Transit.

ennui perhaps, and it is certainly continuous with the concept of *acedia* that we have looked at in relation to noir iconography. Petzold's film is extremely attentive to the ambiguities of *acedic* self-affection, and sensitive, too, to the quality of a 'saving sorrow' that – as Agamben notes – is resident in the experience. Ultimately, in a manner that is reminiscent of Chow's romantic pessimism in *2046*, Petzold's noir-invested antihero appears to savour his intervallic status, the condition of non-identity and statelessness imposed upon him by circumstance, with which he increasingly comes to affiliate himself.

At the close of the film, in a sequence that is quite faithful to Seghers's novel but which also departs from it in certain ways, Georg is fixed to a seat in the café where he has spent so much of his time throughout the film. In Seghers's original finale, the first-person narrator abides here in a condition of life conceived at its most attenuated or desistant, identifying himself with the 'partial scrap of a shadow on the wall' in front of him: his own faint shadow that evaporates each time the door behind him is opened, letting in light.[10] Thus, in the Orphic terms that Seghers – and later Petzold – courts for him, *Transit*'s hero is merely a living 'shade', a mirror of the 'shade' of Marie, who by this point in the narrative has receded into the Underworld. While Petzold foregoes replicating the metaphor of the shadow, Rogowski's performance of studious indifference in the scene, even as enemy sirens wail through the streets outside, captures a similar sense of life in its most indeterminate state. As Massumi – in the vein of Deleuze – insists, such indeterminacy is the residual quality of affect itself. A provocative image such as that of Georg sitting in abeyance at the close of *Transit* can be understood to impart nothing other than the somatic condition of a body gaining and sustaining a sense of 'transitional immediacy' to its own fundamental *indeterminacy*.[11] Importantly, this 'charge of indeterminacy carried by a body is inseparable from it. It strictly coincides with it, to the extent that the body is in passage or in process'.[12] Indeterminacy here defines the background hum of lived experience.

Significantly, given both Seghers's and Petzold's attention to the metaphor of incomplete texts, Orphic iconography and indeterminate states in their respective versions of *Transit*, it is interesting that Blanchot brings all of these elements together in a number of studies, and in particular in *The Space of Literature*. Inspired by Rilke's meditation in his *Sonnets to Orpheus*, Blanchot identifies the space of literature with the 'disinterested gaze' that Rilke associates with an authentic experience of 'the Open': a gaze 'which has no future and seems to come from the heart of death'.[13] Such a gaze very much informs the closing image of Petzold's *Transit*, in which Georg's Orpheus – responding to the opening of a door – gazes back over his shoulder and responds to whatever it is he spies there with a strange serenity reminiscent of the Swede's exalted gaze into the 'Outside' in *The Killers*. Is it Marie – his Eurydice – come back to him? Or is it the enemy arriving with the neutralizing force of fate? The film doesn't offer any clarity but closes instead in a provocative indeterminacy, wishing to communicate only this indeterminacy itself and a minor joy resident in it.

For Blanchot, notably, this 'mystical' Rilkean backward gaze is also the gaze of art. And, for our purposes, we should pay attention to the affective charge of indeterminacy that a visualization of this gaze itself tends to carry when it is configured as an arresting affection-image in cinema or as a surviving image of *zero affect* persistent in the visual arts more generally.

> Everything hinges on the movement of seeing, when in it my gaze, ceasing to direct itself forward with the pull of time that attracts it to goals, turns back to look 'as if over the shoulder, behind, toward things', in order to reach 'their closed existence', which I see then as perfected, not crumbling or being altered by the wear of active life, but as it is in the innocence of being. I see things then with the disinterested and somewhat distant look of someone who has just left them.

In Petzold's *Transit*, Georg is associated with a capacity to inhabit just such a *disinterested* or *distant* perspective, and is therefore repeatedly delivered to us via a corresponding pathos formula which – at times – can communicate precisely this intuitive insight. Indeed, the roots of this characterization stem from Seghers's novel, where at one point the protagonist even attests to a vaguely Spinozist experience of viewing existence *sub specie aeternitatis*, as when – even as German soldiers approach a farmyard in which he is hiding – he opts to do the 'most sensible and most foolish thing' possible, and to 'remain sitting there':

> Suddenly I felt quite calm. I thought, I'm sitting here, and the Germans are moving past me and occupying France. But France has often been occupied – and the occupiers all had to withdraw again ... My fear vanished completely ... I saw the mightiest armies of the world marching up to the other side of my garden fence and withdraw; I saw the cockiest of empires collapse and the young and the bold take heart; I saw the masters of the world rise up and come crashing down. I alone had immeasurably long to live.

Of course, the resonances with Blanchot's autobiographical story 'The Instant of My Death' and its principal image of a life held in abeyance, which we examined in an earlier chapter, are quite striking here. It points us to a significant feature of the Rilkean 'Open', Blanchot's 'space of literature' and the noir experience of the 'dark interval' (as I have termed it, purloining the phrase from Rilke, of course): namely, that during the rupture of such a scintillating and enigmatic moment, one has – as Blanchot puts it – 'already died'.[14] The latter is a quality ascribable to many a noir protagonist, including Bogart, whose screen persona – as André Bazin memorably described it – captures the 'corpse on reprieve ... within all of us'.[15] This, too, is what constitutes the noir antihero as *intervallic*: his or her revenant status. In a very real sense, every intuition of life *sub specie aeternitatis* makes us a revenant thereafter. The same is true of Nietzsche's eternal return. The trick is to make oneself a joyful revenant, where possible, and to align oneself with a will to power that is fundamentally a powerlessness: a receptivity to the potential in any and every moment.

Lest the indeterminacy and powerlessness glimpsed in *Transit* – and in noir of the dark interval more generally – be viewed too negatively as involving a reductive fatalism, it is important to observe that this opening on to the dark passages of indeterminacy can be propitious to action and not simply conducive to melancholy or resignation. In Seghers's novel, the protagonist may identify with an intermittent scrap of shadow, but it is a shadow 'trying to connect with flesh and blood again', and moreover one that – at this point in the novel – has already resolved to join the Resistance.[16] For Blanchot, the death one experiences in the interval is an 'impersonal death'. It doubles and even eclipses the more conventional sense of death as a finitude of the self. This emphasis on the impersonal resonates with Agamben's concept of 'whatever-singularities', of course, which – as we observed at the close of the previous chapter – he associates with the possibilities for a new community of 'being in common' and for strategies of resistance such as those of the demonstration movements in Tiananmen Square.

Significantly, in Petzold's adaptation of *Transit*, Georg never expresses any commitment to join the resistance movement. Towards the film's end, having forfeited his transit papers, he confides to the café barman (the film's narrator) a desire to escape over the Pyrenees – which had been Walter Benjamin's intended escape route also. The barman tells him this will be futile. While Georg never overtly abandons this flight plan, it is significant that it is at this precise moment, when he is made aware of its futility, that he glimpses a vision of Marie – his Eurydice – as if sent from the underworld to herald his impending demise. Afterwards, torn between the diminishing possibility of escape from the enemy and his hope that his vision of her wasn't illusory (that Marie may yet be alive), he does not flee the city, but instead sits waiting for her. The film closes with a range of possibilities in play and Georg, impassively sitting in the midst of them, is thereby left fundamentally intervallic or indeterminate. We can read his radical passivity in many ways. As an iteration of stoic fatalism or joyful Nietzschean amor fati. As a mere knightly prelude to a sudden burst of action and escape from the enemy forces that he has already eluded once before when in similar circumstances. Or we can view his passivity, too, as expressive of an act of faith in the Kierkegaardian sense. In Seghers's novel, in a similar scenario, the hero chooses the 'most sensible and most foolish thing' – to continue sitting there, while embracing a beatitudinal overcoming of his specific temporal moment. If he sits there, Eurydice will return. And, of course, this is true. Some form of Eurydice *will* return. Potential is ever in circulation. In her analysis of *Transit*, Landry places the images of waiting and suspension within the shelter of Siegfried Kracauer's concept of the 'anteroom' or 'waiting room': 'a spatiality that is aligned with a temporality on the threshold of knowledge, beauty, and potentiality'.[17] This would be a more positive articulation of the potential latent in Sobchack's 'lounge time'. The muted utopian strains here are also quite resonant with Berlant's versatile concept of the 'impasse'. On the one hand, the latter is suffused with dismaying experiences of broken 'good life' genres, precarity and 'slow death' that, as Berlant argues, have come to dominate the contemporary 'affectsphere'. Yet, on the other, the impasse is also 'a stretch of time in which one moves around with a sense that the world is at once intensely present and enigmatic, such that the activity of living demands both a wandering absorptive awareness and a hypervigilance that collects material that might help to clarify things'.[18] These qualities might well be regarded as consistent with the properties of an attenuated noir consciousness, or at least qualities of one intervallic form of life in noir, as we have pursued it in this study. Radical passivity in noir is not coterminous with capitulation or acquiescence. It may be a principle of detachment from which a receptivity to action and a reimagining of the human and the social may arise.

'Sometimes it is'

Taking *Transit* as a model, then, noir of the dark interval might designate only the sense that in transitional affective states of passage proper to every living being, in the zones of indetermination within which our lives acutely 'recur', Agamben's formula – *potentiality for darkness/potentiality for light* – obtains above all. Ultimately, a chief concern in noir – asserted through the pathos formula of 'zero affect' – centres on the question of how one responds to the potentiality revealed in the interval. How does one appropriate the passion that one is? The question is fundamentally an open one.

For this reason images of the dark interval remain ambiguous. And noir, of course, is just one site in cinema within which this surviving image of radical passivity – *zero affect* – is sheltered, though it certainly strikes me as the most powerful, provocative and protean of these sites. Given the capacity of such images to resonate across times and temporalities, it is interesting that in Jarmusch's *Ghost Dog: The Way of the Samurai* the patient and graceful Ghost Dog (Forest Whitaker) implicitly aligns himself with an 'untimely' conception of history whereby discrete times collapse into one another, just as they do in *The Long Goodbye* and *Transit*. When Ghost Dog encounters two hunters who – having already lawlessly killed a black bear – proceed to racially abuse and threaten him, the samurai swiftly executes them, in an act of violence that appropriates the force-of-~~law~~ just as Marlowe's similar act did at the close of *The Long Goodbye*. Before slaying the second hunter, Ghost Dog informs him that 'in ancient cultures bears were considered equal with men'. His victim replies, 'This ain't no ancient culture here, mister,' which elicits Ghost Dog's decisive yet ambivalent retort: 'Sometimes it is.' The latter statement, with its evocation of an incoherent temporality and submission to the impersonal, relays the temporal-affective charge of the interval as 'event'. In arresting time, it brings time itself into collapse. The images of the dark interval we have examined feature divergent if related iconographies, ranging from visualizations of supreme passivity to acts of pure violence, and they solicit qualities that range from the redemptive and beatitudinal to the irreparable and the elegiac. Yet throughout all these quiet and disquieting noir images there survive intensities and affects of immense capacity, reverberating across distinct times and epochs, and making these times and epochs tremble, too. In these images, the residual and constitutive affective experience of human existence is resonant, living on in the images that capture it.

Ultimately, the figure of passion – a term that, as we noted, has etymological and iconographic associations with passivity and pathos – has guided my study here. In pursuing the significance of this passion of the interval within film noir, I suggest that – however poorly the term 'film noir' may function in terms of demarcating a stable object of inquiry – the schismatic drifter term 'noir' nevertheless communicates something to us, even if it is only a facet of lived experience that remains stubbornly beyond verbal communication. What it communicates is our immersion in an immanent register of affect: our suffusion in both the powerlessness and the immensely potent folds of our passion.

Above and beyond the taxonomical impasse of defining what noir names, then, this is what film noir 'means', or, at least, it is one of its meanings. It is the sense of film noir that I have tried to retrieve in this study. Operating at the level of affect, of passion, film noir, or at least that strain of noir that we have examined, is a cinematic quality or sensibility that, despite its frequently dark and ominous content, bristles with life and a mercurial condition of self-relation that – if it can be glimpsed at all – can be recognized only as indeterminate and in flux. In this regard, the traditional scholarly understanding of noir as a *failed* name is arguably its most apt feature. It is not just the term 'noir' that is caught in processes of semantic drift, after all. Terms drift; but so, too, do concepts. The concept of the dark interval – of a passion and potential inherent in self-affection – is an elusive figure drifting and mutating in many iterations throughout many epochs. It is akin to a concept without a name. It is frequently articulated as a philosophical figure but also as an aesthetic figure, one residing in a specific set of iconographies. Amorphous and elusive, it has something of the status of Roland Barthes's punctum: a wound on the register of the visual as well as the register of the semantic.[19]

Hence, if noir may not name its object coherently, we should consider the counsel of Barthes, who says, 'What I can name cannot really prick me.'[20] What cannot be named is what wounds us. Noir's struggle or failure to *name* its quarry coherently aligns it all the more faithfully with the elusive wounds of passion, potentiality and beatitude that so mercurially pulsate within the films that nevertheless take its name.

Notes

1 Reiner Schürmann, *Broken Hegemonies* (Bloomington: Indiana University Press, 2003), 16.
2 Massumi, *Parables for the Virtual*, 5.
3 Olivia Landry, 'The Beauty and Violence of *Horror Vacui*: Waiting in Christian Petzold's *Transit*', *German Quarterly*, 93.1 (2020), 95.
4 Benjamin, *Arcades Project*, 462.
5 Lauren Berlant, *Cruel Optimism* (Durham, NC: Duke University Press, 2011), 9.

6   Landry, too, notes the relevance of Berlant's work to Petzold's film in her essay on *Transit*.

7   Jordan Cronk, 'Interview: Christian Petzold', *Film Comment*, February 28, 2018. https://www.filmcomment.com/blog/berlin-interview-christian-petzold/, accessed 2 May 2019.

8   Significantly, like Walker in *Point Blank*, Georg can also be understood as a dead man who does not yet understand he is a ghost – a rewired Hermes, conceived as a dysfunctional psychopomp, an interloping figure caught between worlds, having forgotten his status as go-between. This is a fate similar to that of Christopher Nolan's fugal noir antiheroes: Leonard (Guy Pearce) at the close of *Memento*; Cobb at the close of *Inception*. It is also characteristic of the experience of David Lynch's own fugal noir protagonists in *Lost Highway* and *Mulholland Drive*. In *Transit*, when Georg fixes the broken radio, he is immediately struck by a song on the radio – a lullaby his mother sung to him as a child. The song, in which a range of creatures are called home to rest in ways specific to their nature ('the elephant stomps home/the ant rushes home') may therefore be a communication to Georg from the underworld, akin to the enigmatic messages Orphée receives via radio in Cocteau's film.

9   Anna Seghers, *Transit*, trans. Margo Bettauer Dembo (New York: New York Review Books, 2013), 20.

10 Ibid., 251.

11 Massumi, *Parables*, 5.

12 Ibid.

13 Blanchot, *The Space of Literature*, 150.

14 Ibid., 122.

15 André Bazin, 'The Death of Humphrey Bogart', in *Cahiers du Cinéma: The 1950s*, ed. Jim Hillier (Cambridge, MA: Harvard University Press, 1985), 98.

16 Seghers, *Transit*, 251.

17 Landry, 'The Beauty and Violence of *Horror Vacui*', 101.

18 Berlant, *Cruel Optimism*, 4.

19 Roland Barthes, *Camera Lucida*, trans. Richard Howard (London: Vintage, 1993), 26–7.

20 Ibid., 51.

BIBLIOGRAPHY

Agamben, Giorgio, 'Nymphs', in *Releasing the Image: From Literature to New Media*, ed. Jacques Khalip and Robert Mitchell, Stanford: Stanford University Press, 2011, 60–83.
Agamben, Giorgio, *The Coming Community*, trans. Michael Hardt, London: University of Minnesota Press, 1993.
Agamben, Giorgio, 'Eternal Return and the Paradox of Passion', *Stanford Italian Review*, 6.1–2 (1986), 9–17.
Agamben, Giorgio, *Homo Sacer: Sovereign Power and Bare Life*, trans. Daniel Heller-Roazen, Stanford, CA: Stanford University Press, 1998.
Agamben, Giorgio, *The Man without Content*, trans. Georgia Albert, Stanford, CA: Stanford University Press, 1999.
Agamben, Giorgio, *The Open: Man and Animal*, trans. Kevin Attell, Stanford, CA: Stanford University Press, 2004.
Agamben, Giorgio, *Potentialities: Collected Essays in Philosophy*, trans. Daniel Heller-Roazen, Stanford, CA: Stanford University Press, 1999.
Agamben, Giorgio, *Remnants of Auschwitz: The Witness and the Archive*, trans. Daniel Heller-Roazen, New York: Zone Books, 1999.
Agamben, Giorgio, *The Signature of All Things: On Method*, trans. Luca D'Isanto with Kevin Attell, New York: Zone Books, 2009.
Agamben, Giorgio, *Stanzas: Word and Phantasm in Western Culture*, trans. Ronald L. Martinez, London: University of Minnesota Press, 1993.
Agamben, Giorgio, *State of Exception*, trans. Kevin Attell, Chicago: University of Chicago Press, 2005.
Agamben, Giorgio, *The Time That Remains*, trans. Patricia Dailey, Stanford, CA: Stanford University Press, 2005.
Alloway, Lawrence, 'Iconography and the Movies', *Movie*, no. 7 (1963), 4–6.
Arsić, Branka, 'Active Habits and Passive Events or Bartleby', in *Between Deleuze and Derrida*, ed. Paul Patton and John Protevi, London: Continuum, 2003, 135–57.
Arthur, Paul, 'Philosophy in the Bedroom', *Cineaste*, 30.4 (2005), 6–8.
Auerbach, Erich, '*Passio* as Passion', in *Time, History, and Literature: Selected Essays of Erich Auerbach*, ed. James I. Porter, trans. Jane O. Newman, Princeton, NJ: Princeton University Press, 2014, 165–87.
Azoury, Phillipe, and Jean-Marc Lalanne, *Cocteau et le cinema: Désordres*, Paris: Cahiers du Cinema, 2003.
Bakhtin, Mikhail, *Problems of Dostoevsky's Poetics*, ed. and trans. Caryl Emerson, Minneapolis: University of Minnesota Press, 1984.

Bansak, Edmund G., *Fearing the Dark: The Val Lewton Career*, Jefferson, NC: McFarland, 1995.
Barker, Jennifer Lynda, *The Aesthetics of Antifascist Film: Radical Projection*, London: Routledge, 2013.
Barthes, Roland, *Camera Lucida*, trans. Richard Howard, London: Vintage, 1993.
Barthes, Roland, *The Eiffel Tower and Other Mythologies*, trans. Richard Howard, Berkeley: University of California Press, 1997.
Barthes, Roland, *The Grain of the Voice: Interviews 1962–1980*, trans. Linda Coverdale, Berkeley: University of California Press, 1985.
Bartoloni, Paolo, 'The Open and the Suspension of Being', *CLCWeb: Comparative Literature and Culture*, 7.3 (2005). http://docs.lib.purdue.edu./clcweb/vol7/iss3/10/. Accessed 4 September 2014.
Bataille, Georges, *On Nietzsche*, trans. Bruce Boone, London: Continuum, 2004.
Baudrillard, Jean, *Simulacra and Simulation*, trans. Sheila Faria Glaser, Ann Arbor: University of Michigan Press, 1994.
Baudrillard, Jean, *The Spirit of Terrorism and Other Essays*, London: Verso, 2003.
Bazin, André, 'The Death of Humphrey Bogart', in *Cahiers du Cinema: The 1950s*, ed. Jim Hillier, Cambridge, MA: Harvard University Press, 1985, 98–101.
Bellour, Raymond, *Between-the-Images*, Zurich: JPR Ringier, 2011.
Benjamin, Oliver, *The Abide Guide: Living Like Lebowski*, Berkeley: Ulysses, 2011.
Benjamin, Walter, *The Arcades Project*, trans. Howard Eiland and Kevin McLaughlin, Cambridge, MA: Harvard University Press, 2002.
Benjamin, Walter, *Illuminations*, trans. Harry Zohn, with an introduction by Hannah Arendt (ed.), New York: Schocken, 2007.
Bennett, Jane, *Vibrant Matter*, Durham, NC: Duke University Press, 2009.
Bergson, Henri, *Time and Free Will: An Essay on the Immediate Data of Consciousness*, London: Dover Press, 2001.
Berlant, Lauren, *Cruel Optimism*, Durham, NC: Duke University Press, 2011.
Bettinson, Gary, 'Happy Together? Generic Hybridity in 2046 and In the Mood for Love', in *Puzzle Films: Complex Storytelling in Contemporary Cinema*, ed. Warren Buckland, Oxford: Wiley-Blackwell, 2009, 167–86.
Birault, Henri, 'Beatitude in Nietzsche', in *The New Nietzsche: Contemporary Styles of Interpretation*, with an introduction by David B. Allison (ed.), Cambridge, MA: MIT Press, 1994, 219–31.
Blanchot, Maurice, *Friendship*, trans. Elizabeth Rottenberg, Stanford, CA: Stanford University Press, 1997.
Blanchot, Maurice, *The Infinite Conversation*, trans. Susan Hanson, Minneapolis: University of Minnesota, 1993.
Blanchot, Maurice, *The Siren's Song: Selected Essays*, ed. Gabriel Josipovici, trans. Sacha Rabinovitch, Brighton: Harvester, 1982.
Blanchot, Maurice, *The Space of Literature*, trans. Ann Smock, Lincoln: University of Nebraska, 1989.
Blanchot, Maurice, *The Writing of the Disaster*, trans. Ann Smock, Lincoln: University of Nebraska, 1995.
Blanchot, Maurice, and Jacques Derrida, *The Instant of My Death* / Jacques Derrida, *Demeure: Fiction and Testimony*, trans. Elizabeth Rottenburg, Stanford, CA: Stanford University Press, 2000.

Borde, Raymonde, and Etienne Chaumeton, *A Panorama of American Film Noir*, trans. Paul Hammond, San Francisco: City Lights Books, 2002.
Bould, Mark, *Film Noir: From Berlin to Sin City*, New York: Columbia University Press, 2005.
Bridges, Jeff and Glassman, Bernie, *The Dude and the Zen Master*, New York: Plume, 2012.
Brooks, Peter, 'The Law as Narrative and Rhetoric', in *Law's Stories: Narrative and Rhetoric in the Law*, ed. Peter Brooks and Paul Gewirtz, New Haven, CT: Yale University Press, 1996, 14–22.
Brown, Kristi A., '*Pathétique* Noir: Beethoven and *The Man Who Wasn't There*', *Beethoven Forum*, 10.2 (2003), 139–61.
Buchanan, Ian, 'Deleuze's "Life" Sentences', *Polygraph: An International Journal of Culture and Politics*, 18 (2006), 129–47.
Buscombe, Edward, 'The Idea of Genre in the American Cinema', *Screen*, 11.2 (1970), 33–45.
Calvino, Italo, *t zero*, trans. William Weaver, New York: Harcourt, Brace and World, 1969.
Cameron, Allan, '"Trajectories of Identification": Travel and Global Culture in the Films of Wong Kar-Wai', *Jump Cut: A Review of Contemporary Media*, 49 (2007). https://www.ejumpcut.org/archive/jc49.2007/wongKarWai/text.html. Accessed 1 June 2014.
Chabrol, Claude, and Eric Rohmer, *Hitchcock: The First Forty-four Films*, trans. Stanley Hochman, New York: Ungar, 1979.
Chandler, Raymond, *The Big Sleep*, London: Penguin, 2005.
Chandler, Raymond, *The High Window*, London: Penguin, 2005.
Chandler, Raymond, and Billy Wilder, Screenplay for *Double Indemnity*, http://ubuntuone.com/1LLFc924lbmghsyaxZYdYe. Accessed 23 January 2014.
Christopher, Nicholas, *Somewhere in the Night: Film Noir and the American City*, New York: Simon & Schuster, 1997.
Coen, Joel and Ethan, *Burn after Reading*, London: Faber and Faber, 2008.
Colebrook, Claire, *Gilles Deleuze*, London: Routledge, 2002.
Cook, Terry, 'Evidence, Memory, Identity, and Community: Four Shifting Archival Paradigms', *Archival Science*, 13 (2013), 95–120.
Corliss, Richard, '2046: A Face Odyssey', *TIME*, 1 August 2005.
Cowie, Elizabeth, 'Film Noir and Women', in *Shades of Noir: A Reader*, ed. Joan Copjec, London: Verso, 1993, 121–66.
Cronk, Jordan, 'Interview: Christian Petzold', *Film Comment*, February 28, 2018. https://www.filmcomment.com/blog/berlin-interview-christian-petzold/. Accessed 2 May 2019.
Damico, James, 'Film Noir: A Modest Proposal', *Film Reader*, no. 3, 1978, reprinted in *Film Noir Reader*, ed. Alain Silver and James Ursini, New York: Limelight, 1996.
Darke, Chris, *Alphaville*, London: I.B. Tauris, 2005.
Davis, Whitney, *A General Theory of Visual Culture*, Princeton, NJ: Princeton University Press, 2011.
de Cordova, Richard, 'Genre and Performance: An Overview', in *Film Genre Reader III*, ed. Keith Barry Grant, Austin: University of Texas, 2003, 130–41.

de la Durantaye, Leland, *Giorgio Agamben: A Critical Introduction*, Stanford, CA: Stanford University Press, 2009.
Deleuze, Gilles, *Cinema I: The Movement Image*, trans. Hugh Tomlinson and Barbara Habberjam, London: Athlone Press, 1986.
Deleuze, Gilles, *Cinema II: The Time Image*, trans. Hugh Tomlinson and Robert Galeta, London: Athlone Press, 2000.
Deleuze, Gilles, *Difference and Repetition*, trans. Paul Patton, London: Athlone Press, 1994.
Deleuze, Gilles, *Expressionism in Philosophy: Spinoza*, trans. Martin Joughin, New York: Zone Books, 1990.
Deleuze, Gilles, *Gilles Deleuze from A to Z*, with Claire Parnet and Pierre-André Boutang, trans. Charles J. Stivale, Los Angeles: Semiotexte, 2011.
Deleuze, Gilles, 'Immanence: A Life' in *Pure Immanence: Essays on Life*, with an introduction by John Rajchman, trans. Anne Boyman, New York: Zone Books, 2001, 25–33.
Deleuze, Gilles, *Nietzsche and Philosophy*, trans. Hugh Tomlinson, London: Athlone Press, 1983.
Deleuze, Gilles, 'Postscript on the Societies of Control', *October* 59 (1992), 3–7.
Deleuze, Gilles, *Spinoza: Practical Philosophy*, trans. Robert Hurley, San Francisco: City Lights Books, 1988.
Deleuze, Gilles, and Félix Guattari, *A Thousand Plateaus: Capitalism and Schizophrenia*, trans. Brian Massumi, Minneapolis: University of Minnesota Press, 1987.
Deleuze, Gilles, and Félix Guattari, *What Is Philosophy?*, trans. Hugh Tomlinson and Graham Burchell, New York: Columbia University Press, 1994.
del Río, Elena, *Deleuze and the Cinemas of Performance: Powers of Affection*, Edinburgh: Edinburgh University Press, 2008.
Derrida, Jacques, *Margins of Philosophy*, trans. Alan Bass, Chicago: University of Chicago Press, 1982.
Derrida, Jacques, *On the Name*, ed. Thomas Dutoit, trans. David Wood, Stanford, CA: Stanford University Press, 1995.
Derrida, Jacques, 'The Parergon', trans. Craig Owens, *October* 9 (1979), 3–41.
Derrida, Jacques, 'Passions – An Oblique View', in Jacques Derrida, *On the Name*, ed. Thomas Dutoit, trans. David Wood, Stanford, CA: Stanford University Press, 1995.
Derrida, Jacques, *Spectres of Marx: The State of the Debt, the Work of Mourning and the New International*, trans. Peggy Kamuf, London: Routledge, 1994.
Derrida, Jacques, *Writing and Difference*, trans. and with an introduction by Alan Bass, London: Routledge, 2005.
Didi-Huberman, Georges, *The Surviving Image: Phantoms of Time and Time of Phantoms – Aby Warburg's History of Art*, trans. Harvey L. Mendelsohn, University Park: Pennsylvania State University Press, 2017.
Dimendberg, Edward, *Film Noir and the Spaces of Modernity*, Cambridge, MA: Harvard University Press, 2004.
Dixon, Wheeler Winston, *Black and White Cinema: A Short History*, New Brunswick, NJ: Rutgers University Press, 2015.
Doane, Mary Ann, *The Emergence of Cinematic Time: Modernity, Contingency, The* Archive, Cambridge, MA: Harvard University Press, 2002.

Doane, Mary Ann, '"Pathos and Pathology": The Cinema of Todd Haynes', *Camera Obscura* 57, 19.3 (2004), 1–21.
Durgnat, Raymond, 'Paint It Black: The Family Tree of the Film Noir', *Cinema*, 6.7, 1970, in *Film Noir Reader*, ed. Alain Silver and James Ursini, New York: Limelight, 1996, 37–52.
Dussere, Eric, *America Is Elsewhere*, Oxford: Oxford University Press, 2013.
Eliade, Mircea, *The Sacred and the Profane*, trans. Willard R. Trask, New York: Harvest, 1968.
Elmer, Jonathan, 'Enduring and Abiding', in *The Year's Work in Lebowski Studies*, ed. Edward P. Comentale and Aaron Jaffe, Bloomington: Indiana University Press, 2009, 445–54.
Erickson, Glenn, 'Expressionist Doom in *Night and the City*', in *Film Noir Reader*, ed. Alain Silver and James Ursini, Limelight, 1996, 103–8.
Foucault, Michel, 'The Thought from Outside', in Michel Foucault and Maurice Blanchot, *Foucault / Blanchot*, trans. Jeffrey Mehlman and Brian Massumi, New York: Zone Books, 1987, 7–60.
Frank, Nino, 'A New Kind of Police Drama: The Criminal Adventure', trans. Alain Silver, in *Film Noir Reader 2*, ed. Alain Silver and James Ursini. New York: Limelight, 1999, 15–19.
Freud, Sigmund, *Beyond the Pleasure Principle*, trans. and ed. James Strachey, *The Standard Edition of the Complete Works of Sigmund Freud*, vol. 18, London: Hogarth, 1953–74, 3–64.
Girard, Rene, *Violence and the Sacred*, trans. Patrick Gregory, London: Continuum, 2005.
Goffman, Erving, *The Presentation of the Self in Everyday Life*, Garden City, NY: Doubleday, 1959.
Gombrich, Ernst Hans, *Aby Warburg: An Intellectual Biography*, Oxford: Phaidon Press, 1970.
Gregg, Melissa, and Gregory J. Seigworth (eds), *The Affect Theory Reader*, Durham, NC: Duke University Press, 2010.
Grønstad, Asbjørn, and Henrik Gustafsson (eds), *Cinema and Agamben*, New York: Academic, 2014.
Gross, Larry, 'Film Après Noir', *Film Comment*, 12.2 (1976), 44–9.
Gustafsson, Henrik, 'A Wet Emptiness: The Phenomenology of Film Noir', in *A Companion to Film Noir*, ed. Andrew Spicer and Helen Hanson, Oxford: Wiley Blackwell, 2013, 50–66.
Hammett, Dashiel, *The Maltese Falcon*, New York: Vintage, 1992.
Harris, Oliver, 'Film Noir Fascination: Outside History, But Historically So', *Cinema Journal*, 43.1 (2003), 3–24.
Heidegger, Martin, *Being and Time*, trans. John Macquarrie and Edward Robinson, Oxford: Blackwell, 1962.
Heidegger, Martin, *Contributions to Philosophy*, trans. Parvis Emad and Kenneth Maly, Bloomington: Indiana University Press, 1999.
Heidegger, Martin, 'Letter on Humanism', in *Basic Writings*, trans. David Farrell Krell, London: Routledge, 1993, 234–45.
Heidegger, Martin, *The Question Concerning Technology and Other Essays*, trans. William Lovitt, London: Harper and Row, 1977, 3–48.

Herzogenrath, Bernd, 'On the Lost Highway: Lynch and Lacan, Cinema and Cultural Pathology', *Other Voices*, 1.3 (1999). www.othervoices.org/1.3/bh/highway. Accessed 12 October 2014.

Hughes, David (ed.), *The Complete Lynch*, London: Virgin Books, 2001.

Iversen, Margaret, and Stephen Melville, *Writing Art History: Disciplinary Departures*, Chicago: University of Chicago Press, 2001.

Jameson, Fredric, *Postmodernism, or, the Cultural Logic of Late Capitalism*, Durham, NC: Duke University Press, 1991.

Jay, Martin, *Downcast Eyes: The Denigration of Vision in Twentieth-Century French Thought*, Berkeley: University of California Press, 1993.

Johnson, Christopher D., *Memory, Metaphor, and Aby Warburg's Atlas of Images*, Ithaca, NY: Cornell University Press, 2012.

Johnson, G. Allen, 'Frustrated Romantic Trapped in the Past, with Hope for the Future', *San Francisco Chronicle*, 19 August 2005.

Jones, Jenny M., *The Big Lebowski: An Illustrated, Annotated History of the Greatest Cult Film of all Time*, Minneapolis: Voyageur Press, 2012.

Kael, Pauline, *Diva* review, *New Yorker*, 19 April 1982.

Kaplan, E. Ann, 'The "Dark Continent" of Film Noir: Race, Displacement and Metaphor in Tourneur's *Cat People* (1942) and Welles's *The Lady from Shanghai* (1948)', in *Women in Film Noir*, ed. E. Ann Kaplan, London: BFI, 1998, 183–201.

Kaufman, Eleanor, 'Midnight, or the Inertia of Being', *Parallax*, 12.2 (2006), 98–111.

Keating, Patrick 'Out of the Shadows: Noir Lighting and Hollywood Cinematography', in *A Companion to Film Noir*, ed. Andrew Spicer and Helen Hanson, Oxford: Wiley Blackwell, 2013, 267–83.

Kermode, Frank, *The Sense of an Ending*, Oxford: Oxford University Press, 2000.

Kerouac, Jack, 'Beatific: On the Origins of the Beat Generation', *Playboy*, June 1959, 31–2, 42, 79.

Keyssar, Helene, *Robert Altman's America*, Oxford: Oxford University Press, 1991.

Kierkegaard, Søren, *Fear and Trembling*, trans. Howard V. Hong and ed. Edna H. Hong, Princeton, NJ: Princeton University Press, 1983.

Killeen, Padraic, 'Echoes Beyond Time, Language or Caress: *Orphée, Alphaville, 2046*', *[in]Transition: Journal of Videographic Film and Moving Image Studies*, 6.2 (2019). http://mediacommons.org/intransition/echoes-beyond-time.

Killeen, Padraic, 'Suffering in Rhythm: The "Haunting Melody" in Film Noir', *[in]Transition: Journal of Videographic Film and Moving Image Studies*, 5.2 (2018). http://mediacommons.org/intransition/2018/05/02/suffering-rhythm.

Klein, Richard, *Cigarettes Are Sublime*, Durham, NC: Duke University Press, 1993

Klibansky, Raymond, Erwin Panofsky and Fritz Saxl, *Saturn and Melancholy: Studies in the History of Natural Philosophy, Religion, and Art*, Nendeln/Lichtenstein: Kraus, 1979.

Klinger, Barbara, 'The Art Film, Affect, and The Female Viewer: *The Piano* Revisited', *Screen*, 47.1 (2006), 19–41.

Klossowski, Pierre, *Nietzsche and the Vicious Circle*, trans. Daniel W. Smith, London: Athlone Press, 1997.

Kolker, Robert, *A Cinema of Loneliness*, Oxford: Oxford University Press, 2011.

Kranzfelder, Ivo, *Edward Hopper, 1882–1967: Vision of Reality*, New York: Taschen, 1998.
Kristeva, Julia, *Powers of Horror: An Essay on Abjection*, trans. Leon S. Roudiez, New York: Columbia University Press, 1982.
Krutnik, Frank, *In a Lonely Street, Film Noir, Genre, Masculinity*, London: Routledge, 2006.
Lambert, Gregg, 'Cinema and the Outside', in *The Brain is the Screen*, ed. Gregory Flaxman, Minneapolis: University of Minnesota Press, 2000, 253–92.
Landry, Olivia, 'The Beauty and Violence of *Horror Vacui*: Waiting in Christian Petzold's *Transit*', *German Quarterly*, 93.1 (2020), 90–105.
Lavery, David, '"Secret Shit": the Uncertainty Principle, Lying, Deviation, and the Movie Creativity of the Coen Brothers', *Post Script*, 27.2 (2008), 141–53.
Levinas, Emmanuel, 'On Maurice Blanchot', in *Proper Names*, trans. Michael B. Smith, London: Athlone, 1996, 127–70.
Levinas, Emmanuel, 'Reality and Its Shadow', in *The Levinas Reader*, ed. Seán Hand, Cambridge: Blackwell, 1989, 129–43.
Luhr, William, *Film Noir*, Oxford: Wiley-Blackwell, 2012.
Lyotard, Jean François, *The Inhuman: Reflections on Time*, trans. Geoffrey Bennington and Rachel Bowlby, London: Polity Press, 1991.
Ma, Jean, *Melancholy Drift: Marking Time in Chinese Cinema*, Hong Kong: Hong Kong University Press, 2010.
Maltby, Richard, *Hollywood Cinema*, London: Blackwell, 2003.
Martin, Adrian, *Last Day Every Day: Figural Thinking from Auerbach and Kracauer to Agamben and Brenez*, New York: Punctum, 2012.
Martin, Adrian, 'Recital: Three Lyrical Interludes in Godard', in *Forever Godard*, ed. Michael Temple, James S. Williams and Michael Witt, London: Black Dog, 2004.
Martin-Jones, David, *Deleuze and Film*, ed. David Martin-Jones and William Brown, Edinburgh: Edinburgh University Press, 2012.
Martin-Jones, David, *Deleuze and World Cinemas*, London: Continuum, 2011.
Masierska, Ewa, and Rascaroli, Laura, 'Trapped in the Present: Time in the Films of Wong Kar-Wai', *Film Criticism*, 25.2 (2000), 2–20.
Massumi, Brian, 'The Autonomy of the Affect', *Cultural Critique*, 31 (1995), 83–109.
Massumi, Brian, *Parables for the Virtual: Movement, Affect, Sensation*, Durham, NC: Duke University Press, 2002.
McArthur, Colin, *The Big Heat*, London: BFI, 1992.
McArthur, Colin, *Underworld USA*, London: Secker and Warburg/BFI, 1972.
McGowan, Todd, *Timeless in Space: Desire in Atemporal Cinema*, Minneapolis: University of Minnesota, 2011.
McLuhan, Marshall, *Understanding Media: The Extensions of Man*, Cambridge, MA: MIT Press, 1994.
Meehan, Paul, *Horror Noir: Where Cinema's Dark Sisters Meet*, Jefferson, NC: McFarland, 2011.
Mitchell, W. J. T., *Iconology: Image, Text, Ideology*, Chicago: University of Chicago Press, 1987.
Mitchell, W. J. T., *What Do Pictures Want? The Lives and Loves of Images*, Chicago: University of Chicago Press, 2005.

Mottram, James, *The Coen Brothers: The Life of the Mind*, London: B.T. Batsford, 2000.

Mottram, James, 'Elliott Gould: I Didn't Have a Drug Problem. I Had a Problem with Reality'. *The Independent*, 22 July 2012.

Mulvey, Laura, *Death 24 X A Second: Stillness and the Moving Image*, London: Reaktion Books, 2005.

Murphy, Timothy S., 'Beneath Relativity: Bergson and Bohm on Absolute Time', in *The New Bergson*, ed. John Mullarkey, Manchester: Manchester University Press, 1999, 66–81.

Murphy, Timothy S., 'Quantum Ontology: A Virtual Mechanics of Becoming', in *Deleuze and Guattari: New Mappings in Politics, Philosophy, and Culture*, ed. Eleanor Kaufman and Kevin Jon Heller, Minneapolis: University of Minnesota, 1998, 211–29.

Nancy, Jean-Luc, *The Disavowed Community*, trans. Philip Armstrong, New York: Fordham University Press, 2016.

Nancy, Jean-Luc, *The Inoperative Community*, trans. Peter Connor, Lisa Garbus, Michael Holland and Simona Sawhney, Minneapolis: University of Minnesota, 1991.

Naremore, James, *More Than Night: Film Noir in its Contexts*, London: University of California Press, 1998.

Ness, Richard R., 'A Lotta Night Music: The Sound of Film Noir', *Cinema Journal*, 47.2 (2008), 52–73.

Nietzsche, Friedrich, *The Birth of Tragedy*, trans. and with an introduction by Douglas Smith, Oxford: Oxford University Press, 2000.

Nietzsche, Friedrich, *The Gay Science*, trans. W. Kaufmann, New York: Vintage Books, 1974.

Nietzsche, Friedrich, *Untimely Meditations*, trans. R. J. Hollingdale, ed. Daniel Breazeale, Cambridge: Cambridge University Press, 1997.

O'Brien, Geoffrey, 'Dana Andrews, or The Male Mask', in *Castaways of the Image Planet*, Washington, DC: Counterpoint, 2002, 194–201.

Oliver, Kelly, and Trigo, Benigno, *Noir Anxiety*, Minneapolis: University of Minnesota Press, 2003.

Orr, Stanley, 'Razing Cain: Excess Signification in Blood Simple and The Man Who Wasn't There', *Post Script*, 27.2 (2008), 8–22.

Osteen, Mark, *Nightmare Alley: Film Noir and the American Dream*, Baltimore, MD: John Hopkins University Press, 2013.

Palmer, R. Barton, 'The Divided Self and the Dark City: Film Noir and Liminality', *symploke*, 15.1–2 (2007), 66–79.

Panofsky, Erwin, *Meaning in the Visual Arts*, London: Penguin, 1993.

Pinkerton, Nick, 'Buschel's *Missing Person* Gestures towards Missing Profundity', *Village Voice*, 17 November 2009. www.villagevoice.com/2009-11-17/film/buschel-s-missing-person-gestures-towards-missing-profundity/full/. Accessed 23 November 2010.

Pippin, Robert B., *Fatalism in American Film Noir: Some Cinematic Philosophy*, Charlottesville: University of Virginia Press, 2012.

Place, Janey, 'Women in Film Noir', in *Women in Film Noir*, ed. E. Ann Kaplan, London: BFI, 1998, 47–68.

Place, Janey, and Lowell Peterson, 'Some Visual Motifs in Film Noir', in *Film Noir Reader*, ed. Alain Silver and James Ursini, New York: Limelight, 1996, 65–76.

Plantinga, Carl, 'The Scene of Empathy and the Human Face in Film', in *Passionate Views: Film, Cognition, and Emotion*, ed. Carl Plantinga and Greg M. Smith, Baltimore, MD: John Hopkins University Press, 1999, 239–55.

Poellner, Peter, 'Existential Moments', in *The Moment: Time and Rupture in Modern Thought*, ed. Heidrun Freise, Liverpool: Liverpool University Press, 2001, 53–72.

Polan, Dana, *Power and Paranoia: History, Narrative, and the American Cinema 1940–1950*, New York: Columbia University Press, 1986.

Porfirio, Robert, 'No Way Out: Existential Motifs in the *Film Noir*', in *Film Noir Reader*, ed. Alain Silver and James Ursini, New York: Limelight, 1996, 77–93.

Powell, Anna, *Deleuze and Horror Film*, Edinburgh: Edinburgh University Press, 2005.

Rainer, Peter, 'Skin Deep', *New York*, 5 November 2001.

Rampley, Matthew, 'Iconology of the Interval: Aby Warburg's Legacy', *Word & Image: A Journal of Verbal / Visual Enquiry*, 17.4 (2001), 303–24.

Rayns, Tony, 'The Long Goodbye', *Sight and Sound*, 15.1 (2005), 22–5.

Rayns, Tony, 'Poet of Time', *Sight and Sound*, 5.9 (1995), 12–16.

Rempel, Morgan, 'Epicurus and "Contented Poverty"', in *The Big Lebowski and Philosophy: Keeping Your Mind Limber with Abiding Wisdom*, ed. Peter S. Fosl, London: Wiley, 2012, 67–78.

Richards, Rashna Wadia, 'Loose Ends: The Stuff that Movies are Made of', *Arizona Quarterly*, 63.4 (2007), 83–118.

Ricoeur, Paul, *Oneself as Another*, trans. Kathleen Blamey, Chicago: University of Chicago Press, 1992.

Ricoeur, Paul, *Time and Narrative: Volume 1*, trans. Kathleen McLaughlin and David Pellauer, Chicago: University of Chicago Press, 1984.

Ricoeur, Paul, *Time and Narrative: Volume 3*, trans. Kathleen Blamey and David Pellauer, Chicago: University of Chicago Press, 1988.

Rilke, Rainer Maria, *The Duino Elegies and the Sonnets to Orpheus*, trans. A. Poulin Jr., New York: First Mariner, 2005.

Rilke, Rainer Maria, *Selected Poems of Rainer Maria Rilke*, trans. Robert Bly, New York: Harper and Row, 1981.

Rodowick, David, *Gilles Deleuze's Time Machine*, Durham, NC: Duke University Press, 1997.

Rosenbaum, Jonathan, *Essential Cinema: On the Necessity of Film Canons*, Baltimore, MD: John Hopkins University Press, 2008.

Ross, Alison (ed.), 'The Agamben Effect', *South Atlantic Quarterly*, 107.1 (2008), 1–13.

Rosset, Clement, *Joyful Cruelty*, trans. and ed. David F. Bell, Oxford: Oxford University Press, 1993.

Schatz, Thomas, *Boom and Bust: American Cinema in the 1940s*, Berkeley: University of California Press, 1999.

Schefer, Jean-Louis, *The Ordinary Man of the Cinema*, trans. Max Cavitch, Noura Wedell and Paul Grant, New York: Semiotexte, 2016.

Schickel, Richard, 'Short Takes', *TIME*, 29 October 2001.

Schrader, Paul, 'Notes on *Film Noir*', *Film Comment* 8.1, 1972, reprinted in *Film Noir Reader*, ed. Alain Silver and James Ursini, New York: Limelight, 1996, 53–64.
Schürmann, Reiner, *Broken Hegemonies*, Bloomington: Indiana University Press, 2003.
Scott, A.O., 'First Passive and Invisible, Then Ruinous and Glowing', *New York Times*, 31 October 2001.
Seghers, Anna, *Transit*, trans. Margo Bettauer Dembo, New York: New York Review Books, 2013.
Shadoian, Jack, *Dreams and Dead Ends: The American Gangster Film*, Oxford: Oxford University Press, 2003.
Shouse, Eric, 'Feeling, Emotion, Affect', *M/C Journal*, http://journal.media-culture.org.au/0512/03-shouse.php. Accessed 21 November 2010.
Shuffitt, Scott, and Will Russell (eds), *I'm A Lebowski, You're A Lebowski: Life, The Big Lebowski and What Have You*, Edinburgh: Canongate, 2013.
Silverman, Kaja, and Farocki, Harun, *Speaking About Godard*, New York: New York University Press, 1998.
Smith, Murray, 'Altered States: Character and Emotional Response in the Cinema', *Cinema Journal*, 33.4 (1994), 34–56.
Sobchack, Vivian, 'Lounge Time: Postwar Crises and the Chronotype of Film Noir', in *Refiguring American Film Genres*, ed. Nick Browne, Berkeley: University of California, 1988, 129–167.
Somer, Eric, 'The Noir-Horror of *Cat People* (1942)', in *Film Noir Reader 4*, ed. Alain Silver and James Ursini, New York: Limelight, 2004, 191–206.
Spicer, Andrew, 'The Angel of Death: Targeting the Hitman', in *Crime Cultures: Figuring Criminality in Fiction and Film*, ed. Bran Nicol, Patricia Pulman and Eugene McNulty, London: Continuum, 2010, 155–74.
Spicer, Andrew, *Historical Dictionary of Film Noir*, Lanham, MD: Scarecrow Press, 2010.
Stern, Lesley, 'Ghosting: The Performance and Migration of Cinematic Gesture, Focusing on Hou Hsiao-Hsien's *Good Men, Good Women*', in *Migrations of Gesture*, ed. Carrie Nolan and Sally Ann Ness, Minneapolis: University of Minnesota, 2008, 185–216.
Stewart, Garrett, 'The Long Goodbye from Chinatown', *Film Quarterly*, 28.2 (1974), 26–7.
Strawson, Galen, 'Against Narrativity', *Ratio*, 17 (2004), 428–52.
Taylor, Charles, *Sources of the Self: the Making of the Modern Identity*, Cambridge: Cambridge University Press, 1989.
Telotte, J. P., 'The Big Clock of Film Noir', *Film Criticism*, 14.2 (1989–90), 1–11.
Telotte, J. P., *Dreams of Darkness: Fantasy and the Films of Val Lewton*, Urbana: University of Illinois, 1985.
Telotte, J. P., *Voices in the Dark: The Narrative Patterns of Noir*, Urbana: University of Illinois, 1989.
Teo, Stephen, *Wong Kar-Wai: Auteur of Time*, London: BFI, 2005.
Terada, Rei, *Feeling in Theory: Emotion after the 'Death of the Subject'*, Cambridge, MA: Harvard University Press, 2001.
Thompson, David (ed.), *Altman on Altman*, London: Faber and Faber, 2006.

Thompson, Kristin, *Breaking the Glass Armour: Neoformalist Film Analysis*, Princeton, NJ: Princeton University Press, 1988.
Tong, Janice, 'Chungking Express: Time and Its Dislocation', in *Chinese Films in Focus*, ed. Chris Berry, London: BFI, 2003, 47–55.
Turner, Victor, *The Ritual Process: Structure and Anti-Structure*, Chicago: Aldine, 1969.
Utterson, Andrew, 'Tarzan vs. IBM: Humans and Computers in Jean-Luc Godard's Alphaville', *Film Criticism*, 33.1 (2008), 45–63.
Vernet, Marc, 'The Filmic Transaction: On the Openings of Film Noirs', trans. David Rodowick, in *The Velvet Light Trap*, 20, 1983, 2–9.
Vernet, Marc, 'Film Noir on the Edge of Doom' in *Shades of Noir: A Reader*, ed. Joan Copjec, London: Verso, 1993, 1–31.
Vincendeau, Ginette, *Jean-Pierre Melville: 'An American in Paris'*, London: BFI, 2003.
Walker, Michael, 'Robert Siodmak', in *The Movie Book of Film Noir*, ed. Ian Cameron, London: Studio Vista, 1994, 110–51.
Warburg, Aby, *The Renewal of Pagan Antiquity: Contributions to the Cultural History of the European Renaissance*, ed. Kurt W. Foster, trans. David Britt, Los Angeles: Getty Research Institute for the History of Art and the Humanities, 1999.
Watkin, William, *Agamben and Indifference*, London: Rowman and Littlefield, 2014, 137–78.
Willemen, Paul, 'Notes towards the Construction of Readings of Tourneur', in *Jacques Tourneur*, ed. Claire Johnson and Paul Willemen, Edinburgh: Edinburgh Film Festival, 1975, 16–35.
Wood, Robin, 'Ideology, Genre, Author', in *Film Genre Reader III*, ed. Keith Barry Grant, Austin: University of Texas, 2003.
Woolfolk, Alan, 'Disenchantment and Rebellion in Alphaville', in *The Philosophy of Science Fiction Film*, ed. Mark T. Conard, Lexington: University Press of Kentucky, 2008, 191–205.
Zepke, Stephen, *Art as Abstract Machine: Ontology and Aesthetics in Deleuze and Guattari*, London: Routledge, 2005.
Žižek, Slavoj, *The Art of the Ridiculous Sublime: On David Lynch's Lost Highway*, Seattle: University of Washington Press, 2000.
Žižek, Slavoj, *Enjoy Your Symptom! Jacques Lacan in Hollywood and Out*, New York: Routledge, 2001.
Žižek, Slavoj, '"The Thing That Thinks": The Kantian Background of the Noir Subject', in *Shades of Noir: A Reader*, ed. Joan Copjec, London: Verso, 1993, 199–226.
Žižek, Slavoj, *Welcome to the Desert of the Real: Five Essays on September 11 and Related Dates*, London: Verso, 2002.

INDEX

Note: Page numbers with an 'n' denote Notes.

abiding, in the interval 56, 219–25, 229 n.44
abjection 89–90
acedia 15, 43–50, 55, 63, 68, 120, 162–4, 211, 223, 239
   Agamben's and Benjamin's, comparison between 71 n.34
   melancholy of 48–9
   and phantasms 49
   saving sorrow of 47–8
   and temporality 44
   see also self-affection
acedic arrest 33, 44–5, 50, 53, 91, 114, 139, 209
Act of Violence (Zinnemann) 200 n.6
Adam and Eve (Dürer) 123
adequate ideas (Spinoza) 25
affection-image (Deleuze) *see* Deleuze
affective interval 16, 68, 92, 129, 149, 151
affective stillness 43, 95, 165
affectivity 4, 6, 53, 68, 89, 95–6, 98, 107, 124, 129, 131, 167, 211, 213, 221
affectlessness 52, 57, 77, 92–3, 96, 99, 101 n.2
affect(s) 2–6, 16, 24, 53, 68, 92, 94–5, 98, 114–15, 122, 128, 243
   autonomous transmission of 138
   and body's power 6
   exposure to 134–9
   and music 97
   registering 132, 134–5
   see also zero affect
Agamben, Giorgio 2, 5, 15–16, 17, 24, 50, 105, 109–10, 113–14, 122–3, 157, 195, 200 n.5, 210, 214, 219, 228 n.29, 243
   on *acedia* 46–9
   bare life 121, 193, 195, 202 n.31, 233
   and beatitude 121
   on being-such 215–17, 225, 233
   biopolitical machine 193
   Coming Community, The 42, 229 n.41, 230 n.57
   on erotic anamnesis 42
   on eternal return 143, 162, 169
   on ethics 203 n.38
   on extra-juridical act 183
   on gestures 136–7, 139
   Homo Sacer: Sovereign Power and Bare Life 202 n.31
   on the Irreparable 216
   on *Melencolia I* 48
   on the messianic 17, 46–7, 197, 210, 215, 225, 231 n.61
   on *Nymph and Shepherd* (Titian) 139
   Open, The: Man and Animal 109, 121–2
   on *pathosformel* 50
   potentiality (*see* potential/potentiality)
   on profound boredom 119
   on self-affection 162, 166
   Stanzas 43, 48, 71 n.34, 120, 174 n.19
   State of Exception 192
   on state of 'shame' 42
   on video works of Bill Viola 51–2

INDEX

whatever-being 215–16, 224, 234, 241
Alloway, Lawrence 32
Alphaville: A Strange Adventure of Lemmy Caution (Godard) 2, 16, 119, 127–43, 149–54, 161–3, 165–6, 169–70, 187–8, 194
Altman, Robert 53, 185–6, 200 n.7, 201 n.10, 201 n.13
American Friend, The (Wenders) 13
anarchy/anarchic moment 16, 162, 179–80, 194, 197–8, 233–4
Anaximander Fragment, the 190, 199–200 n.2
Andrews, Dana 56
angel
  and image 211, 227 n.11
  intervallic 'angelic' realm 211
  of melancholy 45, 48, 157, 211
Angel Heart (Parker) 14, 206
animal becomings 105, 110
Antonioni, Michelangelo 57
Aristotle 120, 162, 176 n.48
arrest 45–6, 53
  acedic arrest 33, 44–5, 50, 53, 91, 114, 139, 209
  arresting image 165, 240
  messianic arrest 17, 46–7, 197, 210, 215, 225–6, 231 n.61
Arsić, Branka 67–8
art 117–19, 128, 145 n.19
Artaud, Antonin 100
Arthur, Paul 168
Asphalt Jungle, The 178 n.54
As Tears Go By (Wong) 151
atemporal rupture 140, 149–50
Auerbach, Erich 52
Aumont, Jacques 173 n.12
Aura, The (Bielinsky) 60–1
auto-affection 16, 83, 169, 211
Automat (Hopper) 55
automatism 53, 55–6, 100
L'Avventura (Antonioni) 10
Azoury, Phillipe 153

background hum 97–8, 100, 142, 240
Bakhtin, Mikhail 169

bare life (Agamben) 121, 193, 195, 202 n.31, 233
Barthes, Roland 137–8, 145 n.29, 244
Bartoloni, Paolo 119
Bataille, Georges 200 n.5, 229 n.41
Baudrillard, Jean 212
Bazin, André 241
beat/beatific 141, 223, 230 n.52
beatitude 25–7, 78, 98–101, 114, 163–4, 169–70, 194, 203 n.40
  Agamben's use of 121–2, 233
  Deleuzian 5, 15, 20 n.49, 218
  and eternal return 16 n.48, 141, 161
  in Nietzsche 141, 146 n.48
  noir beatitude 65–8
  quasi-redemptive 15, 129, 233–4
  and self-affection 214, 218–19, 223
  Spinozist 15, 20 n.49, 25, 78, 224
  Žižek's use of 20 n.49
becoming(s) 4, 16, 24–5, 97, 107, 122, 141, 161
  animal becomings 105, 110
  becoming-imperceptible 26, 203 n.40
  impersonal becoming 10, 26, 65, 141, 169
  lapse across thresholds of 129
  time as 10, 150
being missing 207–15, 209, 214
Bellour, Raymond 51
Belmondo, Jean-Paul 137
Benjamin, Walter 17, 121, 168, 192, 194–5, 228–9 n.38, 235–6, 242
Bennett, Jane 90
Bergson, Henri 60, 96, 169
  durée 140–1, 149, 212
Berlant, Lauren 235–6, 242
Bettinson, Gary 174 n.23
Big Clock, The (Farrow) 16, 179–81, 199 n.1, 206
Big Combo, The 228 n.34
Big Heat, The (Lang) 45, 94, 183, 198, 228 n.34
Big Knife, The (Aldrich) 228 n.34
Big Lebowski, The (Coen brothers) 17, 56, 78, 136, 205, 216–23, 225, 228 n.38

INDEX

Big Sleep, The (Chandler) 178 n.54, 200 n.7, 201 n.24, 202 n.25, 228 n.34
biopolitical 192–3, 196, 202 n.31, 215, 233, 235
Birault, Henri 146 n.48
Birth of Venus (Botticelli) 50
Black Angel (Neill) 206, 226 n.2
Blade Runner (Scott) 14, 159
Blanchot, Maurice 5, 8, 21–3, 26, 52, 55, 63–4, 74 n.93, 78, 99, 115, 160, 178 n.58, 235, 240
    on disaster 212–14, 220, 225
    on friendship 123
    'Instant of My Death, The' 65, 169, 178 n.58, 241
    'Outside, the' 26–7, 55–6, 58, 64, 236, 240
    on pathos 52
    and space of 'the Outside' 26–7, 55–6, 58, 64, 236, 240
    on states of 'infinite' waiting 236
    on thought outside of thought 27
blank point 12–13
Blood Simple 78–9
Bodeen, DeWitt 106
body 5, 56–7, 108, 136, 145 n.19, 208, 217–18, 234, 240
    active and passive powers of 6, 213–14
    affective autonomy of 56
    affectivity of 6, 9, 95, 213, 221
    and composure 11
    enigmatic body 100
    gendered 45
    grooming of 89–90
    unthought life of 218
Body and Soul (Rossen) 36–8, 178 n.54
Bogart, Humphrey 165, 168, 178 n.54, 186, 241
Bohler, Olivier 217, 228 n.35
Bohm, David 134
Borde, Raymonde 3–4, 34–5, 203 n.42
Bould, Mark 6
Bout de souffle, À (*Breathless*) 137, 165
Brackett, Leigh 200 n.7

Bridges, Jeff 218
Brooks, Peter 102 n.18
Brown, Kristi A. 96
Buchanan, Ian 121
Burn After Reading (Coen brothers) 78
Buscombe, Edward 32

Calvino, Italo 22–6, 140
Cameron, Allan 172
Campagnola, Giulio 43
Capital of Pain, The (Eluard) 135
captivation 113–16
    of animals 110, 113
    awakening from captivation to captivation 114
    of humans 111, 113, 115, 127
    and opening-to 110
Carpaccio, Vittore 54–5
Cat People (Tourneur) 2, 16, 101, 105–24, 127–8, 136, 139
Chabrol, Claude 41
Chandler, Raymond 184
Chaumeton, Etienne 3, 4, 34–5, 203 n.42
Chinatown (Polanski) 11, 13, 184, 196
Christopher, Nicholas 54, 127
chronological time 8, 12, 23, 35, 44, 51, 179
    and 'law, the' 182
Chungking Express 151
Cigarettes Are Sublime 164
cigarette smoking 36, 80, 85, 116, 152, 163–6, 174 n.23, 193, 218 *see also* figure smoking
classic noir 11–13, 17, 27, 80, 93, 101, 119, 178 n.54, 179–80, 197, 205
clock imagery 33–4, 157, 164, 179–81, 199 n.1
close-ups 9, 37, 92–3, 98–9, 152
Colebrook, Claire 141, 193–4
Comentale, Edward P. 221
community 78, 89, 179–81, 197, 216, 224
contemplation 38–9, 48, 54, 68, 86, 116, 211
Conversation, The (Coppola) 11, 13, 184, 196

Corliss, Richard 151
counter-narrative 92, 96, 99–100
Coup de torchon (Tavernier) 70 n.28
Cowie, Elizabeth 14
Crack-Up (Reis) 119, 226 n.2
Criss Cross (Siodmak) 116
Critique of Judgment (Kant) 72 n.50
Curse of the Cat People, The (von Fritsch and Wise) 110, 117, 123

D'Agostino, Albert 106–7
Dark Corner, The (Hathaway) 119
Darke, Chris 134, 137–8, 153
Dark Passage (Daves) 102 n.10, 175 n.44
Dasein (Heidegger) 47, 110–11, 118
Davis, Whitney 31–2
Days of Being Wild (Wong) 151, 164
Dead Reckoning 178 n.54
de Cordova, Richard 73 n.65
defining noir, problems thereof 2–5
de la Durantaye, Leland 7, 174 n.19
delayed/interrupted movement of film 51
Deleuze, Gilles 2, 4, 5, 8, 11, 21–2, 26, 51, 55, 68, 82, 90, 95, 109, 134, 141–2, 213–14, 233
  on affection-image 9, 92–4, 98, 138–40, 152, 240
  on animal becomings 105, 110
  on beatitude 5, 20 n.49, 67
  on *Cat People* 105
  Cinema I: The Movement-Image 9, 21, 92–4
  Cinema II: The Time-Image 9, 20 n.49, 57, 63, 94, 146 n.46, 208, 213
  Difference and Repetition 67, 176 n.47, 218
  on difference-from-itself 167
  on direct time-image 208
  on eternal return 24, 176 n.47
  on 'forger, the' 80
  on homo tantum 99
  on immanence 66
  'Immanence: A Life ...' 66
  on interval 9, 21–2, 68, 78, 92–5, 105, 141, 212 (*see also* interval)
  on larval selves 67–8, 90, 218
  on 'life, a' 10, 36, 66–7, 77, 88, 93, 99, 121–2, 195–6, 203 n.40, 217, 224, 233
  on movement-image 43
  and Nietzschean 'will to power' 6–7
  on *paramnesia* 22, 60, 96, 212
  on *Passion of Joan of Arc, The* 92–3
  on passive synthesis 67–8, 218
  on powers of the false 79–80, 91, 99
  on 'refrain, the' 97
  on seer 10, 94–5, 190
  on spiritual automaton 100
  Thousand Plateaus, A 26, 95, 97, 107, 203 n.40, 208, 214
  on time-image 9–10, 19 n.30, 20 n.49, 43, 57, 63, 94–5, 143, 146 n.46, 190, 208, 213, 218
  on transcendental field 55, 62, 66
del Río, Elena 6, 10, 56
Departed, The (Scorsese) 206
Derrida, Jacques 23, 28 n.12, 65, 167
  on *différance* 23, 28 n.12
  on justice 189–90
  on secret passion 206
Destroyer (Kusama) 13
Detour (Ulmer) 39
Didi-Huberman, Georges 32, 43, 50, 51
difference-from-itself 141, 146 n.46, 167, 176 n.47
Dimendberg, Edward 199
disaster 55, 91, 207, 212–14, 220–21, 225
dissolution of narrative 90–8
Diva (Beineix) 53, 229
divine violence *see* pure violence
Dixon, Wheeler Winston 107
D.O.A. (Maté) 189
Doane, Mary Ann 29 n.23, 70 n.29, 73–4 n.78
Donne, John 124
Dostoyevsky 169, 178 n.58
Double Indemnity (Wilder) 37–8, 59–60, 102 n.20, 116, 120, 199, 202 n.30, 217
drives 14–15, 45, 169, 234

Duino Elegies (Rilke) 109
duration 118–19, 150–1, 166, 169
durée (Bergson) 140–1, 149–50, 212
Dussere, Erik 217, 221

Eliade, Mircea 200 n.5
Elmer, Jonathan 218, 220, 225–6, 230 n.49
Elsaesser, Thomas 4
Eluard, Paul 128, 170
emotive formulas *see* pathos formulae (*pathosformeln*) (Warburg)
Enframings 111–12, 118, 121, 128, 133, 142
enigmatic body 100 *see also* body
Erickson, Glenn 153
eternal return/recurrence 24, 51, 149, 169, 191, 241
   Agamben on 143, 162, 169
   Deleuze on 24, 176 n.47
   to difference-from-itself 141, 161
   gesture as 143
   pure passion of 161–3, 167
ethics 120, 136, 203 n.38
Ethics (Spinoza) 25
ethos 139, 219–20, 222–3, 225, 229 n.41
Evening Wind (Hopper) 54–5, 58
Excursion into Philosophy (Hopper) 55
extra-juridical acts 183, 192, 194–5, 197, 233 *see also* force-of-law
extra-temporal quality 59–60, 63, 139, 149, 233

Fallen Angels (Wong) 151
false narration 79–80, 91, 99
Farocki, Harun 129, 141–2
fascination 1, 21, 33, 53–4, 59, 62–65, 67, 77, 89, 95, 114, 117, 122, 157, 161, 234
Faulkner, William 200 n.7
Femme Fatale (De Palma) 37
File on Thelma Jordan, The (Siodmak) 156, 206
firstness, affective order (C. S. Peirce) 94

Force of Evil (Polonsky) 54, 127, 178 n.54
force-of-law 192, 194, 197, 234, 243
   see also extra-juridical acts; pure violence
Foucault, Michel 91, 227
freedom 15, 25, 42, 118
Freud, Sigmund 48
   on repetition compulsion 175 n.29
friendship 107, 122–4
fugal/fugue 206, 226 n.2, 228 n.36, 245 n.8
Furthman, Jules 200 n.7
Fury (Lang) 203 n.42

gambling/gambler 168–9, 178 n.54
gaze 14, 43, 54–5, 58–9, 61–4, 67, 70 n.18, 83, 100, 115, 139, 163–4, 169, 236, 240
German Romanticism 54
gesture(s) 6, 10, 31, 36–7, 41, 43, 50–2, 83, 90, 93, 130–1, 135–40, 153, 223–4
   eternal return as 143
   pure gesture 139, 158, 192, 196–7, 211, 213, 221
   slouching gesture 221–3
   vesperal gesture 116
Ghost Dog: The Way of the Samurai (Jarmusch) 214, 243
Gifford, Barry 157
Gilda (Vidor) 116
Girard, Rene 200 n.5
'giving way' 98–9, 149, 198
Godard, Jean-Luc 127, 153, 201 n.1
Gombrich, Ernst 50
Gormley, Anthony 57
Gregg, Melissa 53
Grønstad, Asbjørn 140
Gross, Larry 188–9
groundlessness 199
Guattari, Félix 11, 21–2, 26, 51, 55, 79, 82, 95, 107, 109, 203 n.40, 209, 214
   on 'refrain, the' 97
Gustafsson, Henrik 4, 140, 156

Happy Together 161, 175 n.28
Harris, Oliver 59, 61
haunting melody 49, 96–7, 101, 115, 117, 156
hauntology 23, 28 n.14, 190
Hawks, Howard 200 n.7
Heidegger, Martin 47, 105, 109–11, 113–14, 117, 121, 143, 190
  'Anaximander Fragment, The' 190, 199–200 n.2
  on art 117
  coming to-presence 129
  on Enframing 111–12, 118, 121, 128, 133, 142
  on freedom 118
  'Origin of the Work of Art, The' 117
  on profound boredom 119
  'Question Concerning Technology, The' 117
Heisenberg, Werner 81–2
He Ran All the Way (Berry) 70 n.15
Herzogenrath, Bernd 226 n.2
hiatus ('/') 21, 108–9, 118, 122
High Window, The 202 n.25
Hirsch, Foster 59
Hitch-Hiker, The (Lupino) 199
Holmes, John Clellon 230 n.42
Hopper, Edward 54–8, 63, 73 n.59, 115, 209–11, 238–9
Huston, John 226–7 n.9

iconography 2, 10, 12, 17, 26, 31–2, 35, 37, 64, 92, 105, 138–9, 163–73, 234–5
  acedia (*see* acedia)
  of *acedic* arrest (*see* acedic arrest)
  figure at window 36–8, 45
  figure in fascination 38
  figure in repose 33, 35, 37, 39–44, 53
  figure smoking 36–8, 80, 85–6, 116, 130–1, 152, 163–6, 174 n.23, 175 n.42, 193, 211, 218
  of temptation 86
  zero affect 50–4
iconology 31–3, 51, 69 n.2
idem-identities (Ricoeur) 176 n.48

idleness 116, 138
Il Conformista (Bertolucci) 36
illusions 60, 81–2, 86
immanence 27, 65–7, 68, 78–9, 93, 98–9, 109–10, 114, 169, 195, 203 n.40, 208, 211, 219, 224 *see also* pure immanence
impasse (Berlant) 235–6, 242, 244
impassivity 52, 56, 99
impersonal becoming 10, 26, 65, 141, 169
implicate order, of the universe (Bohm) 134
impossibility of narrative 78–80
impotentiality 7–8, 120–1
inadequate ideas (Spinoza) 25
in-betweenness 3, 53, 105, 108, 211
Inception (Nolan) 13, 74 n.79, 174 n.21, 245
incommunication 213, 218
indeterminacy, and noir 2–5, 11, 239–43
inertia 33, 35–7, 39, 57
inertia of being (Blanchot) 52, 235
infinite resignation 168, 172
  knight of 177–8 n.53, 191–2
inhumanity 118, 132–3, 140, 144 n.11
inoperativity 5, 17, 123–4, 126 n.46, 215
Intermission (Hopper) 56
interval 21, 23, 68, 98, 139–43
  and affective images 93–4
  affective interval 16, 68, 92, 129, 149, 151
  as an originary division 23, 28 n.12
  Blanchotian 21, 27, 56
  as the blank space between the images 51
  Deleuzian 9, 21–2, 68, 78, 92–5, 105, 141, 212
  disaster of 212–13
  embodying 216–19
  as 'event' 243
  of fascination with a radical 'outside' 233
  as a form of socio-juridical lapse 179–99

lapse 8–11
melancholy (*see* melancholy)
between narrative identity and the passions 233
as a philosophical figure 51
as a source of salvation 16
suspension in 15–17
intervallic experience 84, 89, 105
intervallic figures 9, 10, 23, 27, 78, 95, 116, 123, 153, 189, 207, 221, 226, 241–2
intervallic passivity (*see* passivity)
intervallic time/temporality 95, 190, 197, 212, 214–15, 231 n.61
In The Cut (Campion) 37
In the Mood for Love (Wong) 151, 154–5, 157–9, 168, 170, 173 n.10, 174 n.23, 174 n.27, 175 n.28, 178 n.61
Invisible Man films 195
ipse-identity (Ricoeur) 176 n.48
Italian neorealist movement 9
I Travelled 9,000 km to Give It to You 152
Iversen, Margaret 48

Jameson, Frederic 72 n.54
Jay, Martin 54
Johnny O'Clock (Rossen) 199 n.1
Johnson, Christopher D. 32, 52
Johnson, G. Allen 151
jointure/disjointure 190
Jones, Jenny M. 217
Le jour se lève (Carné) 3
justice 185–6
    Derrida on 189–90
    disjointure 190
    and 'law, the' (*see* 'law, the' and justice)
    spectral time of 179–84, 189–90
    and time/temporality 181, 199 n.2

Kaufman, Eleanor 72 n.48
Keating, Patrick 32
Kermode, Frank 211–12
Kerouac, Jack 223, 230 n.52
Kierkegaard, Søren 177–7 n.53, 192
    knight of faith 191–2, 203 n.40

knight of infinite resignation 177–8 n.53, 191–2
    on stages of life 168
Killers, The (Siodmak) 2, 10, 15, 27, 38, 54, 57–66, 77–8, 95, 156, 169, 236, 240
Killing, The (Kubrick) 178 n.54
Klein, Richard 164–5
Klibansky, Raymond 43
Klossowski, Pierre 24, 141–2, 168
knowledge forms (Spinoza) 25–7, 62, 80, 191, 240, 241
Kolker, Robert 185–6, 197
Kracauer, Siegfried 242
Kranzfelder, Ivo 54–5
Kristeva, Julia 89–90
Krutnik, Frank 14

Lacan, Jacques 226 n.2
Lady from Shanghai, The (Welles) 108
Lady in the Lake, The (Montgomery) 175 n.44
Lalanne, Jean-Marc 153
Lambert, Gregg 140
Lancaster, Burt 56, 137
Landry, Olivia 235, 242
language, limitations of 136–7
lapse 16, 129, 235, 237
    across thresholds of becoming 129
    of dark interval 8–11, 56
    socio-juridical lapse 179–84
Last Seduction, The (Dahl) 108–9
Laura (Preminger) 56, 96, 156–7, 199 n.1
Lavery, David 79
'law, the' 179–80, 199, 215, 220 *see also* force-of-~~law~~
    and life, biopolitical distinction between 233
    and time 180
'law, the' and justice 179, 181–2
    disjunction between 197
    extra-juridical acts 183, 192, 195, 197, 233
    interval between 182–4, 189
Levinas, Emmanuel 64, 126 n.36
Lewton, Val 105–6

'life, a' 10, 36, 66–7, 77, 88, 93, 99, 121–2, 195–6, 203 n.40, 217, 224, 233
life-as-singularity 67
light and exposure metaphors 131–4
Locket, The (Brahm) 96, 108
Long Goodbye, The (Altman) 2, 11, 13, 16, 36, 53, 70 n.27, 71 n.40, 119, 179–99, 201 n.18, 205, 217, 219–20, 237, 243
Lost Highway (Lynch) 13, 157, 206, 226 n.2, 245
lounge time (Sobchack) 44, 57, 70 n.27, 236, 242
love 135, 139, 155, 159
  as duration 150–1
  and temporality 149–51
Luhr, William 195
Lyotard, Jean-François 133, 144 n.11
lyrical noirs 39, 90, 105–6, 128, 130–1, 135, 138–40, 152

Maltby, Richard 56
Maltese Falcon, The (Hammett) 226–7 n.9
Maltese Falcon, The (Huston) 3
man and animal
  distinction between 109, 122
  ontological interval between 233
Man Who Wasn't There, The (Coen brothers) 2, 13, 16, 49, 56, 60, 67–8, 77–101, 86–7, 102 n.20, 106, 120, 124, 175 n.42, 182, 206–7, 213, 226 n.1, 237
Martin, Adrian 138, 156
Martin-Jones, David 19 n.30
Massumi, Brian 5, 24, 97, 114–16, 208, 234, 239
Mazierska, Eva 178 n.56
McArthur, Colin 32, 45
McLuhan, Marshall 135, 145 n.19
'meanwhile' 21–3, 51
mediality 136, 138–40, 149, 158, 195–6, 221
melancholy 16, 43–5, 48–9, 157, 169, 211, 234, 236, 241

Melencolia I (Dürer) 45–6, 48, 210–11
Melville, Stephen 48
Memento (Nolan) 13, 37, 69 n.14, 206, 245
Merleau-Ponty, Maurice 166
messianic time of arrest 17, 46–7, 197, 210, 215, 225–6, 231 n.61
meta-noir 37, 55, 60, 216
missingness 206, 218, 228 n.37
Missing Person, The (Buschel) 17, 33–4, 37, 39, 54–5, 63, 119, 205–15, 220, 225
missing persons 206–15, 218, 236
Mitchell, W. J. T. 57
Mitchum, Robert 56, 137
modernism 9, 22
modern noir 11–13, 17, 26–7, 60, 101, 172, 206
Montgomery, Robert 186
Mottram, James 78–9
movement-image 9, 21, 43, 93–4
Mulholland Drive (Lynch) 13, 245
Mulvey, Laura 51
Mummy, The, pictures 194
Murder, My Sweet (Dmytryk) 102 n.10, 175 n.44
music 96–7, 116, 206
Musuraca, Nicholas 106–7

Nachleben (survival, afterlife) 32, 50
Naked City, The (Dassin) 199
Nancy, Jean-Luc 27
Naremore, James 3, 102 n.20, 198, 200 n.8
narrative identities 16, 82–5, 87–8, 176 n.48, 206
narrative time 140, 179
nature and history, distinction between (Benjamin) 121
Neale, Stephen 3–4
Neff, Walter 199
neo-noir films 2, 11–13
Neuromancer (Gibson) 159
New York Movie (Hopper) 55, 209–10, 238
Nietzsche, Friedrich 8, 14, 24, 110, 168, 177 n.51, 200 n.4
  and beatitude 146 n.48

eternal recurrence (*see* eternal return/recurrence)
'will to power' 6–7, 162, 165, 167–8, 241
Night and the City (Dassin) 153
Night Moves (Penn) 13, 184, 196
Night of the Hunter (Laughton) 208–9
9/11 attacks, and disasters 212, 214–15
Nino, Frank 3
No Country for Old Men 78
Nocturnal Animals (Ford) 13
Nora Prentiss (Sherman) 44–5
Nosferatu (Murneau) 134
nullpunkt (Merleau-Ponty) 166, 175–6 n.44
Nymph and Shepherd (Titian) 122–3, 139

objective narrative (master narrative) 85–7
O'Brien, Geoffrey 56
Oliver, Kelly 173 n.14
On Dangerous Ground (Ray) 199
'Open, the' (Rilke) 16, 108–19, 122, 240, 241
opening sequence 15, 22, 33–7, 39–40, 70 n.15, 108, 130, 144 n.7, 159, 163, 186–8, 190–1, 207, 220
opsigns 94–5
Orphée (Cocteau) 134, 152–4, 173 n.12
Orphic myth/noir 139, 150–2, 154–7, 169, 237, 240, 242
Orr, Stanley 91, 99
Our Mutual Friend (Dickens) 66, 169
Out of the Past (Tourneur) 57, 107, 156, 165
'outside of thought' 27, 79

Panic in the Streets (Kazan) 199 n.1
Panofsky, Erwin 31–2, 43, 48
paramnesia 22–4, 60, 62, 96, 212
La Paresse (Sloth) 137
Parnet, Claire 177 n.51
Passenger, The (Antonioni) 13, 100
passion 1, 27, 52, 114, 155, 233, 243–4

of a life 77 (*see also* 'life, a')
passionate passivity 5, 53, 162, 234
pure passion 7–8, 158, 161–3, 166, 169
recurrence of (*see* eternal return/recurrence)
secret passion 167, 206
of self-affection 162–3, 214
supremacy of 206
Passion of Joan of Arc, The (Dreyer) 16, 77, 88, 92–3
passive synthesis (Deleuze) 67–8, 218
passivity 1–2, 4, 6, 10, 42, 51–2, 56–9, 78, 95, 116, 121, 137, 155, 163, 213–14, 217, 233–4, 242
affective state 5
and drive 14
passionate 5, 53
passive body 213
radical passivity (*see* radical passivity)
self-affective 4 (*see also* self-affection)
and sovereign elation (Blanchot) 65
'Pathétique Sonata' (Beethoven) 49
pathos 73–4 n.78
and *passio*, semantic associations between 52
pathos formulae (*pathosformeln*) (Warburg) 27, 50–5, 63–4, 68, 92, 99, 115, 130, 136–7, 139, 143, 145 n.20, 162, 211, 234, 236–7, 240, 243
Peirce, C. S. 94
Pépé le Moko (Duvivier) 3
perception 9, 59, 81–2, 85, 97–8, 105, 109, 134, 140, 228 n.38, 234
performance 6, 10–11, 56–7, 73 n.65, 92–3, 95, 99, 101 n.2, 121, 137, 165, 235
autonomous performance 56, 93
integrated performance 56
style 56–7
personal narratives, revision of 36, 84–5
Peterson, Lowell 32

INDEX

phantasms 23, 41, 43, 48–9, 59–61, 118, 174 n.19, 190, 234
Phantom Lady (Siodmak) 119
Pinkerton, Nick 226 n.3
Pitfall (Toth) 44–5
Place, Janey 14, 32
placeless place (Agamben) 48–9, 118, 237
  of self-affection 50
Plantinga, Carl 64
Poellner, Peter 22
poiēsis 117–18, 128–9, 134, 144 n.8
Point Blank (Boorman) 12–13, 17, 100, 138, 188, 245 n.8
Polan, Dana 82, 116
Polonsky, Abraham 54
potentia (Spinoza) 5, 6, 220
potentia activa 162
potential/potentiality 5–8, 10, 12, 15, 17, 26–7, 48, 68, 78, 91, 114, 116, 118–21, 143, 162, 169–70, 172, 194, 214, 234, 243
potentia passiva 162
potestas (Spinoza) 6, 95, 220
Powell, Anna 105, 126 n.50
Powell, Dick 186
powerlessness 8, 78, 94–5, 169, 241, 244
profound boredom 113–16, 119, 238
pure being-in-language 196
pure gesture 139, 158, 192, 196–7, 211, 213, 221 *see also* gesture
pure immanence 27, 66, 93, 99, 110, 114, 169, 195, 224
pure language 196
pure passion 7, 8, 158, 166, 169 *see also* passion; eternal return/recurrence
pure violence 16–17, 179, 192, 194–8, 243 *see also* force-of-~~law~~

quietude 7, 33, 99

radical passivity (Wall) 4–6, 8, 15, 65, 122, 163, 225, 233, 236, 238, 242–3 *see also* passivity
Rainer, Peter 101 n.2

Rampley, Matthew 31
Rascaroli, Laura 178 n.56
Raskin, David 156
Rayns, Tony 173 n.13
Rempel, Morgan 230 n.55
repetitions 23–4, 37, 51, 161
  repetition compulsion 161, 169, 175 n.29
return
  to difference-from-itself 146 n.46
  see also eternal return/recurrence
revenant 188, 194–5, 207
Richards, Rashna Wadia 165
Ricoeur, Paul 84, 90, 176 n.48
Rilke, Rainer Maria 5, 16, 109–10, 241
Rodowick, David 79, 95, 100–1
Rohmer, Eric 41
Romeo's Bleeding (Medak) 13
Rosenbaum, Jonathan 173 n.9, 195
Ross, Alison 193
Rosset, Clement 141, 146 n.48
Rudolph, Alan 201 n.18

Sacred and the Profane, The 200 n.5
Said, Edward 175 n.43
Saint Augustine in His Study 54–5
Le Samouraï (Melville) 33, 35–7, 39, 63, 214, 217, 229
Sartre, Jean-Paul 55
Saturn (Campagnola) 43, 46
saturnine 43, 55
saved night (Benjamin) 119–24, 139
saving sorrow 47–8, 68, 239
Saxl, Fritz 43
Scanner Darkly, A (Linklater) 134, 206, 221
Scarlet Street (Lang) 45, 119
Schefer, Jean-Louis 100
Schickel, Richard 101 n.2
Schopenhauer, Arthur 110
Schürmann, Reiner 234
Scott, A. O 99
seer, the (Deleuze) 10, 94–5
Seghers, Anna 236, 238–42
Seigworth, Gregory J. 53
self-affection 4, 7, 10, 12, 15, 36, 42–3, 48, 50, 53, 60, 63–5, 68, 87, 95–6,

98–9, 114, 120, 129, 153–4, 156, 162–6, 169–70, 176 n.44, 194, 211, 214, 219, 221–3, 234, 236–7, 239, 244
  and eternal return 164–5
  and fascination 64–5
  intervallic condition 153–4
  passion of 162–3, 214
  placeless place of 50
  see also acedia; zero affect
self-reflexive modern noirs 11, 17, 59, 91, 130, 132, 159, 162, 188–9
sempiternality 211–12, 214, 226
Set-Up, The (Wise) 36
Shadoian, Jack 19 n.36
Shadow of a Doubt (Hitchcock) 39–42, 44, 49, 96
shadows 41, 62, 108, 156, 234, 239, 241
Shannon, Michael 34, 207, 213
Shock (Werker) 116
Shouse, Eric 97
Shutter Island (Scorsese) 13, 206
Silverman, Kaja 128, 141–2
singularity 134
  life as 67
  whatever-singularity 215–16, 224, 234, 241
'slow motion' sequences 95–6, 166
Smith, Murray 74 n.88
Sobchack, Vivian 44, 57, 70 n.27, 236
Somewhere in the Night 206, 226 n.2
sonsigns 94–7
Sound of Fury, The (Endfield) 198–9, 203 n.42
sovereign power 202 n.31, 235
Space of Literature, The 240
Spectres of Marx (Derrida) 190
Spengler, Oswald 127
Spicer, Andrew 12
Spinoza, Baruch 5–6, 11, 14, 25, 66, 90, 121
  beatitude 20 n.49, 25
  duratio 212
  power (*potentia*) 5–6, 220
  power (*potestas*) 6, 220
  third form of knowledge (*sub specie aeternitatis*) 25–7, 62, 80, 191, 240–1
standstill (Benjamin) 235
state of exception 192, 202 n.31, 214, 220
state of things (Deleuze) 92
Stern, Lesley 64
Stewart, Garrett 186
stillness 1, 51–2
  affective stillness 43
  stilled photograms 51
Stranger, The (Welles) 16, 180–1, 199
Strawson, Galen 84
Stromboli (Rossellini) 14–15, 20 n.49
St Thomas Aquinas 211
sub specie aeternitatis (Spinoza) 25–7, 62, 80, 191, 240–1
survivals/surviving images 32, 43, 50–2, 130, 136, 214, 235, 240, 243
  of zero affect 240
suspended time 1, 5, 15, 24, 155
  see also arrest; time/temporal/temporality
suspense 5, 10–11
suspension 5, 10-11, 37, 51, 56, 101, 111, 114–19, 121–2, 139, 162–3, 168, 183, 192, 208–9, 221, 234, 242
  affective state of 115
  condition of 117
  deviant temporality of 45–6
  in interval 15–17

Tarrying with the Negative (Žižek) 20 n.49
Taylor, Charles 84
tech-noir 143 n.2, 159, 166
technology 43 n.2, 111, 117, 132–5, 145 n.19
Telotte, J. P. 77, 82, 91, 105–6, 175–6 n.44, 180, 199 n.1
telotype 217, 228 n.5, 234
Teo, Stephen 159, 161
they-self (Heidegger) 47
'Thing That Thinks, The' (Žižek) 14–15, 20 n.49

This Gun for Hire (Tuttle) 2–3, 33–5, 39, 63
Thompson, Kristin 157
Thornton, Billy Bob 56, 83
time, law and justice 181, 184 *see also* justice; 'law, the'
time-image (Deleuze) 9–10, 19 n.30, 20 n.49, 43, 57, 63, 94–5, 143, 146 n.46, 190, 208, 213, 218
Time Table (Stevens) 199 n.1
time/temporal/temporality 2–3, 21–2, 28–9 n.23, 139–40, 152, 198–9 n.1, 211, 225
  chronology 8, 12, 23, 35, 44, 51
  clock-time 45, 140, 150, 180
  and 'event, the' 51
  halted temporality 1, 5, 23, 44, 59, 61, 189
  intervallic 95, 190, 197, 212, 214–15, 231 n.61
  and justice 199 n.2
  lapse 8, 179–84
  liminal time 183, 200 n.5
  linear temporality 26, 33, 51, 59, 114, 139–40, 149, 182, 189
  lounge time 44, 57, 70 n.27, 236, 242
  and love 149–51
  profane time and sacred time, distinction between 200 n.5
  sempiternal time 211–12, 214
  surveyor of time/the seer 10
  temporal arrest 48, 157, 163–4, 169
  temporal discontinuity 188–9
  temporal lacuna 180, 183
  time-as-becoming 10, 150
  see also arrest; suspended time
tiredness 9, 57, 95, 213, 218
To Each His Own Cinema 152
To Have and Have Not 165
Tong, Janice 152
transcendence 55, 62, 114, 218, 229 n.41
Transit (Petzold) 2, 13, 17, 39, 235–42, 243
Trigo, Benigno 173 n.14
Turner, Victor 200 n.5

2046 (Wong) 2, 16–17, 129, 143, 149–78, 190, 239
't zero' (Calvino) 22–6, 140

uncertainty principle 81–2
underworld of noir 150, 153, 155–6, 242
Unknown Man, The (Thorpe) 16, 179, 181–3, 189, 197, 206
Usual Suspects, The (Singer) 13
Utterson, Andrew 131

Vernet, Marc 33
Vertigo (Hitchcock) 156
vesperal noir 105–6, 116–18, 121, 124, 152, 166
the 'virtual' 7, 60, 86, 91, 96–7, 164, 170, 208
virtual images 60, 95–6
visual style or sensibility, film noir as 3

waiting 9, 22, 56–7, 95, 115, 171, 213, 218, 235–6, 242
Walker, Michael 59
Wall, Thomas Carl 4–5–6, 8, 65, 122, 233
Warburg, Aby 27, 31–2, 43, 48, 50, 52, 55, 71–2 n.46, 92, 136, 139
  concept of survival (*Nachleben*) 32, 50
  Mnemosyne Atlas 51
  'pathos formulae' (*see* pathos formulae (*pathosformeln*) (Warburg))
  on Renaissance 51
Watkin, William 121
whatever-being 215–16, 224–5, 228 n.9, 234, 241
Where the Sidewalk Ends (Preminger) 183, 206
Willemen, Paul 109
will to powerlessness 168, 177 n.51
will to power (Nietzsche) 6–7, 162, 165, 167–8, 241
Window, The (Tetzlaff) 116
windows 36–8, 45, 115–16, 238
Winnicott, D. W. 48

Woman at a Window (Friedrich) 54
Woman in the Window, The
  (Lang) 108
Wood, Robin 40–1, 134
Woolfolk, Alan 140

Yakuza, The (Pollack) 214
You Were Never Really Here (Ramsay)
  13, 37, 206

Zen 229 n.41, 234

Zen Noir 229 n.41
zero affect 26, 53–4, 56, 68, 99, 115,
  216, 234, 236–7, 240, 243 *see also*
  pathos formulae (*pathosformeln*)
  (Warburg)
zero point/vanishing point of narration
  13, 26–7, 78, 91, 95
Žižek, Slavoj 13–15, 20 n.49, 54,
  73 n.59, 169, 212, 224
Zuboff, Shoshana 221

www.ingramcontent.com/pod-product-compliance
Lightning Source LLC
Chambersburg PA
CBHW052219300426
44115CB00011B/1759